AN OUTLINE HISTORY
OF THE WORLD

H. A. DAVIES, M.A.

FIFTH EDITION
REVISED BY
C. H. C. BLOUNT

OXFORD UNIVERSITY PRESS
1968

Oxford University Press, Ely House, London W. 1

GLASGOW NEW YORK TORONTO MELBOURNE WELLINGTON
CAPE TOWN SALISBURY IBADAN NAIROBI LUSAKA ADDIS ABABA
BOMBAY CALCUTTA MADRAS KARACHI LAHORE DACCA
KUALA LUMPUR HONG KONG TOKYO

FIRST PUBLISHED 1928
REPRINTED 1931, 1936
NEW EDITION 1937
REPRINTED 1942, 1946, 1947, 1950
THIRD EDITION 1954
REPRINTED 1957, 1959
FOURTH EDITION 1964
FIFTH EDITION 1968

PRINTED IN GREAT BRITAIN
AT THE UNIVERSITY PRESS, OXFORD
BY VIVIAN RIDLER
PRINTER TO THE UNIVERSITY

THE MODERN WORLD REDISCOVERING THE ANCIENT

Mesopotamian excavators, under European supervision, unearthing the ruins of Babylon

PREFACE TO THIRD EDITION

THE study of World History has been widely neglected in the past, and even to-day it has hardly advanced beyond the experimental stage; it is too frequently a mere appendage, and not, as it should be, a groundwork for the study of all history. Exclusive attention to the record of one's own particular nation is apt to induce feelings of superiority and self-righteousness, which are a barrier in the way of international understanding, and which, in their extreme form, find expression in such ridiculous doctrines as the Nazi theory of a pure German race. 'The historian among his books', said the Greek writer Lucian, 'should forget his nationality.' What is best and most durable in the world is the result of the accumulated and transferred wisdom of many nations. A knowledge, however fragmentary, of these contributions towards progress, of the events which have caused the rise and fall of nations, and of the differing ways in which individual countries have promoted the general welfare, will help to ensure that international outlook without which a League of Nations or a United Nations Organization would have little chance to make headway.

In a work such as this the task of selection is necessarily difficult, and I must therefore ask the pardon of those readers whom I may, inadvertently, have offended by not including, or by passing over lightly, events which are of special interest to them. I am conscious of no bias, apart from an attachment to that particular form of freedom which can only exist in democratic countries, but I have made an honest attempt to explain other forms of political activity, and to reveal their good points. The lack of scientific documentary evidence naturally makes it more difficult to assess the history of the post-war period than that of a time which is so distant that it can be examined with complete historical detachment.

PREFACE TO THIRD EDITION

The reception already given to this book encourages the writer to believe that it has aroused some interest, not only in schools, for which it is primarily intended, but also among general readers, whom it may lead to a more detailed study of world history. I am deeply indebted to the officers of the Oxford University Press and their advisers for suggestions and advice, which have been of the greatest assistance to me, and for the choice of illustrations.

August 1953   H. A. D.

PREFACE TO FIFTH EDITION

CONTINUED demand having called for a new edition of the late Mr. H. A. Davies's book, the publisher invited me to undertake the necessary revision. The book has accordingly been revised throughout in the light of developments and events to the middle of 1967.

July 1967   C. H. C. B.

CONTENTS

PART I
THE ANCIENT WORLD

I. Early Man	1
II. Early Civilizations—Egypt	15
III. Early Civilizations—Babylonia and Assyria	46
IV. Early Civilizations—The Medes and Persians	59
V. Early Civilizations—China	72
VI. Early Civilizations—India	78
VII. The Phoenicians	84
VIII. The Beginnings of Civilization in Europe	89
IX. The Greeks	97
X. The Empire of Alexander the Great	144
XI. Buddha and Confucius	152
XII. The Roman Republic	159
XIII. The Roman Empire	189
XIV. The Conquerors of Rome	226
XV. What Civilization owes to the Jews	233
APPENDIX I. Some important dates in Ancient History	254

PART II
FROM THE BEGINNING OF THE MIDDLE AGES TO THE PRESENT DAY

XVI. Europe after the fall of Rome	259
XVII. The Rise and Spread of Islam	273
XVIII. The Empire of Charles the Great	287

CONTENTS

XIX. The Power of the Medieval Church . . 306
XX. The Growth and Development of Towns during the Middle Ages . . . 338
XXI. The Growth of Nationality during the Middle Ages 359
XXII. The Mongols and the Turks . . . 370
XXIII. The Beginning of Modern Times . . 383
XXIV. Grand Monarchy in the Seventeenth and Eighteenth Centuries . . . 412
XXV. The American and French Revolutions . 429
XXVI. Napoleon Buonaparte 450
XXVII. The Industrial Revolution . . . 469
XXVIII. The Triumph of Nationality in the Nineteenth Century 482
XXIX. Modern Imperialism 496
XXX. Russia and the Near East in the Nineteenth Century 510
XXXI. The United States of America . . . 523
XXXII. The Twentieth Century 533

Some important dates in Medieval and Modern History 567

TIME CHARTS 571

INDEX 579

LIST OF ILLUSTRATIONS

The Modern World rediscovering the Ancient. Photograph by Underwood Press Service . . . . . *frontispiece*

Some typical Stone Age implements. From drawings by Mrs. M. C. Burkitt 5

Palaeolithic Art. A boar from the caves of Altamira. After Breuil . 7

A reconstructed view of a Neolithic lake village, built on piles. Reproduced by kind permission of Messrs. Charles Scribner's Sons, from J. M. Tyler's *New Stone Age in Northern Europe* . 11

A raft-house on the Irrawaddy to-day, showing the modern survival of a very ancient type. Photograph by Mr. R. Gorbold . 11

Neolithic Civilization. Stonehenge from the air. By permission of H.M. Stationery Office 13

Water pouring through the Assuan Dam 19

A village on the banks of the Nile. Photograph by Mr. Percival Hart 19

The step-pyramid of Sakkara, built by Imhotep. Photograph by Mr. Percival Hart 21

The Sphinx and the Great Pyramid of Gizeh. Photograph by Mr. Percival Hart 21

Writing in Egypt: 1, An Egyptian scribe. Photograph Giraudon; 2, Wooden ink-pot and reed pens; 3, An unused roll of papyrus (British Museum) 23

Ploughing, sowing, reaping, carrying, and threshing corn. From a fresco in a Theban grave. Photograph Giraudon . . 25

Life in Egypt. A nobleman inspects his cattle. Photograph Metropolitan Museum of Art, New York 27

The Great Temple of Luxor. Photograph by Sir Alan Cobham . 31

Tutankhamen's Armchair. Cairo Museum 33

Egyptian Religion: 1, The Pharaoh Seti I in adoration before Osiris. Photograph Metropolitan Museum of Art, New York; 2, Raamon. British Museum; 3, Isis, wife of Osiris. British Museum 35

Akhnaton and his wife Nefertiti. Left-hand, Photograph Giraudon; right-hand, Ashmolean Museum, Oxford 43

The Great Temple at Abu Simbel, showing the four statues, each 60 feet high. Photograph by Mr. Percival Hart . . 45

LIST OF ILLUSTRATIONS

An air-view of Nippur, a great Sumerian town, showing the ruins laid bare by modern excavation. By the courtesy of the Royal Air Force	49
Sumerian Art and Handwriting: 1, A specimen of cuneiform writing. Photograph by the courtesy of Professor S. Langdon; 2, A Sumerian priest, 3000 B.C. British Museum; 3, King Gudea of Lagash, 2600 B.C. Photograph Giraudon	51
King Hammurabi. From a contemporary sculpture	53
Some typical Babylonian weights	53
An Assyrian war-chariot. Photograph Giraudon	57
Agriculture in Persia. Using the winnowing fan. Photograph by Mr. R. Gorbold	61
The Might of the Persian Empire: 1, The ruins of Xerxes' palace at Persepolis. Photograph by Dr. Sarre; 2, King Darius and a row of captive rebels. Photograph by Dr. R. Campbell Thompson	65
The Great Wall of China. Photograph by the Underwood Press Service	75
A nomad tribe with their cattle moving down from the hills to the plains	81
Phoenician transport: A Phoenician ship on a coin of Sidon; 'The ship of the desert'. Ashmolean Museum, Oxford	87
Cretan Art. A painting at Cnossos, restored by Sir Arthur Evans	93
Minoan Civilization: 1 and 3, Jewellery. Photograph by G. Maraghiannie, Candia; 2, Minoan Jug, 1600 B.C. Ashmolean Museum, Oxford; 4, Excavation in progress at Cnossos. Photograph by Miss M. V. Taylor	95
The walled citadel of Athens. Photograph by English Photographic Company, Athens	101
Where ancient Sparta stood: the plain below Taygetus	101
Delphi; the ruins of the great shrine of Apollo. Photograph by English Photographic Company, Athens	103
Greek Religion: The goddess Demeter. British Museum; A seated goddess. Photograph by Julius Bard	107
Greek Industries: A fisherman with his baskets. Ashmolean Museum, Oxford; Olive-harvest, whipping the trees. By permission of the Trustees of the British Museum	109
Greek shipping: Slips for launching triremes in the harbour at Aegina; Rowers at the oar in a trireme	113
Coin of Croesus, King of Lydia	114

LIST OF ILLUSTRATIONS

Art under the Tyrants: Above, wrestling. National Museum, Athens; Below, a cat and dog fight. National Museum, Athens . 117

The War with Persia: 1 and 2, Persian soldiers in the bodyguard of King Darius; 3, A Greek hoplite. A bronze statuette dedicated to Zeus by a Greek soldier 121

Athenian girls with lyres; a Spartan girl running. Photograph by Chaundy 125

Athenian Art under Pericles: Head and shoulders of the colossal gold and ivory statue of Athena which stood in the Parthenon, reproduced on an ancient gem; The Parthenon, on the Acropolis at Athens 129

The Greek Theatre: The rows of seats and the orchestra of the great marble theatre at Epidaurus; The front seats of the theatre of Dionysus at Athens 133

Three great Greeks of the fifth century B.C.: 1, Herodotus. Metropolitan Museum of Art, New York; 2, Socrates. British Museum; 3, Thucydides. Holkham Hall, England . . 139

A Greek painted vase of the late sixth century B.C. Athenian girls drawing water from the lion-head spout of a public drinking fountain. Metropolitan Museum of Art, New York . . 143

The Arab village of Siwa, where Alexander visited the shrine of Amon-Ra. Photograph by Sir Alan Cobham . . . 149

The great Buddhist monastery at Lhassa. Reproduced from Sir Charles Bell, *Tibet, Past and Present* 157

An Etruscan chariot, showing the Etruscans' beautiful bronze work. Metropolitan Museum, New York 163

Rome and the Samnites: A Samnite warrior. Photograph by Giraudon; Two Roman soldiers carrying a dead comrade. Photograph by Alinari 167

Agriculture in Italy. Ploughing with oxen in an orchard of olive trees. Photograph by Mr. Percival Hart 173

A Roman warship, manned by legionary soldiers. Photograph by Alinari 179

Julius Caesar. Photograph by Anderson 181

Roman Amphitheatre at Verona, showing the passages and gangways by which the spectators entered and left the theatre, and the main entrance for the competitors 185

A chariot race. A Roman mosaic in Britain 185

Roman religion. A sacrifice in a temple at Rome. Restoration after Carey and Deam 187

The Forum of Trajan at Rome. After E. J. Banks in *Art and Archaeology*, vol. iv 193

LIST OF ILLUSTRATIONS

Roman Trades: 1, A cobbler. Hôtel-Dieu, Rheims; 2, A soap-shop. Museum, Épinal; 3, A butcher's shop. From a relief at Dresden 199

The ruins of Baalbec in Syria. From Th. Wiegand, *Baalbek*, vol. ii (Walter de Gruyter & Co., Berlin) 201

Roman Architecture. The Pont du Gard, near Nîmes. Photograph by Lévy et Neurdein réunis 207

New Religions at Rome. A marble relief of priests and priestesses of Isis in procession. Photograph by Sansaini . . . 209

Roman fashions in hairdressing, first to third centuries A.D. . . 215

Roman furniture. A beautiful bronze stand found at Pompeii. Photograph by Alinari 221

The Roman Army: 1, Trajan's army foraging in the enemy's land. From C. Cichorius, *Die Reliefs der Trajanssäule*; 2, Gravestone of a cavalry soldier. After a painted cast in the Museum, Mainz 223

Rome and the barbarians. From Cichorius, *Die Reliefs der Trajanssäule* 229

An encampment of nomad tribes in Palestine to-day. Photograph by American Colony, Jerusalem 237

An Eastern city gate 239

A model of the Jewish synagogue at Capernaum, where our Lord preached. From H. Kohl and C. Watzinger, *Antike Synagogen in Galilaea*, 1916 247

The interior of Santa Sophia at Constantinople 258

St. Benedict. In the margin a beggar with wooden leg and crutch (British Museum, MS. Egerton 2125) 269

The Cloisters, Gloucester Cathedral. Photograph by Mr. J. R. H. Weaver 271

Moslem architecture. The great mosque in Kairouan, North Africa. Photograph by Sir Alan Cobham 277

Moorish architecture in Spain. A corner of the 'Courtyard of the Lions' in the Alhambra. Photograph by Mr. Percival Hart 279

Street scene in old Bagdad. Photograph by Mr. R. Gorbold . 281

Silver denarius of Charlemagne, struck at a trading station in the Low Countries. In the collection of Dr. D. M. Metcalf, of Oxford 287

Church and State in the days of Charlemagne. St. Peter giving the stole to Pope Leo III, and the banner of Rome to Charlemagne. Photograph by Alinari 289

Capture of Syracuse by Saracens in the ninth century. From the fourteenth-century MS. of Skylitzes at Madrid. Photograph, G. Millet, *Collection des Hautes Études*, Sorbonne, Paris . 299

LIST OF ILLUSTRATIONS xiii

A tournament. From a carved ivory panel of the thirteenth century. Photograph by Alinari 303

The Labourer in the Middle Ages. From reliefs on Notre-Dame in Paris. Left-hand, photograph by Mansell; right-hand, photograph by Giraudon 305

The castle of Carcassonne in France. Photograph by Lévy et Neurdein réunis 311

A Pilgrimage. The Earl of Warwick embarking for the Holy Land, c. 1475. (British Museum, MS. Cotton Julius E. iv) . 317

A crusader's castle above Antioch, built across the old Seleucid Wall. Photograph by Sir Aurel Stein 319

The Knights of the Holy Spirit starting on Crusade, fourteenth century. From H. de Viel Castel, *Statuts de l'Ordre du Saint-Esprit de Naples* 321

The murder of Becket; from an ivory 327

Auto-da-fé. From a painting of about 1500. Photograph by Mansell 329

A friar preaching. From the Fitzwilliam Museum MS. 22 (fifteenth century). 331

The western doorway of the Benedictine Abbey of Ripoll in Spain (about A.D. 1150), showing Old Testament scenes that were probably copied from miniatures in a Spanish illuminated manuscript bible. Photograph by Mr. J. R. H. Weaver . 333

The Palace of the Popes, Avignon 337

The City Walls of Avila in Spain. Photograph by Mr. J. R. H. Weaver 341

The medieval craftsman. A Mason and a Carpenter proving their skill before a Gild Warden. (British Museum, Royal MS. 15 E. 11) 343

Venice. The Grand Canal to-day. Photograph by Mr. Percival Hart 347

Amiens Cathedral, one of the finest examples of Gothic Architecture. Photograph by Lévy et Neurdein réunis 349

A page of the Mainz Bible (c. 1455), reduced. Bodleian Library, Postcard 33 351

The age of the great Italian tyrants. Equestrian statue on tomb of the Scaligers, the great family who ruled Verona. Photograph by Alinari 355

Warfare in Italy. Part of a picture of an army besieging Florence, by the painter Vasari. Photograph by Alinari . . . 357

Country life in medieval England: Knocking down acorns for swine; treading grapes. Harrowing, sowing, and digging. Weeding and picking flowers (?). Barnard wood-carvings, Abington Hall, Northants. From photographs kindly lent by Professor F. P. Barnard 361

LIST OF ILLUSTRATIONS

A Medieval Siege. From a Flemish MS. made for Edward IV about 1480. (British Museum, Royal MS. 16 F. ii) . . 363

Marco Polo's travels. A ship sailing from Venice, from a MS. illustration of the early fourteenth century. (Bodl. Misc. 264) 373

The Buland Darwaza at Fatehpur Sikri, Akbar's capital . . 379

Suleiman the Magnificent. Reproduced, by permission, from *Solyman the Magnificent Going to Mosque*, edited by Sir William Stirling Maxwell, 1877 381

A Renascence schoolmaster and his pupils. A sculptured relief from Giotto's Campanile at Florence. Photograph by Alinari 385

The Loggia dei Lanzi at Florence, itself a fine example of Renascence architecture, and containing a marvellous collection of masterpieces of Renascence sculpture. Reproduced, by kind permission, from a photograph by Dr. M. J. Rendall . . 389

One of the carved panels of the 'Gates of Paradise', by Lorenzo Ghiberti. Baptistery of St. John, Florence. Photograph by Anderson 391

The Quadrant and the Astrolabe were the chief instruments of medieval navigation. An astrolabe of 1574 . . . 395

The introduction of the potato to the Old World. An illustration from Gerarde's *Herball*, 1597 399

The Great Explorers: Columbus's fleet reaching America. From a woodcut of 1494. Magellan's ship *Victoria* . . . 401

Spain in the New World and the growth of slavery: Inside the silver-mines of Potosi. From *The Universal Magazine*, 1751; An African slaving post. From Moll's *Atlas* . . . 405

The Reformation. Preaching at St. Paul's Cross. From an engraving after a picture in the possession of the Society of Antiquaries 409

Interior of the House of Commons in 1742 . . . 415

The Grand Monarchy. Grounds of Louis XIV's palace at Versailles, from a contemporary print 419

The defeat of the French in North America and the Acquisition of Canada. Wolfe capturing Quebec. Photograph from the Rischgitz Collection 427

'The Smoking Club', by Bunbury, about 1780. Cotton-growing in the Mississippi Valley. A woodcut from *The Illustrated London News*, 24 Sept. 1881, by permission of the Editor . 431

Opening of the States-General, 5 May 1789 . . . 439

Siege of the Tuileries, 10 August 1792 441

The Reign of Terror. Pages taken from an alphabetical list compiled about 1795; out of these eighty-five persons, all but sixteen were guillotined, and seven of these sixteen committed suicide 443

LIST OF ILLUSTRATIONS

Napoleon Bonaparte. From an engraving in the British Museum	451
Napoleon's plan for the invasion of England. A fanciful print of 1798 contemplating invasion by air, sea, and a Channel tunnel	455
Napoleon and the growth of the French Empire. A cartoon of 1805 by Gillray; Napoleon helps himself to Europe, while Pitt holds the sea for England	457
Moscow. A general view of the Kremlin in 1913. Photograph by Mr. Louis Cahen	459
The era of steam. The *Great Eastern* off the Isle of Wight; launched 1858. Reproduced, by permission, from a contemporary colour print in the Science Museum, South Kensington	471
The old and the new. A century of progress in the railway engine. Photograph by The Special Press	473
Conditions in the Factories. Children in a rope factory. English factory slaves. Cartoon by Robert Cruikshank	477
The Chartist Movement: The Great Chartist gathering to present the Monster Petition. Police awaiting the procession in Hyde Park. From *The Illustrated London News*	485
Headquarters of Garibaldi, at the convent of San Silvestre in Rome. From *The Illustrated London News* of 1848	491
A *Punch* cartoon of Bismarck, 1883. By permission of the Proprietors of *Punch*	493
Great Britain in Egypt. The Battle of Omdurman. By permission of the Editor of *The Illustrated London News*	499
The earliest view of Canton harbour. From Nienhoff's *Embassy of the Dutch East India Company*, 1655	503
1, Livingstone received by an African chief, 1854, in what is now Northern Rhodesia. From his *Missionary Travels*, 1866. 2, Peace-making in New Zealand. A mission boat accompanying a war expedition, 1831. From Rev. W. Yate, *An Account of New Zealand*, 1835	507
Peasants on a Russian estate before the war. Photograph by Professor Nevill Forbes	513
The Crimean war. Balaclava harbour, with British Fleet and transports. From a photograph taken at the time	519
Neutrality under difficulties. Disraeli and the Bulgarian atrocities. A cartoon from *Punch*, August 1876, reproduced by permission of the Proprietors	521
Slave auctions in Richmond, Virginia, 1861. From *The Illustrated London News*, February 1861	525
American Industrialism in the twentieth century. A view of Pittsburgh. Photograph by Ewing Galloway, N.Y.	529

xvi   LIST OF ILLUSTRATIONS

The Skyscrapers of New York. Photograph by Aerofilms Ltd. . 531
Twentieth Century Communications: (i) Flying. Photograph by the British Overseas Airways Corporation. (ii) Radio. Photograph by the British Broadcasting Corporation . . . 545
Peace or War?: (i) A Meeting of the Security Council of the United Nations Organization. Photograph by Fox Photos. (ii) The Ruins of Hiroshima. Photograph by Associated Press 555

LIST OF MAPS

Egypt and the Nile Valley	17
The Ancient East	47
The Persian Empire at its Greatest Extent, 500 B.C.	62
Aegean Civilization	91
Greek and Phoenician Colonies, Sixth Century B.C.	111
Greece, Fifth Century B.C.	123
The Empire of Alexander the Great	145
Ancient Italy	162
The Roman Empire at its Greatest Extent under Trajan	191
Migrations of the German tribes in the Fifth Century	217
Palestine	235
The Mohammedan Empire in A.D. 750	283
Europe in 814. Death of Charlemagne	293
Ottoman Dominions at the death of Suleiman the Magnificent, 1566	380
Europe at the time of Napoleon's greatest power, about 1810	456
The Divisions of Italy before the Wars of Independence	487
Africa before the First World War	501
Europe in 1914 and 1966	537

EARLY MAN

IN the countless ages of the World's story which preceded the dawn of History, the evolution of life, both animal and vegetable, was profoundly affected by tremendous changes of temperature, whose full significance has only been realized within comparatively recent times. There were cold periods, four in all, known as Ice Ages, which were fatal to many forms of life; these were always preceded or succeeded by Sun Ages, when living things evolved and developed, first great writhing monsters who lived on banks of slime and fought and devoured each other, and who appear to have been destroyed by the intense cold of the Second Ice Age; then mammals such as horses and bears, very small at first, but gradually increasing in size as they became accustomed to their surroundings. The Ice Ages, which were not universal, either killed warmth-loving animals or caused them to migrate to sunnier climes, and it was the last Ice Age which appears to have caused the disappearance from England of such creatures as the elephant, the rhinoceros, and the hippopotamus. During this time the struggle for existence was hard and rigorous, and it gave man the opportunity of developing the brain which has enabled him to assert his mastery over all other created things.

How man originated is still very doubtful. Possibly he is descended from some man-like ape, or it may be that he and the great anthropoid apes such as the chimpanzee, the gorilla, and the orang-outang are all descended from a common ancestor. The earliest evidences of the existence of creatures which may have been human are flints and stones roughly chipped and shaped so that they could be held in the hand and used probably as axes. At Trinil in Java, at Heidelberg in Germany, and in Central Africa remains have been found, such as the top of a skull, teeth and a thigh bone, and a jaw bone, which may have belonged to ancestors of man. The Heidelberg remains probably belong to the warm period before the Fourth Ice Age; those found in Rhodesia and Tanganyika are thought to be much older. With the former were also found remains of rhinoceroses, elephants, lions, and other warmth-loving animals, evidently from a time of great forests and moist climates. Gradually, however, there was a cooling of the temperature and then some great disturbance in Southern Europe, resulting in the separation of Africa and Europe, and so it was no longer possible for animals to wander as they pleased from Europe to Africa or for the hunters to follow them; consequently the men and animals of the two continents would tend to become differentiated. In the gravel and sand-beds of the rivers Marne and Somme in France many of the rough flint implements used by these early hunters have been discovered. At Chelles-sur-Marne so many tools have been found that any resembling them are called Chellean. Here there was probably a flint industry; there was another at St. Acheul on the Somme, near Amiens, where much better tools were made. The stone axes of the Acheulean workers (who have given their name to the cool period which followed the warm Chellean period) had more even edges, and flint knives and awls and a primitive hammer were also made. It is probable that they bartered their wares for the fruits of the chase, and so were spared the necessity of hunting for their food.

As the climate grew colder and wetter, men began to live in caves, which did not, however, mean an end of wandering. When the days became warmer and herds of bison and wild ox came to graze on the fresh grass, the caves would be deserted until the snow and ice returned once more. We owe our knowledge of what these cave dwellers looked like primarily to the discovery of a skeleton at Neanderthal, near Dusseldorf in Germany. Human beings of this type lived probably about fifty thousand years ago ; and careful examination of their remains seems to establish the facts that they stooped, had no chins, and may have been incapable of speech. Their caves were warm and fairly comfortable, for the Neanderthalers were probably acquainted with the use of fire, which they may have got by striking iron pyrites with flints among dry leaves. Fires were very useful to keep wild animals— lions, bears, and hyenas—away, and it was probably the work of the women and children to see that they were kept alight and replenished with fuel when necessary.

The Neanderthal men had very simple, but often beautifully made, weapons of flint or wood which they used for hunting the smaller animals.[1] They also ate the flesh of the big beasts whenever they had the opportunity. They may have followed wounded animals, or killed them when at a disadvantage, when bogged or when in difficulties at awkward river crossings. It was very necessary for these men to live near streams, for they had no pots or vessels in which to carry water. Their clothes consisted of dried skins. Their food was very much varied in character—fish (which they caught with the hand alone), flesh, fowl, and the fruits of the earth such as nuts, crab-apples, pears, cherries, sloes, watercress, and fungi. They lived together in little groups, and the head of each group was head for just as long as he remained the strongest man within it. As he grew older and as his energy abated, some younger man might dispute his authority, kill him, and succeed to his position—a practice which is still quite common in the animal world. When the Dutch discovered Tasmania in 1642 they found a people little more advanced than these early Palaeolithic men. The Tasmanians wore no clothing ; they had not

[1] Their implements improved in quality as time went on. In 1908 a very interesting skeleton of a Neanderthal man was found in the cave of Le Moustier in Southern France, and near him an extremely well-made stone axe.

learned how to build a roofed hut; they could not make bows and arrows; they did not know how to fish; they had no horses, cows, sheep, or dogs; and they had no idea of pottery or of sowing seed or raising crops. But they cooked their meat; they had very good wooden spears tipped with stone, which they threw with great accuracy; they were very dexterous in weaving cups and baskets from bark fibre; and they had a simple language with words to express their possessions and what they did day by day. Their backward condition was due to their isolation from the rest of the human race. They had no stimulating competition, no examples to urge them any farther along the road of progress.

The Neanderthal type of man prevailed in Europe for about twenty-five thousand years. Then, about twenty-five thousand years ago, a new type appeared. It originated in North Africa or Southern Asia or perhaps in lands now submerged beneath the waters of the Mediterranean Sea. Probably these men came into Europe as the climate again became more temperate and the food and plants to which they were accustomed spread there. They seem to have been of two kinds : the Cro-Magnon type, so called because remains of them were first found in the grotto of Cro-Magnon in France, and the Grimaldi type, of whom skeletons were found in the cave of Grimaldi near Mentone. It is possible that there were types intermediate between them and the Neanderthalers. One such type appears to be represented by the skull found at Broken Hill, Rhodesia, in the summer of 1921. The brain is more highly developed than that of the Neanderthal type, the teeth and bones are quite human, and the creature whom it represents was almost certainly able to

---

1. Polished celt; 2. Double-barbed harpoon, Palaeolithic; 3. Eyed needle made of bone, Palaeolithic; 4. Point or javelin head, Palaeolithic; 5. Flint dagger, Neolithic; 6 Winged and tanged arrowhead, Neolithic; 7, 8. Pigmy tools, Palaeolithic and Neolithic; 9. Tanged arrowhead; 10. Sickle blade, Neolithic.

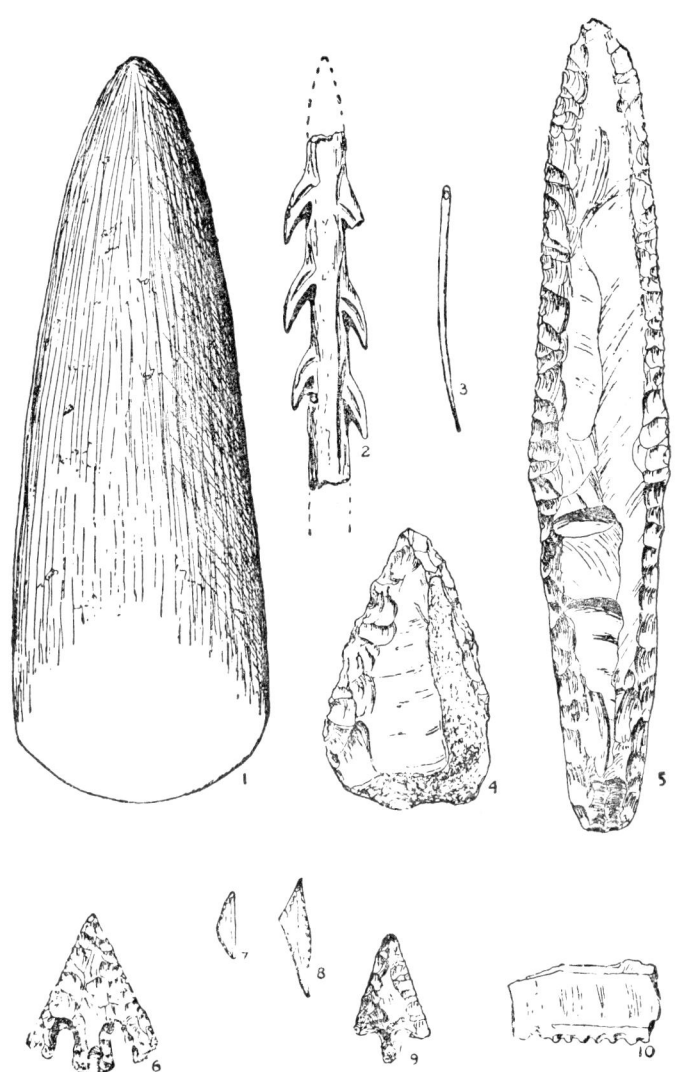

Some typical Stone Age implements
See note opposite

walk without a stoop. His face, however, must have been ape-like in appearance. The Cro-Magnon and the Grimaldi men mark a much higher stage in the evolution of the human race; they were men in every sense of the word; they were not grotesque or bizarre in appearance; they were certainly savages, but savages of a high order.

The Cro-Magnons were tall, with broad faces, prominent noses, and good brains: the Grimaldi men, of whom we know very little, seem to have been negroids. Neither race appears to have had anything to do with the Neanderthalers beyond dispossessing them of their caves and probably exterminating them. Both types—Cro-Magnon and Grimaldi—may have lived in the world at the same time, and both belong to what is known as the later Palaeolithic Age. During this period men used improved flint weapons, and, as time went on, implements of bone as well—harpoons, spear-heads, and very fine needles. They were great hunters and lived much in the open air. They appear to have hunted the mammoth and the horse as well as the reindeer and the bison. Horse was quite a favourite article of food among them, and it is possible that they also domesticated this animal; it is almost certain that they did not domesticate dogs. They were capable artists, increasing in skill as the centuries passed; they drew on bones and antlers, and on the walls of caves and cliffs; they employed colours, black, brown, red, yellow, and white, and some of their work is astonishingly good, such as that found by M. Santuola in 1879 in the caves of Altamira in Northern Spain. M. Santuola was really searching for flints. His little daughter, who was with him, getting tired of watching her father, had wandered away, and he, apparently, did not notice her absence until he heard her call ' Toros, Toros ' (Bulls, Bulls). He found her standing in a cave and pointing to a roof which was covered with coloured drawings or paintings of bulls, horses, deer, and wild boars, some of them life-size, and all of them remarkably realistic. Examples of Palaeolithic

Palaeolithic art. A boar from the caves of Altamira
After Breuil

drawings and paintings have frequently been found a good distance inside the caves, for the artists possessed lamps in which they burned some kind of fat. They also made small statuettes of ivory or soapstone. But no pottery of this period has been discovered; there were no buildings of any kind, possibly not even tents; and the art of cultivating the soil was unknown.

The Cro-Magnon type of human beings lived in Europe probably for about fifteen thousand years, and it is usual to distinguish different varieties of them and to name them after places where important remains have been found. Thus the Aurignacians, who lived twenty-five to thirty thousand years ago, are so called after the cave of Aurignac on a spur of the Pyrenees, where seventeen persons had been buried; the Solutreans after Solutré, near the River Saône, where they had a great open-air camp, and where in addition to the bones of human beings the remains of a very large number of wild horses which they hunted for food have been found; and the Magdalenians after the rock shelter of La Madeleine, where some of them lived. The Aurignacians were skilled artists and engravers who adorned the walls of their caves. The Solutreans had no great artistic talent, but they were very skilful in making spear-heads. They were warriors whose domination does not appear to have lasted very long. The Magdalenians were inferior as tool-makers to the Solutreans, although they were the first to invent harpoons made of bone. They probably made their first appearance in Western Europe about 16000 B.C., and during the six or seven thousand years covered by this period there were changes of temperature which had important results. At first it was very cold: cave-dwelling became essential; and the artists among them relieved the monotony of existence by paintings which still excite wonder and admiration. Then followed a time of icy winds and dust storms, and after that a period of temperate climate when Arctic animals migrated; and the Europe

THE NEW STONE AGE

that we know, a Europe of extremes neither of heat nor of cold, came into being. The Magdalenians were the most skilful of the Palaeolithic artists. The wonderful paintings in the cave of Altamira were done by them. They were engravers as well as painters, and on the rock shelter of Cap Blanc they executed a remarkable frieze of horses. Six horses, each about seven feet long, are carved out of the limestone. There are many other caves in this region of Southern France and Northern Spain, full of wonderful engravings and fascinating paintings, all testifying to the high degree of skill to which the Magdalenian artists had attained.

This race disappeared almost as mysteriously as it had come. It may be that it intermixed with the men and women of the next great age—the Neolithic or New Stone Age, which probably began about ten thousand years ago in Europe, and much earlier in the parts of Asia or Africa whence the Neolithic men came when the open steppes of Europe became wooded and the whole landscape took on a more modern appearance. The Neolithic Age is characterized by the manufacture and use of polished stone implements, in particular the stone axe, which was furnished with a wooden haft ; the beginnings of agriculture, pottery, and proper cooking ; plaiting and weaving ; and the domestication of animals. In course of time gold was discovered, then (about six or seven thousand years ago) copper, and later on tin, bronze, and iron. Neolithic men are the direct ancestors of modern men, and a fair amount is known concerning their habits and mode of life. They buried some of their dead with distinction and constructed great heaps of earth over them. They also built monuments known as dolmens, which in their simplest forms consisted of at least three erect unhewn stones supporting a large flattish stone. These may have marked the graves of people of importance, or, in their most elaborate forms, as at Stonehenge in Wiltshire and at Carnac in Brittany, they may have been temples.

Some tribe or tribes belonging to the Neolithic civilization settled in Switzerland, where they constructed peculiar kinds of villages known as lake villages, constructions of huts on timber platforms supported by piles driven into the bed of a lake. One such dwelling-place was discovered in 1854 when a particularly dry winter caused the water-level of the lake to be remarkably low, and the foundations of the village were revealed. Investigations followed, and discoveries were made of a great number of utensils and ornaments of wood, stone, and bone ; remains of food ; pieces of net ; and garments. Lake villages still exist as the homes of living people in New Guinea, and on the rivers Amazon and Orinoco in South America.

Neolithic men dressed chiefly in skins, but they also made a rough kind of linen. They seem to have been inferior to the later Palaeolithic men in artistic skill. They killed and ate deer, wild boar, and probably fox, but not horse. They did not eat hare, probably because they feared that if they did so the timidity of that animal would be communicated to themselves. Their agricultural methods were crude: ploughs and hoes were made of wood : wheat and barley were cultivated, but not oats and rye. They had a knowledge of sowing and reaping, and it may have come to them originally from their practice of burying wild grain with their dead. They caught fish by hooking or harpooning them. Towards the close of the age they may have practised some primitive form of barter, which would be greatly helped by the discovery of metals.

The Neolithic culture, like those which preceded it, did not end simultaneously in all parts of the world ; the use of metal, which is usually regarded as the harbinger of historic times, came at widely different times in different places. In Polynesia it did not come until the eighteenth century A.D. The oldest metal tools were made of pure copper, then came bronze tools, and after them tools made of iron. In most

A reconstructed view of a Neolithic lake village, built on piles

A raft-house on the Irrawaddy to-day; showing the modern survival of a very ancient type

countries the New Stone Age was succeeded by a Bronze Age, then by an Iron Age, and then, after a considerable lapse of time, by the discovery of writing; but in Egypt and Babylonia writing came before the discovery of iron. Probably writing, which is a way of expressing ideas, was a natural development of the arts of painting, sculpture, and engraving, which are ways of expressing objects. The fact that picture-writing was the earliest form of writing seems to support this conclusion.

Primitive men had some conception of religion. Sun-worship was probably the predominant idea, and Stonehenge may be the ruins of a great temple dedicated to the worship of the sun-god. Human sacrifices were offered to propitiate the angry deity, to secure good harvests, to avert or end pestilences, and to celebrate victory over enemies in war. Another factor in primitive religion was ancestor worship. The influence of the head of the family did not end at death : to avoid his wrath it was necessary to propitiate him afterwards. Sometimes it was considered sufficient merely to preserve his spear or other possessions and taboo their use or perhaps even contact with them. H. G. Wells has a graphic paragraph in which he visualizes the religious life of England three or four thousand years ago before the coming of civilization, and the alternating feelings of fear, awe, mystery, and even cheerfulness which primitive religion invoked :

'Away beyond the dawn of history, 3,000 or 4,000 years ago, one thinks of the Wiltshire uplands in the twilight of a midsummer day's morning. The torches pale in the growing light. One has a dim apprehension of a procession through the avenue of stone, of priests, perhaps fantastically dressed with skins and horns and horrible painted masks—not the robed and bearded dignitaries our artists represent the Druids to have been—of chiefs in skins adorned with necklaces of teeth and bearing spears and axes, their great heads of hair held up with pins of bone, of women in skins or flaxen robes, of a great peering crowd of shock-headed men and naked children. They have assembled from many distant places ; the ground between the avenues and Silbury Hill is dotted with their

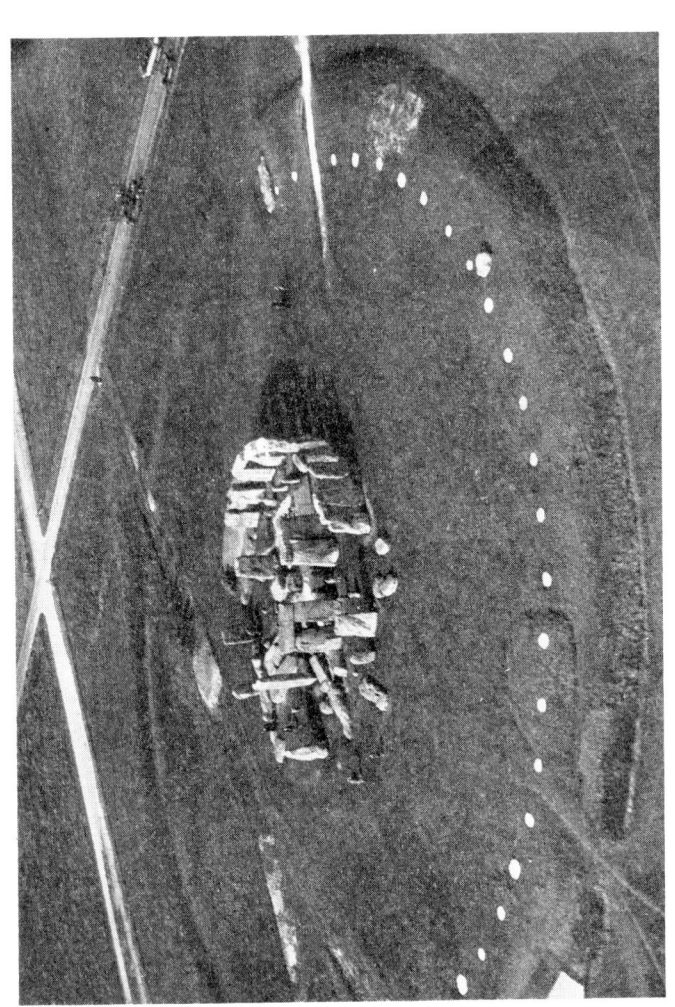

Neolithic civilization. Stonehenge from the air
Reproduced by permission of H.M. Stationery Office

encampments. A certain festive cheerfulness prevails. And amidst the throng march the appointed victims, submissive, helpless, staring towards the distant smoking altar at which they are to die—that the harvests may be good and the tribe increase.'[1]

The men of the Old Stone Age, even the artistic and highly developed Cro-Magnons, were not what we should call civilized. They were barbarians, but splendid barbarians. So too were Neolithic men, who, however, made a great step towards civilization by the practice of a form of agriculture, which tended towards settled habits of life. In the Old Stone Age nomadic customs prevailed. Men were hunters, and therefore wanderers. Comparatively few must have roamed over, and in a sense inhabited, vast tracts of territory, just as, to-day, Labrador, which is bigger than France, is inhabited by a few thousand Indians, who follow one great herd of caribou as it wanders north and then south again in search of food. The wanderings of primitive man would make his differentiation into groups or peoples practically impossible. This is confirmed by the fact that Palaeolithic remains, whether found in Somaliland, on the banks of the Nile, or in the drift deposits of the Seine or the Thames, are astonishingly similar.

Civilization implies settlement in definite territories, the building of cities, the evolution of ordered methods of government, the development of trade and commerce, and a capacity for progress which is unrestricted. The absence of writing and of ships were two things which made it impossible for the men of the Stone Ages to progress beyond a certain point; but while the inhabitants of Europe were still labouring under these disadvantages, in other parts of the world men had actually evolved civilizations which, in some respects, are not inferior to the finest civilizations of modern times. The earliest civilizations were those which sprang up in Egypt, Babylonia, China, India, and Crete, and of these the

[1] *Outline of History*, Chap. XII.

Egyptian and the Babylonian appear to be the oldest. It is not as yet at all certain which preceded the other, and the problem of the extent to which one ancient civilization affected another also awaits solution. It is possible that they were all indigenous and grew up out of their own roots.

II

EARLY CIVILIZATIONS—EGYPT

PROFESSOR FLINDERS PETRIE considers that Egyptian civilization is as old as 10000 B.C., and that even at this remote period of the world's history the Egyptians had well-made pottery modelled by hand, fine flint work, a little copper, but *no* weaving. The earliest governments were probably city-states. These eventually combined to form two kingdoms—one comprising the Nile Delta known as Lower Egypt, the other to the south known as Upper Egypt. The kingdoms were united by Menes, who succeeded to the southern state and conquered the northern, probably about 3400 B.C., although some authorities put it very much earlier.[1] With Menes begins the dynastic period of Egyptian history. He was the first king of the first dynasty, and when Alexander the Great added Egypt to his dominions in 332 B.C. it was the thirty-first dynasty which came to an end.

From very early times, thousands of years before Menes, the Egyptians believed in a future life. Valuable property was placed with the dead, including grain and linen. These discoveries are believed to indicate that Egypt was the country from which the first grain and flax came to Europe about six thousand years ago. In Egypt, too, the earliest taxes may have originated, in the form of measures of flax or grain which the peasants paid to their chieftains, who controlled the irrigation trenches by means of which Nile water was

[1] e.g. Dr. Flinders Petrie and Dr. Wallis Budge.

spread over the country during the annual overflowing of the river. If the peasant refused to pay his tax, the chieftain would stop his supply of water, and a failure of his crops would be the result.

The river Nile has in all ages been the source of the life and prosperity of the people of Egypt. In the early Dynastic period they had no knowledge of whence it came and they spoke of it as surrounding the whole earth. The Nile-god was regarded as a particularly potent deity. Some idea of the respect in which the Egyptians held him may be gathered from a Hymn to the Nile preserved on papyrus in the British Museum :

' Homage to thee, O Hapi (the river Nile or the river-god), thou appearest in this land, and thou comest in peace to make Egypt to live. Thou waterest the fields which Ra (the sun-god) hath created, thou givest life unto all animals, and as thou descendest on thy way from heaven thou makest the land to drink without ceasing. Thou art the friend of bread and drink, thou givest strength to the grain and makest it to increase, and thou fillest every place of work with work. . . . Thou art the lord of fish . . . thou art the creator of barley, and thou makest the temples to endure for millions of years. . . . Thou art the lord of the poor and needy. If thou wert overthrown in the heavens, the gods would fall upon their faces and men would perish. When thou appearest upon the earth, shouts of joy rise up and all people are glad ; every man of might receiveth food, and every tooth is provided with meat. . . . Thou fillest the storehouses, thou makest the granaries to overflow, and thou hast regard to the condition of the poor and needy. Thou makest herbs and grain to grow that the desires of all may be satisfied, and thou art not impoverished thereby.' [1]

It is possible that the art of writing originated in Egypt. The earliest form of writing was picture writing such as is still to be found among some uncivilized communities, e. g. the Indians of Alaska. Thus an Indian of Alaska, if he wished

[1] *A Guide to the Egyptian Collections in the British Museum*, pp. 9 and 10.

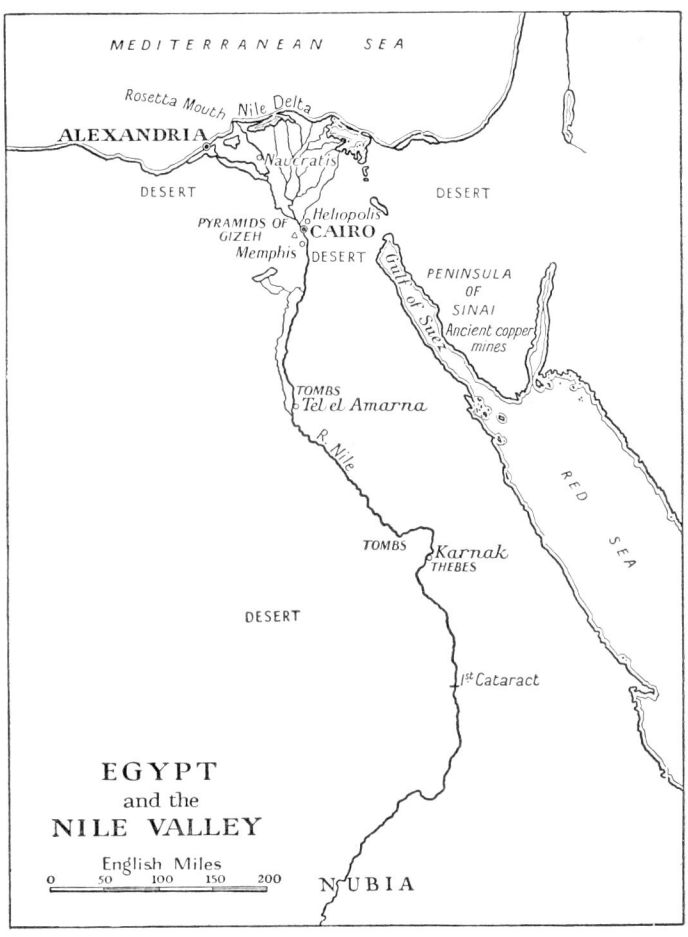

to send a message that he was starving, would carve on a piece of wood a figure with empty hands hanging downwards to denote dejection, and another figure pointing to a tent with one hand and to his mouth with the other to convey the full meaning. The ancient Egyptians advanced far beyond this cumbrous and very imperfect method, and, at least five or six thousand years ago, possibly much earlier, had invented for themselves an alphabet, the earliest known alphabet, consisting of twenty-four signs. They also had pens, inks, and paper (papyrus), and it is to them that the modern world is primarily indebted for these most necessary devices.

Example of the English word 'lake' written in Egyptian hieroglyphic characters. The first sign is the Egyptian letter *L*, the second the letter *K*. The three wavy lines are the determinative for water, showing that 'lake', is meant, and not 'look' or 'like'. The Egyptians had no vowel signs.

Writing materials consisted of papyrus, palette, reed pens, ink, and inkpot. Papyrus was made from the stem of the papyrus plant, a kind of reed which grew in marshes and pools near the Nile. It is no longer cultivated in Egypt, but is found in the Sudan, where it grows to a height of twenty to twenty-five feet and has very thick stems. The method of making papyrus was as follows : the stems were cut into thin strips and laid side by side perpendicularly : upon these another series of strips was laid horizontally : a thin solution of gum or paste was then run in between them, after which the sheet was pressed and dried. By joining a number of such sheets together rolls of great length could be made : one roll in the British Museum is 135 feet long and 17 inches wide. The palette was a rectangular piece of wood, eight to sixteen inches long and two to three inches broad, at one end of which were a number of circular or oval hollows to hold ink or paint, while down the middle was a groove to hold

Water pouring through the Assuan Dam

A village on the banks of the Nile

THE RIVER NILE

writing reeds. These were about ten inches long and from one-sixteenth to one-eighth of an inch in diameter. Ink was made by thickening water with gum and then mixing certain mineral or vegetable substances with it. Inkpots were usually made of porcelain.

There is a theory that Egypt was the country where the Age of Metal dawned. Some Egyptian banking his camp fire with copper ore in the peninsula of Sinai, as he stirred the embers next morning may have discovered globules of bright copper and thus stumbled upon a most important discovery. Before the age of metal the Egyptians built the tombs of their kings from sun-baked brick, but with the manufacture of copper tools it became possible to cut square blocks of limestone, and line the burial chambers of kings with them instead of with bricks. The earliest surviving example of stone masonry is a terraced building, sometimes called a step-pyramid, erected as a tomb for Zoser, who was ruler of Egypt somewhere about 3000 B.C. The architect's name was Imhotep; he was also famed as a physician and wise man. A century or so later, the art of building had progressed to such an extent that the Great Pyramid of Gizeh was being constructed for the Pharaoh Khufu or Cheops. It is a solid mass of masonry covering thirteen acres and containing 2,300,000 blocks of limestone each weighing on an average two and a half tons. The building was 481 feet high and its sides at the base measure 755 feet. According to one story, which is quite credible, a hundred thousand men worked at it for twenty years.[1] It is obvious that the ruler for whom it was constructed was a man of eminence, enjoying the assistance of a great body of officials. The palace of this king and the

[1] It has been usual to regard Khufu as a tyrant whose pyramid was the work of slaves or of workmen toiling under slavish conditions. Some Egyptologists, however, hold the view that he was a great benefactor to his subjects, giving the peasants work to do on the Great Pyramid during the months when the annual overflowing of the Nile made agricultural work impossible.

The step-pyramid of Sakkara, built by Imhotep

The Sphinx and the Great Pyramid of Gizeh

villas and offices of the officials which grew up around made up the royal city of Memphis, the capital of Egypt; the city has long since vanished, for it was built of sun-baked brick and wood. The city of the dead—the pyramids of the Pharaohs and the smaller tombs of relatives and holders of office—was of stone and has therefore proved more durable. So it is that from the summit of the Great Pyramid a wonderful view can be obtained of a line of pyramids stretching southwards as far as the eye can see. Each pyramid is the tomb of a king and bears witness to an epoch in Egyptian history known as the Pyramid Age, which lasted from about 3000 B.C. to about 2500 B.C. These remarkable structures testify to the Egyptian belief in a life after death, and the belief that in order to obtain this life it was necessary to preserve the body from destruction. Hence arose the practice of embalming, and the erection of pyramids and other tombs in which the dead body could be sheltered.

The tombs which cluster thickly around the pyramids of Gizeh are a storehouse of information about the lives of the Egyptians of the Pyramid Age, nearly five thousand years ago. Each tomb contains a chapel chamber in addition to the chamber below the ground where the mummy was laid. In this chapel-chamber food and drink were left daily by the relatives of the dead man, who was believed to be able to return for them; the walls were covered from floor to ceiling with beautifully painted pictures of life on the estate which had once belonged to the occupant of the tomb. These pictures give us a vivid idea of the degree of civilization which the Egyptians had attained at a time when Europeans had not advanced beyond the lake village stage. They tell us that in Egypt at this period there were cunning smiths; potters who made vessels of great beauty; glass workers; weavers of fine linen stuffs; makers of tapestry; goldsmiths whose work is hardly surpassed by that of the best goldsmiths and jewellers of the present day; cabinet-makers who made

An Egyptian scribe

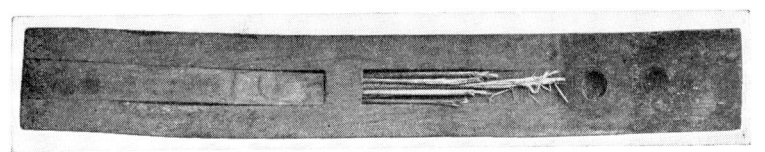

Wooden ink-pot and reed pens

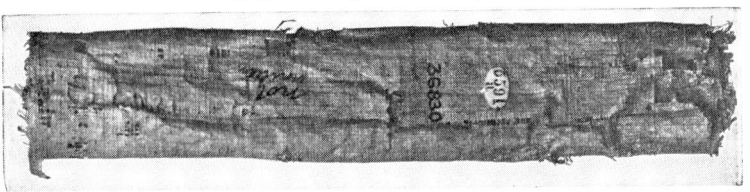

An unused roll of papyrus

WRITING IN EGYPT

chairs and couches for the king and rich people, much of it very beautiful, overlaid with gold and silver, inlaid with ivory and ebony, and upholstered with soft leathern cushions; and musicians who played upon the harp, pipe, or lute. The houses of the Egyptian nobles of this time were apparently much more beautiful than modern houses, and to each of them was attached a large garden where the lotus bloomed luxuriantly, and where the nobleman could enjoy his leisure with his family and friends, playing draughts or listening to music, while the women danced and the children amused themselves by splashing about in the fish pools, or by playing ball, or by teasing a tame monkey. Egypt was obviously a prosperous and affluent country enjoying a remarkable degree of culture. Many other things testify to this fact. Ships had been invented and trading expeditions were undertaken across the Mediterranean as far as Phoenicia. In addition, the Pharaohs were in the habit of sending caravans of donkeys (horses were apparently unknown) far up the Nile into the Sudan to deal with the black people of the south and bring back ebony, ivory, ostrich-feathers, and fragrant gums.

The art of sculpture was very highly developed. The portrait sculptor was the greatest artist of the age. His statues were carved in wood or stone and the eyes inlaid with rock-crystal. No age has produced more life-like portraits. The most famous of them, the largest portrait ever wrought, is the Great Sphinx, representing the head of a man upon the body of a lion. It has been suggested that the head is that of Khafre or Chephren, the king who built the second pyramid of Gizeh, but this is doubtful. The figure is about 160 feet long and about 70 feet high; the head is 33 feet long from crown to chin, and the face 13 feet 8 inches wide. Further examples of Egyptian sculpture were to be seen in the temples erected just outside the pyramids: granite pillars and colonnades, halls of much beauty, and superb statues of the kings to whom the temples were memorials. There was no

Ploughing, sowing, reaping, carrying, and threshing corn. From a fresco in a Theban grave

EGYPTIAN AGRICULTURE

chapel-chamber in a pyramid, merely a mummy-chamber at the end of a long passage. The place of the chapel-chamber was taken by the temple. To this the usual funerary gifts were brought, and its walls were adorned with a pictorial record of the achievements of the king whose mummy lay within the pyramid.

The Pharaohs of the Pyramid Age were absolute monarchs: there can be little doubt that the majority of the Egyptians lived in a state of serfdom, and that they regarded their king as the owner of both their souls and bodies. He was the essence of God in human form upon earth, and in the Other World his power was held to be equal to that of the great gods of the dead. With the close of the age there comes a change. There are long periods of confusion and anarchy; weak kings ascend the throne; some of them fail utterly to maintain their positions (the Seventh Egyptian Dynasty contained seventy kings who reigned for seventy days); temples are robbed, and works of art destroyed; and the country is split up once more into a number of small states or districts. In other words a sort of feudal system prevails in which the allegiance of the great lords to the king is little better than nominal. This period lasted apparently for several centuries until one of the nobles succeeded in founding a new dynasty (the Eleventh, about 2160 B.C.) with the city of Thebes (about 450 miles from Memphis) as its capital. This dynasty and that which succeeded it gradually asserted their authority over the whole of Egypt, and in course of time, with the increase of the power of the royal officials, the power of the feudal lords was almost reduced to nothing. The return of order and efficient government was followed by another burst of prosperity. The boundaries of Egypt were extended forty miles above the Second Cataract of the Nile, and an attempt was made to conquer Syria. The rise of the Nile was regularly recorded, and huge earthen dikes and basins constructed to store water from the river for irrigation purposes. Every few

Life in Egypt. A nobleman inspects his cattle. Models found in a tomb dating from about 2200 B.C.

years a census was taken for purposes of taxation ; some of these census lists have survived. The Pharaohs had by this time a small fleet which coasted along the Mediterranean and through the Aegean archipelago. A canal connected the north end of the Red Sea with the nearest branch of the Nile in the Eastern Delta where the river divides into many mouths. Thus the Mediterranean and the Red Sea were connected, and the Suez Canal had a predecessor over four thousand years ago.

But probably the most striking advance of the age was in literature. There were rolls on a great variety of subjects : science, mathematics, medicine, history, theology, and even fiction. One story known as ' The Tale of Sinuhe ' became so popular that it was even written on shards, or flags of stone, to be placed in tombs for the entertainment of the dead. It was also customary to write texts or directions on the insides of coffins for the benefit of the soul of the dead man, so that he would know how to deal with the demons and serpents whom he would meet on his journey to the Other World. These directions formed the nucleus of what in the Imperial Age became ' The Book of the Dead ', the most famous of all the Egyptian rolls. Some of the recipes prescribed on the medical rolls are still efficacious, others represent diseases as the work of demons. One of the medicines mentioned is castor oil. Another interesting roll of the period is one which sets forth the sufferings of the poor, appeals for justice to the lower orders of society, and speaks of an ideal time in the future when some righteous ruler, ' a Saviour who shall be the Shepherd of all his people,' shall bring in justice and happiness for all. This may have influenced the Hebrew prophets in their proclamation of the coming of a Messiah who should be the Deliverer of his people.

The period of Egyptian history between the end of the Twelfth and the beginning of the Eighteenth Dynasty is one

THE TEMPLE OF KARNAK

of which our knowledge is confused and somewhat contradictory. By some authorities it is considered to cover over five hundred years; others think it less than two hundred. For a considerable part of it Egypt was ruled by Semitic invaders known as Hyksos or Shepherd Kings. The Hebrews probably entered Egypt with them, as allies, and one of these kings may be the Pharaoh of the Oppression. They ruled from some city in the Delta, but for how long is uncertain. They gradually adopted the manners and customs of the Egyptians, and eventually the titles of the old Pharaohs, and became to all intents and purposes Egyptian kings. The Hyksos rule was not confined to Egypt; it almost certainly embraced Syria as well. Their adoption of Egyptian culture was not an unmixed blessing for them, for they never seem to have assimilated it properly; consequently their power slowly decayed, their kingdom broke up into petty states, and Thebes, the largest of them, at length became powerful enough to overthrow the Hyksos domination (about 1580 B.C.) and found the Eighteenth Egyptian Dynasty, inaugurating what is known as the imperial age of Egyptian history, which lasted for about four hundred and fifty years.

One of our chief sources of information for this period is the great Temple of Karnak, which made Thebes one of the most magnificent of the cities of antiquity. The walls of the temple are covered with enormous sculptures in relief picturing the wars of the Pharaohs of the period. They are to be seen in their chariots with the enemy scattered and prostrate before their plunging horses. Both the chariot and horse had been imported into Egypt from Asia during the Hyksos period. The Pharaohs of the Empire were great generals with standing armies chiefly composed of archers and charioteers. Their territories extended from the Euphrates in Asia to the Fourth Cataract of the Nile in Africa. One of them, Thothmes III, ruled for about fifty years, beginning about 1500 B.C. He was a great conqueror—the Napoleon of Ancient Egypt—and the successful issue of his campaigns in the Soudan and in Palestine, Syria, and other parts of Western Asia enabled him to be a generous friend of the priesthood and a great builder. He added considerably to the Temple of Karnak and constructed granite obelisks in Thebes, Heliopolis, and other places. One of these now stands on the Thames Embankment and is known as Cleopatra's Needle. The fleet of Thothmes III was only a little less efficient than his army; it carried his power to the Aegean, and one of his generals became governor of the Aegean Islands. For about ten years of his reign Thothmes ruled in association with his aunt Hatshepset, the first great queen in history; she is commemorated by a huge obelisk, a shaft of granite in a single piece nearly a hundred feet high just behind the great hall of the Temple of Karnak. After her death, Thothmes caused this obelisk to be hidden from sight by a great wall of masonry, lest the world might behold traces of the hated rule of a woman.

The Temple of Karnak took nearly two thousand years to complete and it is nearly a quarter of a mile long. The oldest parts were built during the feudal age and the newest—the front wall—by the Ptolemies, the Greek kings of Egypt. Practically everything which makes the temple famous belongs to the period of the imperial Pharaohs: the obelisk of Queen Hatshepset; the avenue of sphinxes leading from the temple to the Nile; and above all the great Hall of Columns, 338 feet wide and 170 feet long, covering a floor area equal to that of the cathedral of Notre-Dame in Paris, *and this is only a single room of the temple.* In the Hall of Columns there are 136 columns in sixteen rows. The twelve centre columns are each 79 feet high, and on the top of the capital of each a hundred men can stand at once.

The temples of Thebes were once bright with colour; vast battle-scenes were painted on their walls, and they shone with gold and silver in many parts. The colours have disappeared

The Great Temple of Luxor
An air-photograph by Sir Alan Cobham

and the temples are in ruins, but quite enough remains to give the most unimaginative a vivid idea of the magnificence of the age during which they were built, and the colossal scale upon which the Pharaohs undertook their building operations. The Temple of Karnak is not the only witness to this. About a mile distant from it is another temple, the Temple of Luxor, begun by Amenhotep III in the fifteenth century B.C., and on the other side of the river are more temples and two colossal statues of Amenhotep III.[1] These and similar statues were often 80 or 90 feet high and as much as a thousand tons in weight—and they were cut from a single block. Behind the statues of Amenhotep are majestic cliffs in which are cut hundreds of tomb-chapels belonging to the great men of the Empire—the great generals who commanded the expeditions which the Pharaohs sent into Nubia and Asia, and the great architects in whose brains the monumental city of Thebes was conceived. The records of their exploits are preserved in these tombs; here we may occasionally read a story of old romance such as that of the general who saved Thothmes III from an infuriated elephant during a hunt in Asia, by rushing in and cutting off the animal's trunk. Here also much of the elegant furniture of the period has been found, some of it real triumphs of artistic skill. Near Thebes the tomb of the parents of the wife of Amenhotep III has been discovered, containing some of the furniture which their royal son-in-law gave them: chairs covered with gold and silver and fitted with leathern cushions, jewel boxes, perfume caskets, a bed of sumptuous workmanship, and a chariot overlaid with gold. Still more wonderful were the treasures discovered in the tomb of the Pharaoh Tutankhamen in the latter part of 1922: magnificent state couches, boxes inlaid with ebony and ivory, four chariots whose sides were encrusted with precious stones and rich gold decoration, exquisite alabaster vases, a throne or chair

[1] The so-called Colossi of Memnon.

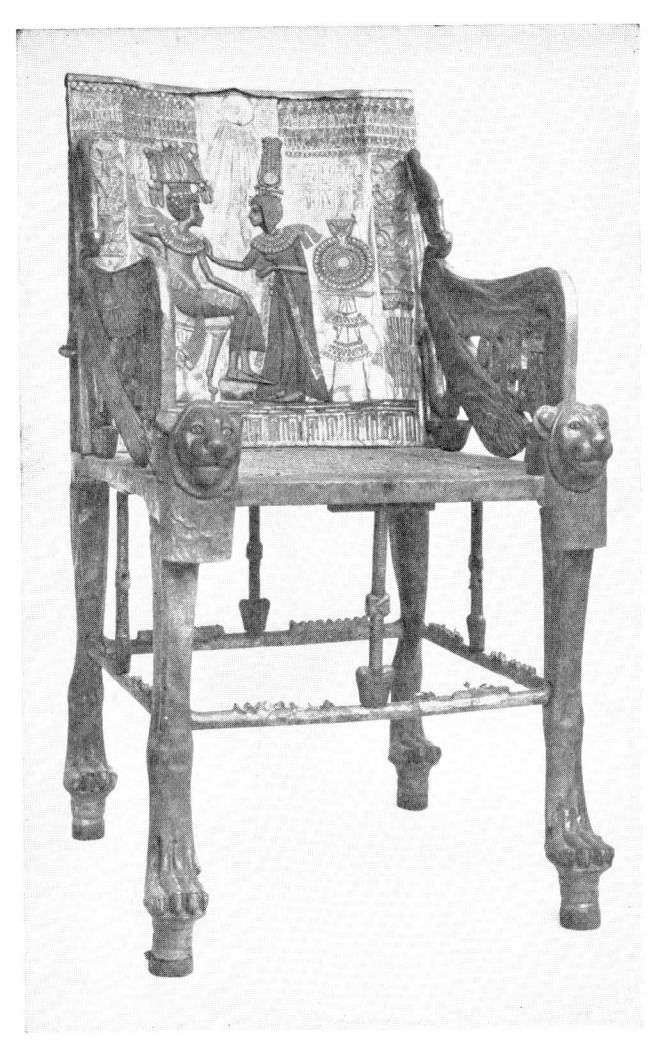

TUTANKHAMEN'S ARMCHAIR

Made of wood, overlaid with gold, and decorated with faience, glass, and stone inlay. The scene on the back shows Tutankhamen and his queen Ankhesenamen. This beautiful chair dates from about 1350 B.C., and is now in the Cairo Museum

of state covered with gold plating, and royal robes of the finest material decorated with elaborate bead and gold work. The best of the chariots, evidently the king's triumphal chariot, was in such excellent condition that the gold and stones which adorned it glistened in the sunshine as it was carried from the tomb.

When Amenhotep III died he was succeeded by his young son Amenhotep IV (1375-1358 B.C.) who, despite the fact that he only reigned eighteen years and was only thirty years of age when he died, carried through one of the most remarkable religious reformations in the history of the world. Although so advanced in other respects, the Egyptians were singularly backward in their religious conceptions. They believed in a multiplicity of gods of whom some were Ra, the sun-god; Osiris, the man-god who rose from the dead, was deified, and became king of the Other World and Judge of the Dead; Isis, his wife; Horus, their son; and Set, the principle of evil, the enemy of Osiris. Every district, city, town, and village possessed a god with a female counterpart and a son, and also a devil or thing of evil. It has been computed that in all there were about two thousand two hundred deities. For this confused and not very elevating religion Amenhotep IV substituted the worship of one God. He commanded that everywhere in his dominions, both in Africa and Asia, Aton the god of the solar disk should be worshipped and Aton alone; the temples of the old gods, including the Temple of Karnak, sacred to Amen-Ra, were closed and the very names of the gods erased from the walls; and the capital of Egypt was moved from Thebes to what is now known as Amarna (or Tel-el-Amarna) lower down the Nile. Amenhotep also changed his name from Amenhotep, which means 'Amen rests', to Akhnaton, which means 'Aton is satisfied'.

The worship of Aton was not new, but Akhnaton's conception of it was. The worship of the sun-god Ra, of whom

The Pharaoh Seti I in adoration before Osiris

Ra-amon

Isis, wife of Osiris

EGYPTIAN RELIGION

Aton was a manifestation, was general throughout Egypt, but it was not a particularly intelligent worship. When the sun was represented it was as a concrete solid ball, an object whose terrors were not under-estimated. One of the stories of the god Ra was that at one time he was so angry with mankind that he sent the goddess Hathor among them to destroy them indiscriminately. He stopped the work of slaughter before it was completed, but was so weary of men that after consultation with the other gods he decided to withdraw from the management of his own affairs : he accordingly created Elysian Fields, where he could spend his time in selfish enjoyment. For this Akhnaton substituted a more refined and philosophical worship. He conceived of Aton as a god who was a kind father to all ; even the birds in the marshes were aware of his goodness, uplifting their wings like arms to praise him. Aton was to be worshipped at sunrise and sunset, when the sun's rays are most kindly and beneficent. Akhnaton's idea was to stress the milder and humaner aspects of the sun and not as in the Ra worship of former times to represent him as a king of terrors. The same conception is to be seen in the rites which were practised in the temples of Aton. The air of terror, the sense of awe which had been artificially created by the priests of Amon-Ra by means of ceremonial processions, inner sanctuaries which no layman might enter, and curses upon those who failed to pay proper respect to the god, were wholly absent from the new religion. There were few priests, and the religious ceremonies which they performed were of a very simple nature, consisting of offerings of vegetables, fruit, and flowers to the deity, the singing of psalms, and prayers. Moreover, Aton was thought to delight less in these ceremonies than in the natural thanksgivings of all living things : the birds singing upon the trees, young calves frisking through the meadows, and man working in a joyous and contented frame of mind.

Akhnaton did not allow any graven image of Aton to be

made. He spoke of God as formless, a kind of divine essence pervading space, and his theory is remarkable not only on account of its nobility but also by reason of its scientific accuracy. No one until this time seems to have realized that the rays of the sun are the means of the sun's action, the source of all life, beauty, and energy. Flinders Petrie says that no conception that can be compared with this for scientific accuracy was reached for at least three thousand years after it. Again, ' How much Akhnaton understood we cannot say, but he had certainly bounded forward in his views and symbolism to a position which we cannot logically improve upon at the present day. Not a rag of superstition or of falsity can be found clinging to this new worship.'[1]

According to beliefs current in Egypt before the time of Akhnaton, when a man died his soul had to undertake a fearsome journey through the Tuat or Other World to the judgement halls of Osiris. The Book of the Dead and The Book of Gates were written so as to give people instructions how to pass the various evil spirits whom they would encounter. Much of what is contained within these books is extraordinarily childish. Thus the Book of Gates relates how it is necessary to pass the serpent Apep, who is guarded by four gods armed with curved knives, and four other gods, each having four snakes as heads. But these are, apparently, not sufficient, for sixteen additional gods are added who are assisted by a hidden hand and five other gods. When the soul arrived before Osiris it had to submit to a rather grotesque form of judgement. If the weight of the dead man's heart failed to counterbalance an ostrich feather, the symbol of righteousness, it was cast to an animal called The Eater of the Dead, which was partly lion, partly crocodile, and partly hippopotamus. When the heart and the feather balanced exactly Osiris rewarded the deceased according to his deserts, the joys of the Elysian Fields apparently being graduated.

[1] *History of Egypt*, in six volumes, vol. ii (published by Methuen).

Akhnaton admitted none of these weird beliefs into his religion. Spirits, monsters, serpents, even Osiris himself and all his court were treated as non-existent. Akhnaton believed that when a man died his soul continued to exist as a kind of immaterial ghost, sometimes resting in the dreamy halls of heaven, sometimes visiting in shadowy form those places which it valued most on earth. The soul could still enjoy the pleasures of sunshine, the singing of birds, and the beauty of flowers. There is no mention of a hell for the souls of the wicked, for Akhnaton would not believe that God would allow any of his creatures, however sinful, to suffer endless torture. Apparently the only punishment that was meted out to those who had led evil lives on earth was annihilation. When death came they simply ceased to exist.

It was quite customary for the Egyptians to compose hymns in honour of their gods. Some of them, like many of the Hebrew psalms, are not of a high moral tone; they glorify war and take evident delight in the wrath and thunders of the gods. Very different is the great Hymn to Aton, probably composed by Akhnaton himself. It is one of the greatest poems of antiquity, full of joy and profound thankfulness for the life and beauty which the sun's rays give to nature and to all living creatures:

[1] ' Thy appearing is beautiful in the horizon of heaven;
The living Aton, the beginning of life,
Thou risest in the horizon of the east,
Thou fillest every land with thy beauty.

Thou art very beautiful, brilliant, and exalted above earth,
Thy beams encompass all lands which thou hast made,
Thou art the sun, thou settest their bounds,
Thou bindest them with thy love,
Thou art afar off, but thy beams are upon the land;
Thou art on high, but the day passes with thy going.

. . . .

[1] F. Ll. Griffith's translation (Flinders Petrie's *History of Egypt*, vol. ii. Pub. by Methuen).

How many are the things which thou hast made:
Thou createst the land by thy will, thou alone,
With peoples, herds and flocks.
Everything on the face of the earth that walketh on its feet,
Everything in the air that flieth with its wings,

.   .   .   .

By thee the people live, they look on thy excellences until
   thy setting,
They lay down all their labours when thou settest in the west,
And when thou risest they grow ...'

There is no mention of war in the poem. Only once, and that on a private tomb, is there any mention of it during the reign. Domestic affection was Akhnaton's ideal of life. His queen and children are shown with him on every occasion. He refers to her in the Hymn as

' the great royal wife, his beloved, lady of both lands,
   Nefertiti, living and flourishing for ever eternally.'

War and vulgar conquest were considered to be utterly repugnant to Aton. Some of Akhnaton's subjects tested the sincerity of the king's beliefs by rebelling against him. Syria was taken by a tribe from Asia Minor called the Hittites, and Palestine was invaded by the Hebrews; but Akhnaton, although loth to lose these lands, refused to win them back by armed force.

Akhnaton was too great for his day and generation. The religion which he founded did not long survive him, probably only a few years. Under his son-in-law Tutankhamen the old religion was restored. Amarna was deserted, the priests of Amon recovered their influence and Thebes became the capital of Egypt once more. Akhnaton was denounced as a villain and heretic; even his mummy was not spared. The name was cut out of the gold ribbons which passed round it, so that (according to a belief current in Egypt at the time) the king's soul was debarred from the benefit of earthly prayers and forced to wander unpitied and unknown through the Other World. Arthur Weigall has thus expressed it:

'Through starry space the execrations of the priests passed, searching out the wretched ghost of the boy, and banning him as they supposed, even in the dim uncertainties of the Lands of Death. Over the hills of the west, up the stairs of the moon, and down into the caverns under the world, the poor twittering shadow was hunted and chased by the relentless magic of the men whom he had tried to reform. There was no place for his memory upon earth, and in the under world the priests denied him a stone upon which to lay his head.[1] It is not easy now to realize the full meaning to an Egyptian of the excommunication of a soul: cut off from the comforts of human prayers; hungry, forlorn, and wholly desolate; forced at last to whine upon the outskirts of villages, to snivel upon the dung heaps, to rake with shadowy fingers amidst the refuse of mean streets for fragments of decayed food with which to allay the pangs of hunger caused by the absence of funeral offerings. To such a pitiful fate the priests of Amon consigned "the first individual in history"; and as an outcast amongst outcasts, a whimpering shadow in a place of shadows, the men of Thebes bade us leave the great idealist, doomed, as they supposed, to the horrors of a life which will not end, to the misery of a death that brings no oblivion.'

The same writer has given us an admirable summing up of what he considers Akhnaton's permanent contribution to the cause of progress to be:

'In an age of superstition and in a land where the grossest polytheism reigned absolutely supreme, Akhnaton evolved a monotheistic religion second only to Christianity itself in purity of tone. He was the first human being to understand rightly the meaning of divinity. When the world reverberated with the noise of war, he preached the first known doctrine of peace; when the glory of martial pomp swelled the hearts of his subjects he deliberately turned his back upon heroics. He was the first man to preach

[1] *Life and Times of Akhnaton,* by Arthur Weigall (pub. by Thornton Butterworth).

DISCOVERIES AT TEL-EL-AMARNA

simplicity, honesty, frankness, and sincerity; and he preached it from a throne. He was the first Pharaoh to be a humanitarian; the first man in whose heart there was no trace of barbarism. He has given us an example three thousand years ago which might be followed at the present day : an example of what a husband and a father should be, of what an honest man should do, of what a poet should feel, of what a preacher should teach, of what an artist should strive for, of what a scientist should believe, of what a philosopher should think. Like other great teachers he sacrificed all to his principles, and thus his life plainly shows—alas— the impracticability of his doctrines; yet there can be no question that his ideals will hold good " till the swan turns black and the crow turns white, till the hills rise up to travel and the deeps rush into the rivers." '[1]

Many interesting discoveries have been made at Tel-el-Amarna on the site of the city which Akhnaton made his capital and which was deserted by Tutankhamen. In 1888, in a low brick room which had served as an archive chamber of the Egyptian foreign office, about three hundred letters and dispatches were found. These constitute the oldest international correspondence in existence. They are written on clay tablets in Babylonian writing and throw light on the relations existing between the Pharaohs and the kings of Western Asia. Another remarkable find was made in 1912— a statue showing the head of Nefertiti, the queen of Akhnaton. One authority has described it as 'perhaps the most life-like portrait in all Egyptian art', and another as work that ' could

[1] Egyptologists do not all agree that Akhnaton was a great man. Some go so far as to assert that he was a misguided fanatic, whose ignorance and obstinacy almost ruined his country; who deserted his loyal servants in Syria and Palestine; forced a religion which they detested upon his subjects; and who may possibly have taken up his attitude of hostility to the cult of Amen-Ra because he coveted the possessions of the god, rather than because he hated the great national religion of Egypt. Akhnaton, according to this theory, was the victim of heredity and circumstances, who, towards the close of his reign, became so conscious of his own disabilities, mental as well as physical, that he appointed one of his sons-in-law, whose name was Sakara, to rule with him.

only be compared with the finest work of any country or period whatsoever '.

Akhnaton was the last great king of the Eighteenth Dynasty. Not long after his death—probably about eight years—the Nineteenth Dynasty began. Two of its kings, Seti I and his son, Rameses II, succeeded in winning back some of the lost military glory of the Egyptian Empire, although Syria was never fully recovered. Rameses II[1] ruled for sixty-seven years (1292-1225 B.C.). He fought wars in the Soudan and in Syria, but he was not a great soldier like Thothmes III, and the only striking exploit of his military career appears to have been the battle of Kadesh in Syria, the details of which he caused to be recorded on every temple which he built or restored. Very often illustrations of Rameses' gallantry are accompanied by a poem, which does not fail to flatter the king, the work of one of the court poets, once wrongly believed to be Penta-ur, a young scribe who made a copy of the composition on papyrus. Kadesh was a town on the river Orontes, which the Egyptians attacked, and the poem relates how Rameses had charged far ahead of his troops who had either been killed or had run away. His position was desperate, but undismayed he cut his way back through his foes, alone and unaided, for none of his soldiers were bold enough to come to his assistance. Rameses was by no means loth to sing his own praises, or even to claim the credit for achievements which were not his. His record as a builder proves this : he frequently caused his own name to be inscribed on statues or monuments which he did not make. And yet his own personal record ought to have been sufficient to satisfy the most covetous desirer of fame, for Rameses II was a very great builder. He completed the Hall of Columns at Karnak ; he added to the Temple at

[1] There is a popular theory that Rameses II was the Pharaoh who oppressed the Israelites, and that it was under his son and successor Menephthah that the Exodus took place.

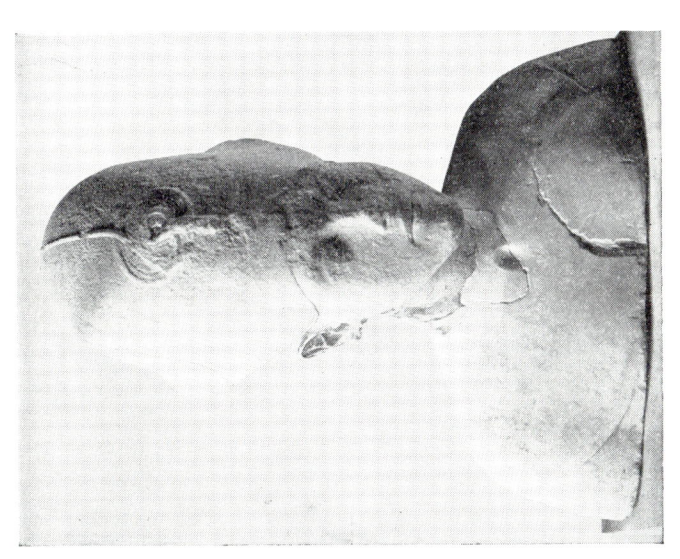

Akhnaton and his wife Nefertiti

Luxor begun by Amenhotep III and carried farther by Tutankhamen; he set up several statues of himself and two granite obelisks, each about 80 feet high; and, above all, he was responsible for the great Temple of Abu Simbel in Egyptian Nubia. This temple was cut out of the sandstone cliffs; it is 185 feet long and 90 feet high. In the large hall are eight square pillars each 30 feet high, each with a colossal figure of Osiris 17 feet high leaning against it. In front of the temple are four huge statues of the king, 60 feet high and hewn out of the sandstone cliff. The temple was dedicated to Ra-Harmakhis, the Rising Sun, and it was so situated that at sunrise the rays of the sun shone into it, illuminating the figures in the innermost shrine.

Towards the close of the imperial period the Egyptians employed numbers of foreigners in their armies—a sure indication of weakness and decline. The subsequent history of the country is somewhat chequered. The great days are over; the various dynasties have frequently to fight for their very lives against African and Mediterranean invaders; we read of confederations of people from Philistia, Cyprus, Crete, and the northern shores of the Mediterranean invading Egypt by both land and sea; there is often trouble in Western Asia (about 930 B.C. the Pharaoh Shishak plundered Solomon's Temple);[1] and in 670 B.C. the Assyrians conquered Egypt. Under Psammetichus I (664–610 B.C.) native rule was restored for a while. His successor Necho II recovered former Egyptian possessions in Syria while the Medes and Chaldeans were attacking Nineveh. He was the king who defeated and slew Josiah, King of Judah, in the valley of Megiddo (2 Kings xxiii). He was in turn defeated by Nebuchadnezzar the Chaldean and forced to give up his conquests in Western Asia. The Jews who had allied themselves with him were taken as captives to Babylon. In the sixth century B.C., after the fall of Babylon, Egypt was conquered by the Persians.

[1] 1 Kings xiv. 25–6.

The Great Temple at Abu Simbel, showing the four statues, each 60 feet high

Later on, a successful rebellion resulted in sixty years' independence (*c.* 400–340 B.C.). Then followed about eight more years of Persian overlordship, until in 332 B.C. Alexander the Great was welcomed as the saviour of the country from the hated rule of the Persians. Since then Egypt has been subject to various foreigners—Greeks, Romans, Arabs, Turks, and British. In 1952 King Farouk of Egypt abdicated; a Republic was proclaimed in 1954, and four years later Gamal Nasser was made President of the United Arab Republic.

III

EARLY CIVILIZATIONS—BABYLONIA AND ASSYRIA

CONTEMPORARY with Egyptian civilization and possibly of even earlier origin was that which sprang up in Western Asia in the river valleys of the Tigris and Euphrates, the region which is sometimes called Mesopotamia. Before men and women can settle down in cities three things are necessary : a plentiful or at least a sufficient supply of food ; water ; and building materials. In both Egypt and Mesopotamia these conditions were easily satisfied. In Egypt there were the Nile, limestone quarries, and sun-baked brick, and lands rendered fertile by Nile mud after the annual overflowing of the river. In Mesopotamia there were the rivers Tigris and Euphrates, clay that became brick in the sunshine, and trustworthy harvests year by year. The cultivation of wheat may have originated in this part of the world, for here alone has it been discovered growing wild.

The earliest people to found cities in Mesopotamia were the Sumerians, a mysterious race, neither Aryan nor Semite, probably dark-white in complexion. They used a kind of writing which they scratched with a reed pen upon soft clay, which became very hard when exposed to sunlight. Their first writing was picture-writing; then, at a very early date, it became phonetic. Sumerian writing finally possessed over three hundred and fifty signs, each sign representing a syllable. It was never alphabetic: there would be a sign for KAR but none for the letters composing that syllable.

[Map: THE ANCIENT EAST. English Miles 0–500. Pal. = Palestine. Features shown include Black Sea, Caucasus Mts., Greece, Troy, Asia Minor, Crete, Cnossos, Cyprus, Mediterranean Sea, Nile Delta, Sahara Desert, Egypt, Sinai, Red Sea, Arabia, Armenia, Media, Tigris, Sargonburg, Nineveh, Assur, Assyria, Ecbatana, Byblos, Euphrates, Phoenicia, Damascus, Akkad, Babylon, Sumeria, Ur, Chaldea, Susa, Persia, Persian Gulf, Jerusalem, Desert.]

Owing to the curious wedge-shaped character of this writing it is called cuneiform (Latin *cuneus*, a wedge). Paper and parchment seem to have been unknown to these people. ' Their books and memoranda, even their letters, were potsherds ' (H. G. Wells).

The chief city of the Sumerians was Nippur (on the Euphrates, a little south of Babylon). Excavations conducted there by the University of Pennsylvania have revealed evidence of a city community existing as early as 5000 B.C. and possibly

6000 B.C.—an earlier date than any city we have any record of in Egypt. At Nippur the Sumerians built a great tower to their chief god, Enlil, god of the air. Other towns did the same, and the tower at Babylon (Babel) may have inspired the Biblical story of the Tower of Babel.[1] Sumeria at this time was divided into city-states, which often fought for mastery among themselves. Each of them, probably, had a king; an aristocracy of royal officials and priests; a middle class of merchants, landowners, craftsmen, and shop-keepers; and, lowest of all, slaves who did the rough and menial work. The priests were evidently very powerful: before the institution of kingship, cities were ruled by chief priests; and the first of all known empires was that founded by the high priest of the city of Erech, extending, according to an inscription found at Nippur, from 'the lower to the upper sea', that is, from the Persian Gulf to the Mediterranean or the Red Sea. Very famous was the city of Ur, whence the patriarch Abraham emigrated to the land of Israel (Canaan).[2] Recent excavations on the site of ancient Ur have revealed evidences of wealth and fine craftsmanship during a period stretching from about 3200 to 2000 B.C. They include statues which once adorned the temples of the gods; vessels and ornaments of gold, silver, alabaster, ivory, and lapis lazuli; silver harps, chariots, exquisitely inlaid furniture, golden helmets, beautifully designed necklaces, bracelets, and other jewellery.

About 2750 B.C.[3] the Sumerian Empire came to an end when the whole of Sumeria was overrun by a Semitic people known as the Akkadians—nomads who came from the inhospitable, almost desert lands to the north. Under their leader Sargon I, they conquered the Sumerians and founded an empire reaching from the Persian Gulf to the Mediterranean. This empire endured for over two hundred years,

---

[1] Gen. xi. 1–10.   [2] Gen. xi. 27–32.
[3] Authorities differ on this date. Some put it a thousand years earlier, some at about 2500 B.C.

An air-view of Nippur, a great Sumerian town, showing the ruins laid bare by modern excavation. The mound is a tower built in honour of Enlil, god of the air (see top of p. 48)

R.A.F. official photograph: Crown copyright reserved

and is known as the Sumerian-Akkadian Empire. It is fitting that it should be so called, for though the Akkadians conquered the Sumerians, Sumerian civilization conquered that of the Akkadians, who learnt the Sumerian writing and the Sumerian language, and adopted the Sumerian calendar and system of weights and measures. They also learnt the Sumerian art of sculpture, but in this they soon surpassed their teachers.

As the Sumerian-Akkadian Empire declined, other Semitic tribes appeared in Mesopotamia. The Elamites conquered some of the southern cities, while the Amorites from Syria settled in the north somewhere about 2200 B.C. and established themselves in the as yet small village of Babylon. Under their great king, Hammurabi (about 2100 B.C.), they succeeded in overthrowing both the Sumerians and the Elamites, and Babylon became the capital of a new empire which was much more prosperous than anything that had preceded it. The country was rich in grain and also in sheep and cattle, the weaving of woollen cloth became an important industry, and merchants conveyed the products of the land on the backs of donkeys to various parts of Western Asia. There seem to have been no painters at this time and no notable sculpture; otherwise the community over which Hammurabi ruled was a highly developed one. Perhaps the most notable achievement of the reign was the codification of the laws, which were engraved on a piece of stone eight feet high, at the top of which was a sculptured scene representing Hammurabi receiving the law from the Sun-God. The code is not written in Sumerian, but in the Semitic language of the Akkadians and Amorites. Some of it is very good, such as the laws enacting that justice shall be done to poor people, widows, and orphans; some of it is characteristic of the age and would not satisfy modern conceptions of justice. Thus, if a house fell down and caused the death of the householder's son, the code directs that the son

A specimen of cuneiform writing

A Sumerian priest
B. C. 3000

King Gudea of Lagash
B. C. 2600

SUMERIAN ART AND HANDWRITING

of the builder shall be put to death, the old conception of 'an eye for an eye and a tooth for a tooth', also to be found in the law of Moses, which closely resembles the Code of Hammurabi in many respects.

Other important remains of this period which have been unearthed are some fifty-five letters written on tablets of clay, from Hammurabi to some of his officials in the conquered cities of Sumeria. They throw considerable light on the life of Babylonia four thousand years ago. They deal with a variety of subjects. There are instructions relating to the collecting of taxes ; to the clearing of the Euphrates after a flood ; to the attendance of officials at a sheep-shearing festival to be held in the spring ; and to the punishment of bribery.

There were schools in Babylonia at this time. The scholars wrote on slates of soft clay, from which they could rub out their exercises at any time by smoothing the surface with a flat piece of wood or stone. The chief and perhaps the sole object of such schools was to teach children the art of writing, which was not an easy task since it meant the memorizing of some three hundred and fifty signs. The esteem in which those who could write were held is shown by a proverb of the time found on the walls of an old school-house—' He who shall excel in tablet writing shall shine like the sun.' This old school-house was discovered in 1894 by French excavators : it was about fifty-five feet square, and has a peculiar interest as the oldest school-house in existence.

The priesthood was still a powerful and influential class. More than one deity was worshipped, particularly Marduk, who took the place of Enlil as the chief of the gods, and Ishtar, the Asiatic goddess of love, who afterwards became the Aphrodite of the Greeks and the Venus of the Romans. Among the benefits conferred by the gods was supposed to be ability to foretell the future. Priests claimed to be able to

King Hammurabi. From a contemporary sculpture

Some typical Babylonian weights

interpret mysterious signs on the liver of a sheep which had been sacrificed, and so predict coming events. This practice afterwards spread westwards ; it was much used in republican Rome. Another way of foretelling the future was by observation of the movements and positions of stars and planets, a practice which developed under the Chaldeans into astrology, the parent of astronomy.

Meanwhile, higher up the Tigris, on uplands which might be expected to produce greater vigour than the plains of Babylonia, another Semitic people had settled. These are known as the Assyrians, and their first settlements were made even before the downfall of the Sumerian Empire. Their chief cities were Assur and Nineveh. Among them great beards and ringletted hair were fashionable. Sargon I conquered them, but they soon regained their freedom. They were mighty warriors and exacters of tribute ; they were frequently at war with the Hittites ; the adoption of the horse and chariot gave them a military advantage over their enemies, and probably about 1100 B.C. they conquered Babylon; but their hold was not secure, and some centuries elapsed before they established a real supremacy. Nineveh at this time was a poor place. It was not until the time of Sennacherib that it became the most magnificent city of the East and the capital of the Assyrian Empire.

For something like four hundred years the expansion of Assyria towards Egypt and the Mediterranean was hindered by another Semitic people—the Arameans, whose chief city was Damascus, and from whom the Syrians of to-day are descended. The Arameans were a highly civilized race. By 1000 B.C. they were using alphabetic writing which they had borrowed from another Semitic people, the Phoenicians : they used papyrus, the reed-stylus, and ink like the Egyptians : their merchants were rich and prosperous, and together with their wares they carried the alphabet (which was to displace cuneiform signs) through the land of the two rivers and

RELIGION AND SCULPTURE

thence down the Euphrates to other Asiatic lands as far as the frontiers of India. Their language became well known, in course of time displacing the Assyrian speech to such an extent that public business in Assyria was finally carried on in both languages. Assyrian tablets have been found with marginal notes in Aramaic, and it was a common thing in the Assyrian Empire to find Aramean and Assyrian clerks in government offices; the former keeping their records by writing with pen and ink on a roll of papyrus, the latter by writing cuneiform characters on tablets of clay. The Aramean language seems to have displaced the Hebrew of Palestine entirely, and it was the language spoken by Jesus and the Jews of his time.

The art of sculpture was more highly developed by the Assyrians than by the contemporary Babylonians. The valiant actions of kings are recorded in elaborate stone pictures cut in flat relief on great slabs of alabaster, which were set up in long rows along the palace walls. This architectural sculpture was an art not practised in Babylonia, probably because of the lack of stone. In the uplands of Assyria, on the contrary, there were promontories of rock which furnished quarries of limestone and alabaster. In religion there was little difference between the two peoples. The Assyrians took over and revered the sacred stories and god-like symbols of Babylonia, and they were great worshippers of Ishtar, goddess of love. But they clung to their old tribal god Assur, a fierce god of war whom they identified with the sun. He is represented by the sculptor as a winged sun disk (a symbol borrowed through the Hittites from Egypt) shooting deadly arrows among his foes.

In 745 B.C. Tiglath Pileser III, the Tiglath Pileser of the Bible (2 Kings xvi. 7) became ruler of Assyria. He is the real founder of the Assyrian Empire. He conquered and ruled Babylon, and in 732 B.C., with the fall of Damascus, Syrian opposition to Assyrian schemes of aggrandizement was at length broken down. Tiglath Pileser was succeeded by his son Shalmaneser IV, who died during the siege of the Jewish city of Samaria and was succeeded by a usurper, an Assyrian general who took the name of Sargon II. He and his son Sennacherib were great builders and conquerors: under them the Assyrian Empire became the greatest that had yet appeared in the land of the two rivers. Sargon II built a great palace at Sargonburg (Dur-Sharrukin, north-east of Nineveh), which covered twenty-five acres and whose enclosure was a mile square, large enough to accommodate 80,000 people. Sennacherib destroyed Babylon and made Nineveh the finest city in Western Asia—a city of vast palaces and imposing temples.

The Assyrian Empire was essentially military, owing its foundation in no small part to the discovery and use of iron weapons. Its armies were composed of spearmen, archers, and charioteers, and its methods were merciless in the extreme. Piles of corpses, pyramids of skulls, traitors flayed alive and stuck to stakes, were some of the signs of the advance of an Assyrian army. Conquered territories groaned under a heavy weight of tribute, and the Egyptians often tried to organize rebellion among the tribute payers. At last Sennacherib determined to conquer Egypt, but the outbreak of a pestilence which decimated his army defeated his intentions (2 Kings xix), and it was not until the time of his grandson Assurbanipal that Egypt was conquered. Assurbanipal was the last great Assyrian emperor. It was his boast that his father had instructed him not only in riding and in shooting with bow and arrow, but also in writing on clay tablets, and in all the wisdom of his time. He had a magnificent library of 220,000 clay tablets (now in the British Museum), a depository of the literary, scientific, and religious ideas of his own and past ages.

Although such ruthless and barbaric conquerors, the Assyrians were by no means blind to culture. The art of

An Assyrian war-chariot. A sculptured relief of about 650 B.C. in the Louvre

sculpture was highly developed among them. The ruins of their palaces are full of excellent examples of it—vast human-headed bulls cut in alabaster, pictures in relief on the lower walls also of alabaster, illustrating the great exploits of their emperors in war and on the hunting field—but the art and industries of the Assyrians were not native. They got from Egypt their knowledge of how to glaze coloured brick : all their decorative patterns and their furniture of ebony and ivory were copied from the same source. Cotton-trees, the planting of which laid the foundations of an important industry, came from India.

The encouragement which the Assyrian emperors gave to industry was, unfortunately for the stability of their rule, more than counterbalanced by the demands of their numerous campaigns, and in 612 B.C. Assyria experienced the fate of all military empires, when the Medes and a Semitic tribe, the Chaldeans, destroyed Nineveh. Then followed what is known as the Chaldean Empire, which did not last very long. In 539 B.C. it was in its turn overthrown by the Medes and Persians under Cyrus the Great. The greatest of the Chaldean emperors was Nebuchadnezzar, who reigned from 604 to 561 B.C. He figures largely in the Bible, for the Jews of Palestine caused him some trouble, and in the end he took many of them as captives to Babylon, his chief city, which he rebuilt and raised to a hitherto undreamed-of pitch of magnificence. The gardens which he caused to be made on the roof of the imperial palace were the famous Hanging Gardens of Babylon which the Greeks regarded as one of the Seven Wonders of the World. Commerce and industry received as much encouragement from the Chaldean as from the Assyrian emperors ; literature and art were fostered ; the old divinities of Babylon were revered and their temples rebuilt ; and science made notable progress in the branch of astronomy. The Chaldeans continued the old practice of foretelling the future from the positions and movements of the heavenly bodies, but their investigations led them to some important scientific conclusions. The stars were divided into twelve groups, which we call the Twelve Signs of the Zodiac, and five planets were known and named—those which we know as Mercury, Venus, Mars, Jupiter, and Saturn, for the old Chaldean names have been changed into the corresponding Roman forms. Thus Ishtar, the name of the goddess of love, has become Venus, and the planet named after Marduk, the greatest of the Babylonian gods, is known to us by the name of Jupiter, the greatest of the Roman gods. The Chaldean astronomers were subsequently able to carry their researches so far as to be able to foretell an eclipse, and their work was the foundation upon which the Greek astronomers built.

IV

EARLY CIVILIZATIONS—THE MEDES AND PERSIANS

THE conquerors of the Chaldeans—the Medes and Persians—belonged to quite a different race from the former rulers of Mesopotamia. They were Aryans, that is to say, descended from the same original stock as almost all the peoples of Europe, including the inhabitants of the British Isles. The contest for supremacy between Aryans and Semites, which in this case resulted in favour of the former, was but the prelude to future clashes of the two races almost invariably ending in the defeat of the Semites. The wars between Rome and Carthage are instances of such clashes, but contest for supremacy in the world was to be quite as intense among Aryans as among Aryans and non-Aryans. The great struggle between Greece and Persia, and the subsequent defeat of the Greeks by the Romans, illustrate this.

THE MEDES AND PERSIANS

The conquest of Babylon was by no means the first instance of contact between the Medes and Persians and the Chaldeans. Medes and Persians had helped the Chaldeans to overthrow Nineveh, but after the fall of the Assyrian Empire their interests became divergent. The Chaldeans settled down to the overlordship of the land of the two rivers: the Medes and Persians formed a powerful empire east of the Tigris, an empire which extended from the Persian Gulf to the region of the Black Sea. The Medes were far the more powerful of the two nations; the Persians, who were a rough mountain folk leading an agricultural life and occupying a region about four hundred miles long just north of the Persian Gulf, were their vassals. Then, about fifty years after the fall of Nineveh, there arose a great conqueror among the Persians named Cyrus, who succeeded in uniting his countrymen, and in the space of three years making himself master of the whole of the Median territory as well. These were by no means the last of Cyrus' conquests. His army, consisting mainly of skilled archers and swift cavalry, was everywhere irresistible, and the surrounding nations regarded him with so much alarm that Babylonia (Chaldea), Egypt, Lydia in Asia Minor, and even Sparta in Greece, formed a combination against him, which in no way checked the progress of the great conqueror. By 546 B.C. Lydia, the chief author of the hostile combination, had fallen, and its king, Croesus, whose name has become a kind of synonym for fabulous wealth, was a prisoner in the hands of Cyrus. In 539 B.C. the Chaldeans were conquered and Babylon fell without a struggle, despite the vast walls which Nebuchadnezzar had built to protect it. Eleven years later (528 B.C.) Cyrus was killed while fighting against nomads to the north-east of his dominions, and his place taken by his son Cambyses, who in 525 B.C. conquered Egypt. As a result, the Persian Empire extended from the Nile Delta along the whole eastern end of the Mediterranean to the Aegean and thence eastwards almost to

Agriculture in Persia. Using the winnowing fan

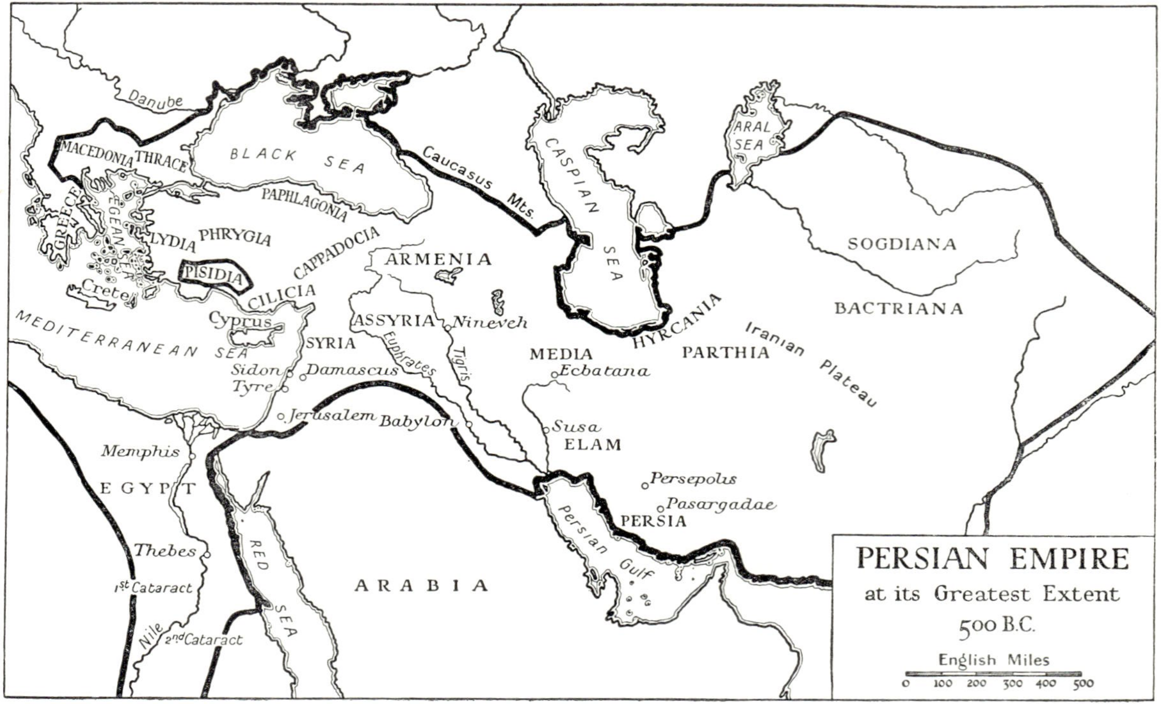
PERSIAN EMPIRE
at its Greatest Extent
500 B.C.
English Miles
0 100 200 300 400 500
Danube
MACEDONIA
THRACE
GREECE
EGEAN SEA
Crete
BLACK SEA
PAPHLAGONIA
LYDIA
PHRYGIA
PISIDIA
CAPPADOCIA
CILICIA
Cyprus
MEDITERRANEAN SEA
Caucasus Mts.
CASPIAN SEA
ARAL SEA
SOGDIANA
BACTRIANA
HYRCANIA
PARTHIA
Iranian Plateau
ARMENIA
ASSYRIA
Nineveh
SYRIA
Sidon
Tyre
Damascus
Euphrates
Tigris
MEDIA
Ecbatana
Jerusalem
Babylon
Susa
ELAM
Persepolis
Pasargadae
PERSIA
Persian Gulf
Memphis
EGYPT
Thebes
1st Cataract
Nile
2nd Cataract
RED SEA
ARABIA

DARIUS

the borders of India. The task of governing this vast territory was finally systematized by Darius the Great, who succeeded Cambyses in 521 B.C. and ruled until 485 B.C.

Darius was king of Babylonia and Egypt: the rest of the empire he divided into twenty provinces, each of which was called a satrapy and ruled by a governor called a satrap, who was appointed by and subject to the Great King, as the King of Persia came to be called. These provinces enjoyed a good deal of independence in local matters as long as they paid tribute regularly and furnished a sufficient number of recruits for the Great King's army. Tribute was sometimes paid in kind, but in the case of Lydia it was certainly paid in coined money which had been common there since about 600 B.C.

The capital of the Persian Empire was the city of Susa, but there were royal residences also at Babylon, Pasargadae (near the battle-field where Cyrus had defeated the Medes), and Persepolis, some forty miles to the south. Magnificent roads ran from end to end of the empire, and the postal system was in the hands of swift messengers, who maintained a much more efficient service than anything that had been previously known in the East. Business was for the most part carried on in Aramaic, but the Persian language was not altogether superseded. Scribes devised an alphabet of thirty-nine cuneiform signs and used it to write Persian on clay tablets, and also when they wished to make records on monuments of stone. The idea of an alphabet probably came from the Aramaic.

Darius was particularly anxious to make Persia a great sea-power. He restored the canal which the Egyptians had made between the Nile and the Red Sea; he treated the Phoenicians with much kindness and organized a great Phoenician war fleet; and he encouraged navigation. Perhaps the greatest of his navigators was a foreigner, a Mediterranean sailor named Scylax whom Darius sent to explore the river Indus, and afterwards to sail along the coast of Asia from the mouth of the Indus westwards to the Isthmus of Suez, a very famous voyage in those days (about 500 B.C.). When Darius' son and successor, Xerxes, invaded Greece in 480 B.C., his fleet numbered 1,200 vessels, three hundred of which were supplied by the Phoenicians.

Persian architecture, which must have been very impressive, was not original. Thus the enormous terraces on which their palaces stood were copied from Babylonia; the winged bulls at the palace gates from Assyria; the vast colonnades in front of the palaces (and often found inside as well) and the gorgeously coloured walls of enamelled brick from Egypt. But the Persians deserve praise for their powers of assimilation.

The Persian religion was much superior to anything that had previously appeared in the world with the exception of the religion of the Egyptian King Akhnaton. It was the religion founded about 1000 B.C. by Zoroaster, who taught that there were two great principles striving for mastery in the world—the principle of goodness and light, and the principle of evil and darkness. Goodness was represented by Mazda or Ormuzd, which means 'Lord of Wisdom', who had followers or angels, one of whom was Mithras, the Light. Evil was represented by Ahriman and his followers: here we have the origin of the idea of Satan. Zoroaster called upon all people to range themselves on one side or the other, and declared that whatever they did they would not be able to escape the final judgement. This is the first appearance in Asia of a belief in the doctrine of the Last Judgement. Some of Zoroaster's hymns and teachings survive and form what is known as the Avesta, the Persian Bible. In the world of to-day his religion is followed and practised by the Parsees of India.

The decline of Persia was partly the result of its conflict with the Greeks, another Aryan people. The Ionian or Asiatic Greeks who lived on the coasts of Asia Minor bordering the Aegean Sea were the vassals of Persia, but the Persians and

The ruins of Xerxes' palace at Persepolis

King Darius and a row of captive rebels. From a bas-relief high up on
the rocks at Behistun, on the road from Babylon to Ecbatana

THE MIGHT OF THE PERSIAN EMPIRE

the European Greeks did not come into contact until the time of Darius the Great. Darius had been much troubled by the attacks of the warlike Scythians upon the northern and northeastern parts of his dominions, so he determined to teach them a lesson and march to their homes in South Russia to do it. He crossed over into Europe at the Bosphorus (520 B.C.), and for some time waged an unequal contest in what are now known as Roumania and Bulgaria, against enemies who avoided pitched battles and hung upon his flanks and rear, causing infinite annoyance and no small degree of damage—the methods which, many centuries later, enabled the Russians to defeat Napoleon. After the failure of this expedition, and indeed probably in consequence of it, Darius was faced with a revolt of his Greek subjects on the eastern coast of the Aegean, a revolt instigated by Histiaeus, tyrant of Miletus, and his nephew Aristagoras. The Greeks appealed to the Spartans and to the Athenians for assistance, in the former case without success, on account, so it is said, of an unfortunate remark of Aristagoras that Susa, the capital of the Great King, was three months' journey from the coast. The Athenians, however, sent twenty ships, and the people of Eretria, one of the chief towns of the island of Euboea, five ships out of gratitude to the men of Miletus for help which they had formerly received from them. These ships sailed to Ephesus, and there all available forces were disembarked for an attack on the important city of Sardis, which the Greeks occupied without resistance and afterwards plundered and burned. This was an insult which the Great King could not forget, and when, six years later, Miletus had been destroyed, its people sold as slaves or carried away into captivity, and Histiaeus and Aristagoras were both dead—Darius thought that his next duty was to punish the people of Eretria and Athens. An expedition sent out partly for this purpose in 492 B.C. under Mardonius, the son-in-law of the king, was defeated by a great storm which crippled the Persian fleet.

Two years later (490 B.C.) another expedition set sail under Datis, a Mede, and Artaphernes, the son of the king's nephew. After subduing Naxos and other islands in the Aegean Sea, and sparing Delos because it was reputed to be the birthplace of Apollo and Artemis, it reached Eretria, which capitulated after a siege of six days. The temples of the city were then plundered and burnt, and its inhabitants made slaves as Darius had commanded. A similar fate was designed for Athens. From Eretria the Persian fleet sailed to the Bay of Marathon, where their troops were disembarked in full strength for the march to Athens, which was about twenty-five miles distant. The Athenians, however, decided to anticipate matters. Upon the advice of their most able general, Miltiades, they marched to Marathon and attacked the Persians, rather than wait in Athens to be themselves attacked. The Greek forces were about ten thousand strong, consisting of about nine thousand Athenians and a contingent of one thousand from Plataea, who thus requited the Athenians for protection which they had once given them against the men of Thebes. The Persian army was probably about twice as strong as the Athenian. The most striking feature of the battle appears to have been a charge of the Athenian hoplites, or heavy armed spearmen, who amazed the Persians, because they attacked without support from archers or cavalrymen, and because, according to Herodotus, they were so few in number. Six thousand four hundred Persians are said to have been killed in the Battle of Marathon. Callimachus, the nominal commander of the Athenians, was also among the slain, but Miltiades survived to give the defeated Persians one further example of his skill as a general. When the issue of the battle was no longer in any doubt, the Persians embarked on their ships and made all haste to Athens by sea, intending to arrive there before their conquerors, but when they reached the Bay of Phalerum they found that the Athenian forces were already in camp near the city awaiting their arrival. The Persians had no desire to fight a second Marathon, and so they sailed back to Asia Minor.

This great frustration of his hopes did not in any way turn Darius from his purpose; on the contrary, it strengthened his resolution to punish the Greeks. They must be taught that the wishes of Persia could not be defied with impunity, and preparations were at once made for a greater and more formidable expedition. A revolt in Egypt, inspired perhaps by the example of Marathon, caused some delay, and in 485 B.C., before his plans had been perfected, Darius died. His son and successor, Xerxes, was, however, as determined to conquer Greece as his father had been, and after a successful expedition against the Egyptians he set himself to the task with such energy that his victory seemed assured. How could a small country like Greece, no bigger then than it is to-day and not even united, hope to withstand a great empire which stretched from Macedonia to the borders of India, and which included Egypt, Arabia, Syria, Palestine, Mesopotamia, Asia Minor, Armenia, Persia, and Afghanistan? Moreover, no precautions which might ensure success were neglected. Roads were made, bridges constructed, and harbours improved so as to facilitate the advance of the expedition, which was to consist of an army and a fleet, which, after the Hellespont (Dardanelles) had been crossed, were to keep in as close touch and communication with each other as possible. Two bridges were constructed across the Hellespont from Abydos to Sestos. (Abydos is about three miles from the forts of Chanak and Kilid Bahr, where British warships attempted to force the passage of the Dardanelles in March 1915.) According to Herodotus it took the Persian army seven days and seven nights of continuous marching to cross these bridges. The numbers of this great host have been variously estimated from three million to eight hundred thousand; probably four hundred thousand would be a more correct figure. It was a motley host in which all the races who formed the Persian Empire had representatives. Naked Sudanese marched side by side with fur-clad Turkomans; Arabs on dromedaries rode near Libyans in war chariots; cultured Greeks from Asia Minor and Persians found themselves members of the same host as half-wild Nubians and spiritless peasants from Syria and Babylonia. The cosmopolitan nature of the army was a great source of weakness; it was only the Persians who would have any real interest in the success of Xerxes, and the interest of the Asiatic Greeks would tend to verge upon hostility or at least indifference, for they were being asked to fight against their kinsfolk—and they furnished three hundred of the twelve hundred ships which composed the Great King's fleet.

The task of resisting this huge array devolved chiefly upon the Spartans and the Athenians, of whom the former naturally assumed the leadership by land, while the Athenians bore the brunt of the naval warfare. After much wrangling it was decided to try to stop the Persian advance at the pass of Thermopylae, so called from some hot springs in the neighbourhood.[1] The highway from Thessaly into Greece led through this pass, which was extremely narrow, with precipitous mountains rising on one side and the sea beating against the road on the other, so that it was possible for a small number of determined men to hold up a multitude. When Xerxes arrived there in the summer of 480 B.C. to find his way blocked by a force of less than eight thousand men under the command of Leonidas, one of the Spartan kings, he was, says Herodotus, so astounded at their impudence that for four days he forbore to attack because he confidently expected the Greeks to run away. On the fifth day, seeing that they had not moved, he sent Medes and Kissians against them with orders to bring them alive into his presence. But this attack was so easily repelled that Xerxes commanded his picked

[1] The hot springs are still there, but the physical features of the country have so changed that the pass no longer exists.

guardsmen, the famous Immortals, to assault the pass. These were perfectly fresh, and they greatly outnumbered all the defenders, but they fared no better than the Medes; they too were hurled back with fearful slaughter. The next day was a repetition of this one, and Xerxes began to feel anxious. His whole enterprise seemed about to be brought to naught by the valour of a few thousand men. At this crisis, however, a Malian Greek, an inhabitant of these parts, craved audience with the king and offered for money to lead the Persians over a steep circuitous path which he knew, which would enable them to attack the defenders of the pass in the rear. The offer was eagerly accepted. But even now the Persian project need not have succeeded. Leonidas, apparently anticipating something of the kind, had posted a thousand Phocians on the heights to safeguard this track. When the Persians saw them they were taken by surprise; so too were the Phocians, who, if they had shown ordinary courage, might easily, considering their numbers and the fact that the path which they had to guard was a rough and narrow mountain track, have held the invaders at bay. But instead they retreated to higher ground, leaving the road open to the Persians. When news of this was brought to the defenders of the pass, most of them marched away, possibly at the command of Leonidas, but he and his three hundred Spartans, with seven hundred Thespians and four hundred Thebans, remained. The fight which followed is one of the epics of war, and it is wonderfully described by Herodotus. The invaders came on in wave after wave, lashed on by their officers, who used their whips unsparingly. The Greeks slew and slew. Many of the enemy fell into the sea and were drowned. The Thebans appear to have surrendered at the first opportunity, but the Spartans and Thespians had no thought of self-preservation. Two half-brothers of Xerxes were slain; then Leonidas was killed. In after years it was believed that he had deliberately sacrificed himself in order

DECLINE OF PERSIA

to save Sparta, since the Delphic oracle had predicted that the Persians must either destroy Sparta or a king of Sparta. After his death his followers fought on with their swords and then, when these were broken, with hands and teeth until they had all been slain. The road was now clear for the Persians, who advanced upon Athens, which they captured and burned, but only after it had been abandoned by its inhabitants, who, realizing the futility of resistance, had withdrawn to Argolis, Aegina, and Salamis, leaving behind a very small force to defend the Acropolis or citadel of Athens. This force made a spirited but ineffectual resistance, and after it had been overcome and Xerxes was completely master of Athens he was so elated with his somewhat empty success that he at once dispatched a horseman to carry the great news to Susa. Before the end of the year (480 B.C.) he was to realize how barren his success had been, when the Athenian fleet won a signal victory over the Persians in the Bay of Salamis. Shortly afterwards Xerxes returned to Persia, leaving the subsequent conduct of affairs to his generals. They fared no better, and in 479 B.C. the land defeat of Plataea and the sea defeat of Mycale completed the discomfiture of the Persians and compelled their retreat from Greece.

The subsequent history of Persia is somewhat squalid, a history of intrigues, assassinations, and contests for supremacy among rival kings, which show to what an amazing extent decline and demoralization had set in. In 465 B.C. Xerxes was assassinated in his palace; then follow various rulers, none of them very capable—Artaxerxes I, Xerxes II, Darius II, Artaxerxes II, Artaxerxes III. The reign of Artaxerxes II is notable because of a contest for supremacy between him and his younger brother Cyrus, who had the assistance of ten thousand Greeks. Cyrus defeated his brother in the battle of Cunaxa (401 B.C.), but was killed in the moment of victory. The Greeks then made a famous march back to the coast, which has been described by their leader Xenophon in a masterpiece—the *Anabasis*. The fact that it was possible to march in this way right through the Great King's dominions convinced the Greeks that the Persian Empire was not such a powerful thing as they had at one time imagined, and it is not surprising to see it falling an easy prey to the arms of Alexander the Great seventy years later (330 B.C.).

V

EARLY CIVILIZATIONS—CHINA

CHINESE legends speak of a Golden Age three thousand years before the birth of Christ and of emperors who were almost impossibly virtuous. Setting aside these accounts as purely imaginary, it is nevertheless certain that by 1000 B.C. the civilization of China had reached a high stage of development. This civilization appears to have been indigenous; it grew up spontaneously and unassisted; it is quite safe to reject the theory that it was an offshoot of the Sumerian civilization, but it is not unlike other civilizations in some respects. Like Sumeria and Egypt, China was originally a land of city-states; the art of writing originated with pictorial signs in China as in Egypt; there were Chinese dynasties, the Shang (1750–1125 B.C.), the Chu (1125–250 B.C.), and then the Tsin and the Han; there was a feudal age in China as in Egypt, followed by a centralizing empire; Chinese civilization, like that of the Egyptians and the Sumerians, owed much to its rivers, the Hwang-ho and the Yang-tse-kiang.

From the tenth century B.C. to about 220 B.C. China was under a feudal system, and the various feudal nobles were constantly at war with one another; but, when they were not engaged in killing each other, the Chinese of this period enjoyed a high degree of civilization. The men occupied them-

SHI-HWANG-TI

selves in hunting, fishing, and agriculture, the women in spinning and weaving; there were skilled workers in gold, silver, iron, and bronze; there are vessels of bronze in existence to-day which date from the Shang dynasty; the written language was almost as far advanced as it is to-day; the art of silk-weaving seems to have been highly developed; and the attention paid to it at the courts of the emperor and the princes must have aided its progress. Little is known of Chinese pottery. Proofs exist of the production of pots and tiles of clay in the second and third centuries B.C., but there is no doubt that earthenware had been made very much earlier. Porcelain ware, however, does not appear until the sixth or seventh century A.D.

The books which were read in ancient China consisted of thin slips of wood or bamboo on which the characters were written by means of a pencil of bamboo slightly frayed at the end so as to pick up a coloured liquid easily and transfer it to the tablets. The Chinese did not, as was once supposed, scratch their characters on the wood with a knife; the knife was only used to scratch out what had been wrongly written. Later in Chinese history, paper made of silk was used for writing purposes, and then, about A.D. 105, a more serviceable kind of paper was discovered, made of the bark of trees, hemp, rags, and old nets. Silk paper, however, remained in use until A.D. 418, if not later.

About 220 B.C. the feudal system came to an end in China. Its continued existence was certainly a menace to good order and security; in the valleys of the Hwang-ho and Yang-tse-kiang there were no fewer than five or six thousand small states with a dozen powerful states dominating over them. The man who put an end to this condition of affairs and ultimately made himself ruler of a united China called himself Shi-Hwang-ti, which means First Emperor. Among his feats were the defeat of the Huns, who were menacing his northern frontiers, and the building of the Great Wall of

China, largely by convict labour, criminals being sentenced to long terms of penal servitude at the work. The Great Wall was erected as a protection against the Huns. It is eighteen hundred miles long, about twenty-two feet high, and twenty feet broad. At intervals of a hundred yards are towers forty feet high. The whole structure was originally of brick. It has been glorified as the last trace of man's handiwork on the earth which would fade from the view of an imaginary person receding into space. The building of the Great Wall was not popular among the Chinese, largely because of the forced labour which it entailed : it is reputed to have taken only ten years to complete. It was not, of course, an entirely new structure ; it linked up, extended, and fortified a number of previously existing walls. Still more unpopular was another act of Shi-Hwang-ti. He desired to give a stimulus to literary effort, but adopted a singularly unfortunate method of so doing. Listening to the flattery of his courtiers, he determined that literature should begin again with his reign. He therefore ordered that all existing books should be destroyed except those dealing with medicine, fortune-telling, and agriculture. Many scholars were put to death for concealing books ; many others were sent to hard labour on the Great Wall ; and numbers of valuable books were destroyed. The wonder is that any were preserved, particularly the writings of Confucius,[1] against which there was special enmity, for they upheld the feudal institutions which it was the emperor's mission to overthrow.

In 210 B.C. Shi-Hwang-ti died. His son, who succeeded him, only reigned four years. Then followed the Han dynasty, which ruled over China for over four hundred years. During this time the Chinese were very warlike. There were frequent conflicts with the Tartar tribes to the north, whom the Great Wall failed to keep out ; with the Huns and the Koreans ; and before the end of the second century B.C.

[1] See Ch. XI.

The Great Wall of China

Chinese armies had penetrated far into Central Asia, annexing the Pamirs and Kokand. At home the stability of the empire was endangered by constant intrigues: for about thirteen years in the middle of the first century B.C. the imperial power was in the hands of a usurper named Wang Mang, who secured it by treachery and poison, and ultimately lost it when his own soldiers revolted against him and killed him. But despite foreign wars and unrest at home, the period of the Han dynasty was one in which Chinese civilization made very pronounced advance. Paper and ink were invented and also the camel's-hair brush, which gave a great impetus to the art of painting; the custom of burying slaves with the dead was abolished; literary degrees were established; efforts made to repair the injury done to literature by the unbalanced enthusiasm of Shi-Hwang-ti; the writings of Confucius restored to favour once again, and perpetual nobility conferred upon the eldest male descendant of the teacher. Their military campaigns in Central Asia brought the Chinese into contact with Bactria, at that time an outlying province of Greece. Thus we get the first outside influences upon Chinese civilization. The grape was imported and a wine made from it which remained a favourite drink in China until a few centuries ago; the water-clock was introduced as an improvement upon the sundial, upon which the Chinese were formerly wholly dependent for their knowledge of time. It now became possible to divide the day into twelve accurate divisions of two hours each. The calendar was regulated anew, and music modified and reconstructed so that it closely approximated to that of Greece.

The art of sculpture in bas-relief was widely spread throughout China in the second century B.C. Tombs have been discovered in the province of Shan-tung, with various figures carved in stone on the inside walls, representing chariots, riders, battles, hunting, fishing, imperial receptions, and solemn processions of elephants, camels, and apes. The

SOCIAL CLASSES

scenes give a characteristic picture of ancient China, and may be compared with the sculptured records of the life of ancient Egypt which are to be seen on the walls of the old tomb chapels.

Although the history of China contains the records of numerous wars, Chinese civilization was most decidedly organized for peace ; but the demands of modern power politics and the maintenance of large armies have obscured the old Chinese contempt for the soldier's occupation. From very early times until the beginning of the twentieth century, four main classes below the emperor have been recognized : the mandarins or literary class, the cultivators of the soil, the artisans, and the mercantile class. The military class has for the most part been recruited from utterly impecunious people and those of doubtful reputation. The fact that the leading class is an intellectual one suggests comparison with India, where the chief class from long before the time of Alexander the Great right down to the present day has been the Brahmans, who are priests and teachers. But the Brahmans have always been a caste, whereas the Chinese have never become mandarins by birth but by education ; the distinction is thus open to all classes of the community, and for centuries it depended upon the result of competitive examination. Under the Han dynasty, however, the system of competitive examination had not been devised, and the crude method was followed of electing scholars on the recommendations of local dignitaries. Thomas Carlyle, commenting upon the high regard in which the Chinese have ever held men of letters, writes :

' By far the most interesting fact I hear about the Chinese is that they *do* attempt to make their Men of Letters their Governors. The man of intellect at the top of affairs : this is the aim of all constitutions and revolutions, if they have any aim. For the man of true intellect, as I assert and believe always, is the noble-hearted man withal, the true, just, humane, and valiant man. Get him for governor all is got; fail to get him, though you had Constitutions plentiful as blackberries, and a Parliament in every village, there is nothing yet got.'

VI

EARLY CIVILIZATIONS—INDIA

INDIAN civilization is very old, much older than was at one time supposed. Discoveries made in the present century in Sindh[1] and in the Punjab[2] have established that it goes back at least 3,000, and possibly 5,000 years before the birth of Christ. It was contemporary with that of ancient Sumeria, and it is clear from the discovery of Indian seals and other objects in cities like Ur and Kish, that Indian merchants traded with the Sumerians; they may even have got as far as the Nile valley.

The Indians of these early days appear to have been highly civilized in many ways. They had massive public buildings and comfortable dwelling-houses, built mostly of brick; well-planned streets and open spaces; good sanitation, and an elaborate drainage system. They knew how to write, but their language, which has not yet been deciphered, was not alphabetic, but syllabic like the Sumerian language. Their cities were obviously well governed, and the discovery of copper knives, shell spoons, pestles, cruets, and dishes of various kinds points to a good level of domestic comfort. They do not appear to have been very artistic, but there are evidences that their women were fond of jewellery—gold, silver, and copper—and that they used cosmetics. The discovery of variegated toys—carts, birds, whistles—seems to show fondness for their children—and they appear to have been more devoted to the arts of peace than to those of war—

[1] At Harappa (Sindh), 1924.
[2] At Mohenjo-daro (Punjab), 1923.

THE RIGVEDA

the weapons which have been found are more likely to have been used to clear the jungle, and for defence against brigands, than to attack their neighbours. They probably worshipped many gods, and perhaps one supreme goddess, a Mother Goddess, who in some respects is like Ishtar (Aphrodite) or the Egyptian Isis.

A very different culture was brought in by invaders from the north, probably about 1500 B.C., Aryans, who spoke Sanskrit, and who gradually conquered Northern India and imposed their language on the conquered. They ultimately spread over the whole of India, and it is their culture which most powerfully influenced subsequent development. We can reconstruct this from the Vedas, four books which the Hindus consider to be inspired, of which the oldest is the Rigveda, a collection of hymns, liturgical directions, and philosophical discussions, composed probably between 1200 and 800 B.C. The Rigveda contains many slighting references to the conquered people, but gives no account of the manner of the conquest. But it gives us much information about the habits and mode of life of the Aryan conquerors. They were a fair-skinned race, divided into many tribes with a chieftain over each. Women were held in high esteem, and the marriage tie was regarded as sacred. Both husband and wife were described as 'rulers of the house', and the later Hindu custom of burning widows on the funeral pyres of their husbands was quite unknown. So too was the caste system, which was a much later development, probably about 800 B.C., although its origins can be discerned very much earlier in the growth of a social system in which the descendants of the conquered occupied a status which tended to be permanently lower than the descendants of the conquerors.

The Veda describes the Aryan tribes as having blacksmiths, coppersmiths, goldsmiths, carpenters, barbers, and other artisans. They fought from chariots, and used the horse but not the elephant in war. There were some among them who loved a wandering life, but on the whole they had settled down to agricultural pursuits; they tilled their fields with ploughs, and lived in villages or towns. But cattle was their chief wealth; they paid fines with them; and one of their words for war means 'a desire for cows'. They ate beef (unlike the modern Hindus), and drank a kind of beer, made from the soma plant. They knew something of the sea, and built ships or river boats. It is supposed that merchants, trading in the seventh century B.C. from the western ports of India with Babylonia, brought back a Semitic alphabet, from which all the alphabets used in India, Burma, Siam, and Ceylon have been derived. In the course of the next few centuries, considerable intellectual progress was made in India. Two great epic poems—the Ramayana and the Mahabharata, both very long,[1] and both mixing myth with some amount of moral teaching, had been composed, possibly as early as 500 B.C.; and Indian philosophy had emerged in the writings of Kanada, who taught the immortality of the soul, and Kapila, whose ideas are remarkable for their scientific insight. In the sixth century B.C. lived Gautama Buddha, the founder of Buddhism, and Vardhamana, called Mahavira, the founder of the Jain religion. Buddhism was ultimately defeated in India by Hinduism, but it spread and prevailed in other parts of Asia.[2] The Jains have never been numerous, but they still survive in India; they are pacifists and vegetarians, whose influence can be compared to that of the Quakers in Great Britain and the United States of America.

At the beginning of the sixth century B.C. India was divided into sixteen independent states, some of them monarchical and others republics. In the extreme south, opposite Ceylon, was the Pandya kingdom, whose chief port, Korkay, was one of the famous cities of antiquity, owing its origin

[1] The Ramayana contains 48,000 verses, and the Mahabharata is eight times as long as Homer's Iliad and Odyssey combined. See Ch. IX.
[2] See Ch. XI.

'Cattle the chief wealth of India.' A nomad tribe with their cattle moving down from the hills to the plains

and prosperity to the pearls of the Gulf of Malabar on which it stood. By this time the caste system was widespread. The Aryans recognized four social grades—the Brahmans or sacrificing priests; the Kshatriyas or nobles, who claimed descent from their early leaders; the Vaisyas or clansmen; and the Sudras, who were descended from the conquered. Below these were those who had no caste, Outcastes who were beneath contempt. Slaves were Outcastes: so too were those who had lost caste by intermarrying with members of a lower caste or perhaps by neglecting an important religious ceremony. Gautama Buddha welcomed followers irrespective of caste. He said that 'as the four streams that flow into the Ganges lose their names as soon as they mingle their waters in the holy river, so all who believe in Buddha cease to be Brahmans, Kshatriyas, Vaisyas, and Sudras'. But the influence of the priestly caste was ultimately too strong for Buddhism. Caste prevailed, and even extended: from the sixth century B.C. there were subdivisions of the Sudra caste in the form of guilds of work-people. Eventually there were eighteen of them—workers in wood, metal, and stone, weavers, potters, dyers, fishers, flower-sellers, basket-makers, and painters.

The religion of the modern Hindu villager, with its belief in charms, its complicated ritual, and its countless prayers, bears little resemblance to the religion of the primitive Aryans as described in the Rigveda. They worshipped the great and striking phenomena of nature, which they personified and called 'the shining ones', which seems to indicate that it was the phenomenon of light which primarily influenced the Aryan mind. The same tendency is found in the Persian acceptance of the teaching of Zoroaster, for Ahura Mazda, the Supreme God in his system, was a god of light.[1] The Vedic hymns mention thirty-three gods—eleven in heaven, eleven on earth, and eleven dwelling in glory in mid-air. Among

[1] See p. 64.

HINDU RELIGION

them are Surya, the bright sun-god, who gives light, warmth, and air, and is naturally highly venerated; Ushas, the morning dawn, who 'shines upon us like a young wife, rousing every living being to go forth to his work'; Agni, the fire-god, who lights and warms every hearth, and drives away all evil and impure things; and Indra, the god of the atmosphere, who gives rain and harvest, and governs the winter and the thunderstorm. He became the chief of the Aryan gods, and of him they sang—'The gods do not reach unto thee, O Indra, nor men; thou overcomest all creatures in strength.' Other gods were Mother Earth, The Encompassing Sky, and The Maruts, storm gods, 'who make the rocks to tremble, who tear in pieces the forest'.

For the most part the Vedic hymns are addressed to bright and friendly gods. Human sacrifices are not mentioned, and Rudra, who afterwards became Siva, the god of destruction, is merely the god of roaring tempests. A similar spirit of cheery optimism pervaded the early Aryan conception of death. The Aryans did not bury their dead like their predecessors; they burned them on funeral pyres. They believed that a man got his natural birth from his parents; his second birth from the performance of religious rites; and that fire by setting the soul free from the body completed the third or heavenly birth. During the funeral ceremony the friends of the dead man stood around the pyre, and bade his eye go to the sun, his breath to the wind, and his limbs to the earth whence they had been severally derived, but 'as for his unborn part, do thou, Lord, quicken it with thy heat; let thy flame and thy brightness quicken it; convey it to the world of the righteous'. The doctrine of the transmigration of souls, which became a prominent feature of later Hindu theology, was unknown at this time. The singers around the pyre assumed that their departed friend went to a place of blessedness and of joyful reunion with loved ones who had gone before.

VII

THE PHOENICIANS

THE Phoenicians were a very small nation, but their influence in the ancient world was considerable, not because of any civilization which they developed, but because of what they did to spread the civilizations of others. The Phoenicians were sailors whose vessels sailed from end to end of the Mediterranean, and were the means whereby the benefits of civilization were first carried to many barbaric peoples.

The Phoenicians were of Semitic origin, and they appear to have believed that their ancestors came originally from Babylonia. The nature of the country into which they migrated made them sailors. It was a narrow strip of land shut in by the mountains of Lebanon, which made communication with the interior difficult; many rocky promontories jutting out into the sea indented the coast with bays, some of which formed good natural harbours; and the cedar-trees of Lebanon gave them abundant wood from which to build their ships. Their towns were all ports such as Acre, Byblos, Tyre, and Sidon; they were all independent of one another, and each had its own god or Baal, which means 'lord and master'. Generally speaking Baal-worship was a form of sun-worship which emphasized the fierce qualities of the sun. Thus human sacrifices were frequently offered to the deity. More humane was the worship of Astarte, the goddess of love, whom the Phoenicians identified with the moon. They feared Baal, who typified the storms and dangers which were part of their seafaring life: they loved Astarte, whom they associated with the good things of life, the joy of rest after a voyage, and whom they worshipped with sailor-like riotousness when on shore. They communicated

NAVIGATION, TRADE, AND COMMERCE

this worship to the Greeks, for the Greek Aphrodite is identical with the Phoenician Astarte.

It was once thought that Phoenician ships were the first to sail on the Mediterranean, but most authorities now believe that the Cretans were before them. The art of navigation owes much, however, to the Phoenicians: the discoveries in Crete do not weaken their claim to be regarded as the foremost mariners of the ancient world. Their vessels were rowing-boats with curved sides and a keel, and when the wind was suitable sails were used as well. They had no compasses, and most of their sailing was done by day. At night they generally cast anchor in some roadstead or beached their vessels, and they rarely steered them out of sight of land. When they did steer at night they got their bearings from the North Star. Their trading was pure barter, and they did not scruple to supplement it by acts of piracy. Traders worked individually and kept the routes which they traversed a close secret; a master would run his ship aground rather than reveal to another where he was going. In order to be able to trade successfully it was necessary to know how to read, write, and reckon easily. The Phoenicians learnt how to calculate from the Assyrians, and they adopted or rather adapted the Egyptian alphabet which they afterwards taught to the Greeks. Phoenician art was very unoriginal, a slavish imitation of that of Egypt. Voyaging and trading absorbed so much of their time that there was hardly sufficient left to develop an art of their own. Their trade was enormous. In addition to their activities on sea they organized a system of caravans which linked up the Caspian Sea and the Persian Gulf with the Mediterranean. Among the goods which they traded were incense, myrrh, and onyx from Arabia; spices, ivory, and precious stones from India; flax and cotton from Egypt; gold, ebony, ivory, and ostrich feathers from Africa; corn from Spain; copper, tin, marble, and shell-fish for dyes from the isles of Greece; carpets from Persia; and minerals and slaves from the Caucasus. In addition there were the articles which they manufactured themselves; vases, jewels, materials of fine texture beautifully embroidered, and above all transparent glass and purple dye.

The two chief Phoenician cities were Tyre and Sidon. Sidon was the first to attain a sort of pre-eminence. In the fifteenth century B.C. as the vassal of the Egyptians it reached a high degree of prosperity. The kings of Egypt gave Sidonian sailors the right to carry on the foreign commerce of Egypt, and allowed them to establish depots in the Nile Delta and even in Memphis. Sidonians colonized Cyprus, Rhodes, and many of the islands of the Aegean. They even entered the Black Sea and explored the unknown country around, whence they brought gold, silver, tin, and slaves. Their riches excited the envy of the Philistines, who captured the city and destroyed its supremacy in the thirteenth century B.C.

Tyre then became the chief Phoenician city, but whereas the Sidonians had confined their activities mainly to the Eastern Mediterranean, the Tyrians dealt principally with the West. Coasting along the shores of Greece they sailed thence to Sicily, Malta, Northern Africa, and Spain. After going through the Straits of Gibraltar they came to a country rich in corn, oil, wool, and silver which they called Tarshish (modern Andalusia); some of the bolder spirits among them sailed north and discovered the Cassiterides (possibly the Scilly Islands), where they obtained tin. Some appear to have coasted the shores of Africa as far as Senegal, and recent discoveries in South Africa seem to indicate that Phoenicians worked gold deposits near the river Limpopo. The internal history of Tyre is hardly as fortunate. Apart from the time when Hiram, the friend of David and Solomon, was ruling, it is the record of a sordid struggle for power between aristocracy and people; and, just as in the Italian cities during the Middle Ages, a contest for supremacy would frequently be followed by the emigration of the defeated side. It was a

A Phoenician ship on a coin of Sidon

'The ship of the desert.' A bronze statuette found in Syria

PHOENICIAN TRANSPORT

defeat of the nobles which brought about the founding of Carthage, the greatest of the Tyrian colonies, in 814 B.C.

Phoenician colonies were of three kinds. In civilized countries like Egypt the Phoenicians were content with trading rights, which allowed them to have independent quarters in the towns and to build bazaars and docks. In uncivilized countries they established trading stations consisting of depots, factories, a temple, and some fortifications. In other parts they built towns, conquered the original inhabitants, and governed the country; such colonies were Palermo in Sicily, Gades (Cadiz) in Spain, Utica in North Africa, and of course Carthage.

No account of the Phoenicians is complete without some reference to the great voyage of the Carthaginian Hanno, which is described in a Greek book translated from the Carthaginian, called *The Periplus of Hanno*. Starting with sixty ships in about 520 B.C., Hanno and his men sailed southwards from the Straits of Gibraltar past the Senegal river and beyond the Gambia, probably getting as far as Liberia. From one of their landing-places they were frightened away by the noise of flutes, drums, and gongs, and the burning of bush fires; for days on end the coast seemed a perfect blaze of fire; and they once landed on an island where were 'wild, hairy men and women whom' the interpreters called 'gorillas'.[1] Some of these they captured, but they proved impossibly violent on board ship, so they killed them and brought their skins back to Carthage. An even more remarkable Phoenician sea-voyage was that which is described by the Greek historian Herodotus. He relates how Pharaoh Necho of the Twenty-sixth Egyptian dynasty (612 B.C.) commissioned some Phoenicians to sail round Africa, which they did, although it took them nearly three years:

'Libya (Africa) shows itself to be surrounded by water, except so much of it as borders upon Asia. Neco, king of Egypt, was the

[1] H. G. Wells suggests that they were chimpanzees.

first whom we know of that proved this ; he, when he had ceased digging the canal leading from the Nile to the Arabian Gulf, sent certain Phoenicians in ships with orders to sail back through the pillars of Hercules (Straits of Gibraltar) into the northern sea (Mediterranean Sea) and so return to Egypt. The Phoenicians accordingly, setting out from the Red Sea, navigated the southern sea ; when autumn came they went ashore, and sowed the land by whatever part of Libya they happened to be sailing, and waited for harvest ; then having reaped the corn they put to sea again. When two years had thus passed, in the third, having doubled the pillars of Hercules, they arrived in Egypt, and related what to me does not seem credible, but may to others, that as they sailed round Libya they had the sun on their right hand. Thus was Libya first known.'[1]

VIII

THE BEGINNINGS OF CIVILIZATION IN EUROPE

THE Mediterranean Sea was the great highway of commerce in the ancient world ; Egyptian ships were sailing upon it as early as 3000 B.C. ; over its waters the Phoenicians came to Cornwall in search of tin ; and probably ships sailing on the Mediterranean from Egypt first brought copper to Europe, thus starting the Age of Metal in that continent. The Egyptians almost certainly brought it to the Aegean coasts, and thence it was taken by land as far north as Norway, Sweden, and Denmark. By 2000 B.C. copper was in general use in Northern and Western Europe, and bronze also in Norway.

The use of metals did not, however, lead to a considerable development of culture in the north and west of Europe. In these parts we find great monuments like Stonehenge and Carnac, but no fine architecture whatsoever. It is in the islands of the Aegean and the neighbouring countries that we must look for the first signs of culture in Europe, and that

[1] Cary's Herodotus, Bk. IV.

BEGINNINGS OF EUROPEAN CIVILIZATION

because they were favourably situated with regard to the civilized Orient. For two or three thousand years before the Christian era there was trade between the civilized communities of the East and the people living in what we now know as Asia Minor. In the north-west corner of Asia Minor commanding the trade routes, almost at the entry of the Dardanelles or Hellespont, was the city of Troy. As early as 2500 B.C. the Trojans had mastered the art of pottery; they knew how to manufacture textiles; and they had a citadel of sun-baked brick, the earliest fortress in the Aegean world. Bordering on Troy and undoubtedly influencing its culture were the Hittites, who had a hieroglyphic alphabet of their own invention, and also used cuneiform characters in order to facilitate their trading relations with the Assyrians and Babylonians. They were warlike and ambitious; they are often mentioned in the Bible; but the language of their monuments has only recently been deciphered.

Just as Asia Minor was the link between the Aegean world and the civilized East, so the island of Crete was probably the link between that world and Egypt. By 1800 B.C., possibly much earlier, the Cretans were a highly civilized people; recent excavations on the island have revealed evidences of a civilization which is thought to be as old as that of Egypt. By 1600 B.C. its zenith had certainly been reached. The pottery, ivory, and gem work of the Cretans, and the paintings which they executed on the walls of their palaces and on the vases which they manufactured, are as good as anything which has survived to us from this period of the world's history. At Cnossos, in the centre of the island, was a great palace with innumerable rooms clustered round a central court-yard, and many passages. The labyrinth in the well-known legend of the Minotaur probably signifies this palace. The ruler of Crete took the title of Minos just as the ruler of Egypt took the title of Pharaoh, and the story of how a certain number of Athenian youths and maidens had to be sacrificed every

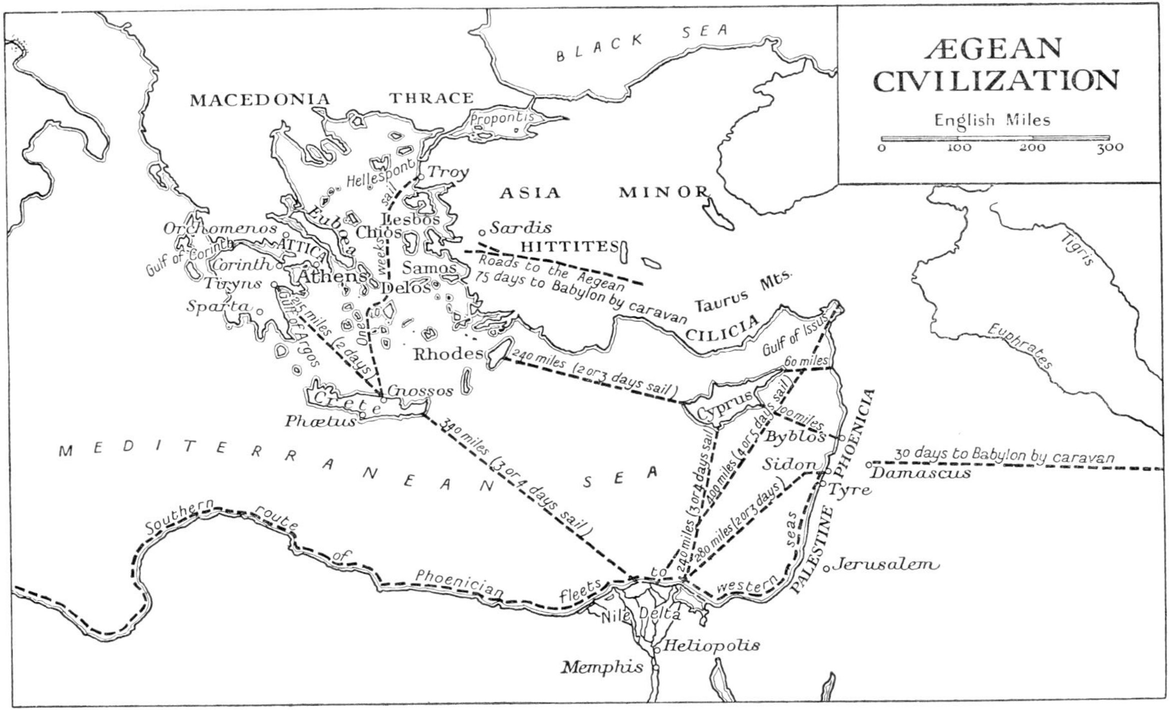
ÆGEAN CIVILIZATION
English Miles
0 100 200 300
BLACK SEA
MACEDONIA
THRACE
Propontis
Hellespont
Troy
ASIA MINOR
Sardis
HITTITES
Roads to the Aegean
75 days to Babylon by caravan
Taurus Mts.
CILICIA
Gulf of Issus
60 miles
Orchomenos
Gulf of Corinth
ATTICA
Corinth
Athens
Tiryns
Sparta
Euboea
Chios
Lesbos
Samos
Delos
weeks sail
One
215 miles (2 days)
Gulf of Argos
Rhodes
240 miles (2 or 3 days sail)
Gnossos
Crete
Phæstus
340 miles (3 or 4 days sail)
MEDITERRANEAN SEA
Cyprus
100 miles
Byblos
Sidon
PHOENICIA
Tyre
Damascus
30 days to Babylon by caravan
Tigris
Euphrates
240 miles (3 or 4 days sail)
400 miles (4 or 5 days sail)
280 miles (2 or 3 days)
PALESTINE
Jerusalem
Southern route of Phoenician fleets to western seas
Nile Delta
Heliopolis
Memphis

year to the Minotaur and how Theseus of Athens eventually slew the monster probably means that at one time the Athenians paid tribute to the Cretans, but that eventually the Athenians threw off the yoke and destroyed the palace of Cnossos. The palace was certainly destroyed (probably by Greeks) in 1000 B.C., after having been sacked four hundred years earlier (1400 B.C.).

The excavations which have been made at Cnossos reveal the fact that in many respects the customs of the ancient Cretans were singularly like those prevailing in the civilized world to-day. Bath-rooms have been discovered with terra-cotta baths, and a drainage system which filled the excavators with astonishment. It is the opinion of experts that the drains of this ancient palace were superior to anything known subsequently in the world until the middle of the nineteenth century. The drain-pipes were so well made that many of them can be used to-day. The fact that London and Paris had no sewage systems at the end of the sixteenth century will perhaps help us to realize the perfection of Cretan civilization. The palace walls at Cnossos are adorned with beautiful frescoes which show men and women of an apparently joyous care-free disposition, some of them looking astonishingly modern. The women wear low-necked bodices and flounced skirts reaching to the ground; they are almost Parisian in appearance, and corsets are among the articles found in the ruins. The life of the people generally seems to have been surprisingly good, far superior to what it was in contemporary Egypt and Babylonia. Excavators have come across ruins of houses belonging to artisans, with six or eight rooms in them. One contained a full set of carpenter's tools made from bronze. It is possible that the first flying-machine was constructed in Crete; it may be that the Greek legend of Daedalus, who made wings for himself and flew from Crete to Cumae in Italy is an allegorical description of the adventures of the first aeronaut.

Cretan art. A painting at Cnossos, restored by
Sir Arthur Evans

It is thought by some that the Cretan civilization was an offshoot of the Egyptian, but recent investigations have led other authorities to believe that it was an original development giving as much to Egypt as it received from that country. We know that the Egyptian King Thothmes III had a general who bore the title of ' Governor of the Aegean Islands '; these may have included Crete. It is far more probable that Crete was quite independent of Egypt. At one time the Cretan civilization was probably as extensive as that of Egypt or Babylonia. Troy may have been a Cretan colony, and traces of Cretan influence have been found as far west as Sicily. The Etruscans, that mysterious people of North Italy, whose origin is wrapped in obscurity, have been thought by some to have been Cretans, and there are many who believe that the Philistines were an offshoot of the same race. If so, then their warlike character as described in the Bible shows a change of nature, for the original Cretans were almost certainly a peace-loving people. No war pictures, such as are to be found in great abundance in Egypt and Babylonia, have been discovered in Crete, and no trace of fortifications. Their fleet was evidently used for trade and defence, and not for purposes of aggression. Their prosperity probably depended mainly on the skilful seamanship of their sailors and on their lucrative carrying trade.

Cretan and Egyptian ships frequently carried articles of commerce to the mainland of Greece, and this was probably the means whereby civilization was first carried to that part of the European continent. At Tiryns and Mycenae in the south of Greece, great ruins of buildings with stone foundations have been found, and among the ruins examples of Cretan and Egyptian pottery and metal work. Excavations were carried out at Mycenae before any were undertaken in Crete : that is why this period of Pre-Greek art in the Aegean is often spoken of as the Mycenean Period rather than the Cretan Period, which would be a more accurate appellation,

Minoan jewellery    Minoan jug, 1600 B.C.    Minoan jewellery

Excavation in progress at Cnossos

MINOAN CIVILIZATION

96 BEGINNINGS OF EUROPEAN CIVILIZATION

for Mycenae was the debtor of Crete. The ruins of Mycenae were first explored in 1876 by the German archaeologist Schliemann, who discovered that the town consisted of two parts—an acropolis or citadel, and a lower town. The acropolis was approached through a gate called the Lion Gate, because the door was surmounted by a pediment, a great triangular stone on which were carved in bas-relief the figures of two lions standing on their hind legs. The heads of the lions were made of bronze. In the acropolis were discovered six tombs carved in the solid rock. The corpses inside were adorned with gold ornaments, crowns, jewels, and armour, and one of them had been embalmed just like an Egyptian mummy. The chief feature of the lower town was a domed building showing traces of very beautiful decorative work, probably also a tomb, although it is known as the Treasure House of Atreus. Mycenae figures much in the Homeric poems. Its king, Agamemnon, described as 'the king of men', was the leader of the Greeks in the war against Troy; and the city itself is declared to be 'abounding in gold'. The discoveries of Schliemann seem to justify the epithet. Mycenae owed its wealth to its position; it commanded the mountain pass over which ran the shortest road from the Gulf of Argolis to the Gulf of Corinth. Many merchants used this road, and all of them would have to pay toll for the passage of their wares to the people of Mycenae. The art of Mycenae was of exquisite quality; it reached its highest level in painting, gem-engraving, and metal work; in sculpture and architecture it was somewhat inferior.

This early period of culture only affects the southern part of Greece; in the plain of Thessaly the people were still living in a semi-barbarous condition, hardly superior to that of the men of the Late Stone Age. The use of metals did not become at all general in Thessaly until 1500 B.C.

IX
THE GREEKS

HOW Greek civilization originated cannot be determined with any degree of definiteness. The ancient Greeks were certainly a mixture of races, who ultimately evolved a remarkably unified idea of culture. But what the mixture was is not definitely known. The Cretan civilization which spread into Greece had little in common with that of the Greeks of the thousand years before Christ. Its art and architecture were mainly conventional; its political systems were those of Egypt and Assyria, with whom it had come into frequent contact—a system of castes, pageantry, and dynasties. Nevertheless, the existence of this great culture exercised a profound effect upon the subsequent history of Greece, because it had laid a foundation of vigorous craftsmanship in an area which was afterwards to produce the historic Greeks.

Somewhere between 2000 and 1500 B.C. invaders from the north, from the direction of what we now know as Macedonia, began to make their appearance in Greece. At first there was probably no definite invasion. It is almost a rule in history that before any definite invasion of a new territory takes place there is a long period of more or less peaceful penetration. In the beginning we have the settlements of adventurers and traders; then mercenaries are invited in by some chieftain anxious to get the better of a fellow chieftain, or perhaps a few families move a little farther up a mountain or a little to the other side of a pass. Then follow disputes and violence. From this it is not a far cry to definite invasion. By 1500 B.C. this latter process had almost certainly started in Greece, and the names of the various tribes of whom the invaders were composed are probably preserved for us in the lands which they conquered. There were Hellenes, Thessalians, Boeotians, Achaeans, Phocians, and Dorians. They appear to have mixed with the former inhabitants in varying proportions. Attica was not subdued, but met and received the invaders on equal terms : here the native race predominated. In Sparta, on the other hand, the invading Dorians kept their race pure. Mycenae was destroyed: the Mycenaean culture submerged: and the native languages gave way to the Aryan language of the invaders, which we call Greek.

When Greece had been conquered, a task which took centuries to accomplish, the migrating tribes crossed the sea to the western coast of Asia Minor, where three groups of settlements—Aeolian, Ionian, and Dorian—preserve the names of the conquering tribes. In one of these migrations Troy was destroyed, and its siege, blended with the recollections of earlier battles, forms the subject of Homer's *Iliad*, the first epic of Europe, sung in the metre which the conquerors had brought with them from the north.

The Greeks crossed over to Asia Minor by sea, but some centuries were to elapse before they became a maritime people. The conquest of Greece, Asia Minor, and the Aegean Islands had probably been completed by 1000 B.C., but as late as 700 B.C. it is obvious from the writings of Hesiod that the Greeks regarded the sea with disfavour. Originally they were nomads counting their wealth by flocks and herds ; then, as they formed settled communities, they became agriculturists, although for some time the work of tilling the fields and growing crops was left to the women, while the men tended the cattle or fought the battles of their tribe. As nomads they had no such thing as law ; its place was taken by customs, such as the custom of the next of kin being responsible for revenging a murdered man. They were all split up into tribes and frequently there were subdivisions of the tribe. Each tribe had a king or leader, but generally speaking a kind of rough equality prevailed. There were no rich and no poor, and nothing approximating to government

EVOLUTION OF GOVERNMENT

with the exception of a council of elders which decided some matters of tribal importance or arbitrated disputes, and an assembly of warriors which met annually or at some festival to decide migrations or the making of peace and war. When the Greeks settled into communities new problems faced them, such as the adjustment of the relations between rich and poor, and the passing of laws in order to protect the landowning class which had come into existence and power. The period from 1000 to 600 B.C. witnessed a determined attempt to grapple with these problems, and the difficulties of the task were complicated by the absence of writing, which necessitated the existence of such officials as 'rememberers' whose work it was to remember the terms of a contract or agreement, or the conditions of a treaty.

In course of time groups of villages coalesced to form cities, and the city-state was the only nation which the Greeks ever knew. Each city governed itself, had its own council and assembly, made peace and war, and raised its own taxes. In the centre of each of them, on an eminence, was the king's castle or acropolis or citadel. Down below, grouped around it, were the houses of the citizens, and the market-place where the king and council adjusted business and settled disputes. The council was composed of nobles or 'eupatrids' who had secured power and wealth for themselves by adding considerably to their lands by force, fraud, intermarriage, or oppression. The assembly consisted of the poorer citizens and of peasants from country districts which belonged to the city-state. It had little power in early times; as a matter of fact it did little more than confirm what the council had already decided. The council was the powerful body; and its members were the chief protectors of the state in time of war, for they alone could afford costly weapons and equipments. The peasants soon found it a waste of valuable time to attend the assembly, and their attendances became less and less frequent. When they were there they exercised no real authority, and in the meantime their lands were being neglected. In many cases it was all that they could do to extract a bare livelihood from them, and it often happened that, in order to discharge debts which they had incurred, they had to sell themselves into slavery to some wealthy landowner. Slaves had no rights whatsoever, and could not vote in the assembly.

Politically, ancient Greece was always weak because of its division into city-states. At one time there were hundreds of them, all independent of one another, and, as in the Italy of the Middle Ages, the larger and more powerful cities were constantly trying to absorb the smaller and weaker ones. This tendency towards disunion was aided by the geographical configuration of the country; its mountains and deep bays kept communities apart. Thus local habits and dialects would develop, as distinct as those of North and South Germany, or of Brittany and Provence. Such differences made union difficult. Only two permanent unions were ever effected among the various groups of Greek city-states: one in Laconia under the leadership of Sparta, and the other in Attica under the leadership of Athens. Consequently Greek patriotism was narrow, but it was very intense. No people have ever loved their country more passionately than the ancient Greeks loved their cities. The Athenians of the time of Pericles did not regard their lives as their own, but as the property of the state.

There were, however, some influences which tended to bring ALL the Greeks together. There were the 'amphictyonies' or religious councils which controlled the great national temples or shrines such as that of Apollo at Delphi, or arranged religious festivals like the great annual festival of Apollo in the island of Delos. To these councils *all* the city-states sent representatives. The great games such as the Olympic Games were a further unifying influence, and the councils which controlled them were also representative

The walled citadel of Athens

Where ancient Sparta stood : the plain below Taygetus

of the whole of Greece. Trade, which often brings peoples together, had the very opposite effect in ancient Greece. A merchant who settled for purposes of trade in a foreign city had no legal rights whatsoever, and in order to protect himself he became the guest or was appointed to be the guest of some citizen. The Homeric writings made strongly towards unity, for they were regarded as the common property of all Greeks, and they told of a time when all Greece was united against the Asiatic city of Troy. Finally, the Greek idea that all who were not Greeks were 'barbarians' showed some kind of national consciousness, but it was never fully awakened. Even the Persian invasions produced nothing like complete unity. The Athenians received no help from Sparta at Marathon, and when Xerxes invaded Greece he received much support from the Thebans, who seemed really anxious that the Persians should be successful.

It was the nobles who reduced the mass of the people to political insignificance in early Greece; it was they also who undermined the power of the king. Between 750 and 650 B.C. kingship disappeared from the Greek states, and elective officers took the place of the kings, such as the archons at Athens, whose period of office was one year. In Sparta, however, kingship was not abolished, but its powers were much curtailed by the device of two kings at the same time and the appointment of administrative officials called ephors, five in number, and holding office for one year. These could and actually did arrest, try, and fine kings. They were appointed by the popular assembly, which was, however, becoming more and more aristocratic in character; it was dominated by the wealthier citizens who were owners of numerous slaves and who were rapidly developing into a military caste which was to give Sparta its peculiar position among the Greek city-states.

With the disappearance of kings went the necessity for royal palaces, but the shrines which were attached to, or often

Delphi; the ruins of the great shrine of Apollo. In the centre of it, the subterranean chasm above which the priestess sat to deliver the oracles of the god

a part of the palaces, remained. Thus the palace of King Erectheus at Athens disappeared, but the little shrine of the goddess Athena in the palace developed into a temple in her honour known as the Erectheum. On this same hill—the Acropolis of Athens—was built in later times a still more magnificent temple—the Parthenon.

During the period when the nobles were gradually gaining the ascendancy in Greece, the civilization of the Aegean underwent great changes. In course of time the Greeks overcame their original antipathy to the sea, and Greek trading vessels became a very common sight on the Aegean, particularly the vessels of the Ionian Greeks of Asia Minor. The greatest traders of the time were the Phoenicians, who brought to Greece from their ports of Tyre and Sidon exquisite metal work, pottery, and linen of fine texture, the work of Phoenician craftsmen, who showed themselves clever imitators of the Egyptians from whom they had learned their art. This work was finer than anything that the Greeks could yet produce. Accordingly Phoenician mariners were always welcome in Greek ports; their merchandize could always find ready buyers. But the Greeks owed them a still greater debt, for it was from them that they learned the art of writing. The Phoenicians had long given up cuneiform writing; they had adopted alphabetic writing—an adaptation of the Egyptian variety—somewhere about 1000 B.C. Their alphabet consisted of twenty-two letters with no vowels; the Greeks were the first to invent vowel sounds, so it was they who had the first complete alphabet. At first the art of writing was not popular; but shortly after 700 B.C. it became fairly common among all classes. The Greeks often called the papyrus which they used 'byblos', after the Phoenician city of Byblos, which imported it from Egypt and then exported some to Greece, and when they wrote their books on such rolls they called them 'biblia'. Thus we get our word 'Bible'. It is worth remembering that not only the Greek alphabet, but all the alphabets of Europe and Western Asia are descended from the Phoenician alphabet.

As yet Greek art was very crude, very much inferior to that of the Aegeans. There was no real architecture; sculpture was in its infancy; painting was confined to the simplest decorative work, such as that of the painter of pottery jars; buildings were constructed of sun-baked brick. It was in literature that the Greek genius first manifested itself, and probably its place of origin is the vale of Thessaly, where the sight of the snowy summit of Mount Olympus would act as a powerful incentive to the imagination. The mountain came to be regarded as the abode of the gods, and songs were composed about them and their relations with men; often new interest was added to these songs by weaving into them memories of bygone battles or sieges in which the favour or anger of the gods had been strikingly manifested. In time the songs made their way across the Aegean to the Ionian Greeks, and it was among them that professional bards first appeared—who recited or sang these old tales to the accompaniment of a harp in the halls of the nobles. Then the songs were collected into a cycle and committed to writing about 700 B.C. One of the most notable of the bards was named Homer; indeed, so notable was he that the whole cycle, which really took a couple of centuries to complete, was attributed to his authorship. Afterwards he was represented as the author of the *Iliad* and the *Odyssey* alone—the former the record of the Greek war against Troy, the latter an account of the wanderings of one of the Greek warriors, Odysseus (Ulysses), and his followers after the fall of Troy. Perhaps even this limited authorship is more than can justly be attributed to Homer.

The Homeric songs were immensely important in the minds of the ancient Greeks. Their authors were the first Greeks to put into permanent literary form their thoughts about gods and men, and the songs can rightly be regarded as the Bible of the Greeks of that time. We gather that they believed in a variety of gods and goddesses—Zeus the father of the gods, Hera his wife, Apollo the god of the sun and also of archery and much else. Pallas Athena goddess of the arts, Aphrodite goddess of love, Ares god of war, Hermes, Dionysos, and many others. These deities were singularly prone to human weaknesses; indeed their only claim to superiority appears to have been their immortality. After death it was believed that the spirits of the departed led particularly dreary existences in Hades—good and bad alike —although heroes were sometimes rescued from this by the gods, and permitted to enjoy lives of endless bliss among the Elysian fields, or in the Islands of the Blessed situated to the far west in the unexplored ocean.

The Homeric songs are singularly impersonal. The authors do not intrude at all. In striking contrast are the poems of Hesiod (seventh century B.C.), an obscure farmer who lived under the shadow of Mount Helicon in Boeotia, and who cries out against the tyranny and greed of the rich and the increasing miseries of the poor. He makes bitter attacks on the princes who ruled the land,[1] 'bribe-swallowing lords, fools who know not how much more the half is than the whole.' 'The people', he tells us, 'pay for the mad folly of their princes, who evilly minded pervert judgement.' This can be contrasted with Homer, whose princes rule by divine right, and whose only agitator is soundly beaten amidst universal laughter and approval. But since the time of Homer a great change had come over Greece. Literature had ceased to be inspired exclusively by princely patrons, and the character of the princes had altered considerably. Greedy landlords with law courts to support them in their exactions had taken the place of the benevolent military autocrats of earlier times. The poems of Hesiod can be compared with those of the

[1] Hesiod's *Works and Days* (Loeb Classical Library) (H. Evelyn White's Translation).

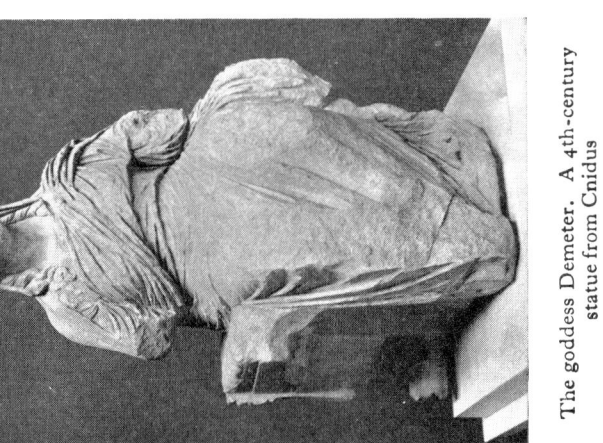

The goddess Demeter. A 4th-century statue from Cnidus

A seated goddess. Archaic statue of the 5th century B.C.

GREEK RELIGION

Jewish prophet Amos, the herdsman of Tekoa. Their subject-matter is very similar, but the results were somewhat different—in Greece the growth of democracy, in Palestine the development of a more humane religion. The rugged sincerity of Hesiod is in some respects reminiscent of a great modern thinker—Thomas Carlyle. Both men had no sympathy for shams and artificialities, and both preached the perennial nobleness and sacredness of work. Work was for Hesiod the law of life. He boldly declares that[1] 'both gods and men are angry with the man who lives idle, for in nature he is like the stingless drones who waste the labour of the bees, eating without working. . . . Work is no disgrace. It is idleness that is a disgrace.'

The tyranny of the nobles and the increasing misery of the peasants were undoubtedly the original causes of Greek colonization, although there were other reasons too, such as love of adventure, and the desire for greater wealth than their own country afforded them. Once the Greeks had become accustomed to the sea they produced a very hardy and adventurous race of seamen, and the humble Greek sailor who sailed across the Mediterranean to the countries of the far west such as Spain, France, and Britain probably did as much to spread Greek culture as Alexander the Great and his generals, who in much later times made it their mission to take it to the remote corners of the earth. Early Greek ornaments have been found in Britain and in France, especially in the Somme region and in Provence, and still more in the Saar valley and along the upper Rhine, and it is quite clear that the Greeks established trade with the west of Europe in the sixth century B.C. or even earlier. The most westerly of their colonies was probably Tartessus in Spain, and the most easterly the remote city of Gelonus in the Caucasus, built of wood, surrounded by a stockade and inhabited, according to Herodotus, by a Greek people who were trappers and hunters of the otter and the beaver. There were other settlements

[1] See note, page 106.

A fisherman with his baskets. A fragment of an Athenian wine-cup

Olive-harvest. Whipping the trees. A painting on a wine-jar

GREEK INDUSTRIES

on the shores of what we now know as the Black Sea. But the harsh climate of these regions was not favourable to the development of culture, and for that reason the cities which grew up there were less civilized than those situated in the milder Greek climate. The colonies round the Black Sea were invaluable to the Greeks as granaries, but almost impossible as places where the Greek genius could thrive. It was in Southern Italy and Sicily that the most famous of the Greek colonies were founded. Southern Italy became a kind of new Greece, and it had its full share of the culture which afterwards came to the Greeks. This is a matter of considerable importance, because it was through the Greeks that literature, art, architecture, and the knowledge of how to write came into Italy, so that the Roman civilization is the debtor of the Greek, just as the Greek is the debtor of Phoenicia, and the Phoenicians the debtors of Egypt. Thus it will be seen how interdependent the various branches of the human race are one upon the other and how civilizations benefit from those which precede them. One of the most famous Greek cities in Italy was Neapolis (new city), the modern Naples. Rome at this time was a perfectly insignificant place consisting of the rude settlements of semi-barbaric people ; as yet there was nothing to indicate its future greatness. In Sicily the Greeks founded in the city of Syracuse what was at one time the most powerful and cultured city in the Greek world ; the Phoenicians, the former colonizers of the island, were driven to its western extremities. In Egypt Greek colonizers were welcomed, and settlements were made at Naukratis and Cyrene. In 696 B.C. Ionian Greeks assisted an Assyrian governor who was in revolt against Sennacherib, but they were defeated. This is the earliest known collision between the Greeks and a great power of the Tigris–Euphrates region. The island of Cyprus was almost entirely occupied by Greek colonists, and for a long time it was the most easterly outpost of the Greek world.

GREEK & PHOENICIAN
COLONIES
Sixth Century B.C.

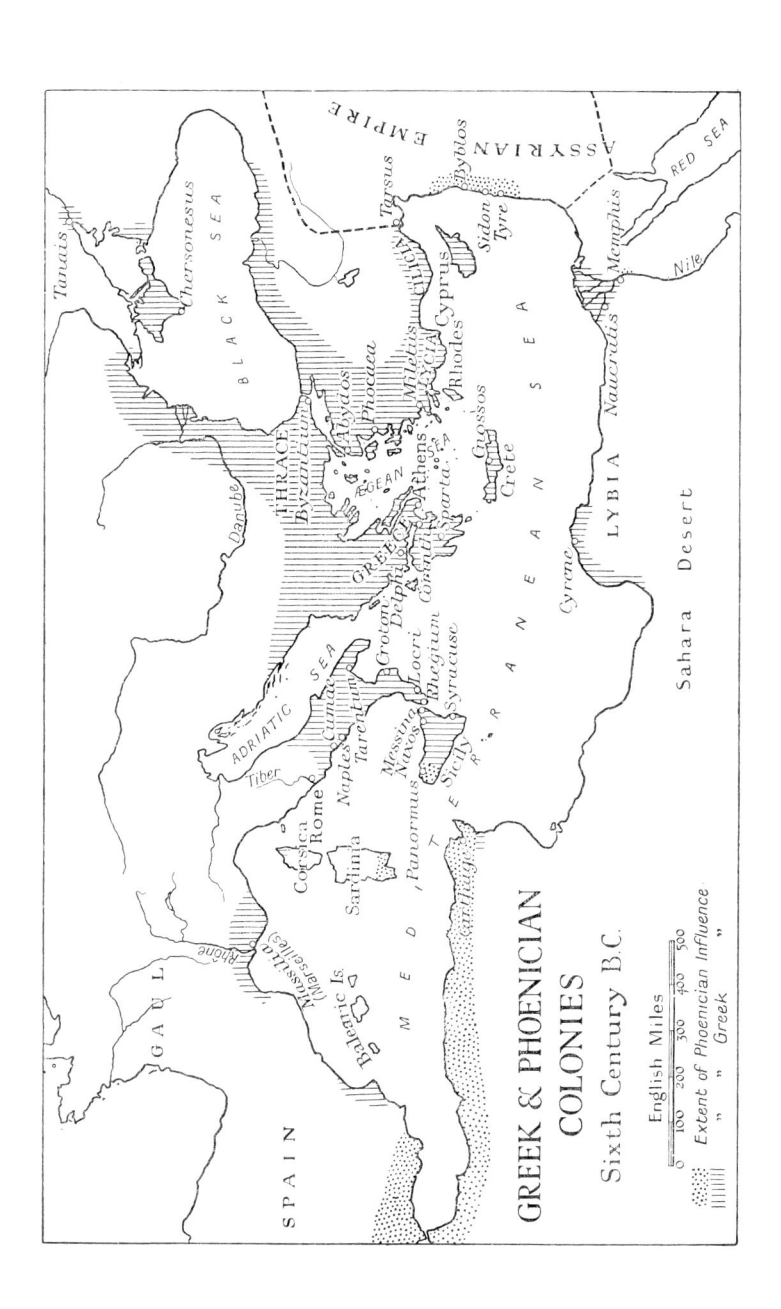

English Miles
0 100 200 300 400 500

Extent of Phoenician Influence
"   "   Greek   "

THE GREEKS

In the wake of colonization there went commercial and industrial development. Greek colonists settled on the sea coasts had dealings with the inhabitants of the interior of the islands or countries where they had taken up their abodes, and the consequence was an exchange of commodities—woven stuffs, metal-work, and pottery which were manufactured in Greece, for such things as amber, grain, fish, and the bronzes of the Etruscans. Thus there resulted an immense development of sea-borne commerce, and the shops of Greece developed into large factories worked by slaves. The Ionian Greeks led the way; the Athenians followed and soon outstripped all others, as they subsequently did in art, literature, and philosophy. Of the painted Greek vases that have been found signed with the name of the artist, more than half come from six great factories in Athens. These vases have been found in diverse regions—in the far interior of Asia Minor, in the Nile Delta, and in Etruria.

The development of commerce naturally led to improvements in the art of shipbuilding. The old galley rowed by fifty oars of Homeric times became obsolete, and sailing-vessels came into general use. Also ships were built on a much larger scale; harbours became necessary; and the first anchor was invented. The expansion of commerce also necessitated a navy—ships-of-war as distinguished from pure merchantmen—to protect and render safe the activities of the merchants. This industrial and commercial development had a further result—the rise of a new and very important class, the capitalist class, whose wealth was reckoned not in land or in flocks and herds, but in money. The use of money the Greeks learned from the Lydians, among whom it is found as early as the seventh century B.C. Originally values were assessed in the East in bars and rods of metal of a given weight: when the kings of Lydia began to cut up these bars into small pieces of a fixed weight, and stamp each piece with their own image, coined money had been invented.

Slips for launching triremes in the harbour at Aegina

Rowers at the oar in a trireme. A Greek marble relief
GREEK SHIPPING

In the meantime the lot of the peasants had been growing worse and worse. Foreclosure of mortgages, great burdens of debt and slavery in discharge of them, while they benefited the moneyed classes, caused profound discontent among the peasants. Sometimes a nobleman would fan this discontent and take advantage of it in order to secure a sort of preeminence over all others—noble and non-noble—in the state. Thus a 'tyranny' was established. The word 'tyrant' did not signify to a Greek quite the same thing as it does to us. Very often a Greek tyrant ruled well and justly, and Greek philosophers afterwards declared that the best government is the government of the perfectly just tyrant. Yet there was a feeling that the existence of a tyranny, however benevolent, was an outrage on liberty, and the assassination of a tyrant was eventually regarded as a heroic and laudable exploit.

Coin of Croesus, King of Lydia (enlarged), see p. 112

One of the remedies which the poorer classes esteemed as a means of redressing their wrongs was the writing down of their laws. When laws were oral, handed down by word of mouth from generation to generation, it was much easier to evade them, perhaps by getting a judge to interpret them in a way which suited the person who gave him the largest bribe, as happened in the case of Persis, who thus swindled his brother Hesiod out of their father's lands. In 624 B.C. the Athenians secured a written code of law, arranged by a man named Draco. These laws, which did nothing to relieve the peasants, were very severe, and the word 'Draconian' is still a synonym for severity.

Less harsh and more just were the laws of Solon (594 B.C.), the first great Greek statesman. Originally prominent as a writer of verses, he had declaimed against the distressing condition of the Athenian peasants, and had roused his countrymen to recapture the island of Salamis which had been taken by the merchants of Megara. He was made archon with full powers to take what steps he considered necessary to remedy the evils of Athens. He immediately declared all mortgages void; ordered the freeing of all Athenians enslaved for debt; and purchased with state money the freedom of those who had been sold into slavery abroad. He also set a limit to the amount of land which a noble might hold, but refused to accede to the demands of the lower classes that there should be a new apportionment of land. Solon did not establish a democracy, although he gave all free craftsmen the right to vote in the Assembly, and accorded equal rights in the law courts to all freemen. The highest offices in the state were not within the reach of all; they still remained the prerogatives of the nobles.

At the end of his term of office Solon retired into private life. In 560 B.C. a tyranny was established in Athens by Pisistratus. He was succeeded by his two sons, Hippias and Hipparchus, but although all these tyrants ruled efficiently and were not unmindful of the interests of the state, the old hatred of tyranny remained, and when Hipparchus was assassinated by two youths, Harmodius and Aristogiton, who paid for it with their own lives, his murderers were regarded as heroes, and in 511 B.C. Hippias, the last of the tyrants, was forced to flee. The chief credit for this must go to a certain nobleman named Cleisthenes, who had bribed the Delphic Oracle to tell the Spartans to march on Athens and expel the tyrant. Subsequently Cleisthenes carried through a remarkable law whose object it was to prevent a recrudescence of tyranny. It was that the people of Athens might once a year declare any prominent citizen dangerous to the state, and by a vote of six thousand or over expel him for ten years. This was known as ostracism, because the name of the person whose expulsion was desired was written on a piece of pottery called an 'ostrakon', and then put into an urn.

THE GREEKS

The Age of the Tyrants (about 600 to 500 B.C.) saw a marked development of Greek art. Limestone was being used in place of sun-baked brick for building, and the front of the temple of Apollo at Delphi was of marble; sculptured figures of gods also adorned it. In Athens, on the hill of Areopagus, the people erected figures of Harmodius and Aristogiton, the slayers of Hipparchus. These were subsequently carried off by the Persians, but restored to their original positions by Alexander the Great.

In literature we have the songs of Sappho and Stesichorus, the pastoral poet of Sicily. Music too was cultivated: a system of writing musical notes arose, and one musician wrote a composition for the *flute* (the favourite musical instrument) which was intended to tell the story of Apollo's fight with the dragon of Delphi. The literature of the time shows a grander conception of deity: Zeus and the other gods were now pictured as always doing what was right and men were enjoined to do likewise; they were further told that in the world of the dead there was punishment for the evil-doer and blessedness for the good. There were some who came very near an utter disbelief in the gods, notably Thales of Miletus, the founder of philosophy. In 585 B.C. he correctly predicted an eclipse of the sun, and boldly declared that the movements of the heavenly bodies were not due to the whims of the gods but to fixed laws of nature.

In 490 B.C. occurred the battle of Marathon, the first great battle between the Greeks and the Persians. The credit for frustrating this deliberate attempt upon the liberties of the European Greeks belongs almost entirely to the Athenians. An urgent appeal for assistance was sent to Sparta, the message being entrusted to a trained long-distance runner named Philippides,[1] who is reputed to have covered the distance—about one hundred and fifty miles up hill and down

[1] Browning calls him Pheidippides, and this name is probably better known than the real name (Philippides).

Art under the Tyrants. Above, wrestling. Below, a cat and dog fight. Athenian sculpture of the time of Pisistratus.

dale and over roads which were in parts rocky and precipitous—so quickly that he reached Sparta on the second day after leaving Athens. The Spartans promised help, but they could not, so they said, march until it was full moon, six days later.[1] With this answer Philippides hurried back to Athens, and on the way, when near Mount Parthenios, it was afterwards related that the god Pan met him and promised help to the Athenians, which after the victory of Marathon they acknowledged by building a temple to him under the Acropolis, and by instituting yearly sacrifices and torch races in his honour. The runner Philippides fought at Marathon, and after the battle ran back to Athens with the news of victory, but died after giving his message.

' He flung down his shield,
Ran like fire once more : and the space 'twixt the Fennel-field
And Athens was stubble again, a field which a fire runs through,
Till in he broke: "Rejoice, we conquer!" Like wine through clay,
Joy in his blood bursting his heart, he died—the bliss ! '[2]

To the Athenians Marathon was ever an abiding glory, for there, so they imagined, they had stood alone against the whole might of Persia and had prevailed. On the epitaph of Aeschylus the fact that he fought at Marathon is recorded and not his fame as a dramatist. Another prominent Athenian who fought at Marathon was Themistocles, a great believer in sea-power, and what happened in this year undoubtedly gave him considerable prestige. If Athens had possessed an efficient navy the passage of the Persian fleet across the Aegean to the Bay of Marathon might, possibly, have been prevented. By 480 B.C., the year of Xerxes' great invasion, Themistocles had persuaded his fellow citizens to build a war fleet of 180 triremes, and it was sea-power more than any-

---

[1] The Spartans kept their promise and, as soon as the moon was full, made all haste to Athens, but too late to take part in the defeat of the Persians. So after visiting the battlefield and praising the victors they returned to Sparta.

[2] ' Pheidippides ' (Robert Browning).

THEMISTOCLES

thing else which ensured the ultimate success of the Greeks. The original plan of Themistocles was that the Greek navy should at once fight the Persian navy, and if successful sail northwards and cut the Persian lines of communication; meanwhile the land forces of the Greeks were to avoid pitched battles and content themselves with the defence of the northern passes, particularly the pass of Thermopylae. This plan was only partially successful. Leonidas, King of Sparta, and his troops covered themselves with deathless glory at Thermopylae and delayed the Persian advance, but the Athenian fleet could only manage a drawn battle with their opponents, who probably outnumbered them to the extent of five hundred to three hundred ships. Themistocles did not lose heart, but went on building ships, confident in the ultimate success of his policy, and before the year was out the victory of Salamis justified his confidence. He then proposed that the Greek fleet should sail to the Hellespont so as to cut off the Persians from Asia. His counsel was not followed; if it had been Greece might have been spared another year of war, and Themistocles would not have fallen from power, for, ironically enough, the Athenians deprived him of his command because the battle of Salamis was not decisive.

The Persians were, in many ways, a highly civilized people, and they had many admirable qualities, of which perhaps the most striking were their love of truth, their belief that it was disgraceful to fall into debt, and their courage. Their religion, Zoroastrianism, was very much superior to what passed for religion among the Greeks of this time. But their lack of self-control, their inordinate love of luxury,[1] and the colossal vanity of their leaders ruined everything, and it was certainly a good thing for the world that Xerxes' great

[1] Some of the richest Persians took costly furniture, couches overlaid with gold and silver, and golden drinking-vessels with them when they went to war.

expedition failed. If it had been successful, the Greek genius would have been hampered at a very important stage of its development, for the Persian system of government was not consistent with free citizenship or indeed with any form of political progress. Herodotus relates of Xerxes that when a storm had destroyed some of the boats which supported the bridge which he was constructing across the Hellespont, he commanded that the sea should be given three hundred lashes and that fetters should be thrown into it for daring to treat its master, the King of Persia, with such scant respect. On another occasion, when a certain rich Lydian named Pythius, who had hospitably entertained him, and with whom Xerxes was much pleased, asked that his eldest son should be excused from service against the Greeks, in consideration of the fact that the services of four other sons had been willingly surrendered, Xerxes fell into a great rage and ordered the instant execution of the favourite son, and the cutting of his body into two halves, which were to be placed one on each side of the highway along which the Persian army was to pass. Contrast with these a story which is told of Pausanias, King of Sparta, the nephew of Leonidas. After the battle of Thermopylae, Xerxes and his general Mardonius cut off the head of Leonidas and crucified him. This same Mardonius was in command of the Persian forces at Plataea, where he was defeated and killed by the Spartans under Pausanias, to whom it was suggested that he should avenge his uncle's death by decapitating and crucifying the dead body of Mardonius. But the Spartan king scornfully refused, declaring that such conduct was more suitable to foreigners than to Greeks, and blameworthy even in foreigners, and that Leonidas had already been amply avenged in the unnumbered Persians who had been slain since Thermopylae. If the stories of Xerxes and the Hellespont and Xerxes and Pythius are true, and there is very little reason for disbelieving them, they exhibit Oriental despotism at its worst; they reveal an attitude of

Persian soldiers in the body-guard of King Darius. Persian sculpture of the 6th–5th centuries B.C., from the palace at Susa

A Greek hoplite. A bronze statuette dedicated to Zeus by a Greek soldier.

THE WAR WITH PERSIA

mind which is irrevocably opposed to the free development of the human spirit, and which is the very antithesis of those ideas which are at the root of all progress, for whose evolution and development the world is deeply in the debt of ancient Greece.

The defeat of Persia had a very disturbing effect upon the Athenians : many of them began to dream of a Greek empire which should rule the world. The Spartans, on the contrary, were quite content with their position and had neither the inclination nor the imagination for imperial authority. Thus the years that followed the Persian collapse witnessed a great struggle between the Athenian spirit and the Spartan spirit. The Spartans were conservative, the slaves of tradition, devoid of imagination, esteeming nothing virtuous but military excellence. They looked to the past and the dominance of the few. The Athenians, or at least the best among them, were progressive, liberal minded, highly imaginative, with their eyes fixed on the future and the dominance of the many.

' Suppose ', wrote Thucydides, ' the city of Sparta to be deserted, and nothing left but the temples and the ground plan, distant ages would be very unwilling to believe that the power of the Spartans was at all equal to their fame. And yet they own two-fifths of the Peloponnesus and are acknowledged leaders of the whole, as well as of numerous allies in the rest of Greece. But their city is not regularly built and has no splendid temples or other edifices ; it resembles rather a straggling village, like the ancient towns of Greece, and would therefore make a poor show. Whereas if the same fate befell the Athenians the ruins of Athens would strike the eye, and we should infer their power to have been twice as great as it really is.'

This prediction has been amply verified. What remains of Sparta is so insignificant that it is very difficult to locate the ancient site at all, whereas the Acropolis of Athens with its marble buildings can be seen twenty miles away. But Sparta

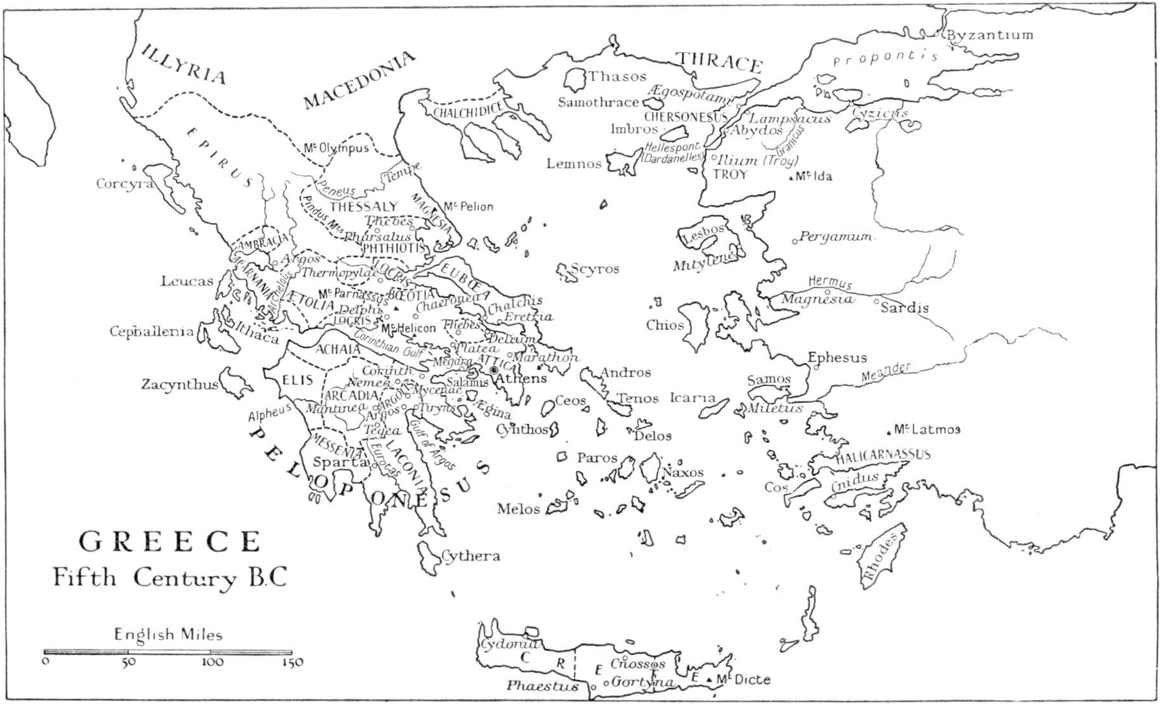

GREECE
Fifth Century B.C

had not always been 'a straggling village'. Recent excavations make it clear that in the seventh and part of the eighth century B.C. it was the leading city of Greece. In the days of the poet Alkman (about 630 B.C.) it was a centre of culture delighting in music and dancing, and in the work of artists, sculptors, potters, and craftsmen. But early in the sixth century B.C. culture and luxury were banished from Sparta, strangers were expelled, and Spartan art and literature came to an end. Henceforth ideals of beauty were discouraged, and the city was put under a system of martial law, state training took the place of family life, and rigorous and even brutal tests of endurance were imposed upon youths in order to ensure that they should be brave men. 'In the matter of education', said the great Athenian statesman Pericles, 'whereas the Spartans from early youth are always undergoing laborious exercises which are designed to make them brave, we live at ease and yet are equally ready to face the perils that they face.'

After the Persian invasions the chief man in Athens was Themistocles. Under his guidance, the Athenians began the rebuilding of their city, constructed long walls around it, and fortified the Piraeus, the harbour of Athens. Themistocles was among the foremost champions of the idea of an Athenian Empire, and circumstances were distinctly favourable to the development of his projects. Many of the Greek cities, particularly those of Asia Minor and the islands of the Aegean, fearing Persian vengeance, agreed to form a league of protection with Athens as its leader. Thus was formed the Delian League, so called because its funds were originally kept in the Temple of Apollo on the island of Delos. The more powerful members of the league furnished ships; the weaker members contributed money. In the time of Pericles the treasury was moved from Delos to Athens and its contents used for purely Athenian purposes. Thus the Delian League was the real nucleus of the Athenian Empire.

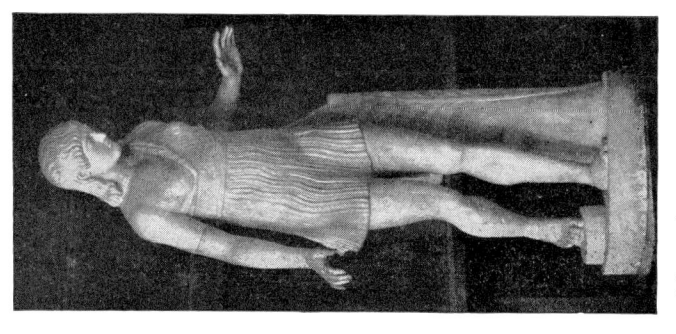

A CONTRAST: Athenian girls with lyres; a Spartan girl running

The ships of the league under Cimon, son of Miltiades, the victor of Marathon, were very successful in clearing the Aegean of the Persians. Cimon was a strong supporter of friendship with Sparta; opposed to him was Themistocles, who urged war with Sparta. He failed, however, to carry the Assembly with him and in 471 B.C. was ostracized and forced to flee; curiously enough, he entered the service of the King of Persia, whose plans he had been mainly instrumental in frustrating. Ten years later (461 B.C.) Cimon persuaded the Athenians to send assistance to the Spartans, who were experiencing difficulty through a revolt of some of their subjects. Before the rebellion had been crushed the Spartans asked the Athenians to withdraw. This was regarded as a deadly insult, and Cimon, who had been responsible for sending the Athenian troops to Sparta, was ostracized.

The leadership of Athens now devolved upon Pericles, the greatest of the Greek statesmen. He was a descendant of Cleisthenes, and like him a strong upholder of popular liberties. There was a marked extension of democratic ideas, and it became possible for all Athenians, with the exception of the very poorest labourers, to fill any of the offices of state. Like Themistocles, Pericles was an exponent of the imperial idea and in favour of war with Sparta. In 459 B.C. the first Spartan (Peloponnesian) War broke out. It lasted for thirteen years, and at its close Athens was in a state of exhaustion. Worse than that, in 459 B.C. an Athenian fleet of two hundred vessels, which had been sent against the Persians in Egypt, was entirely lost. The peace which ended the first Peloponnesian War was intended to last for thirty years, and Athens was left in possession of the island of Aegina, the conquest of which (by Athens) had been one of the original causes of the war.

The Age of Pericles is the most brilliant in the history of Greece, and indeed in the history of the world, because of its tremendous achievements in art, literature, and most things that make up the higher life of man. At this time the state of Athens consisted of about 280,000 people, of whom about 100,000 were slaves and 20,000 resident aliens who had no political privileges. This leaves 160,000 made up of the free citizens and their families. Of this number, probably about forty to forty-eight thousand would be freemen. All these were in a very real sense the rulers of the state. Athenian democracy was not a delegated democracy like those of modern times. The Athenian did not elect any one to represent his interests at meetings of the Assembly ; he went there himself and recorded his vote. The Assembly was held at least ten times a year, and at least six thousand votes were necessary before it could ostracize a citizen. Assisting it in the work of government was the Council, which had five hundred members, fifty from each of the ten tribes into which the Athenians were divided, but the really important body was the Assembly. There were very few civic duties which the Athenians did not perform in person ; one of the exceptions was the task of policing the city, which was done by Scythians, whose practice of wearing trousers must have caused the Athenian youths endless amusement. Practically all the other ordinary duties of the citizen were performed by the freemen of Athens as their turns came along : such as the duty of serving in the army or the navy, or the duty of serving on a jury. Juries were very large, two hundred or over, and fulfilled the function of the modern judge as well as that of the modern jury. Pericles was the first to introduce the practice of paying the juror for his services. The pay was low—about $4\frac{1}{2}d.$ a day—but not too low to make it a much desired privilege for those Athenians who were not overfond of work.

Most of the citizens of Athens were farmers—peasant proprietors with holdings of their own—although some few were tenants of the state or of a religious corporation. A striking feature of their lives was their intense patriotism. A wealthy citizen would consider it a privilege to build and equip a trireme at his own expense ; to provide the money for literary or athletic contests ; to pay the expenses of a chorus at one of the great religious festivals ; or, if he happened to be the leader of a successful chorus, to help to beautify the city by erecting a fitting memorial of his good fortune. Other citizens would show their patriotism in the work which they did. Craftsmen and professional men would work for a drachma (about four shillings) a day ; this was the fixed wage beyond which there was no advance. When one considers what the best-known artists and sculptors of the present day are paid for their works and compares it with the pay of Pheidias, one gets some idea of the outlook of the Athenian upon life.

Pericles was the dominant personality in Athens for thirty years. The first fifteen of these witnessed a gradual unfolding of the civilization which has made the city famous, but its development was retarded by the wars with Sparta and Persia. The fifteen years of peace which followed were the really important years. Obviously the first thing for Pericles to do was to erect fitting memorials of the gratitude which the people of Athens felt towards the gods for their deliverance from Persia. The Persians had destroyed the temples of the Acropolis,[1] and it was Pericles' task to erect finer ones in their place—and the finest monument of all was the Parthenon on the south side of the hill. This was dedicated to the goddess Athena, and the architect of the temple was Ictinus. Collaborating with him was the great sculptor Pheidias, whose frieze work, although considerably mutilated, may still be seen in the British Museum (The Elgin Marbles). It represents a Pan-Athenaic festival, which occurred every four years, when the people gathered together in stately processions, and trials of athletic, literary, and musical skill were

[1] The Acropolis of Athens was a flat-topped rock, about a thousand feet long and five hundred feet broad, and about a hundred and fifty feet above the level of the plain.

Head and shoulders of the colossal gold and ivory statue of Athena which stood in the Parthenon, reproduced on an ancient gem. The statue was the work of Pheidias

The Parthenon, on the Acropolis at Athens; the strip of black stone marked with a cross was the base on which the statue of Athena stood

ATHENIAN ART UNDER PERICLES

held. Despite the mutilated nature of the work, sufficient of it remains to show the complete technical mastery which Pheidias and his pupils—for it is not the work of Pheidias alone—had attained. The rich variety of crease and fold in the draperies is worth noticing; so too is the grave dignity and simplicity of the whole work. The greatest achievements of Pheidias were two statues, one of Zeus in Olympia, and the other of Athena in the Parthenon. This was in the central chamber of the temple. It was made of wood and overlaid with ivory and gold, ivory for the flesh and gold for the garments, and was about forty feet high. With her left hand the goddess supported her spear and the edge of her shield. On her outstretched right hand was a winged Victory, six feet high, holding a wreath. The helmet of the goddess was adorned with a Sphinx and Gryphons, two figures of Pegasus (the winged horse of Zeus), and a row of small horses. All available spaces were covered with reliefs. In particular there was a battle between Greeks and Amazons on the outside of the shield. The statue is known to have been in existence about A.D. 430, but not long after this date the figure was removed and the Parthenon converted into a Christian church. Since that time it has suffered much from the iconoclastic fury of churchmen, Turks, and Venetians, and it is a melancholy reflection that its present dilapidated condition is due more to human foolishness than to the influence of time.

The Parthenon was not the only feature of the Acropolis. To the west of it was a Temple of Victory, inferior to the Parthenon, but none the less a remarkable achievement, and on another side of the hill was a great bronze statue of Athena, whose shield and helmet could be seen flashing far out at sea on a sunny day.

If it had produced nothing but sculpture the Age of Pericles would be very notable, but it also marks a development of the art of painting (generally scenes depicting the

THE DRAMA

achievements of gods and heroes), of literature, of rhetoric and philosophy, even of mathematics, medicine, and science. At this time lived the three great tragic poets of ancient Greece: Aeschylus, Sophocles, and Euripides. Their plays were performed in open-air theatres, seats being arranged semicircularly and in tiers, and each citizen attended as the guest of the state, which made itself responsible for his entrance fee. Aeschylus had fought at Marathon and Salamis, and Sophocles had, as a boy of sixteen, witnessed from the island of Salamis the defeat of the Persian fleet in the adjoining bay in 480 B.C. Thus it is not surprising to find that the works of both these playwrights recall the stirring days of the Persian invasions and do not fail to laud the gods. They were, therefore, very popular with their audiences, probably far more popular than the plays of Euripides, a younger poet, the son of a farmer on the island of Salamis, who often seems to cast doubt upon the wisdom and goodness of the gods, and who is full of gloomy forebodings about mankind.

The great tragic poets were not the only writers of the period. Herodotus and Thucydides, two of the greatest historians the world has known, lived through the Periclean age. Xenophon was a child and Socrates a young man when the building of the Parthenon was begun in 447 B.C., and Aristophanes, the great writer of comedies, a child when it was completed in 438 B.C. Pericles was the patron of all forms of culture, and in this he received the enthusiastic support and approval of his mistress, Aspasia of Miletus.

This age is also remarkable for the rise of a class of professional teachers—the Sophists—who were prepared to teach something beyond the ordinary subjects of the day—reading, writing, the study of the old poets, music, dancing, and gymnastic exercises. The Sophists were great doubters, much more so than Euripides, eager to get at the root of things, merciless exposers of shams, accomplished orators and writers, and it was they who gave the first stimulus to oratory and good prose among the Greeks. They also taught the rudiments of arithmetic, geometry, and astronomy. They were peripatetic teachers, wandering about from city to city. In the eyes of the ordinary Greek they had one defect, more marked in some than others : their impiety. One of the Sophists went so far as to deny the existence of the gods. This was a very dangerous thing to do, for the Greek took his religion very seriously, and it was comparatively easy to rouse him to a state of fanaticism. Pericles could not save his friend, the philosopher Anaxagoras, from banishment when he hinted that there were no gods, but only a great spirit animating the universe. Indeed flight saved Anaxagoras from almost certain death, which Pericles would have been powerless to avert. The great Pheidias was accused of impiety because in a representation on the shield of Athena of a fight between Greeks and Amazons he had dared to depict himself and Pericles among the Greeks : he was thrown into prison and died there of disease in 432 B.C. This was shortly after his return to Athens from Olympia, where he had just executed the statue of the Olympian Zeus, his greatest work. Even Pericles was not immune from the suspicions of the multitude : a charge of peculation was brought against him, and when that failed his enemies sought to wound him by procuring the banishment of Aspasia, and it was only the tearful remonstrances of Pericles which saved her.

So great is the debt of the modern world to ancient Greece that a modern mind suddenly transported to the Athens of Pericles would find much that it could appreciate and enjoy—but some things would have the opposite effect, such as the existence of slaves, the treatment of women, and the absence of many of the ordinary comforts of civilization such as drains and soap. Olive-oil served instead of soap and electric light. Women had no political rights whatsoever : generally speaking, they had nothing more exciting than household duties to live for. Greek slavery varied in character. Many

The rows of seats and the orchestra of the great marble theatre at Epidaurus

The front seats of the theatre of Dionysus at Athens

THE GREEK THEATRE

of the Athenian slaves were skilled craftsmen and worked at the temples and public buildings with their masters : occasionally some few of them obtained their freedom. But the slaves of the silver mines of Laurium (which belonged to Athens) worked naked in galleries two or three feet square under conditions so appalling that they hardly survived for more than three years. And yet the Greek record is much better than that of other nations. All nations had slaves, and in Rome and Carthage they were often treated with disgusting cruelty ; in Greece alone were there any who argued whether it was right to have slaves ; some writers went so far as to condemn slavery altogether, a point of view which is in advance of that held by St. Paul.

Politically the Age of Pericles is important because it witnessed the development of the Confederacy of Delos into the Athenian Empire. Not only was the treasury of the League transferred to Athens, and League money used to beautify the city ; cases of dispute between members, which had originally come before a court of arbitration connected with the League, were decided by the Athenian courts ; and members who endeavoured to flout Athenian authority were severely dealt with. Thus when in 439 B.C. the island of Samos, a powerful member which paid tribute in ships and men and not in money, and had a government quite independent of Athens, and strong fortifications, refused to accept Athenian arbitration in a dispute with Miletus, another member of the League, over some land in Asia Minor, the whole force of the Confederacy was assembled against it ; its fortifications were dismantled ; and a democratic government substituted for the oligarchy which had previously ruled. The Samians got some assistance from the Persians ; they also applied for aid to Sparta, an application which was unsuccessful, chiefly on account of the opposition of Corinth, who contended that a confederacy had the right to punish its recalcitrant members. Yet, eight years later (431 B.C.), when

DEATH OF PERICLES

there was a dispute between Corinth and Corcyra [1] (originally a Corinthian colony) over some assistance which Corinth had given to Epidamnus,[2] a Corcyrean colony in Illyria, Athenian ships were dispatched to save the Corcyreans from conquest by Corinth. After this the feelings of the Corinthians towards Athens became bitterly hostile. They gave assistance to Potidaea,[3] a revolted member of the Delian League ; and aroused fear and hatred towards Athens amongst the Spartans, so that the Thirty Years' Truce was broken and the Second Peloponnesian War broke out.

Practically all the Peloponnese, except Argos, was hostile to Athens ; so too was Boeotia in Northern Greece, led by the city of Thebes. The strength of Athens lay in its fleet ; that of Sparta in its army, against which the Athenians could not hope to fight on equal terms. Accordingly all the country people of Attica, sending their live stock to the island of Euboea, withdrew for safety within the fortifications of Athens. Overcrowding was the result, and in the second year of the war there was a great plague which destroyed about one-third of the people, including Pericles, who could ill be spared. This plague had much to do with the ultimate defeat of Athens, but it was by no means the sole cause. After the death of Pericles, Athens was like a ship without a rudder. A succession of leaders who lacked ability, such as Nicias or Cleon the tanner (whom Aristophanes ridiculed unmercifully in his comedies), vacillating counsels, silly superstitions, and the moral delinquencies of Alcibiades (the one brilliant leader of the period) could have but one result. The treatment of Mitylene is an example of Athenian policy or lack of it. Mitylene had rebelled and been subjugated, and the Assembly decided that all the citizens should be put to death. A ship was dispatched from Athens with orders to that effect, but

[1] Modern, Corfu.   [2] Modern, Durazzo.
[3] A town in Macedonia, originally a Corinthian colony, which had become tributary to Athens.

before it reached Mitylene another ship overtook it with later orders that only the leaders of the insurrection should be executed; the Assembly had met again and changed its mind. In 421 B.C. Nicias negotiated a kind of truce with Sparta called the Peace of Nicias. He favoured a policy of conciliation, but opposed to him was the brilliant but erratic Alcibiades, who, in 415 B.C., persuaded the Assembly to prosecute the war vigorously once more by sending a great expedition against the important city of Syracuse, which was a Corinthian colony, and after the conquest of Sicily, Italy, and Carthage he proposed that the victors should return to Greece, subdue Sparta and establish Athenian supremacy over the whole peninsula. The expedition sailed with Alcibiades and Nicias in command, but before it had accomplished anything Alcibiades was recalled to answer a charge of impiety; according to his accusers he had been responsible for mutilating certain images of the god Hermes. Instead of returning, he fled to Sparta and persuaded the Spartans to send help to the Syracusans—the result being the complete defeat of the Athenian forces, an event which was rendered more certain by the superstitious foolishness of Nicias, who allowed himself to be shut up in the harbour of Syracuse because an eclipse of the moon would make withdrawal unlucky. About seven thousand prisoners were taken by the victors and enslaved, but Nicias, who was one of the captives, was put to death, some, and especially the Corinthians, fearing that, being rich, he might by bribery escape and do them further mischief.[1]

These events discredited the Athenian democracy, and an oligarchy was established in Athens: its life was short-lived, however, for the fleet refused to obey it and democratic government was tried again. But the city's star was not in the ascendant. Alcibiades was recalled after negotiating an alliance between Athens and Persia, and put in command

[1] Thucydides (Jowett's translation), Bk. VII, § 86.

of the fleet, but he was defeated in 406 B.C. at Notium through the indiscretion of one of his lieutenants. Two years later, near Aegospotami, a small river which flows into the Hellespont, the Spartan admiral Lysander captured the Athenian fleet. Spartan troops advanced into Attica ; the loss of the fleet made it impossible for the Athenians to get grain from the Black Sea, and surrender to Sparta was the only thing left for them to do. The victors refused to take the advice of Corinth that Athens should be destroyed, but insisted that the fortifications of the Piraeus [1] and the Long Walls [1] should be demolished, that the people of Athens should join the Spartan League, and that their ships should be handed over to Sparta.

The great war with Sparta did not stop the development of the intellectual life of Athens. Probably during the early years of the struggle Herodotus completed his history, which does not fail to bring into prominence the achievements of the Athenians in the wars with Persia and for which they are reputed to have voted him the sum of ten talents (about £3,000). The comedies of Aristophanes brought some gleams of light into the darkness of the period ; sometimes this great writer was performing a public service, as when he exposed the charlatanry and incompetence of Cleon, but he was influencing his fellow citizens badly when he poked fun at the ugly face and ill-fitting garments of the philosopher Socrates, who was at this time a familiar figure on the marketplace, questioning the citizens of Athens, convincing them of their lack of knowledge, leading them to realize that the only lasting foundations of any community are truth and virtue, and earning a reputation for wisdom which has lived and will always live in the dialogues of his great disciple Plato. The

[1] The Piraeus was the harbour of Athens, and among the achievements of Pericles was the building of the Long Walls connecting the fortifications of Athens with the Piraeus, thus forming a road completely walled in between the city and its harbour.

Delphic Oracle declared that he was the wisest of living mortals. Socrates, however, had his enemies: he was accused of corrupting the youth of Athens—among his pupils were Plato and Xenophon, but also Alcibiades—and in 400 B.C. he was condemned to death by a tribunal of his fellow citizens. His magnificent defence and the nobility of his last days have been admirably described by Plato and Xenophon. His condemnation is the most discreditable thing that the democracy of Athens ever did, and if the object was to obliterate his teaching it failed utterly. The spirit of inquiry which Socrates did so much to foster can be exemplified in much that happened after his death, perhaps nowhere more effectively than by comparing the work of Thucydides with that of Herodotus. The latter made no attempt to treat history scientifically: events were regarded as resulting from the will of the gods rather than from natural processes.[1] Thucydides, on the other hand, in his great account of the Peloponnesian War, no longer discerns the mere will of the gods in the events which were hastening the destruction of the Athenian Empire, but traces them to their natural causes in the world wherein they occur.

The ascendancy of Sparta lasted from 404 to 371 B.C. Spartan rule was more aggressive and domineering than that of Athens had been. Autocratic forms of government were established in the conquered cities and military garrisons in some as well. The Athenians, however, succeeded in re-establishing democratic government, but the Athenian democracy of this time was not a very desirable form of government. For instance, it aided the Persians to subjugate the Greek cities of Ionia (387 B.C.) simply because the

[1] It should not be assumed from this that Herodotus was not a great historian. His defects, his credulity, and his belief in oracles and miracles are considerably more than outweighed by his merits—his eager spirit of inquiry, his powers of observation, and the fact that he is a very prince of story-tellers. His History recreates, as no amount of research can do, the world through which he moved.

Herodotus Socrates Thucydides

Three great Greeks of the fifth century B.C.

Spartans were on the side of the Ionian Greeks. In 371 B.C. Spartan dominion was overthrown by the Thebans at the battle of Leuctra. Then followed a brief period of Theban ascendancy, ended in 362 B.C. by the battle of Mantinea, a victory of the Thebans and Athenians over the Spartans, but one of those victories which are more disastrous than defeats, for among the slain was Epaminondas, the Theban leader, and with his death the ascendancy of his city both by land and sea came to a rapid end. The great Greek states, having mutually destroyed one another, were now ready to fall before an outside conqueror, who appeared in 338 B.C. in the person of Philip of Macedon. These last years of Greek independence are notable for the speeches in which the orator Demosthenes warned his countrymen of the danger from Macedon, and for the political pamphlets of Isocrates, whose appeals to the Greeks to unite, overthrow the decadent empire of Persia, and found a Greek empire on its ruins, fell for the most part on deaf ears. The philosophers, turning aside from the bickering, jealousies, and recriminations of the politicians, tried to fix men's minds on the ideal. Plato fancied an ideal state of philosophers whose material wants should be provided by slaves and by artisans who were denied citizenship. Following Plato came Aristotle, a Macedonian, the tutor of Alexander the Great. He wrote on a great variety of subjects—philosophy, politics, ethics, poetry, physics, biology, and medicine—and probably no other thinker has exercised so much influence on the world as he. The speculations on the art of government which we find in the writings of Plato and Aristotle, particularly the latter, mark a new development of human thought, and show the Greeks as the inventors of the science of government.

It is not only the works of the philosophers which make Greek history notable in the years between Aegospotami and Chaeronea. This period also witnessed the sculpture of Praxiteles, whose best-known works are a marble statue of

PHILOSOPHY AND ART

Aphrodite which has been lost, and a statue of Hermes (with the right hand broken off) playing with the child Dionysos, which was discovered at Olympia, and is the only statue in existence which can be proved indisputably to be the work of one of the great Greek sculptors. Praxiteles, like Pheidias, was an Athenian, but the love for sculpture and beautiful things was by no means confined to Athens, although it reached its highest point of development there. Temples and statues, theatres, literary and athletic contests were to be found in almost every centre of Greek life (Sparta was a notable exception)—at Rhodes, Corinth, Syracuse, and in the Greek cities of Asia Minor and Southern Italy. At Rhodes once stood the Colossus [1] (about 280 B.C.), a huge bronze figure one hundred and five feet high, between whose legs it is popularly supposed ships passed in order to enter the harbour. There is no justification for such a supposition.

Most of what the Greeks accomplished in the domain of art has been lost; we have only fragments of the songs of Sappho; their painting survives only on antique vases, and it was so wonderful that Zeuxis is said to have painted grapes so well that the birds of the air pecked at them. But enough remains to convince the most sceptical of the genius of this astonishing people; and much of what we esteem most highly in the modern world, such as the faculty of appreciating beauty, the love of freedom, the love of truth, owes its existence very largely to the thinkers of ancient Greece. Even when they had ceased to count for much politically, the Greeks still ruled the realm of thought. In Zeno and Epicurus they produced two philosophers who founded schools which were destined to exercise much influence upon modes of life and thought in the world for many centuries

[1] The Colossus was a statue of the sun-god Helios (Apollo), and it was overthrown by an earthquake in 224 B.C. Numerous attempts were made to restore it to its place, but they were all unsuccessful. Eventually in A.D. 672 the Arabs sold it as waste metal to a Jew, who is said to have carried away three hundred tons of bronze.

after the deaths of their original members. Zeno, who taught about 310 B.C., was the first of the Stoics, so called after the Stoa [1] or Painted Hall at Athens where he lectured. He taught the need for mastering desire, and that the soul should be trained to control pain. The key-note of his system is *duty*, and among his subsequent disciples were Seneca, Epictetus, and the Emperor Marcus Aurelius. There are many living in the world to-day to whom this Stoic philosophy is a religion. It is usual to contrast it with Epicureanism, the key-note of which was *pleasure.* But the pleasure which Epicurus advocated was not of a low or sensuous type. It had its roots in prudence and temperance. 'We cannot', he declared, 'live pleasantly without living wisely and nobly and righteously.' The stories spread by certain Stoics that the community which he established at Athens in 307 B.C. was licentious are groundless.

To the Greeks also belongs the credit of producing the greatest mathematician of ancient times in the person of Archimedes of Syracuse (287 to 212 B.C.). His experiments in hydrostatics established the principle on which the doctrine of specific gravity is based. A Greek, Aristarchus of Samos (250 B.C.), was the first person to state that the earth moves round the sun, thus anticipating Copernicus, who did not know of Aristarchus' discovery. The works of two Greek physicians, Hippocrates (460 to 357 B.C.) and Galen (A.D. 130 to 200) were the standard text-books on medicine until the end of the Middle Ages, and the work of Euclid (about 300 B.C.), a Greek of Alexandria, was the standard geometrical text-book in schools until very recently. Scientific text-books do not generally remain in use for many years; new knowledge and new methods of investigation cause them to be superseded, but more than two thousand years passed by before Euclid was superseded. Even a grammar written by an obscure Greek, Denis of Thrace, was in

[1] Literally a porch.

A Greek painted vase of the late sixth century B.C. Athenian girls drawing water from the lion-head spout of a public drinking fountain

use in English schools less than a hundred years ago. 'We are all Greeks,' wrote the poet Shelley. 'Our laws, our literature, our arts, have their root in Greece.' Probably the Greeks themselves would have regarded love of freedom as their greatest contribution to civilization. Their attitude towards the Persians no less than their attitude towards the tyrants was deeply coloured and even actuated by this idea. There was much that the Greeks admired in Persian civilization, such as their system of education and the threefold ideal of the young nobles : to ride and shoot well and to tell the truth. But it would have been impossible for them to submit to the yoke of Persia, for in that empire there was no individual freedom. All were subject to the will of one man, who was subject to no one. The Greek ideal was that no man should be the master of another, but that all should be subject to the Law, 'whose service is perfect freedom.' This ideal is emphasized over and over again by the greatest of the Greek thinkers—Herodotus, Plato, Demosthenes, and the great tragedians.

X

THE EMPIRE OF ALEXANDER THE GREAT

THE speeches of Demosthenes against Philip of Macedon were highly coloured and prejudiced. He referred to Macedonia as a land from which the Greeks did not get 'even a decent slave' and to Philip as a barbarian from a country which was not respectable, and in no way akin to Greece. On the contrary, the Macedonians were of Aryan stock like the Greeks, and Philip and his son Alexander put in the forefront of their policies the spread of Greek culture and civilization. Both Philip and Alexander were well educated after the Greek model, and both appreciated the Greek genius. Philip was the friend of Aristotle (who was a

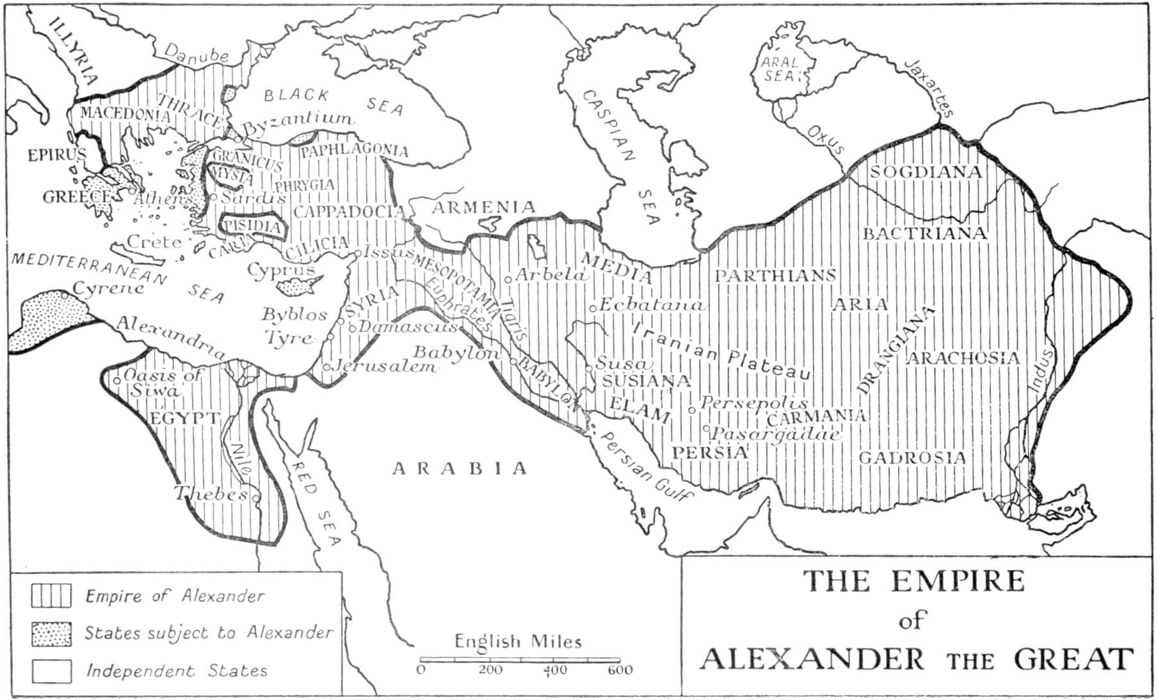
THE EMPIRE
of
ALEXANDER THE GREAT
Empire of Alexander
States subject to Alexander
Independent States
English Miles
0
200
400
600
ILLYRIA
Danube
MACEDONIA
THRACE
EPIRUS
GREECE
Athens
BLACK SEA
Byzantium
GRANICUS
MYSIA
Sardis
PAPHLAGONIA
PHRYGIA
PISIDIA
CAPPADOCIA
CILICIA
CARIA
Crete
MEDITERRANEAN SEA
Cyrene
Cyprus
Byblos
Tyre
Alexandria
Oasis of Siwa
EGYPT
Nile
Thebes
RED SEA
ARABIA
Issus
SYRIA
Damascus
Jerusalem
MESOPOTAMIA
Euphrates
Tigris
Babylon
BABYLON
ARMENIA
CASPIAN SEA
Arbela
MEDIA
Ecbatana
Iranian Plateau
Susa
SUSIANA
ELAM
Persian Gulf
Persepolis
Pasargadae
PERSIA
CARMANIA
PARTHIANS
ARIA
DRANGIANA
ARACHOSIA
GADROSIA
BACTRIANA
SOGDIANA
ARAL SEA
Oxus
Jaxartes
Indus

Macedonian), and he made him his son's tutor. When, just before his Persian expedition, Alexander ordered the city of Thebes to be razed to the ground as a warning against rebellion, he gave instructions that the house of Pindar the poet should be left standing; and just as in after days Napoleon's armies spread the principles of the French Revolution, so those of Alexander spread the culture and civilization of the Greeks.

Philip was King of Macedonia from 359 to 336 B.C. When he came to the throne his country was poor and inconsiderable, composed mainly of peasants, with no seaports and no large cities. Philip changed all that, and the subsequent successes of Alexander were very largely due to the work of his father. It was Philip who created the formidable Macedonian phalanx; it was Philip who conquered the Greeks (Athenians and Thebans) at Chaeronea in 338 B.C. and forced them to agree to a common expedition against the Persians with the King of Macedon as their captain-general. He might, had he led the expedition, have been quite as successful as his son was, but fate had decided otherwise, for in 336 B.C. Philip was assassinated at his daughter's wedding feast.

Two years later (334 B.C.) Alexander started upon his career of world conquest. In the course of eleven years he won the most astonishing successes. On the river Granicus and at Issus he defeated the Persians so thoroughly that their king Darius III suggested that the Euphrates should be the boundary line between his own dominions and those of Alexander. Parmenio, one of Philip's generals and counsellors, advised the acceptance of this offer, pointing out that the presence of a Persian fleet in the Aegean made the further advance of the Macedonians very dangerous. But Alexander, with all the impetuosity and enthusiasm of youth, rejected his advice and decided for advance. However, he first eliminated any possible danger from the Persian fleet by

WAS ALEXANDER 'GREAT'?

conquering the Phoenician ports, including Tyre, thus depriving the Persians of their harbours. Then he conquered Egypt with great ease, and then, after crossing the Euphrates and the Tigris, at a place called Arbela he completely defeated Darius III, who fled precipitately and was killed by some of his own men. Subsequently Alexander occupied Babylon, Susa, and Persepolis; marched through what is now known as Turkestan; crossed the Hindu-Kush mountains, received the submission of the native princes of the Punjab, and would have made his way into the Ganges valley but for the fears and discontents of his followers. He therefore returned through Beluchistan to Babylon and died there in 323 B.C. from a fever brought on by excesses, at the early age of thirty-two, sighing for new worlds to conquer. It had been part of his ambition to add Carthage, Italy, and Spain to his conquests, and had he lived longer he might have attained his desire.

Does Alexander deserve the title 'Great'? That he was a great general there can be no doubt. In other respects too he showed himself far above the ordinary run of men. His ideal—a world-state dominated by Greek ideas—was excellent, and he did much to promote it. He built cities on the lines of his marches, which were to be radiating points of Hellenism, and it was through him that the influence of Greek art penetrated to the Far East—to India, China, and Japan; he was the patron of learning and scientific enterprise—he sent expeditions to solve the problem of the rise and fall of the Nile, and to explore the Caspian Sea; and his campaigns proved advantageous to the development of natural science, for he sent numerous specimens to his old master Aristotle at Athens. But in some respects he was by no means great. He made no great roads through the Persian Empire; he did little or nothing to secure his conquests for his successors; it cannot be said that he wrought any improvements in the method of governing Eastern states; and although the marriages of himself and ninety of his generals and leading men with Persian ladies may be regarded as a step towards the racial fusion of East and West, it was far more probably a step towards Oriental pomp and luxury. There can be little doubt that his successes turned Alexander's head. One indication of it is to be found in his aping of Persian dress and customs, and his injunction that all who entered his presence should bend the knee to him and kiss his feet. A still more remarkable proof is the command that his subjects should regard him as a god and pay him divine honours; he took advantage of his Egyptian expedition to visit the oasis of Siwa in the Sahara Desert where was a shrine of the god Amon-Ra, and when he came out from the holy place the high priest hailed him as the Son of Amon. These pretensions to divinity and his love of Oriental display cost Alexander the fidelity of many of his Macedonian friends. There were conspiracies against him which were cruelly punished when detected. Among those executed for taking part in them were Parmenio and his son Philotas, and Callisthenes, the nephew of Aristotle. The execution of Callisthenes cost Alexander the friendship of Aristotle. More shameful was the death of Clitus, the man who had saved his life at Granicus, whom Alexander killed in a fit of drunken fury for reproving him on account of his Median costume and his monstrous pretensions. The case of Alexander has been paralleled in modern times by that of Napoleon. Both Alexander and Napoleon were great generals; both were inordinately ambitious; both aimed at world dominion; both drank deep of the cup of military glory, and the result in each case was intoxication. Alexander made little or no attempt to render his empire permanent; perhaps he died too soon to think of such things. Napoleon made elaborate attempts but failed.

The death of Alexander was in a sense a great tragedy, for it meant the shattering of the hope of a world empire dominated by Greek ideas. Alexander's empire split up into

The Arab village of Siwa, where Alexander visited the shrine of Amon-Ra
Photograph by Sir Alan Cobham

three divisions under three of his generals. The Asiatic part between the Euphrates and the Mediterranean fell to Seleucus; the European part consisting of Macedonia and Greece to Antigonus; and the African part became a new kingdom of Egypt under Ptolemy. The Seleucids, under pressure from the Parthians on the one side and the Romans on the other, were ultimately reduced to the rulership of Syria. The Ptolemies of Egypt built a formidable fleet, and for a time the eastern Mediterranean was an Egyptian sea. Strife between the three parts into which the empire had split was common, and just as the disunion of the Greek cities rendered them an easy prey to the Macedonians, so the failure of Egyptians, Macedonians, and Syrians to combine against the Romans led to the separate conquest of their countries by that intensely practical people. Egypt was the last to fall—in 30 B.C.

Alexander had striven to spread Greek ideas throughout the world which he conquered, and even if his empire fell to pieces when he died, this part of his policy survived. For centuries after his death the whole of the ancient world was dominated by Greek culture, and even over the all-conquering Romans its influence was not inconsiderable. The great cities of Macedonia, Syria (whose capital was Antioch), and Egypt were almost altogether Greek. The Greek language was spoken in the streets; Greek temples, sculpture, theatres, and gymnasiums were prominent features of them; and some of the greatest of the Greek thinkers, such as Euclid and Archimedes, and the pastoral poet Theocritus lived to prove that Greece still maintained its dominance in matters intellectual. The Greek language had got such a hold over the world that the Jews of Alexandria thought it necessary to translate their sacred scriptures (The Old Testament) into Greek. The translation was supposed to be the work of seventy persons: hence it is called the Septuagint.

The most notable of the subdivisions of Alexander's em-

ALEXANDRIA UNDER THE PTOLEMIES

pire was undoubtedly Egypt under the Ptolemies. For a time that country caught a sort of blaze of glory which recalled its famous past. Alexandria became one of the foremost commercial cities of the world, and at the mouth of its harbour, on an island known as Pharos, was built a colossal lighthouse also known as Pharos, three hundred and seventy feet high. It stood for over sixteen hundred years, the greatest lighthouse in the world; A.D. 1326 is the date of its fall. The design of its tower owed something to Oriental architecture, and it is notable as the model for the first church spires and the minarets of Mohammedan mosques. Alexandria under the Ptolemies is also famed for its possession of the first university of the world. This was the famous Museum (or home of the Muses), which included among its teachers Euclid, Eratosthenes, who calculated the diameter of the world to within fifty miles of what it actually is, and Hero, who devised the first steam-engine. There were also medical and astronomical departments of the Museum, and closely connected with it was the great library, the first great library of the Greek world, containing many thousand rolls. All foreign writers settling in Alexandria were expected to present copies of their works to the library. It differed from a modern library inasmuch as it was a publishing and a bookselling agency as well. Callimachus, who was librarian under Ptolemy III and Ptolemy IV, started the practice of dividing rolls so as to render them more convenient for purposes of reference. Thus the works of Herodotus would be in many rolls or volumes. The teachers at the Museum were paid by the Ptolemies, an unsatisfactory arrangement, which accounts for the decline of learning at Alexandria when rulers who were not inclined to favour scholarship and research ascended the throne of Egypt.

A feature of the world at this time was the spread of toleration. In the Greek cities there was none of that narrow spirit which had been so fatal to Anaxagoras and Socrates :

new ideas did not mean persecution. Even religion was becoming more cosmopolitan. Greeks visited the shrine of Amon in the Sahara Desert; the Egyptian Osiris and the Greek Zeus were merged together in the minds of the people of Alexandria; the Old Testament of the Jews was translated into Greek. Thus with the breaking of the barriers against foreign religions the way was prepared for the subsequent spread of Christianity.

XI

BUDDHA AND CONFUCIUS

GENERALLY speaking, it is probable that the civilization of India was more pacific and happier in character than most early civilizations. It was in this country, in a small state which his family ruled north of Bengal, that Siddhartha Gautama, the founder of Buddhism, was born, somewhere about 560 B.C.

Up to the age of twenty-nine Gautama seems to have lived the ordinary life of a young Indian aristocrat—mainly occupied with hunting, love-making, and a thoughtless drinking of the cup of pleasure. Then his way of life began to worry him, and his worries were increased by four sights which he beheld—an old man bent and enfeebled, a man suffering from some loathsome disease, a dead body unburied and eyeless, pecked at by the birds of the air, and an ascetic seeking some deeper reality in life. A sense of the unsatisfactoriness and instability of human happiness took possession of Gautama's mind, and he rode away from his home accompanied by his charioteer Channa, in the midst of festivities organized to celebrate the birth of his first-born son. After a time he sent Channa back with his horse, sword, and costly ornaments; then he exchanged his clothes with a ragged man whom he met; then followed a period of fasting and abuse of the body

GAUTAMA BUDDHA

in a gorge among the hills of Bengal, until Gautama got into such a feeble state that the effort of walking to and fro in order to stimulate thinking proved too much for him and he fell down from sheer exhaustion. Whereupon he horrified the five disciples who had attached themselves to him by demanding ordinary food and refusing to continue his self mortifications. They left him and went off to Benares. Gautama continued his wanderings alone, until under a great tree, now called the Bo tree (i.e. the tree of Enlightenment), after a day and night of profound meditation, he had his great vision of spiritual regeneration, and came to the conclusion that he was the *Buddha* (i.e. the enlightened one). He then sought out his five former disciples in Benares. At first they turned away, but, catching the light in his face, they afterwards sat down to listen. He told them that he was the Buddha, and expounded to them his system in detail. Finally they yielded one by one and accepted him as the Buddha. Gautama and his disciples immediately founded a sort of academy in the deer park at Benares, where they made huts for themselves and attracted about sixty other disciples. During the rainy season they remained at this settlement discoursing with one another; during the dry weather they went about the country teaching. All their teaching was oral : writing was as yet used only for business purposes in India. Each disciple at once gave up the life of the family and the world, and became an ascetic. He spent most of his time in carrying out the Buddha's system of self-discipline, in order thoroughly to change his own mind, heart, and will. When Gautama died, about 480 B.C., he had many thousands of followers, each of them either a monk or a nun.

Gautama taught that all the miseries of humanity have their origin in desire, and that the selfish cravings of mankind are threefold—the desire to gratify the senses, the desire for personal immortality, and the desire for prosperity. All these must be overcome and, when they are, true serenity or Nirvana is attained. To reach Nirvana, Gautama prescribed an Eightfold Path consisting of Right Views (Truth), Right Aspirations, Right Speech, Right Conduct, Right Livelihood, Right Effort, Right Mindfulness, and Right Rapture.

The religion of Gautama differed from most early religions in that it had no temples and no sacred order of priests, and no theology strictly speaking. It did not deny the divinity of the numerous gods worshipped in India; it merely ignored them and made its appeal purely on lines of conduct. After his death some of Buddha's disciples exalted him into a god, miracles were attributed to him, and a Buddhistic theology came into being. In the third century B.C. Buddhism had got much wealth and power, and substantial monastic buildings took the places of the huts of earlier times. During this time too, Buddhistic art flourished, an art which owes much to the Greeks, which is not surprising, when one takes into consideration the fact that the Seleucids still ruled in the Punjab and that there were numbers of Greek adventurers in India; it also owes something to the Alexandrian cult of Serapis and Isis. Thus the painted or sculptured figure of Hariti (a pestilence goddess whom Buddha converted and made benevolent) and her child is very like that of Isis and her son Horus. Very similar too is the Chinese image of Kuan-yin.

The development of kingship in India meant a struggle between the new leaders and the Brahmanical or priestly caste, and the kings saw in the spreading cult of Buddhism a possible ally against the priests. When Alexander the Great was in the Punjab, a certain low-caste adventurer named Chandragupta had visited his camp with suggestions for the conquest of the Ganges country. But the Macedonians were in no mood for further adventures and he had to flee. He then wandered among the tribes of the north-west, and with their aid after the departure of Alexander overran the

Punjab and conquered the Ganges country. He soon came into conflict with the Brahmans and therefore endowed and encouraged the Buddhists. He was succeeded by his son and then by Asoka (264–227 B.C.). Asoka is one of the great rulers of history, and his dominions extended from Afghanistan to Madras. He is somewhat unique in that he abandoned warfare after victory. He had invaded and conquered Kalinga, a small country on the coast of Madras, but what he then saw of the horrors and cruelties of war disgusted him, and he determined to rely upon the power of religion rather than the power of arms for future conquests. He endowed Buddhism liberally and sent missionaries to spread its teachings in Kashmir, in Ceylon, and in the territories of the Ptolemies and the Seleucids; he founded hospitals, public gardens, and gardens for the growing of medicinal herbs; he created a ministry for the care of subject races, and made provision for the education of women; and by a high standard of Right Aspiration, Right Effort, and Right Livelihood set an example which few kings have, unfortunately, followed, but which gives him a sure claim to be regarded as one of the great benefactors of the human race. 'If', says Koellen, 'a man's fame is to be measured by the number of hearts that honour his memory, by the number of lips which have mentioned and still mention him with reverence, then Asoka is greater than either Caesar or Charlemagne.'

Some people consider that the benefactions of Asoka corrupted Buddhism, because it attracted many to it whose motives were mercenary and unworthy; but it must be borne in mind that Asoka's zeal and generosity were also responsible for the spread of Buddhism. To-day it is the chief religion of Tibet, Ceylon, Burma, and Siam, and also holds a great place in China and Japan. As with most religions, the passage of time has been fatal to its primitive simplicity. Were Gautama Buddha to come to life to-day he would probably fail to recognize the religion which

BUDDHA AND CONFUCIUS

bears his name. He was a man of earnest faith and simple habits, singularly like that most famous of medieval saints, Francis of Assisi. Many of his modern followers, whatever the nature of their faith, are certainly not exponents of simplicity in religious matters. To Tibetans, the Dalai Lama is a sort of god-king; at Lhassa, the capital of the country, there is a huge temple filled with priests and a great idol called 'Gautama Buddha' over the high altar. The members of the expedition which attempted to climb Mount Everest in 1922 found high up in the Himalayas a monastery of Buddhist monks, the Rongbuk Monastery, of whose existence they were previously ignorant. They discovered that the Chief Lama of this monastery was regarded as an especially sacred person, because he was believed to be the incarnation of a god. There was an elaborate ritual attached to the religious services of the monastery, including solemn dances, often called devil-dances, the idea of them being to teach the devout what spirits, good or bad, they would meet in the next world, so that, having learned to recognize them during this life, they would not be afraid when they met them in the hereafter; the idea is very similar to the old Egyptian belief that it was possible to learn charms and spells in this life which would enable the soul after death to exorcize the evil spirits which it would encounter on its journey to the judgement hall of Osiris; it is singularly unlike anything that Gautama taught or believed.

When the Buddhist missionaries first visited China they found other religions or teachings there—Taoism, the philosophical teachings of Lao-tse, and Confucianism. Practically speaking, the two former of these have been incorporated,[1] and have developed along the same lines as Buddhism, so that nowadays their outward practice is very much alike. Tao means a Way and corresponds closely to the Buddhistic idea of a Path.

[1] Lao-tse taught the doctrine of the Tao.

The great Buddhist monastery at Lhassa

BUDDHA AND CONFUCIUS

Confucius, like Buddha and Lao-tse, lived in the sixth century B.C. His life is very similar to those of some of the Greek philosophers of the fifth and fourth centuries B.C. He was a native of the state of Lu at a time when the empire of China was about one-sixth the size of modern China, and when state was fighting against state and all left themselves open to the attacks of the barbarians of the north. Confucius spent his time in editing the classical scriptures of China, and in travelling about from state to state seeking a prince who would make him his counsellor. Two centuries later Plato, actuated by the same spirit, went as adviser to Dionysus of Syracuse, and the same idea is at the root of the attitudes of Aristotle and Isocrates towards Philip of Macedon. At length Confucius had his opportunity when the ruler of Lu made him magistrate in the city of Chung-tu. There Confucius sought to make devoted public men by an elaborate system of regulation. Everything was regulated—rules of conduct, the food which people ate, the keeping apart of males and females in the streets, even the thickness of coffins and the size of graves. Later on the influence of Confucius was undermined and he withdrew into private life, his last days being saddened by the deaths of some of his best disciples. His influence over Chinese national character has been considerable, and, as in the cases of Jesus and Buddha, no small part of this has been due to the blamelessness of his personal character.

The religions of Buddha and Confucius have at least two things in common. They are pacific and they are not theological. In these respects they resemble the teachings of some of the best of the Greek philosophers, Socrates for example, who was quite prepared to conform to the religious customs of the state, and contrast with the Jewish idea of religion, which is that there is but one true God and that all others are false and idolatrous. The original conception of the one God was that he was a jealous god, 'visiting the sins of the fathers upon the children,' but this conception was softened and humanized by the prophets, and the teachings of Jesus, like those of Buddha and Confucius, are essentially pacific.

XII

THE ROMAN REPUBLIC

THE Italian peninsula is four times as large as the Grecian; a ridge of mountains, the Apennines, runs through it; but its plains and valleys are more extensive, rain falls more frequently, and the soil is more fertile. Hence agriculture developed there before and more naturally than trade, for the harbours are on the whole inferior to those of Greece.

The earliest inhabitants of Italy of whom we have any very definite records were lake dwellers, who probably came from Switzerland and settled on the lakes of the north and over the marshes of the Po valley. In time contact with civilization was established and utensils made by the craftsmen of Egypt and Crete found their way into Italy. In the later period of the Egyptian Empire, Sardinians armed with heavy bronze shields and swords took service in Egypt; thus they formed part of the bodyguard of Rameses II, as shown on the wall of the temple of Abu Simbel. At the same time the western coast of Italy opposite Corsica was occupied by sea rovers who are known as Etruscans and who probably came from Asia Minor and were the means of introducing many Oriental customs into Italy, such as the custom of foretelling the future from certain markings on the liver of an animal or bird which had been sacrificed. The Etruscans rapidly developed into the most civilized people north of the Greek colonies of Sicily and Southern Italy. Greek religion and arts flourished among them; they mined copper, and their bronze work was so good that it found a ready market even in Greece. They learned to write with Greek letters and they have left behind them thousands of inscriptions which, unfortunately, cannot yet be read. Their power at one time extended from the Bay of Naples almost to Genoa and inland as far as the Apennines.

The Etruscans were not the only immigrants whom the warmth and fertility of Italy attracted. Probably shortly after the Greeks occupied Greece other Aryan tribes began to pour into the Italian peninsula, where they spoke dialects which were almost wholly unintelligible to any but the members of the particular tribe to which they belonged. South of the Tiber, a tribe known as the Latins occupied a plain known as Latium, about thirty by forty miles in extent. Like their neighbours, they maintained themselves by cultivating grain and keeping flocks; but their land was not very fertile, so that their struggle for existence naturally produced a hardy and practical race. They had little to do with their neighbours, but sometimes found themselves obliged to fight with the Samnites, a powerful group of mountain tribes in the south. Their weapons, first of bronze and then of iron, they purchased from the Etruscans at a market near a ford over the river Tiber. This traffic resulted in a settlement on a hill in the vicinity called the Palatine Hill ; other straggling settlements were made on the hills around, seven in all, and gradually they were all merged into the city of Rome. The traditional date for the founding of Rome is 753 B.C., but this, like the story of the city being founded by two brothers, Romulus and Remus, is purely fanciful. For some time Rome was under Etruscan kings, the last of whom was Tarquinius Superbus, whose attempts to recover his authority, after the Romans had expelled him and established a republic, have been commemorated by Macaulay in his *Lays of Ancient Rome*.

The early Romans owed much to the Greeks. It was from them that they learned how to build ships ; from them

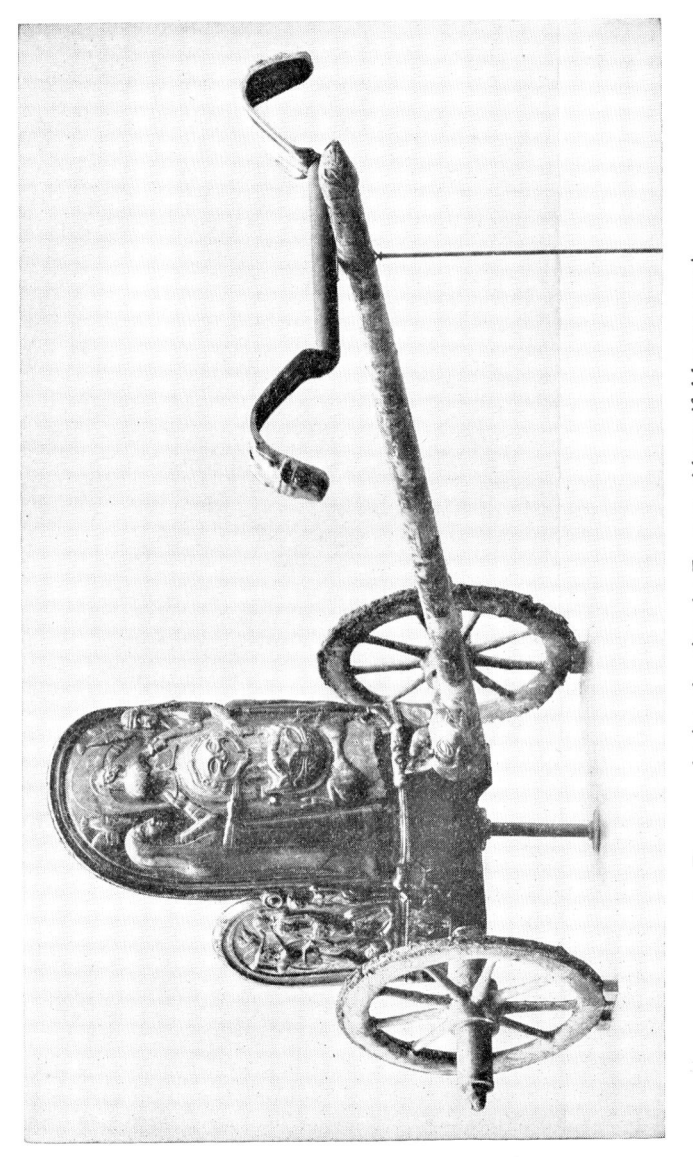

An Etruscan chariot, showing the Etruscans' beautiful bronze-work

they got the alphabet which has come through the Romans to us; Roman coins, weights, and measures have also a Greek

origin. The Greeks were a far more imaginative people than the Romans, so when Greek mythology was woven into that of Rome, the list of heroic adventures in which the Roman gods had played a prominent part was considerably enlarged.

EARLY GOVERNMENT OF ROME

The Romans as a people had little of the culture and vivid imagination of the Greeks. The typical Roman mind was cold and calculating, fitted for great achievements in politics and law rather than in religion, art, literature, or science. There never was anything in the history of Rome to compare with the Age of Pericles; Roman thought has never dominated the world like that of the Greeks. But, on the other hand, there was unity in Italy; an obscure city grew to be the centre and arbiter of a mighty empire; and for practical wisdom and organizing ability it is doubtful if the Romans have ever been surpassed or even equalled.

After the expulsion of the kings Rome was ruled by nobles known as 'patricians', and for some time the city developed on much the same lines as the Greek cities. In 450 B.C. the laws were codified and written down on twelve tables of bronze; forty-four years before, the struggle of the people or 'plebs' to secure rights against the patricians had started with the first secession to the Sacred Mount outside Rome—a very early 'strike'. Ultimately, after two more secessions, the plebeians secured most of their demands. Marriage between patricians and plebeians was legalized, and the chief offices of the state and membership of the Senate were thrown open to plebeians.

The Senate was really the chief authority in the Roman republic, although theoretically it was purely an advisory body. Most of the magistrates, the two consuls in whom full military authority was reposed after the expulsion of the kings, the praetor, who was the chief judicial officer, and the tribunes of the plebs, held office for one year only; while the censor, the controller of the finances, was in office for eighteen months. The Senate, originally, as its name implies, an assembly of old men, was a permanent body; the senators were members for life and were mainly composed of ex-magistrates of the age of twenty-eight or over. Thus it would contain people of experience and authority, and it gradually assumed control of the public expenditure, foreign affairs, the levying and disposition of troops, and the government of the provinces. These powers, if abused, might become a grave menace to the stability of the state ; indeed, the decay of the Senate meant the decay of the Roman republic. But, if properly used, the existence of such a body as the Senate was a great source of strength to the republic. It made impossible in Rome such a state of affairs as existed in Athens after the death of Pericles, when the city languished and declined for lack of a real leader ; and during the great crises of Roman history, such as the period of the Second Punic War, it is natural to find that the Senate was the body round which the resistance and unconquerable spirit of the Romans were concentrated.

Rome was thus an aristocratic republic. But the people were not without protection from possible injustice on the part of the nobles. One of the earliest results of the demand for rights by the plebs was the appointment of two officers called tribunes, whose work it was to look after their interests (494 B.C.). These were elected annually and their chief powers and rights were : to protect citizens from the actions of magistrates ; to veto the intended acts of all other magistrates, including one another ; to preside over the assembly of the plebs ; and to coerce and punish plebeians, subject to appeal. An example of the power of the tribune is the Licinian Law of 367 B.C. (named after the tribune Licinius Stolo) which relieved the peasantry from the financial oppression of the landowners and limited the amount of land which a rich man might hold. A further concession to the people was the Lex Hortensia of 287 B.C., which made the laws (*plebiscita*) made by the plebeian assembly (the Comitia Tributa) binding on the whole community ; previously they had been binding on the plebs alone. The Comitia Tributa elected the tribunes and the minor officers of state and acted as a judicial body to try offences against the 'majesty of the people'. All crimes

THE RISE OF ROME

committed against the state were brought before the Comitia Centuriata, to which people were summoned by classes based on property qualification. Here wealth had the preponderance of votes. All cases involving the life of a Roman citizen were brought before this court. It elected the consuls and heard appeals against the judgements of consuls.

In times of great stress it was possible to appoint a special officer known as a dictator, who superseded all existing authorities and from whose actions there was no appeal to the people; he could take what measures he chose to protect the state. He was nominated by the consul and was appointed for six months only, and for some definite object; as soon as this was achieved he resigned. He could not leave Italy during his term of office, and he had no control over the Treasury. The first great dictator in Roman history was Quintus Fabius Maximus, whose policy of delay was instrumental in bringing about the defeat of Hannibal.

While the struggle for rights on the part of the plebeians was still going on, the Roman state had started its career of expansion. The Latins naturally looked to Rome as their leader in campaigns against hostile tribes like the Samnites and the Volsci, and Rome proved a most efficient leader. Between 489 and 266 B.C. the city triumphed over all rivals: Aequians, Volscians, Etruscans, Samnites, and Greeks, and when the Greek cities of Southern Italy submitted, the conquest of the peninsula had been completed. The Latins asked for the privileges of Roman citizenship in return for the military service which they had rendered; at first Rome was not disposed to grant their request, but wiser counsels ultimately prevailed, another instance of the political sagacity of the Romans. While the Greek cities always guarded their citizenship zealously and would not grant it to any born outside their borders, the Roman Senate eventually realized that such a policy of exclusiveness meant weakness, and when new territories were conquered, although colonies of citizens were first planted therein, full citizenship for the defeated populations not infrequently followed. In Italy the arrangement of granting civic rights to conquered territories worked well. It placated the conquered; furnished Rome with more citizen soldiers; and in no way threatened her ascendancy, for, generally speaking, citizens in distant parts did not consider it worth their while to leave their occupations in order that they might go to Rome to vote.

While the steady expansion of Rome was going on, a tremendous migration of Gauls almost ended the independent career of the rising city. The Gauls were Aryans whose lands stretched from the English Channel to the valley of the Po. Some of them entered the Balkan peninsula and even penetrated to Asia Minor. The famous figure of the Dying Gaul, once set up in Pergamum in Asia Minor, represents one of the Gauls who invaded Asia Minor. In 390 B.C. they defeated the Romans in a great battle and captured and burnt the whole of the city of Rome with the exception of the Capitol. That was almost captured, being only saved, according to legend, by the cackling of some sacred geese which warned Marcus Manlius, the commander, of an attempt to scale the walls, when it had almost succeeded. Ultimately, either because the malarious atmosphere of the city did not suit them, or because the Romans bribed them, the Gauls departed after having held Rome for two months. A hundred years later the Romans defeated an alliance of Gauls and Samnites in a great battle at Sentinum in Umbria. The Gauls were always regarded as a very great menace by the Romans : their alliance with Hannibal added to the terror which the astonishing achievements of the great Carthaginian caused ; and the success of Julius Caesar's campaigns against them produced a tremendous impression in Rome.

The conquest of Italy by the Romans brought them up against the great commercial republic of Carthage, which, with the decline of Greek influence, was practically supreme

A Samnite warrior. A bronze statuette of the 5th century B.C.

Two Roman soldiers carrying a dead comrade. A bronze of the 4th century B.C.

ROME AND THE SAMNITES

in the neighbouring island of Sicily. There were three wars between Rome and Carthage: they are frequently called Punic Wars. The first lasted from 264 to 241 B.C. and resulted in Sicily becoming a Roman province; it is also notable because it affords a striking illustration of the practical genius of the Romans. The Carthaginian fleet was much superior to the Roman, and, at the beginning, this was an enormous handicap to Rome, but they overcame it so successfully that before hostilities ended the supremacy of the seas had been wrested from the Carthaginians. Three years after the conclusion of this war Rome seized Corsica and Sardinia, which became one province seven years later (231 B.C.).

The loss of Sicily caused the Carthaginians, or rather the great family of Barca to which Hannibal belonged, and their adherents to concentrate all their energies upon the founding of a new empire in Spain. Here again they came into conflict with the Romans, and the Ebro was fixed as the boundary line between the two peoples. South of the Ebro, however, was a town, Saguntum, which was Roman. A Carthaginian attack upon this in 218 B.C. was the signal for the outbreak of the Second Punic War, which is sometimes appropriately called the Hannibalic War, for it was Hannibal's hatred for the Romans which caused it, the genius of Hannibal which inspired it, and the withdrawal of Hannibal from Italy which ended it. The war lasted until 202 B.C. At first it was little but a series of Roman disasters. Hannibal, who is one of the greatest military geniuses of all time, made a famous march across the Alps into Italy and defeated the Romans at the river Trebia, at Lake Trasimene, and at Cannae. Then the real greatness of the Roman character, and particularly of the Roman Senate, was manifested. Quintus Fabius Maximus was appointed dictator, and his policy of delay, which earned him the nickname of 'Cunctator' (the Delayer), ultimately proved too much for Hannibal. The methods of Fabius sug-

HANNIBAL AND SCIPIO

gest comparison with those of the Scythians against Darius the Great, and those of the Russians against Napoleon in more recent times. He knew that the Romans were no match for the Carthaginians in the open field, therefore he avoided pitched battles and pursued wearing tactics which proved eminently successful in the end. Three other circumstances contributed to Hannibal's defeat: the fact that no Italian city of any note with the exception of Capua opened its gates to him, and the fate of Capua was not such as to encourage others to do likewise; the rise among the Romans of a military commander of genius, Publius Cornelius Scipio, who thoroughly defeated the Carthaginian forces in Spain; and the very meagre assistance which Hannibal got from Carthage. The family of Barca had many foes in Carthage, and there were some who disapproved entirely of Hannibal and thought that the interests of the state could be more adequately secured by pacific means. Hannibal was in Italy for fifteen years; he was then forced to leave because the Romans had so far recovered from their earlier reverses as to be able to cross over into Africa and attack Carthage itself. This enterprising policy was opposed by Fabius, but the time had come when cautious tactics could be abandoned with advantage, and in 202 B.C. at Zama, near Carthage, Hannibal was defeated by the Roman army commanded by Publius Cornelius Scipio (Africanus) and assisted by Numidian cavalry under Masinissa. The peace which followed stipulated that the Carthaginian fleet should be reduced to ten vessels; Spain was to become a Roman province; the Carthaginians were to pay an indemnity of ten thousand talents (£2,400,000); and Hannibal was to be handed over to the Romans. There was singularly little generosity to conquered foes in the Roman character, and the war had narrowed sympathies and stiffened prejudices. Scipio Africanus, the conqueror, is reputed to have pleaded for magnanimity towards Hannibal, but his plea fell for the most part on deaf ears. Scipio's generosity and nobility of character were exceptional. Hannibal was not handed over because he contrived to escape, but he did not succeed in eluding the virulence of the Senate, and when he finally took refuge with Prusias, king of a small state in Asia Minor called Bithynia, and the Romans demanded that he should be surrendered to them, he took poison rather than suffer that crowning indignity (183 B.C.). Perhaps it should be mentioned on behalf of the Romans that Hannibal was still plotting schemes of revenge against them, but generous treatment after Zama might have averted this.

The Third and last Punic War owed its origin almost entirely to the blind rage of one man, Marcus Porcius Cato, working upon the worst passions of the Romans. The city of Carthage, despite the disastrous consequences of the Punic War, had recovered much of its former prosperity. Cato visited Carthage as a Roman commissioner to help to settle a frontier dispute between Carthage and Numidia. The flourishing condition of the city filled him with fear lest it should produce another Hannibal. He returned to Italy, and henceforth the burden of all his speeches was 'Delenda est Carthago' (Carthage must be destroyed). At length his constant iterations carried conviction. By the peace which ended the Second Punic War, Carthage was not to make war without the consent of Rome. The Senate now encouraged the Numidians to encroach upon Carthaginian territory, and to make themselves such nuisances that the Carthaginians, goaded to desperation, retaliated by force of arms. Thus a condition of the treaty had been violated: Rome demanded hostages and the surrender of arms, and the Carthaginians complied. Then they were told that they must move their city ten miles inland. This was a virtual sentence of death: it left the Carthaginians with no alternative but resistance. A very fierce and harrowing siege followed, and in 146 B.C., the third year of the siege, after six

FALL OF CARTHAGE 171

days' furious street fighting, Carthage fell. Of the half million original inhabitants only fifty thousand were left, and these were sold into slavery. The city was razed to the ground, the land upon which it had stood ploughed as a symbol of final destruction, and a solemn curse invoked upon any who should attempt to rebuild it. Such was the effect of successful war upon the Roman mind. There can be no valid excuse for the destruction of Carthage, for the trade of the city when Rome decided to end its existence was in no sense a serious rival of Roman trade.

The third century B.C., which saw Rome establishing her military and naval supremacy in the Mediterranean, also witnessed the beginning of the conquest of Rome by Greek civilization. This seems to have been started by Greek slaves from the cities of Sicily and Southern Italy. One of these, Andronicus, who shortly after the First Punic War was given his freedom by his master, translated Homer's *Odyssey* into Latin for the use of Roman children, and Greek tragedies and comedies for the use of Romans of more mature years. The Romans, like all other peoples, had their primitive folk-songs and verse-forms, but these now disappeared before the influence of a higher and more finished literature. Latin literature did not, like the Greek, develop along its own lines from native beginnings. For books, music, works of art, and everything that contributes to refinement the Romans were at first entirely dependent upon the Greeks.

At the very time when Greek ideas were beginning to influence Roman thought so powerfully, Roman political and military power was making itself felt in the Greek world. The alliance which Philip, King of Macedon, had made with Hannibal, was made an excuse for a war against him, in which the Romans were assisted by Athenians and Spartans. The complete defeat of Philip at Cynoscephalae in 197 B.C. was followed by a war against Antiochus of Syria which resulted in a great victory for the Romans, led by Lucius Scipio and his brother Africanus, at Magnesia in the north-west of Lydia (190 B.C.). At first the Romans did not desire a conquest of the East. What they desired was such a control of that region as would prevent the rise of a power dangerous to Rome. Thus, after the Second Macedonian War, the Roman Senate proclaimed the Greek cities free, and Macedonia, although humiliated, was not deprived of its independence. But Roman control ultimately developed into Roman sovereignty. In 148 B.C. Macedonia became a Roman province and in 146 B.C. the destruction of Corinth by Mummius gave the Greeks an illustration of what rebellion against Rome meant. At the same time the Romans were fighting against the tribes of Spain, a war which lasted for twenty years and which was marked by considerable cruelty and treachery on the part of the Roman generals. It was ended in 133 B.C. by the capture of the great fortress of Numantia (near the source of the Douro), which Scipio Aemilianus, the destroyer of Carthage, took after a siege of fifteen months.

The supremacy of Rome in the world was now indisputable, but it had been won at a ruinous cost for the majority of the Roman people. The long wars and the resulting conquests caused money to flow into the Roman treasury, and Roman officials were able to enrich themselves at the expense of the conquered provinces. The city of Rome reflected the new prosperity in the many public buildings that sprang up; the gardens and villas of the rich, filled with sculpture from the cities of Asia and Greece; the reading of Greek books and the sending of Roman youths to Athens to receive a Greek education; and the many fine roads spreading in all directions from the city. But the condition of the Roman farmers was lamentable in the extreme. Military service in Africa and Spain had torn them away from their small holdings, and when they returned it was to find that the holdings of their neighbours had been gradually absorbed by the large estates of wealthy landowners, worked by slaves.

Agriculture in Italy. Ploughing with oxen in an orchard of olive trees

The returned soldiers could not hope to compete with these and it was only a matter of time before their estates were also absorbed and they themselves obliged to drift into the capital, where living was cheap, where candidates for office were ready to buy votes, and where were the distractions of the theatre and the circus. Another circumstance that helped to reduce so many of the Roman people to a swarm of state-fed paupers—for the state also gave doles—was the fact that with the expansion of the Roman Empire great corn ships sailed up the Tiber from Sicily, Sardinia, and the Nile country. The result was that the produce of the small farmers was undersold in the Roman market, and they themselves were forced to sell their lands, and flock into the capital. The slaves who worked the large estates which thus came into being were a motley crew consisting of some who had been captured in war and others who had been bought from the pirates who at this time infested the Mediterranean Sea. Sometimes there were slave rebellions, and very fierce struggles followed, marked by great cruelty on both sides.

Two young nobles, the brothers Tiberius and Caius Gracchus, realizing how the real strength of Rome was being sapped and undermined, endeavoured to improve the situation by limiting the amount of land which any one could hold (in accordance with the Lex Licinia of 367 B.C.) and redistributing what was left over among the poorer citizens, as property which could not be alienated and for which they paid a nominal rent to the state. When Tiberius became tribune in 133 B.C. he tried to rouse the Romans to a sense of their position: 'The beasts which roam over Italy', he declared, 'have each his den, his resting-place; they who fought for Italy have only light and air as their share in it ... Called masters of the world, you have not really a clod to call your own.' But the work of Tiberius and his brother Caius ended in failure: senatorial authority was too strong; the Roman mob was little better than *canaille* utterly demoralized and unprincipled; it was easy to work upon their ignorant prejudices; and at the end of his year of office in 133 B.C. Tiberius Gracchus was murdered by them, while eleven years later his brother Caius experienced the same fate. Two reasons for the unpopularity of Caius are illuminating illustrations of the mind of the Roman mob. Caius proposed to make all freemen of the Latin name full citizens and to give all other Italian freemen the right of voting in the Comitia. His unselfish soul never dreamed that those who shouted for their own freedom would deny liberty to others. The other reason was his plan to establish a colony on the site of Carthage and give the colonists the full privileges of Roman citizenship. It was easy for Gracchus' enemies to work upon the prejudices and superstitions of the ignorant, and depict the terrible consequences of building again upon a site which had been so solemnly cursed. One of Caius Gracchus' reforms, a corn law, although conceived in the best spirit, was short-sighted. In his desire that the poorer classes should reap the benefits of empire he set up great corn depots in Rome, where they could purchase corn at an exceptionally low price. He also proposed to pay the citizens for their share in government, a scheme that worked well under Pericles. But Rome was not Athens. The only result of paying the citizens of Rome was to turn them into the most shameless species of paupers, ready to support Gracchus when he gave them what they wanted, but quite as ready to go against him when a fellow tribune named Drusus, put up to it by the Senate, outbid him in the Comitia with wild promises which he never intended to fulfil.

The century which followed the death of Caius Gracchus was one in which the Romans had ample opportunities of witnessing the evil effects of militarism. From 112 to 106 B.C. a war was fought against a certain Jugurtha, who had served in the Roman legions in Spain and then crossed over to Africa and made himself ruler of Numidia. By a lavish use of bribes he overcame the Roman generals who were sent against him, until Metellus succeeded where others had failed, only to be superseded after his successes by Caius Marius, who brought Jugurtha in chains to Rome, where he is said to have died of starvation. Marius was of lowly origin but a most ambitious man. He was consul seven times and is notable as the first great leader of professional soldiers in Italy. His most famous victories were against the Teutones at Aquae Sextiae (Aix in Provence) in 102 B.C. and against the Cimbri, a Gallic tribe, on the Raudine Plain in the following year. Four years before this the Cimbri had slaughtered 80,000 Romans at Arausio on the Rhone. From 91 to 88 B.C. occurred what is known as the Social War, when the Italians fought for the privilege of Roman citizenship. During this war Roman generals marched ruthlessly up and down Italy burning farms, sacking towns, and carrying off men, women, and children to sell them in the open market or work them in gangs on their estates. Marius and a general of noble birth named Sulla, who had been with him in Africa and was his bitter rival, both commanded on the side of Rome. But neither brought the war to a conclusion: it was ended by the Romans conceding practically all the demands of the Italians. This was followed by civil war in Rome. The republic had had trouble with Mithridates, King of Pontus, a land bordering on the southern coasts of the Black Sea. The Senate appointed Sulla to the command of the Roman legions; the people transferred it to Marius. Civil war followed and the victory of Sulla, but when he had left Italy to proceed against Mithridates, Marius and his followers returned to Rome, many of Sulla's supporters were executed, and their estates confiscated. Sulla returned to Italy and pursued exactly the same policy towards the supporters of Marius. Over five thousand are said to have been executed. Then, in 79 B.C., after having defeated Mithridates and been dictator for two years, Sulla retired into private

POMPEY THE FORTUNATE

life to enjoy the great riches which he had amassed. A year later he died, the victim, it is said, of abominable vices ; but this may be nothing more than the fabrication of his enemies. Four years after the death of Sulla there was a third war against Mithridates, in which the Roman commander Lucullus won most of the victories and another Roman commander, Pompey, who superseded him, got practically all the credit. During two years of the time when this war was being fought the Romans had also to deal with a revolt of slaves and gladiators, who, under a leader named Spartacus, entrenched themselves in the apparently extinct crater of Vesuvius and defeated many of the armies sent against them. This rising seems to have inspired considerable terror, and when it was at last ended it was followed by a disgusting display of cruelty, six thousand of Spartacus' captured followers being crucified, forming miles of victims along the Appian Way.[1]

The actual credit for the military suppression of the slave revolt belongs to Marcus Crassus, but Pompey arriving on the scene when all was nearly over gained part of the honour by defeating some of the stragglers from the slave army. Pompey does not appear to have been a man of outstanding ability; most of his successes seem to have been due to a remarkable run of good fortune, and perhaps the best instance of this is his termination of the Spanish War. For nine years (83 to 72 B.C.) the Spaniards were in rebellion against Rome, and under a former Roman commander named Sertorius they won success after success against the legions. Pompey fared no better than other commanders until the murder of Sertorius gave him his opportunity ; it needed little ability to end the war then, and the subsequent triumphal procession through the streets of Rome was the crown of Pompey's good fortune rather than an indication of outstanding genius. His successes in the East were easy of

[1] The great southern road from Rome through Capua and Beneventum to Brundisium (modern Brindisi).

achievement after the work of Lucullus.[1] His other great military success against the pirates of the Mediterranean in 67 B.C. was nothing noteworthy considering the resources at his disposal.

After his successful campaigns in the East, Pompey returned to Italy in 62 B.C. and immediately disbanded his army, a somewhat unwise step from the personal point of view, as he soon saw, for the Senate fearing him no longer refused to ratify his settlement of the East. This threw Pompey into the arms of the popular party, and he, Crassus, and an ambitious young patrician named Julius Caesar formed a triumvirate to further their designs (60 B.C.). They received considerable popular support, and so successful were they that in 59 B.C. Caesar was elected consul, Pompey secured the ratification of his Eastern settlement, and Crassus got the command of an army, with disastrous consequences for himself, for plunging recklessly into the deserts of Asia against the Parthians, he paid for his rashness with complete defeat and death.

After his consulship Caesar proceeded as governor to Gaul, the country which corresponds to modern France. His complete conquest of that territory during the next eight years stamps him as one of the great generals of antiquity. He also proved himself a writer of distinction, and he wrote the record of his wars in books which are of great historical value,[2] and which are models of brevity and simplicity. His Gallic campaigns are also notable inasmuch as they were responsible for the introduction into France of the Latin language, the ancestor of modern French. Caesar also found time to cross over into Britain and give his countrymen their first real idea of that country.

The end of Caesar's governorship marks a crisis in the history of Rome. Unlike Pompey, Caesar knew that his

[1] Pompey's subsequent administration of the East was wise, tolerant, and enlightened.   [2] The *De Bello Gallico* (see also p. 200).

A Roman warship, manned by legionary soldiers. A marble bas-relief

strength lay in the possession of a strong and well-organized army, and he knew that the Senate was ill disposed towards him. He therefore refused to disband his troops, and, crossing the river Rubicon into Italy, prepared for battle with the senatorial forces who were commanded by Pompey. The two armies met at Pharsalus, in Thessaly, in 48 B.C., and Pompey's troops proved no match for the seasoned veterans of the Gallic wars, commanded by the greatest general of the age. Pompey fled to Egypt and was murdered shortly after landing there. Caesar too landed in Egypt, where he was for a time captivated by the charms of the Egyptian queen Cleopatra, the last of the Ptolemies.

The battle of Pharsalus was the death-knell of the Roman republic, although Caesar made no attempt to abolish its outward forms. He got himself appointed dictator for life and consul for ten years; he filled the Senate with his own supporters and nominees, so that it was always prepared to do his bidding; divine honours were paid to him; and to all intents and purposes Rome was ruled by one man. The Republic was dead: military dictatorship had taken its place. There were some who would not submit to this, and in 44 B.C. Caesar was assassinated by a group of conspirators, of whom the chief was Marcus Brutus, whom he had befriended. But if those who killed Caesar hoped that by so doing they would restore the Republic, their hopes were sadly disappointed. World dominion and militarism had killed republicanism, and all Caesar's death did was to frustrate great schemes which he had planned (such as the conquest of Germany), and plunge Italy and the Roman Empire into civil war with all its attendant horrors. A year after the death of Caesar the great orator and writer Cicero, a man of strong republican ideas, was executed by some soldiers at the bidding of Mark Antony, who thus gratified private spite. After Caesar's assassination, Antony, Lepidus, and Octavius Caesar, the nephew and adopted son of Julius, divided the rule

JULIUS CAESAR

of the Roman world between them. To Lepidus, the least noteworthy of the three, fell the province of Africa ; Antony took the East; while Octavius consolidated the West. It was obvious that a contest for supremacy between Antony and Octavius was a mere matter of time, and Antony played into his rival's hands by sacrificing everything to his infatuation for Cleopatra, Queen of Egypt. In 31 B.C. the fleet of Octavius defeated that of Antony and Cleopatra at Actium, the sudden flight of the Egyptian ships being the deciding factor. In the following year Antony committed suicide ; so too did Cleopatra after her wiles and charms had failed to produce any effect upon Octavius, whose legions had proceeded to Egypt after the victory of Actium. Three years later, after having made himself master of the Roman world, Octavius voluntarily resigned his authority to the Senate, who, however, gave him the command of the army, the control of the leading provinces, and the title of 'princeps', meaning the first of the citizens. His appointment was not permanent but for a term of years, after which he was reappointed. Octavius always regarded himself as an official of the Roman Republic, but there was no danger of his authority lapsing during his lifetime. More than once the Senate increased his powers purely on their own initiative, for they could not dispense with his services. They gave him the title of 'Augustus' (the august one) and 'imperator', from which our word emperor is derived; so it was that Octavius Caesar became the Emperor Augustus.

Rome by this time was a very different place from the original small stronghold of citizen soldiers who cultivated their farms when they were not fighting. It was now a large city of about six hundred thousand inhabitants. Of these the nobles, merchants, and rich professional classes formed a very small part; more than three hundred thousand were poor freemen who received periodic doles of corn from the state ; the rest were slaves or freedmen who came from all parts of

LIFE IN ROME AND THE PROVINCES 183

the Empire. There were Syrians from Asia Minor, Moors from Africa, Iberians from Spain, Greeks from Greece and Macedonia, and an ever-increasing number of Gauls and Germans. There were no policemen to keep this motley population in order, and life was more insecure in Rome than in other parts of the Empire. No attempts had been made to improve the general condition of the city, the streets were ill kept and badly paved, and there were insufficient bridges over the Tiber. The rich people lived in separate houses in the upper part of the city ; the poorer classes herded in flats or tenements in the lower part. Here there must always have been overcrowding, starvation, plague, and crime. Investment in slum property appears to have been very profitable, as it often is to-day. Among the investors was the orator Cicero. How rents were collected is unknown, for the poorer people seem always to have been in the hands of moneylenders. But living in Rome was cheap. Wheat, fruit, and vegetables were the ordinary fare; wine only cost a penny a gallon, and the Romans drank it mixed with water.

One of the most noticeable features of the time was the increased wealth of the richer classes. This wealth came from the conquered provinces. Most of the Roman governors looked upon provinces as legitimate prey. The unfortunate inhabitants were shamelessly taxed, bribes were accepted without scruple, and a provincial's hope of justice generally depended upon his ability to pay for it. From 73 B.C. to 71 a man named Verres was governor of Sicily, and his exactions during these three years are said to have desolated the island more than the war between Rome and Carthage for its possession. As chief judge he sold all his decisions, and he plundered the farmers of their crops, keeping the proceeds for himself. He was fond of art, and as he journeyed through the island he stole pictures, statues, vases, and any other objects of value which appealed to him from both private houses and temples. He crucified on the beach a trader who resisted his demands, so as to discourage similar conduct in others. Asked if he did not fear judgement when he returned to Rome, he replied that he intended to use two-thirds of his wealth to bribe the lawyers and judges, and that the third which remained would be quite sufficient to make him rich for life. His subsequent trial gave Cicero the chance of enhancing his reputation, and the result of his brilliant case for the prosecution was that Verres was heavily fined. He fled to Massilia (Marseilles), taking much of his plunder with him, but in 43 B.C. he was put to death by the orders of Mark Antony, who coveted the stolen art treasures which Verres still possessed. The richer classes were not the only ones who benefited from the plunder of the provinces: the free doles of corn to the people came from the same source, and joint-stock companies were formed to collect taxes in the provinces. It was to their interest to fleece the provincials as much as possible, and profits were made with as little regard for the feelings and comforts of the natives as Leopold of Belgium and his advisers had for those of the natives of the Congo Free State in very recent times. If one imagines British landowners living in idleness on money wrung from the natives of India, one has a fair idea of what the provinces meant to Rome.

The Romans had few if any of the refined tastes of the Greeks. The Athenians loved to watch plays being acted in their theatres or to witness the great athletic contests at Olympia. Rome did not possess a permanent theatre until Pompey built one in 55 B.C., and there is on record the complaint of a Roman playwright that while one of his plays was being performed the whole audience deserted it for a bear fight. The chariot races which took place in the great circuses were far more popular than the theatre, and still more popular were the wild beast shows and the gladiatorial contests. In one of Pompey's entertainments the beast show lasted five days. All parts of the Empire supplied animals.

Roman amphitheatre at Verona, showing the passages and gangways by which the spectators entered and left the theatre, and the main entrance for the competitors

A chariot race.   A Roman mosaic in Britain

Bears and wolves came from Europe, tigers and panthers from Asia, lions and crocodiles from Africa. When a rich man was organizing a wild beast show he would ask any friend of his who happened to be the governor of a province to get him wild animals. When Cicero was in Cilicia, an acquaintance asked him to send him as many panthers as he could procure. In the arena the animals were matched against one another; often a large number would be turned loose at once, and then would follow a most nauseating scene, but one that appealed strongly to the Roman populace. The gladiatorial shows were even more popular. They began in 264 B.C., and until the great amphitheatre called the Colosseum was completed by the Emperor Titus, took place in one of the forums. In early times the gladiators were slaves or condemned criminals. Later on, schools for gladiators were established, to which ruined freemen sold themselves. In the arena they fought in every possible way: singly, in pairs, and in companies. When a gladiator was wounded he appealed to the spectators for mercy by stretching out his forefinger, and they indicated with their thumbs whether he was to be spared or otherwise. Those who wished his death turned their thumbs towards their breasts as a signal to his opponent to stab him; those who wished him to be spared turned their thumbs downwards to show the victor that they desired him to drop his sword. At the end of each bout, if there were any dead bodies, they were dragged out with hooks. The number and lavishness of these shows increased when Rome was ruled by emperors. Generals and officials gave them to please the people; magistrates arranged them in connexion with public festivals; and wealthy citizens provided them for their friends after banquets. Nothing reveals the difference between Roman civilization and ours better than the existence of these shows.

The religion of the early Romans was a kind of animism, a worship of spirits rather than of gods who could and did

Roman religion. A sacrifice in a temple at Rome

take human shapes. These spirits were localized : each had its sphere—a hill top, a wood, or a spring—and even they help to reveal the practical genius of their worshippers, for although the Romans could occasionally allow themselves such a wide conception as that of Jupiter, the spirit of the sky, their deities were for the most part such as would be useful to them in their daily occupations, their fields, and their homes. Hence the establishment of great agricultural festivals like the Saturnalia, and the belief in household gods and goddesses, such as Janus, spirit of the door ; Vesta, spirit of the hearth ; the Penates, spirits of the store-room ; and the Lares, probably field spirits, who became the guardian spirits of the household slaves.

When Rome developed from an agricultural community into a city-state, new functions were assigned to these old rustic spirits. Jupiter, the spirit of the sky and therefore of all oaths sworn under the sky, became the god of justice ; Mars, originally an agricultural deity, became the god of war. When the city-state came into conflict with other peoples, the gods of the conquered were gradually assimilated into the Roman system of theology, a striking instance of that talent for toleration and adaptability which was one of the chief reasons why Rome was able to hold together such a motley and heterogeneous collection of peoples as the Roman Empire ultimately comprised. Thus the goddess Minerva was probably introduced from Etruria, and one consequence of contact with Greece was that the Roman deities were identified one by one with those of Greece. Jupiter was Zeus; Juno, his wife, was Hera ; Mars was Ares ; Minerva was Athena. The conquest of Egypt brought the cult of Isis (with its fastings and festivals and the resurrection drama of Osiris) to Rome, and the soldiers of Sulla's eastern army brought home with them the worship of the Persian Mithras, who eventually became the god of the soldiers. His worship was carried by them into the remotest parts of the Empire ;

ROMAN RELIGION

there are traces of a shrine to him on the Roman Wall in the North of England. When Christianity became the official creed of the Roman Empire, it assimilated, as far as was possible without suspicion of compromise, many of the old pagan beliefs. Thus the practice of holidays at Christmas time, the giving of presents, and the general feeling of good will and geniality, grew out of no Christian custom but out of the great pagan winter festival of the Saturnalia.

One feature of Roman religion which distinguishes it from the Greek is that the Romans linked Church and State together. Religious considerations governed the activities of the state. Magistrates would not hold their assemblies nor would generals take the field without first obtaining the sanction of the auguries ; there were certain days when the Senate could not meet, when the law courts were closed, and no public business could be transacted ; and a victorious general ended his triumphal career by climbing the winding road to the Capitol in order to consecrate his spoils in the Temple of Jupiter. The care of religious matters was entrusted to a college of priests or pontiffs, one of whose duties was to keep in repair the bridges over which religious processions passed. The head of the college was called 'Pontifex Maximus', a title afterwards held by the emperors and still later by the Christian bishops of Rome.

XIII

THE ROMAN EMPIRE

THE Roman Empire lasted for five centuries. For two centuries, from the time when Augustus (Octavius Caesar) was made princeps (27 B.C.) to the death of the Emperor Marcus Aurelius, it enjoyed comparative unity and internal peace. From A.D. 180, when Marcus Aurelius died, to A.D. 476, when it was finally overthrown, its history is one of decline, of dissension within, and of frequently changing rulers, most of them characterized by the possession of neither moral nor intellectual qualities.

The first emperor fixed the northern boundaries of his dominions along the Rhine and Danube, and the eastern on the river Euphrates. He attempted to conquer northern Germany but was badly beaten, so that he advised his successor to make no further effort to extend the Roman boundaries. Augustus was an efficient organizer and he did something to check the abuses of government in the provinces by giving the provincials the right to appeal to the emperor. He was a great builder, and it was his boast that he had found Rome a city of brick and left it a city of marble. His successor, Tiberius, further extended the power of the emperor by taking away from the people the right to elect the consuls and praetors and giving it to the Senate, the members of which were appointed by himself. The most notable event of his reign was the crucifixion of Christ in Palestine, which was part of the Roman Empire. The next emperor, Caligula, was insane, and after ruling four years was murdered in his palace by his servants. Claudius, his successor, like all subsequent emperors, owed his elevation to the support of the army. During his reign the southern part of Britain was added to the Empire. He was murdered by his wife, Agrippina, the mother of Nero, who now became emperor. Nero ruled from A.D. 54 to 68. His name has become a sort of synonym for cruelty and disgusting vices. He certainly murdered his mother and his wife, and persecuted the Christians, and it may be that the great fire which destroyed half of Rome in the year 64 was instigated by him. But his unpopularity and subsequent death—he committed suicide in order to escape the army of Galba, which was marching on Rome to depose him—were not due to any of these things, but rather to the defeat of the Roman forces in Britain by Boadicea and to a great earthquake in Southern Italy which the superstitious

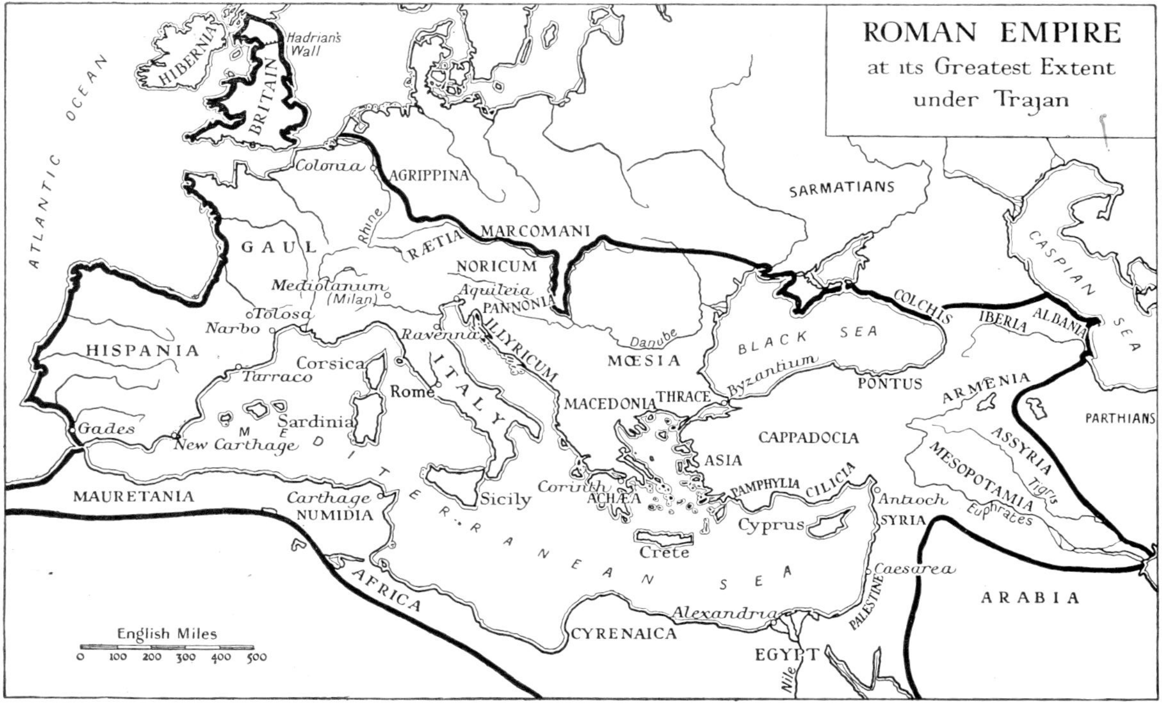
ROMAN EMPIRE
at its Greatest Extent
under Trajan
ATLANTIC OCEAN
HIBERNIA
BRITAIN
Hadrian's Wall
Colonia
AGRIPPINA
SARMATIANS
CASPIAN SEA
GAUL
Rhine
RÆTIA
MARCOMANI
NORICUM
Mediolanum
(Milan)
Aquileia
PANNONIA
Tolosa
Narbo
Ravenna
ILLYRICUM
Danube
HISPANIA
Corsica
Tarraco
ITALY
Rome
MŒSIA
BLACK SEA
Byzantium
COLCHIS
IBERIA
ALBANIA
PONTUS
ARMENIA
PARTHIANS
MACEDONIA
THRACE
Sardinia
Gades
New Carthage
MEDITERRANEAN SEA
CAPPADOCIA
ASSYRIA
MESOPOTAMIA
Tigris
Euphrates
ASIA
PAMPHYLIA
CILICIA
Antioch
SYRIA
Corinth
ACHÆA
Sicily
MAURETANIA
Carthage
NUMIDIA
Cyprus
Crete
Caesarea
PALESTINE
ARABIA
AFRICA
Alexandria
CYRENAICA
EGYPT
Nile
English Miles
0 100 200 300 400 500

Romans regarded as proving that they were ruled by an unlucky emperor. Of subsequent emperors between A.D. 68 and 180 the most important are Vespasian (70–79), in whose reign Jerusalem was destroyed, the Colosseum begun, and the Roman dominion in Britain extended to a line of fortresses between the Firths of Forth and Clyde; Titus (79–81), in whose reign the Colosseum was finished, and the towns of Pompeii and Herculaneum, pleasure resorts where wealthy Romans were wont to escape from responsibilities of state, destroyed by an eruption of Vesuvius; Trajan (98–117), a Spaniard, under whom the Roman Empire reached its greatest extent (see map); Hadrian (117–138), who built the famous wall in the North of England as a protection against the Picts and Scots (compare the Great Wall of China), abandoned Northern Britain, and also gave up the eastern conquests of Trajan—Armenia, Syria, and Mesopotamia—and Marcus Aurelius (161–180).

In many ways Marcus Aurelius is the most remarkable of the Roman emperors. Of his ability as a ruler there can be little doubt; he succeeded in maintaining social order despite a succession of years of bad weather, floods, famines, barbaric raids, and finally a great pestilence. Among his public services were a curtailment of national expenses, the limitation of gladiatorial games, the care of roads, the appointment of none but worthy magistrates, and the regulation of street traffic. So many were his activities that they often kept him at work from early morning until long after midnight. With true stoical fortitude he refused to allow his indifferent health to interfere with what he conceived to be his duties to his subjects, and if he had spared himself more there can be little doubt that he would have lived much longer than he did. He is the author of a remarkable volume of *Meditations*, and he is easily the finest spirit among all the Roman emperors. But despite his charitable sentiments he persecuted the Christians, and it was during his reign that

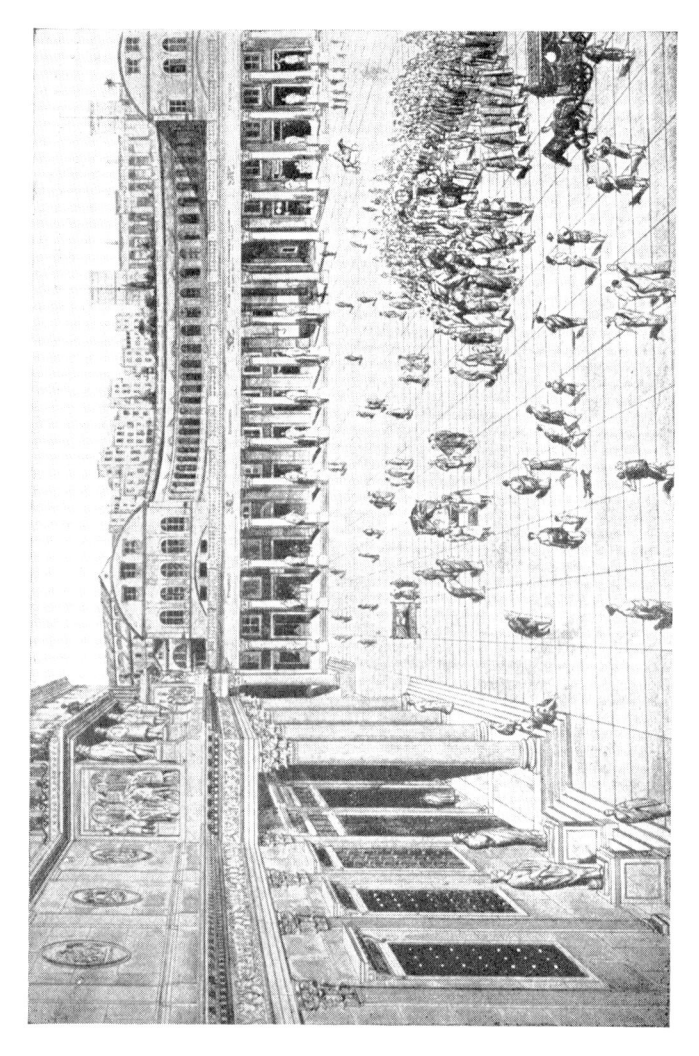

The forum of Trajan at Rome. Extensive ruins still exist to-day

Justin Martyr and Polycarp suffered martyrdom. Curiously enough, his wife was an extremely wicked woman, and his son and successor, Commodus, was one of the most detestable of the Roman emperors.

Life in the Roman world between 27 B.C. and A.D. 180, like life in modern Europe, presented strange contrasts of great wealth and direst poverty. The wealthy people lived in very beautiful mansions on the hills, the poorer classes were crowded into poor and thickly populated tenements in the valleys. The money which some of the worst of the Roman emperors spent on sensual enjoyment is perfectly astounding. Caligula spent as much as £20,000,000 in one year; the roses for one of Nero's banquets cost £35,000; Vitellius squandered £7,000,000 in a few months on eating and drinking : and Domitian spent £2,400,000 on the gilding of one temple on the Capitol. But luxury, idleness, and self-indulgence were probably confined to a very small class. The civil servants who carried on the administration of the Empire were extremely industrious, and there was a marked improvement in the treatment of the provinces. Even the worst of the emperors found it to their interest to rule them wisely, and when they were in need of money they generally wrung it from wealthy nobles at Rome and not from the provinces as had been done by the governors of the later republic. The letters of the younger Pliny throw light upon the life of a studious country gentleman of the year 100. Pliny had a country-house at Como, on one of the Italian lakes, and when he was there he was accustomed to rise at six o'clock in the morning ; he then read or dictated letters to a clerk until midday, when he indulged in a short sleep followed by gymnastic exercise, estate management, and sometimes hunting, until the evening dinner, during which a book would be read aloud. Afterwards until bedtime there would be music and acting. Pliny's gifts to his native town included £4,000 for baths, and £9,000 and a yearly endowment of £800 for a

THE AUGUSTAN AGE

library. There was widespread interest in literature during the first two centuries of the Roman Empire. Books, which took the form of rolls of parchment, were numerous and not very expensive; the elder Pliny consulted as many as two thousand when he was writing his *Natural History*. They were produced in book factories where the work of copying was done by slaves. Roman literature reached its highest level during the reign of Augustus. Maecenas, the Emperor's chief minister, was the friend and patron of literary men, and among those who made the age glorious incomparably the greatest are the poets Horace and Virgil. The poems of Horace will always be one of the richest legacies from the ancient world; they are invaluable not only for their beauty and polished elegance, but also as a treasury of information on the men and life of the Augustan Age. His friend Virgil in the *Georgics* has given us a delightful description of rustic life in Italy, but he is far better known as the author of the *Aeneid*, an epic poem which traces the history of the house of Augustus from the Trojan heroes of former times. Virgil took his materials very largely from the old Greek stories, and his work was a conscious and definite attempt to do for Rome what Homer had done for Greece. Cato and his contemporaries had despised the Greeks and the Greek language. That feeling was by this time conspicuously absent from Roman life. Greek culture was highly valued, and where a rich man lacked it himself he would almost invariably rely upon some slave, whose learning had been guaranteed by the dealer, to supply the deficiency. Not infrequently the slaves were themselves Greek.

There was a very large number of slaves in Rome; they were twice as numerous as free men in Italy, and probably the proportion was still higher throughout the whole empire. Every ancient civilization enslaved prisoners captured in war, and the Roman wars had been numerous and successful. In Rome itself the slaves were mainly domestic and not cruelly treated. Well-educated slaves might even be on terms of friendship with their masters. Pliny, in his anxiety for the health of a favourite slave, sent him to Egypt and afterwards to the Riviera. Sometimes Romans would administer their estates or factories through the agency of clever slaves. These men might even become partners with their masters and purchase their freedom, and former slaves who had been freed often became very prosperous. There is a record of one who did so well that he was able to buy five taverns in Rome from which he derived a considerable income. But slavery had its dark as well as its bright side. The slaves who were employed in agricultural work in the rural districts were generally scandalously overworked and housed like cattle, and sometimes in private households the most revolting cruelties were perpetrated. Pliny writes of a master whose slaves surrounded him in his bath and tried to murder him, and of another who left Como with a retinue of slaves and was never heard of again, while the satirist Juvenal speaks of slaves being 'thrown to the fishes'[1] by angry mistresses. It is, however, worth remembering that there were laws in Rome before the end of the first century B.C. which checked the cruelty of masters and gave slaves the right of appeal to the courts. The Stoics, whose influence in the city was considerable, taught that all men were brothers and that slavery was therefore wrong.

The condition of free-workers in Rome was probably better than that which any workers have enjoyed before or since. They numbered about three hundred thousand of the million inhabitants of whom the city was composed. Their hours of labour were not long. They began working early in the morning but finished at about three o'clock in the afternoon. The days of labour were fewer than they are in the world of to-day. There were 175 days set apart for public games, in addition to occasional festivals. After work there was the

[1] A poetical expression for 'thrown into the river'.

A cobbler

A soap-shop

A butcher's shop

ROMAN TRADES

luxury of bathing in public baths which were often of a perfectly palatial character. Besides the great marble basins of hot and cold water there were gymnastic rooms, libraries, and marble colonnades or lounges where the game of dice could be played. These baths were built by the emperors, and the charge for admission was only the equivalent of a farthing of our money. The Antoninian Baths were capable of accommodating 1,600 bathers. The Roman worker generally got his entertainments without paying anything for them; they were supplied free by the Emperor or the municipality, or by some wealthy noble anxious for popular favour. The Great Circus held 380,000 spectators, and there is reason for supposing that the sports provided—chariot races, foot races, conjuring, and tight-rope dancing—were far more popular than the brutal gladiatorial games of the Colosseum. Free corn, free elementary education, and in the city of Rome free medical treatment, were further privileges which fell to the lot of the Roman workers. They also had trade unions or 'colleges' which were partly provident societies, and partly, it is clear, used to keep up wages. The practice of combining in this way was borrowed from the Greeks, and the gilds of the Middle Ages were continuations of the Roman trade combinations. Each class of workers had separate unions—builders, bakers, smiths, carpenters, the boatmen of the Rhone, the muleteers of the Alps and Apennines—and they became so numerous that in the second century B.C. the authorities at Rome forbade the formation of new ones.

Rome plundered the world in order to enrich her patricians and supply her free workers with many of the amenities of civilization. The historian Gibbon has a graphic paragraph in his great book, *The Decline and Fall of the Roman Empire*, in which he gives us a vivid idea of what this world dominion meant:

'The most remote countries of the ancient world were ransacked to supply the pomp and delicacy of Rome. The forests of

Scythia afforded some valuable furs. Amber was brought overland from the shores of the Baltic to the Danube, and the barbarians were astonished at the price which they received in exchange for so useless a commodity. There was a considerable demand for Babylonian carpets and other manufactures of the East; but the most important branch of foreign trade was carried on with Arabia and India. Every year, about the time of the summer solstice, a fleet of a hundred and twenty vessels sailed from Myoshormos, a port of Egypt on the Red Sea. By the periodical assistance of the monsoons, they traversed the ocean in about forty days. The coast of Malabar or the island of Ceylon was the usual term of their navigation, and it was in those markets that the merchants from the more remote countries of Asia expected their arrival. The return of the fleet to Egypt was fixed to the months of December or January, and as soon as their rich cargo had been transported, on the backs of camels, from the Red Sea to the Nile, and had descended that river as far as Alexandria, it was poured without delay into the capital of the empire.'

If Rome took much from other parts of the world she also gave much to those countries into which her legions marched as conquerors. If Rome plundered she also civilized the world. From one end of the empire to the other there arose large and well-built cities with temples, theatres, baths, and amphitheatres. There are magnificent ruins testifying to the nature of Roman civilization in places so far afield as Britain, Gaul, Spain, North Africa, and Asia Minor. Thus there are the Roman baths at Bath in England; a beautiful temple, a bridge, and an aqueduct nearly nine hundred feet long and one hundred and sixty feet high at Nîmes in France; ruins of temples dedicated to the sun-god, some of the greatest buildings ever erected, at Baalbec in Syria; and in North Africa on the edge of the Sahara Desert a very wonderful ruin, the Roman colony of Thamagudi (Timgad), a town built by the Third Legion as a protection against the desert tribes, with a forum, a senate house, statues of the emperors (it was built in the time of Trajan), and fountains in the main street.

Roman rule afforded security everywhere except perhaps on some of the frontiers. There never was a more practical people than the Romans. The network of fine roads spreading all over the Empire, the schools and law courts which they established, and the skill shown in adjusting their rule to the needs of many different peoples prove this. In consequence of the necessity for modifying their rule according to circumstances, a mass of laws arising from the decisions of various judges was gradually formed : these decisions were collected into one code by the Emperor Justinian in the sixth century A.D. This code is the foundation of nearly all European law, so that it is no exaggeration to say that the Romans gave the world law.

The Romans did not have the imaginative genius of the Greeks, and in some respects their literature is singularly defective. Although their empire was so extensive, the accounts which they have written of the peoples with whom they came in contact are few and scanty. Tacitus wrote an admirable description of the customs and manners of the Germans, but his work is almost unique in Latin literature. Caesar's *Commentaries* contain valuable information, but they exhibit little imagination, and they were written for strictly practical purposes—to justify the political career of their author and to give a picture of the qualities which had enabled Rome to subdue and govern the world. Even great poems, like the *Aeneid* of Virgil and the *De Rerum Natura* of Lucretius, were written with some definite object apart from the mere desire to produce great literature. It is possible that the *Aeneid* was written at the bidding of the Emperor Augustus in order to teach duty and loyalty to the state. The practical wisdom of the Romans seems to colour all their actions, artistic and spiritual as well as political and material. But this did not prevent them from producing some very great literature, whose influence upon the subsequent course of human development it is very easy to underestimate.

The ruins of Baalbec in Syria

It is true that nearly everything of value in Roman literature has borrowed either its form or its ideas from the Greeks; the only form of literary composition which the Romans invented was the satire, a strictly practical form of writing consisting of comments friendly or unfriendly on men and affairs. But it must be borne in mind that without the Romans Greek civilization would not have been spread and adapted to the needs of humanity, and the great literatures of the modern world are quite as much indebted to the Roman as the Roman is to the Greek. But the Roman writers were something much more than mere adapters and disseminators. Two of them, Livy and Tacitus, are among the very greatest historians of all time, and it may be fairly claimed that Cicero is the creator of modern European prose. Livy's history of the Roman Republic is no mere record of facts; it is almost a moral treatise, sanctifying such virtues as fidelity to the pledged word and the subordination of personal ambition to public duty, the qualities which made Rome great. Tacitus, on the other hand, exposes the vices which brought her down from her high position: the conservatism of the governing classes, the loss of the old civic spirit, the general apathy and hedonism of the people.

'To study the history of the Roman Empire in the lurid light which he throws on it is to realize, more vividly than one can do with the events of one's own time, how the reconstruction of a world and the organization of a larger civilization can be thwarted by failure in faith, hope, love; and how, without these, the springs of effective action (as well as those of good literature) dwindle away and run dry.'[1]

In the writings of Cicero, who lived from 106 to 43 B.C., Latin reached its highest perfection both as a written and as a spoken language. It became the most perfect language of prose that the world has ever known. In profundity of

[1] Article on 'Literature' by J. W. Mackail in *The Legacy of Rome* (Oxford Press).

thought Cicero was far inferior to the Greeks, but no one has ever excelled him as a master of language. He made thought attractive, and although he was eminent both as a statesman and as an orator, he is very much greater as a writer. 'He created a universal language, and did for the Republic of Letters what it was his unfulfilled ambition to do for the Republic of Rome, established in it the custom and law of civilized human life.'[1] Fifty-six of Cicero's orations are extant, much of his philosophical work, and hundreds of letters to friends and political connexions, which give us a vivid picture of life in Rome during the latter days of the Republic.

It is astonishing what influence is still exerted by Roman writers of less eminence than Cicero and Tacitus. The ethical writings of Seneca, the tutor of the Emperor Nero, have had a profound effect upon standards and ideals of conduct ever since. Educational theorists of to-day still make use of Quintilian's great treatise on education, the *Institutio Oratoria*. The *De Architectura* of Vitruvius inspired the architecture of the sixteenth and seventeenth centuries, and Pliny's *Natural History*, a book much studied during the Middle Ages, is still used by modern scholars and investigators. Of great importance too are the Christian writings which were written in the Latin language, such as the works of Tertullian, the *Confessions* and *The City of God* of St. Augustine, and above all the Latin translation of the Bible completed by Jerome in A.D. 405 and known as the Vulgate. It has, with some revisions, remained ever since the scripture in daily use throughout the Catholic Church, and its language no less than its substance has profoundly affected all European literature.

Latin verse contains some of the finest poetry ever written. The names of Virgil, Lucretius, Horace, the great narrative poet Ovid, and Catullus, a lyrical poet of supreme genius, challenge comparison with the most illustrious poets of any country, and their influence, direct or indirect, upon the poetry

[1] Ibid.

of other European nations is almost incalculable. Ovid was the model poet of the Middle Ages. 'The common intellectual occupation of the Middle Ages, it has wittily and not without a good deal of truth been said, was writing enormous quantities of bad Latin verse; and much the greater part of that verse was written in the Ovidian couplet.'[1] But Ovid was never a poet of the rank of Virgil, Horace, and Lucretius. Virgil, particularly, is one of the world's great poets; he was also a preacher of ideals which have profoundly affected civilization. Thus in his great pastoral poem—the *Georgics*—he paints the alluring picture of a world at perfect peace and harmony with itself and with Nature, a world of hard work, sincere faith, and simple pleasures. 'In the *Aeneid* he became the voice of Rome, the spiritual founder of the Holy Roman Empire, and the pilot light for that universal Commonwealth or League of Nations on which men's eyes are now more and more earnestly fixed. He was the poet and prophet of the fusion of Rome with Italy (only in our own day imperfectly accomplished) and the incorporation of the whole world in the Italo-Roman civilization.'[1] His famous contemporary, Horace, was less idealistic. 'He gave mankind the type of the man of the world and the gentleman; he showed how it is attainable without birth or wealth, without anxiety or ambition, without either high intellectual gifts or unattainable saintliness of life. . . . His *Odes* became a sort of Psalter of secular life.'[1] Of still another type is the *De Rerum Natura* of Lucretius, who lived many years before the Augustan Age, and whose masterpiece is considered by some critics to be as great a work as the *Aeneid* of Virgil. In it Lucretius set himself a tremendous task, that of expounding the whole system of the universe, and he was astonishingly successful. His object was to kill superstition, to take fear from men's minds, to expose ignorance to the devastating test of truth. He wished his countrymen to give up their

[1] Mackail's article on 'Literature' in *Legacy of Rome*.

beliefs in Hades and in gods who took no real interest in human affairs. Lucretius was a great scholar with an unrivalled knowledge of primitive men and ways of thought, and he anticipated some of the most important modern discoveries in chemistry, physics, the atomic theory, and the theory of light : but the moral effect of his writings is even greater than the scientific. No more bracing message, no nobler exposition of a simple virtuous life has ever been penned by any writer. In the beauty of his diction and the majesty of his thoughts he suggests comparison with the English poet Milton.

Even the Roman drama, which was not original, and whose influence upon the Roman people was brief and transitory, has had a subsequent influence which is considerable. Seneca wrote nine tragedies, probably to please the Emperor Nero, and these served as the model for the plays of the sixteenth century, when the drama flourished in a way which it had not known since the great days of Athens. The principles of Greek drama were not at this time understood : hence the great influence of Seneca. This is clearly to be seen in the plays of Marlowe and the other predecessors of Shakespeare, and also in the work of Shakespeare's early and middle period. In comedy the Romans were more successful than in tragedy. Here again they were the imitators of the Greeks, but they showed great skill in the adaptation of their models, and in Terence and Plautus they could boast the possession of two very great comedians. Plautus was the creator for Europe of burlesque and farce, and he is the 'literary ancestor' of Shakespeare and of the great French dramatist Molière. The posthumous influence of the Latin drama is certainly greater than the influence which it exerted during the lifetime of its creators, for, generally speaking, the Roman people found more enjoyment in gladiatorial games, ballet dances, and costly and gorgeous shows.

The once prevalent idea that Greek art was poetic and

inspired, whereas Roman art was prosaic and dull, can be carried too far. So too can the belief that the Romans were destitute of artistic ideas. They certainly owed much to the Greeks, just as the great architects of the Middle Ages owed much to the Romans, but at least two of their structures—the bath and the aqueduct—were original. In architecture, as in all else, utility was the guiding principle, but it would be a great mistake to imagine that the Romans were blind to the appeal of beauty. The visitor to the town of Nîmes, in the South of France, cannot fail to be impressed with the exquisite taste of the architects who designed the Roman baths which he will see there, and the colossal aqueduct near the town—the Pont du Gard—is a testimony to the magnificence as well as to the permanence of Roman work.

During the imperial period the statues in the streets of Rome are reputed to have been so numerous that it was said that the city had two populations—one of flesh and blood, the other of marble and bronze. The flesh and blood population was Roman—or at least a considerable part of it; the statues of marble and bronze were very largely Greek, for the most part spoils of war. Thus when Marcellus captured Syracuse in 212 B.C. he brought numerous art treasures back with him to Rome; Flaminius brought the art treasures of Philip of Macedon there in 197 B.C.; and the plunder of Corinth in 145 B.C. and of Athens in 86 B.C. meant the bringing of many more. But Rome did have a distinctive sculpture of her own. About A.D. 50 there arose a school of portrait bust-makers, whose method contrasts rather strongly with the Greek. Their aim was to make a speaking likeness of their original; Greek portraits, on the other hand, were not expressions of what the originals actually were, but the highest expression of what they should be There is a fine collection of Roman busts in the British Museum, real likenesses of the emperors whom they represent. Some of these are of great historical value. Thus Merivale deduces

Roman architecture. The Pont du Gard, near Nîmes

from the bust of Trajan that the look of painful thought which it depicts 'seems to indicate a constant sense of overwhelming responsibilities, honourably felt and bravely borne, yet ever irritating the nerves and weighing upon the conscience'.

In religious matters the Romans were on the whole very tolerant. One of the features of the first century of the Roman Empire is the spread of new religions like the Egyptian cult of Isis, and the worship of Mithras, a development of Zoroastrianism. But the toleration which was shown to the devotees of these two religions was not extended to Christianity, another eastern religion which was destined to make still greater progress throughout the Empire. This was partly due to the fact that the emperors did not clearly distinguish the Christians from the Jews, and the Jews were the only people who caused the Romans trouble by reason of their religious fanaticism. Those who professed other religions were quite content to admit the divinity of the Emperor, a legend carefully fostered by Augustus and his successors as a means of maintaining unity. But the Jews would never admit the claim, and when Caligula gave an order that his statue should be placed in the Holy of Holies, the most sacred part of their Temple, they threatened to rebel. Caligula was not the only emperor who came into conflict with them. Tiberius deported four thousand Jews from Rome to Sardinia: Titus, after one of the most terrible sieges in history, captured Jerusalem, destroyed the Temple, and massacred a very large number of Jews, as many as a million according to one account; under Trajan they rebelled in Egypt, Cyprus, and Cyrene, killing many thousands of their opponents, and they were repressed with great severity; when Hadrian, determined to make them conform, ordered that a temple of Jupiter should be built on Mount Zion, there was another rebellion which was only ended after Judea had been almost depopulated. Like the Jews, the Christians refused to pay

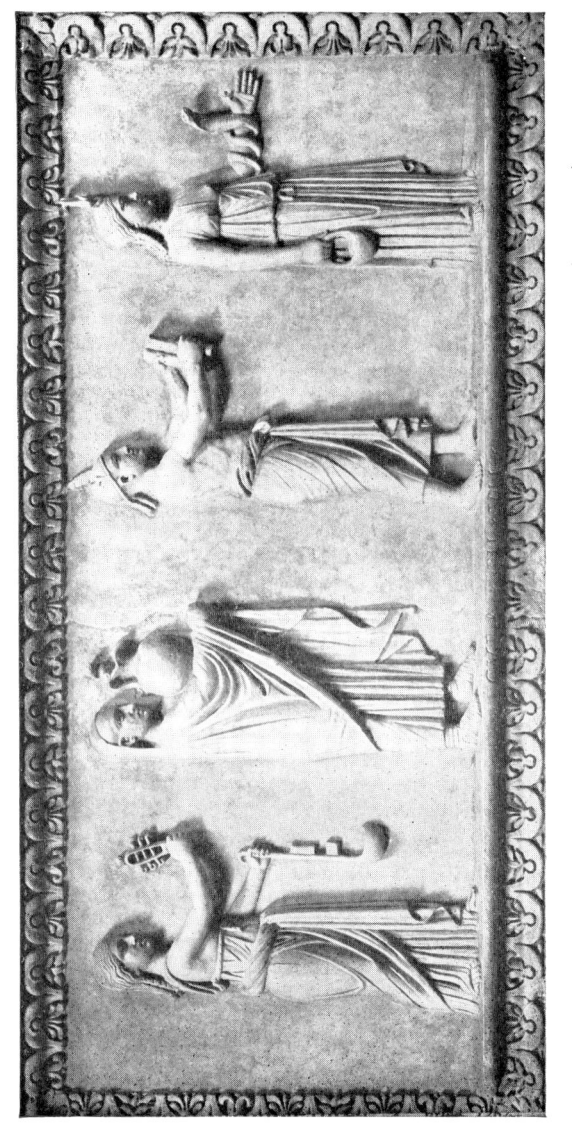

New religions at Rome. A marble relief of priests and priestesses of Isis in procession

divine honours to the Emperor, and many of them went even further and refused to serve in the Roman legions, declaring that they would be false to their religion if they took any part in the shedding of human blood. A letter from the younger Pliny to Trajan and the Emperor's reply throw much light on the Roman attitude towards Christianity. Pliny was governor in Asia Minor at the time and, feeling some perplexity as to the treatment of certain people against whom an accusation of being Christians had been laid, he writes :

'An anonymous information was laid before me containing a great number of names. Some said they neither were nor ever had been Christians ; they repeated after me an invocation of the gods, and offered wine and incense before your statue (which I had ordered to be brought for that purpose, together with those of the gods), and even reviled the name of Christ ; whereas there is no forcing, it is said, those who are really Christians into any of these acts. These I thought ought to be discharged.'

Trajan replies :

'Do not go out of your way to look for Christians. If they are brought before you and the offence is proved you must punish them, but with this restriction, that when the person denies that he is a Christian, and shall make it clear that he is not by invoking the gods, he is to be pardoned, notwithstanding any former suspicion against him. Anonymous informations ought not to be received in any sort of prosecution. It is introducing a very dangerous precedent, and is quite foreign to the spirit of our age.'

Trajan, as this letter makes evident, was one of the most enlightened of the emperors, but he had no doubt that Christianity ought to be suppressed. Even Marcus Aurelius persecuted Christians, and the only reference to them in his *Meditations* is a contemptuously expressed opinion that their readiness to die was due to a mere love of opposition. It is not surprising therefore that there should have been persecutions under half-insane rulers like Nero and Domitian,

THE EARLY CHRISTIANS

and that the ignorant masses should have believed that national calamities, like the inroads of barbarians on the northern frontier of the Empire and the depredations of a great pestilence in the time of Marcus Aurelius, were due to the anger which the gods felt at the spread of the Christian doctrines.

The early Christians held their meetings in secret. Like the Jews who lived in Rome, they used to bury their dead in tombs hollowed out of the rock on which much of Rome was built. During Domitian's persecution, they began to use these tombs as places of refuge; subterranean galleries were made, and eventually passages which communicated with disused sand-pits through which the Christians could escape to the open country. These catacombs, as they are called, are still to be seen in Rome. Christianity made a great appeal to those of lowly circumstances and to those whom fortune had not favoured, and so it is natural to find that many of its disciples were slaves, who got some compensation for the misery of their earthly lives in the confident expectation of a happy existence beyond the grave. But it was by no means confined to the down-trodden, and the Emperor Diocletian (284-305) was so alarmed at the number of Christians in his dominions and the spread of their beliefs, that he instituted one of the most ruthless persecutions in the history of the Church. But persecution failed to break the spirit of the Christians, and in the year 313 the Emperor Constantine, by the Edict of Milan, announced that Christianity was to be tolerated everywhere throughout the Empire. The writer Eusebius says that the Emperor was induced to do this by the vision of a flaming cross which appeared in the sky at noonday together with the inscription in Greek, 'By this conquer.' It is far more probable that it was a political move. The Christian religion had made such progress among his subjects that it occurred to the keen mind of Constantine that it might be used as a means of maintaining unity and solidarity in the Empire. Christianity became firmly established as the official religion; other religions rapidly disappeared or were absorbed, and from the fifth century onwards the only priests and temples in the Roman Empire were Christian.

Between the years 180 and 476 there were more than sixty emperors, many of whom reigned for a very short time, and there were frequent civil wars between rival candidates and the armies which supported them. The best known of these later emperors are Septimius Severus (193-211), Caracalla (211-17), Decius (249-51), Aurelian (270-5), Diocletian (284-305), Constantine (306-37), and Theodosius the Great (379-95). Many of them were not Romans: thus Severus and his son Caracalla were Africans, Aurelian was a peasant of Illyria, Diocletian was the son of a Dalmatian freedman. Caracalla is chiefly known to fame as the man who built the celebrated baths in the city of Rome which are named after him, but he is really of more importance as the emperor who conferred the rights of Roman citizenship on every free-born inhabitant of the Empire. Constantine moved his capital from Rome to a city which was named Constantinople in his honour; this was built on the site of the old fortress of Byzantium and its position was an admirable one, commanding the entrance to the Black Sea and access to the rich cornlands north of the Crimea. Theodosius was the ruler under whom Christianity became the official creed of the Empire. Just before his death he divided his dominions between his two sons, Honorius and Arcadius, the former to rule the West from Milan, the latter to rule the East from Constantinople—a serious blow to the dominance of Rome.

The invasion of the Empire by Teutonic tribes was a constantly recurring event during the last two centuries of its existence. Caracalla fought the Alemanni; Aurelian showed his greatness as a soldier by driving the Vandals and the Goths back across the Danube, and by clearing the Alemanni out

ALARIC AND THE GOTHS

of Lombardy; and the Goths were allowed by Theodosius to settle in Thrace and Asia Minor when the pressure of the Huns made it imperative for them to seek new territories. The consolidation of China by Shi-Hwang-ti and the rulers of the Han Dynasty, and the effectiveness of the Great Wall cut off the Huns from the rich grass plains of that country, and when the Chinese began to advance northwards and westwards it became necessary for the Huns to move in other directions. The ultimate result was their invasion of Europe, which was in no small degree responsible for the incursions of the Teutonic barbarians into the Roman Empire. All the Germans did not, however, come in as enemies. German soldiers served in the legions, and some of them attained very high rank. There were German consuls under Theodosius, and German customs were becoming so fashionable under Honorius that he issued a decree that the people of Milan, his capital, were not to wear trousers, long hair, or fur coats. Stilicho, the commander of this emperor's army, was a Vandal, and when the Visigoths under Alaric first invaded Italy in A.D. 400 it was Stilicho who was mainly responsible for their defeat. Alaric's invasion was the invasion of a nation rather than of an army, for the Goths brought their wives and children, their valuables and their spoils of war with them. They were evidently determined to establish new settlements for themselves on the soil of Italy. Their descent by way of the Julian Alps into the valley of the Isonzo so alarmed the degenerate Italian nobles that some of them spoke of leaving Italy to the barbarians and emigrating to Corsica and Sardinia, while others spoke of founding a new Rome on the banks of the Saône or the Rhône. Stilicho was the one leader who did not forget his manliness, and who realized the necessity of presenting a bold front to the invaders. By his efforts Alaric was ultimately checked in the battle of Pollentia.[1] The poet Claudian, the panegyrist of Stilicho, claims this

[1] Modern Pollenzo, about 23 miles south-east of Turin.

as a great defeat for Alaric; the claim is doubtful, but it is certain that two years later (A.D. 404) the Goths had left Italy, and Honorius and Stilicho were celebrating a triumph in Rome, remarkable not only because a Roman emperor visited Rome, but because it was the last occasion upon which gladiatorial games were held. The protest of a monk named Telemachus, who boldly entered the arena and in his efforts to part the combatants was stoned to death by the spectators, is said to have made such an impression on the mind of Honorius that he decided that such shows should never be held again.

Shortly afterwards the Emperor moved his capital to Ravenna, 'anxious only', says Gibbon, 'for his personal safety.' In the following year there was another Teutonic invasion [1] of Italy under Radagaisus, a pagan whom the writer Orosius describes as the most savage of all the past or present enemies of Rome, and again it was Stilicho who marched against the invaders and defeated them. Yet less than three years later Stilicho was assassinated at the instigation of Honorius, who suspected him of plotting with Alaric. The death of Stilicho was followed by the massacre of the wives and children of the thirty thousand Teutonic soldiers in the legions. These accordingly deserted to Alaric, who in this year (408) crossed the Alps once more and marched towards Rome, laying waste the intervening country and plundering towns and villages. His appearance before the city caused the cowardly Romans to put to death Serena, the widow of Stilicho, 'lest she might traitorously open the gates of the city to him.' [2] Famine and pestilence followed, and an embassy was sent to Alaric suggesting peace 'on moderate terms', and declaring that 'if Alaric refused them a fair and

---

[1] Gibbon says that Burgundians and Vandals formed the main strength of this army. Dr. Hodgkin (*Italy and her Invaders*) speaks of it as a Gothic invasion.

[2] *Italy and her Invaders* (Hodgkin), pub. Oxford University Press.

Early 1st century A. D.

Early 2nd century A. D.

Mid 2nd century A. D.

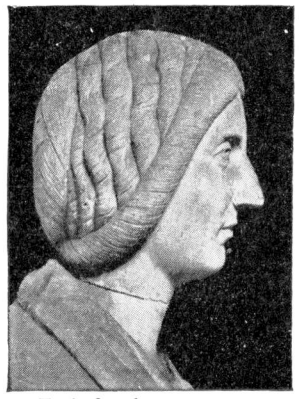

End of 2nd century A

End of 2nd century and early 3rd century

ROMAN FASHIONS IN HAIRDRESSING

honourable capitulation, he might sound his trumpets, and prepare to give battle to an innumerable people, exercised in arms and animated by despair.'[1] The Gothic leader laughed at this bombastic utterance, and, declaring that thick grass was more easily mowed than thin, said he would raise the siege of the city on payment of all its gold and silver, all its valuable movables, and all its slaves of barbarian origin. When asked what he proposed to leave to the citizens, he replied that they might have their souls. Ultimately Alaric consented to raise the siege on payment of five thousand pounds weight of gold, thirty thousand of silver, four thousand robes of silk, three thousand hides dyed scarlet, and three thousand pounds of pepper, a list which suggests that with the extension of their conquests the tastes of the Goths were becoming more luxurious.

There were many in Rome who would now have liked to see Alaric succeed to the position of Stilicho, and become the commander of their armies and the defender of their independence. It was a position which the Gothic general eagerly desired himself, but Honorius would have nothing to do with him. Safe himself behind the marshes of Ravenna, he cared nothing for his less fortunately situated subjects. His attitude is difficult to understand. He expressed himself quite ready to share the Empire with a common soldier named Constantine, whom revolted legionaries from Britain had raised to the overlordship of Britain, Gaul, and Spain, but resisted all Alaric's requests for territory and reasonable rations for his troops, in return for which he was prepared to give military assistance against any enemies who might disturb the peace of Honorius and the Roman people. The result of the Emperor's obduracy was that the Goths besieged Rome a second time, but Alaric, despite a conviction that he was marked by destiny to render the city desolate, was most reluctant to do so. He set up a rival emperor, a Greek named

[1] *Decline and Fall of the Roman Empire*, Chap. XXXI.

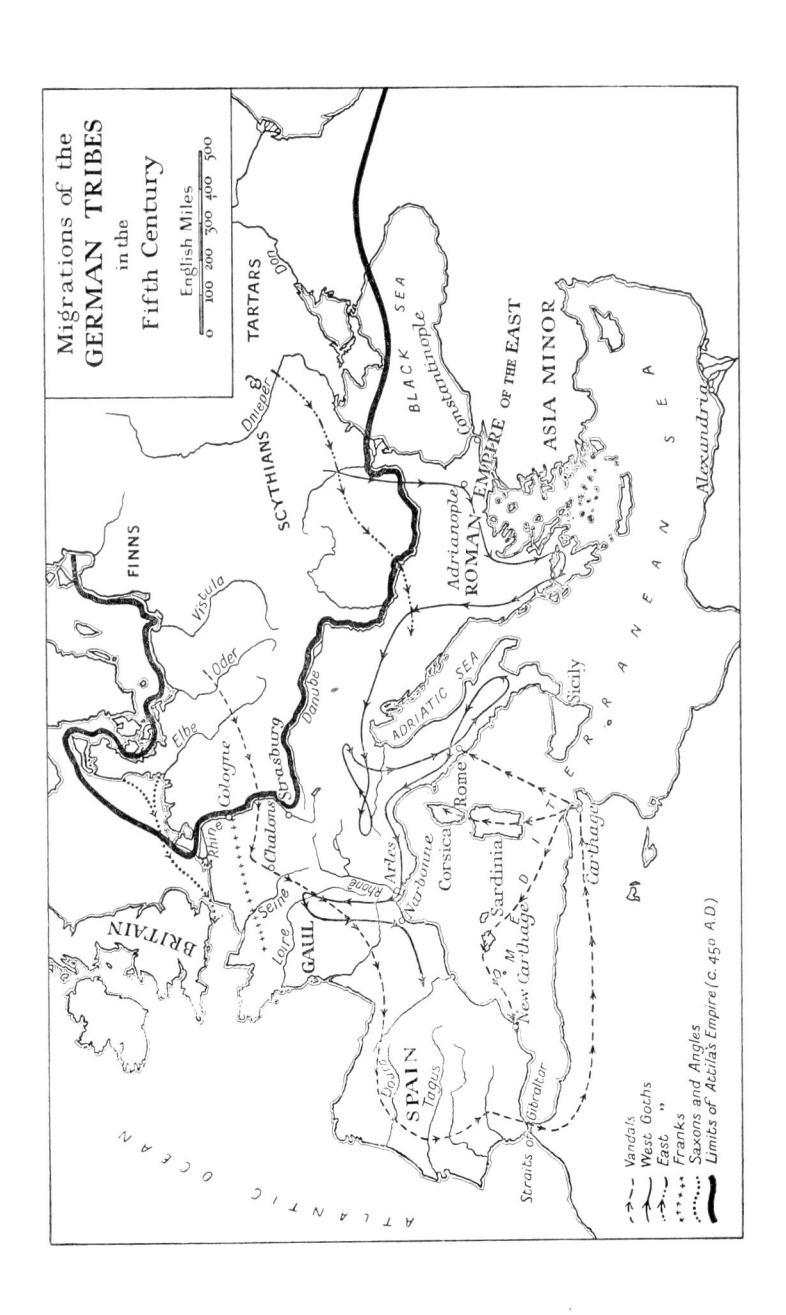

Migrations of the GERMAN TRIBES in the Fifth Century

English Miles
0 100 200 300 400 500

-→- Vandals
--→- West Goths
-↑- East "
+++ Franks
···· Saxons and Angles
━━ Limits of Attila's Empire (c. 450 A.D.)

Attalus, whose rule at Rome does not appear to have annoyed Honorius at Ravenna. Attalus proved himself unworthy of the dignity conferred upon him, so Alaric deposed him, and once more made overtures to Honorius, but again without success. The patience of the Gothic chieftain was now utterly exhausted, and so he began his third siege of Rome. There was no longer any thought of compromise. The city was captured and given over to sack and pillage. The Visigoths were not savages. They were Christians, led by a man who, whatever his record as a destroyer, certainly had no love for the work of mere destruction. Before entering Rome, he had given strict orders, which do not appear to have been disobeyed, that no Christian churches should be harmed and no one who sought refuge within them. There is no doubt that the ruin and desolation spread by the Goths has been much exaggerated by some writers, and, as Gibbon has pointed out, 'the ravages of the Barbarians whom Alaric had led from the banks of the Danube, were less destructive than the hostilities exercised by the troops of Charles the Fifth,[1] a Catholic prince who styled himself Emperor of the Romans. The Goths evacuated the city at the end of six days, but Rome remained above nine months in the possession of the Imperialists; and every hour was stained by some atrocious act of cruelty, lust, and rapine.'[2] Many incidents of the Gothic conquest show that some at least of the invaders were capable of generosity and Christian forbearance, but such incidents were in the nature of things exceptional. The sack of a city, whether it be conducted by pagans or by professing Christians, must abound in incidents of mere savagery.

'We may suspect, without any breach of charity or candour,' writes Gibbon, 'that in the hour of savage licence, when every passion was inflamed and every restraint was removed, the precepts of the gospel seldom influenced the behaviour of the Gothic Christians. The writers, the best disposed to exaggerate their

[1] 1527.   [2] *Decline and Fall of the Roman Empire*, Chap. XXXI.

SACK OF ROME

clemency, have freely confessed that a cruel slaughter was made of the Romans; and that the streets of the city were filled with dead bodies, which remained without burial during the general consternation. The despair of the citizens was sometimes converted into fury; and whenever the Barbarians were provoked by opposition, they extended the promiscuous massacre to the feeble, the innocent, and the helpless.'[1]

Works of art were wantonly destroyed; gold and jewels, furniture, plate, and costly fabrics were piled irregularly upon the wagons which always accompanied the Gothic armies; and so complete was the degradation of the city that St. Jerome in his cell at Bethlehem wrote of it as if it were the forerunner of the end of all civilization.

After the sack of Rome the Goths marched southwards, plundering a good deal on the way. Their objective appears to have been Africa, which Alaric was anxious to conquer because he realized that Africa was the granary whence Rome got her corn-supply, and thus its possession was essential to an effective control of the city. He was, however, never destined to cross the sea. A storm wrought considerable damage to his fleet, and delayed his departure, and before the year which witnessed his greatest triumph (410) was at an end Alaric died after a very brief illness. Nineteen years later, another German people, the Vandals, under Genseric, conquered the Roman province of Africa and founded a new state with Carthage as its capital. The needs of Rome had caused Honorius to withdraw his troops from Britain and Gaul, and Teutonic tribes also poured into these countries—Angles, Saxons, and Jutes into Britain, and Vandals and Burgundians into Gaul.

As if to increase the confusion which the movements of the Germans caused, the Huns now threatened Europe under a chief named Attila. Between the years 445 and 450 they ravaged the Eastern Empire between the Black Sea and the

[1] Ibid.

Adriatic. Tribute was exacted from the emperor who ruled at Constantinople, and then Attila crossed the Rhine into Gaul at the head of a considerable army. So great was the danger that Goths, Franks, Burgundians, and Romans joined forces against him, and after a desperate battle defeated him at Châlons in the north of Gaul (A.D. 451). Attila then marched south with what was left of his army. The legions in Italy were not strong enough to check him, and it looked as if Rome would be sacked again. From this she was saved, so it is said, by the earnest entreaties of Leo, Bishop of Rome, who entered Attila's camp and warned him not to risk the vengeance of heaven by plundering the city, and the Hun leader was so impressed with the bishop's sincerity and intensity of purpose that he withdrew his troops. Attila died in the next year, and his Huns gradually disappeared out of history. They became absorbed into the surrounding populations. They did not, as has been supposed, occupy Hungary, although many of them must have settled in that country and intermarried with the inhabitants. The Magyars, the dominating class of Hungary in modern times, were an altogether different race who came there much later.

The withdrawal of Attila by no means ended the troubles of Rome. In the year 455 a Vandal fleet from Carthage, led by Genseric, sailed up the Tiber. Bishop Leo again pleaded for the city, but Genseric, although he spared the lives of the inhabitants, would not give up the chance of plunder. For fourteen days Rome was rifled of its treasures and thirty thousand citizens were carried away into slavery. Finally, in 476, the Western Empire came to an end. For some time the Roman provinces had been in the possession of the barbarians, and German troops in the service of the Empire had been accustomed to set up emperors as they pleased; in 476 Odoacer, the most powerful of the German generals in Italy, banished the last of the emperors of the West and ruled in his place, nominally as the viceroy of the Eastern Empire,

Roman furniture. A beautiful bronze stand found at Pompeii

which continued to exist until 1453, when Constantinople was taken by the Turks. It is interesting to note that although between the years 395 (when Theodosius died) and 476 there were really two empires, an eastern and a western, writers of the time do not speak of two states, but continue to refer to 'the Empire', just as if its administration were in the hands of one person. Theoretically the two emperors were supposed to govern one empire conjointly. The idea of one government for the whole of the civilized world persisted even after it had ceased to have any basis in reality, and it continued to influence men throughout the whole of the Middle Ages. There is one notable instance in the history of the later Roman Empire where the desire for unity led to an attempt to enforce uniformity, which is an altogether different idea. The Theodosian Code, a great collection of the laws of the Empire completed in 438, made it unlawful for any one to differ from the beliefs of the Christian Church. Those who dared to disagree with its teachings were called 'heretics', and if heretics ventured to come together their meetings were broken up and their teachers heavily fined. Their books were burned; concealment of them was made a capital offence; and houses in which heretical doctrines were taught were confiscated. Thus the Christian Church in power was no more tolerant of the religious opinions of others than the persecuting emperors had been of the Christian gospel.

The extent of the Roman Empire had been recognized as a possible source of weakness as early as the time of Augustus. To hold it together it was necessary that the Romans should exhibit their finest qualities, the qualities of patriotism and intense concentration in the pursuit of an object, which had made them great. Augustus thought that the expansion of the Empire had gone far enough, and he advised his successor to make no attempt to increase his dominions. Diocletian endeavoured to strengthen his position by dividing the Empire into two parts, each of which was to have a separate

Trajan's army foraging in the enemy's land

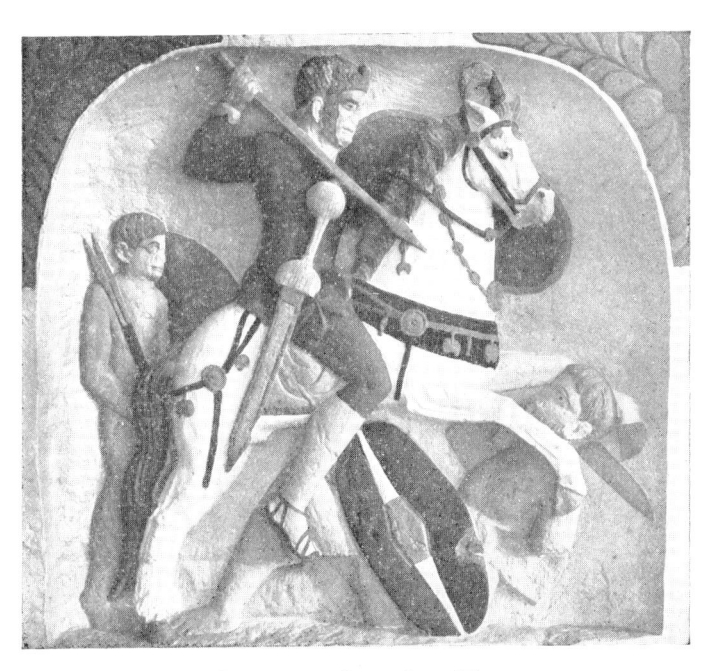

Grave stone of a cavalry soldier
THE ROMAN ARMY

ruler, one ruling from Milan and the other from Nicaea. The same idea accounts for Theodosius' division of his territories between his two sons, but the succession of weak rulers who followed ruined any chance of success that there may have been. In order to maintain possession of the vast territories which comprised the Roman Empire a very large army was necessary, and this had become mainly a mercenary force ; in course of time more than half of it was recruited from the barbarian tribes whose inroads finally brought about the fall of Rome. Obviously such troops were a source of greater weakness than strength. Many of them were openly contemptuous of their employers ; they respected no authority but that of their general ; they were ready to overthrow the civil government at his bidding ; and not infrequently they sympathized with the enemies whom they were paid to fight. A good deal of money was necessary to support them, and this was got by oppressive taxation. Very often the burden of a tax would be increased by the unfair way in which it was collected. Thus in the case of the land-tax, the chief source of revenue, the government made a group of the richer citizens in each town permanently responsible for the whole annual amount due from all landowners in their district. If there were any deficiencies, no matter what the reason, it was their business to make it up. The consequence was that many landowners were ruined ; only the very rich could stand the constant drain upon their resources. The middle class sank into poverty and despair, and it is not surprising to find that great political events were regarded with indifference by the mass of the population. When the barbarians were actually in Italy during the time of the Emperor Honorius, Stilicho preferred to enlist slaves in his army rather than adopt the expedient of a general call to arms. There was no popular uprising against any of the invaders. Obviously it was felt that the Roman Empire was not worth fighting for. Even literature and art had declined,

DECAY AND DESTRUCTION

and law had become 'an accumulation of ill-considered, inconsistent edicts'.[1] The barbarian could be no worse evil than the tax-gatherer and the slave-driver.

'So far', writes a distinguished modern historian, 'had decay advanced through the negligence of those most vitally concerned that, if Europe was ever to learn again the highest lessons which Rome had existed to teach, the first step must be to sweep away the hybrid government which still claimed allegiance in the name of Rome. The provincials of the fifth century possessed the writings in which those lessons were recorded, but possessed them only as symbols of an unintelligible past. A long training in new schools of thought, under new forms of government, was necessary before the European mind could again be brought into touch with the old Roman spirit. The great service that the barbarians rendered was a service of destruction. In doing so they prepared the way for a return to the past. Their first efforts in reconstruction were also valuable, since the difficulty of the work and the clumsiness of the product revived the respect of men for the superior skill of Rome. In the end the barbarians succeeded in that branch of constructive statesmanship where Rome had failed most signally. The new states which they founded were smaller and feebler than the Western Empire, but furnished new opportunities for the development of individuality, and made it possible to endow citizenship with active functions and moral responsibilities. That these states laboured under manifold defects was obvious to those who made them and lived under them. The ideal of the world-wide Empire, maintaining universal peace and the brotherhood of men, continued to haunt the imagination of the Middle Ages as a lost possibility. But in this case, as so often, what passed for a memory was in truth an aspiration.'[2]

[1] Davis, *Medieval Europe* (Home University Library).
[2] Ibid.

XIV

THE CONQUERORS OF ROME

ALL the German tribes were a branch of the Aryan race who migrated into Europe from the neighbourhood of the Black and Caspian Seas at a period long before the existence of historical records. Julius Caesar in his *Commentaries* has given us valuable information about the Germans with whom he came into contact during the time that he was proconsul in Gaul. But of much greater value is the account which the Roman historian Tacitus (*c.* A.D. 60 to A.D. 120) gives in the *Germania* regarding the habits and modes of life of the people who were ultimately destined to conquer Rome.

Tacitus divides them into three great branches: the Ingaevones, who lived nearest the ocean; the Hermiones, who lived in the middle of Germany; and the Istaevones, who included all the rest. When they first began to threaten the Roman Empire these names had disappeared and been replaced by others, such as Franks, Suevi, and Saxons; but neither these names nor those used by Tacitus included all the Germans. They formed rather the division which we know as the West Germans. In addition there were the Germans of the north, afterwards known as the Danes, Norwegians, and Swedes; and the Germans of the east, such as the Goths and Vandals.

The Goths and Vandals originally came from Germany. The Vandals once lived on the north coast of that country, and before they crossed over into Africa under Genseric in A.D. 429 they had traversed Dacia, Pannonia, Gaul, and Spain. Their name is still preserved in the Spanish province of Andalusia (Vandalusia). When we first hear of the Goths they were living on the Prussian coast of the Baltic at the mouth of the Vistula. About A.D 150 they began to move

TRIBAL MOVEMENTS—CUSTOMS

south, and within fifty years had reached the Black Sea and the lower course of the river Danube. From about A. D. 238 onwards they made many incursions into the Roman Empire, burning and sacking many towns, such as Trapezus, Chalcedon, and Nicea. In A. D. 262 or thereabouts they burnt the temple of Diana at Ephesus and overran Cappadocia, Thrace, Macedonia, Achaia, and in the year 272 the Emperor Aurelian surrendered the whole of the province of Dacia to them. By this time they had become separated into two great divisions, the Ostrogoths or Eastern Goths, and the Visigoths or Western Goths. The Ostrogoths settled in Moesia and Pannonia, while the Visigoths remained north of the Danube. Both took part in the great migrations which took place between the middle of the fourth century and the end of the fifth, when whole tribes taking with them all their possessions left their homes and passed over into the Roman Empire, where they either took by force or received as gifts large areas of land (see Map). The Visigoths under Alaric invaded Italy and plundered Rome, afterwards settling in the south-west of Gaul and in Spain. The Ostrogoths extended their dominions almost up to the gates of Constantinople, and in 493, under their king Theodoric the Great, obtained possession of the whole of Italy (493).

In their methods of government the German tribes were democratic. The North Germans had kings whom they elected from one family : there was no fixed law of succession, but the most suitable man was chosen. The West Germans in all probability only had leaders in time of war. They had a clearly defined system of government. There were three political divisions : the tribe or nation, the county (or hundred), and the village. All matters that concerned the village were discussed by all the freemen of the village in a public meeting ; in similar manner the freemen of the county looked after their own affairs, while matters that affected the whole nation were discussed in an assembly of all the freemen of the tribe. In social rank there were three classes: nobles, freemen, and slaves. In the assemblies the vote of an ordinary freeman was as good as that of a nobleman. The slaves were of two kinds: some were attached to the soil and could not be removed from their lands, while others were personal slaves and were treated as chattels. Tacitus says that it sometimes happened that young men gambled themselves into slavery, but that slaves thus acquired 'were generally exchanged away in commerce, so that the winner may get rid of the scandal of his victory'. Chattel slavery seems to have been introduced among the Germans as the result of their contact with the Romans. It was unknown in Tacitus' time. After speaking of those who became slaves in consequence of ill luck at games of dice, he writes:

'The rest of their slaves have not like ours particular employments in the family allotted to them. Each is the master of a habitation and household of his own. The lord requires from him a certain amount of grain, cattle, or cloth, as from a tenant; and so far only the subjection of the slave extends. His (i.e. the lord's) domestic work is performed by his own wife and children. It is unusual to scourge a slave or punish him with chains or hard labour. They are sometimes killed by their masters; not through severity of chastisement, but in the heat of passion like an enemy; with this difference, that it is done with impunity.'

The condition of these slaves was evidently very like that of the serfs or villeins of the Middle Ages, and much better than the condition of most ancient slaves.

It was customary for the young men of the German tribes to attach themselves to some man of established courage and military ability, thus forming what is known as the 'comitatus'. These young men lived with their chieftain and accompanied him on all his expeditions. The relation between them was entirely voluntary and might be terminated if either party failed in its duties. What those duties were Tacitus has told us.

Rome and the barbarians. Trajan (on the right), surrounded by his staff, receiving an embassy of German and Thracian chiefs

'In the field of battle it is disgraceful for the chief to be surpassed in valour; it is disgraceful for the companions (the members of the comitatus) not to equal their chief; but it is reproach and infamy during a whole succeeding life to retreat from the field surviving him.[1] To aid, to protect him; to place their own gallant actions to the account of his glory, is their first and most sacred engagement. The chiefs fight for victory; the companions for their chief. If their native country be long sunk in peace and inaction, many of the young nobles repair to some other state then engaged in war. For, besides that repose is ungrateful to their dispositions, and toils and perils afford them a better opportunity of distinguishing themselves, they are unable without war and violence to maintain a large train of followers. The companion requires from the liberality of his chief, the warlike steed, the bloody and conquering spear; and in place of pay he expects to be supplied with a table homely indeed but plentiful. The funds for this munificence must be in war and rapine; nor are they so easily persuaded to cultivate the earth and await the produce of the seasons, as to challenge the foe and expose themselves to wounds; for they think it base and spiritless to earn by sweat what they might purchase with blood.'

To have a numerous and gallant retinue was regarded by the chieftain as a great mark of distinction, 'an ornament in peace and a bulwark in war.'

The religion of the Germans was a kind of nature worship. There was no priestly caste; each father of a family acted as its priest, and on special occasions it appears that any one might be appointed to act as priest. Contact with the Roman Empire led to the introduction of Christianity. The first of the German tribes to accept this new religion were the Goths, and their conversion is undoubtedly to be referred to

---

[1] The Roman historian Ammianus Marcellinus (died about A.D. 380) relates that when Chonodomarus, king of the Alemanni, was taken prisoner by the Romans, 'his companions, two hundred in number, and three friends peculiarly attached to him, thinking it infamous to survive their prince, or not to die for him, surrendered themselves to be put in bonds'.

the influence of Christians whom they captured and reduced to slavery during their early raids on the Empire. The great missionary of the Goths, however, was himself a Goth, Ulphilas (311-81), who was ordained their bishop, and who translated parts of the Bible into the East Gothic dialect. The conversion of the northern and western Germans came very much later, and even among the Goths the progress of Christianity was for a time very slow. Many of Ulphilas' followers suffered martyrdom, and eventually the Emperor Constantine gave them lands in southern Moesia, where they settled and continued an existence separate from the main Gothic tribes for several centuries. As late as the ninth century A.D. Gothic was still spoken in the province of Moesia.

The main German occupations during peace times were cattle-rearing, agriculture, and hunting. The nomad inclinations of many of them were largely due to ignorance of agriculture; indeed, this must be regarded as one of the chief reasons of the great migration of the fourth and fifth centuries. Their agricultural implements and methods were of the most primitive kind; it is probable that they had only very small areas under cultivation; and a scarcity of game or the destruction of cattle by a pestilence would be an extremely serious matter for a vigorous race who were multiplying so rapidly that Ammianus Marcellinus remarked that they were numerous enough to cause one to suppose that death never visited their land. It is said that within sixty years the tribe of the Aduatuci increased from six thousand to fifty-nine thousand. Most of the agricultural work was done by slaves and women. This does not imply that the status of women was low. On the contrary, the Germans held them in high honour, and often took their advice in the most vital matters. Caesar relates how on one occasion the German leader, Ariovistus, postponed an engagement with the Romans because the matrons had pronounced that he would not be victorious if he fought before the new moon.

It was characteristic of this people that they were for a long time reluctant to live in compactly built towns. Tacitus writes : 'It is well known that none of the Germans inhabit cities, or even admit of contiguous settlements. They dwell, scattered and separate, as a spring, a meadow, or a grove may chance to invite them. Their villages are laid out, not like ours in rows of adjoining buildings, but every one surrounds his house with a vacant space, either by way of security against fire, or through ignorance of the art of building.' This aversion to cities was of long duration, and the subsequent development of town life among them was one of their many debts to Rome.

Roman writers seem to have been much impressed with the high stature, great bodily strength, fair complexions, blue eyes, and light coloured hair of the Germans. They also bear testimony to their bravery, their faithfulness to their obligations, their love of liberty. But they are not blind to their faults—drunkenness, gambling, and an excessive partiality for war. The Germans undoubtedly varied a great deal in character, and in the degree of civilization which they had attained. Goths differed from Franks and both differed from Vandals. But all were alike in their ignorance of the art, literature, and science which had been developed by the Greeks and adopted by the Romans. For a time the effect of their spread over Europe was that the declining civilization of the Empire was extensively submerged. Libraries and works of art were neglected or destroyed, and the Western world fell back into a condition similar to what it had been before the Romans conquered and civilized it. But the loss was only temporary. The great heritage of Greece and Egypt and of Rome did not wholly perish. Centuries of turmoil followed the break up of the Roman Empire : the period is appropriately known as the Dark Ages, but then came a recovery The great works of Greece and Rome were esteemed once more ; a new form of architecture arose, partly modelled on that of the Greeks and Romans; and science made far greater strides than it had ever made in the ancient world.

XV

WHAT CIVILIZATION OWES TO THE JEWS

THE Jews or Hebrews[1] were originally nomads who came from the Arabian Desert into Palestine. Some of them had been slaves in Egypt, but had escaped from bondage under the leadership and inspiration of Moses, who must have been a supremely great man. It is always something of a miracle to get slaves to fight for their freedom, as the experience of the American Civil War during last century proved, but that miracle Moses accomplished. Yet he did not live to enter Palestine at the head of the people whom he had roused from the apathy of centuries. When he died the task of leadership devolved upon a young Israelite named Joshua. Under him a struggle began with the native inhabitants of Palestine. There was doubtless much fighting, but there was not, as is sometimes supposed, anything of the nature of a war of extermination against the Canaanites, the former inhabitants of Palestine. The Canaanites were far more cultured than the invaders. They lived in walled towns, and their position between Egypt and Mesopotamia had exposed them to the influence of both civilizations. From the Egyptians they learned how to manufacture many articles of commerce; the Assyrians taught them how to write in cuneiform characters on letters of clay. There is no doubt that Hebrews and Canaanites intermarried and ultimately became one people, and that the Hebrews learned much from the more cultured Canaanites. One of the things they learned from them

[1] Although the words 'Jew' and 'Hebrew' are often used interchangeably, strictly speaking 'Jew' means 'man of Judah', and is only applicable to the whole race after the destruction of the northern kingdom.

was cuneiform writing, which they used for a few centuries, until Phoenician merchants taught them how to write on rolls of papyrus or sheepskin, using pen and ink and alphabetic characters.

The position of Palestine was not a strong one, situated as it was between the two great empires of Egypt and Assyria. Fortunately for the Hebrew invaders, who were coming into Palestine continuously between 1400 B.C. and 1200 B.C., the Egyptian Empire became feeble and impotent after 1150 B.C., while the Arameans of Syria were a bulwark between them and the people of Assyria and Babylonia. A more pressing enemy were the Philistines, who had come from Crete to the coasts of Palestine, where they settled. Between them and the Hebrews there were constant wars. The exploits of Samson, of Saul, of David, and of others against these enemies occupy prominent places in the heroic literature of the Hebrews.

Before 1000 B.C. the Hebrews had elected their first king, Saul, who lived in a tent, a striking testimony to the hold which nomadic ideas still had upon this people. His successor, David, realizing the need for a capital and for some dwelling place more permanent than a tent, attacked and captured Jerusalem, the fortress of the Jebusites, one of the old Canaanitish tribes. From Jerusalem he extended his dominions over the greater part of Palestine, and Jerusalem has remained, from that day to this, the most important city of that land.

The deeds of David appealed much to the imagination of his fellow countrymen, and in Hebrew literature he figures as a great warrior and a great poet, the 'sweet Psalmist of Israel' (although not one of the psalms can with certainty be attributed to him). David was the most mighty among many mighty men, the conqueror while still a boy of the Philistine giant Goliath of Gath. And yet he had also moral qualities which caused the writer of the Biblical narrative to tell us that he was 'a man after God's own heart'. His

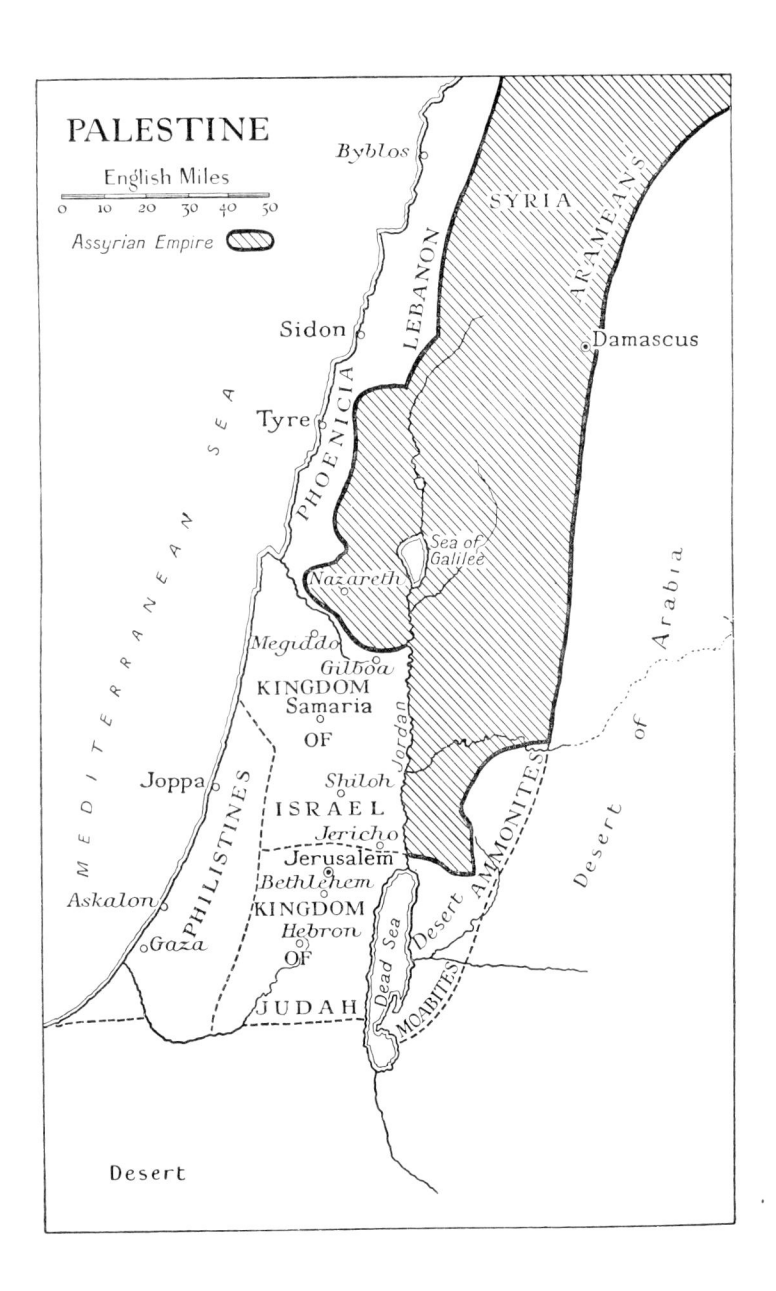

PALESTINE

English Miles
0 10 20 30 40 50

Assyrian Empire

Byblos
Sidon
Tyre
Damascus
MEDITERRANEAN SEA
PHOENICIA
LEBANON
SYRIA
ARAMEANS
Sea of Galilee
Nazareth
Megiddo
Gilboa
KINGDOM
Samaria
OF
Joppa
Shiloh
ISRAEL
Jericho
Jerusalem
Bethlehem
KINGDOM
Hebron
OF
JUDAH
Askalon
Gaza
PHILISTINES
Jordan
Dead Sea
AMMONITES
MOABITES
Desert
Desert of Arabia

Desert

son and successor, Solomon, was fond of Oriental splendour and voluptuousness. He built the first Temple in Jerusalem. Although in Hebrew literature Solomon has an unsurpassable reputation for wisdom, this may be doubted when we consider the nature of his numerous amours, and the heavy taxes which he imposed upon his people. These taxes were mainly responsible for the defection of the ten northern tribes in the reign of Solomon's son and successor, Rehoboam (*c.* 930 B.C.). The northern tribes formed what was known as the kingdom of Israel, whose capital became Samaria; the two southern tribes formed the kingdom of Judah, whose capital remained Jerusalem. Israel was far more fertile and prosperous than Judah. It was a land of busy cities, bustling markets, and much wealth. In Judah nomadic habits of life were still strong, and the inhabitants had much difficulty in earning scanty livelihoods for themselves. The relative wealth of the northern kingdom explains why it tempted a conqueror, so that many of its people were taken into captivity by the Assyrians in 722 B.C., whereas the feeble little kingdom of Judah survived until 586 B.C., when Nebuchadnezzar, the Chaldean king, destroyed Jerusalem and carried the people away captive to Babylonia.

When Cyrus the Persian overthrew the Chaldean Empire he allowed these Babylonian captives to return to Jerusalem, and in 537 B.C. a large number of them under the leadership of Zerubbabel came back to Judah. Seventeen years later they began to build the second temple, which was completed in five years. For nearly a hundred years, however, they were a spiritless and ineffective community. Then two men, Ezra and Nehemiah, transformed this weak, poverty-stricken remnant into a vigorous religious community, whose influence upon the subsequent history of the world has been very great. During the period which had elapsed since the return from Babylon, while some of the Jews had been rebuilding Jerusalem on a modest scale, some had been copying

An encampment of nomad tribes in Palestine to-day

and arranging their sacred manuscripts and adding others, thus helping to bring into existence what we know as the Bible. There can be little doubt that to this time belongs the elaborate body of law and ritual which figures in the Bible as the last half of Exodus, the whole of Leviticus, and most of Numbers. Armed with this, Ezra and Nehemiah went to Jerusalem with seventeen hundred followers, and in 444 B.C. a great gathering of the people was held at which the people bound themselves by oath to observe the laws as revealed in the sacred books. A period of religious revival followed. A body of teachers and commentators known as Scribes came into being; and the position of the priests was secured by the elaborate system of religious taxation which the law ordained. This was a doubtful benefit, because it resulted in the priestly class developing into a thoroughly worldly aristocracy, the Sadducees of the New Testament.

The conquests of Alexander the Great brought Judah within the sphere of Greek influence, and for a time it appeared as if the spirit of Plato might prove too strong for the spirit of Ezra. That it did not was due partly to the opposition of the Scribes, and partly to the fact that in 165 B.C. Antiochus Epiphanes, the ruler of the Syrian division of Alexander's Empire, attempted to extirpate Judaism by force of arms. This rallied all to the standard of Judas Maccabaeus, and support of the old law, the law of Ezra, became synonymous with patriotism. Antiochus was defeated, and with him the chance of the triumph of Greek culture in Judah. At the close of the Maccabaean period the religion of the Jews had become cemented into a legal system. This became controlled by special teachers called rabbis. The priest was now in the background and synagogues were being built where the law could be expounded.

The arrival of Pompey in Judaea in 63 B.C. brought the Jews into close contact with the Romans. At first, however, they did not definitely become part of the Roman Empire.

An Eastern city gate

The government of Judaea was entrusted to an Idumaean chieftain, called Herod the Great, who enjoyed his independence conditional upon his efficiency and his friendliness to Rome. His reign ended in the year when Christ was born. His descendants were very feeble rulers and were consequently deprived by Rome of most of their authority. When Christ was crucified Herod Antipas was ruling in Galilee, Judaea was under an unimportant Roman official named Pontius Pilate, and both were subject to the Roman governor of Syria. Forty-one years later, in A.D. 70, the history of the Jewish state came to an end with the destruction of Jerusalem by Titus, the son of the Emperor Vespasian.

The great contribution of the Jews to civilization is religion. Their Bible has done more for the moral and religious progress of mankind than any other book or collection of books. It is composed of two parts, the Old Testament and the New Testament. In some English Bibles, placed between the Old and New Testaments, are fourteen books or fragments of books, which are known as the Apocrypha. The Jews of Palestine regarded these as not inspired, but the Jews of Alexandria accepted them as part of the Bible. In the modern world opinions vary as to their value. Eleven out of the fourteen books are regarded as inspired by the Roman Church; in the Church of England passages from the Apocrypha are read 'for example of life and instruction of manners', but they are not to be used 'to establish any doctrine'.

The Old Testament is a collection of thirty-nine books written at different times between 850 B.C. and 150 B.C. The books vary considerably in length, quality, and usefulness. Some of them are fairly reliable as history, some are not; some, like the Book of Psalms, Job, and most of the prophetic books are poetry of a very high order. But the main value and interest of the Old Testament do not lie in its literary excellence or in the sidelights which it throws upon contem-

TO THE JEWS

porary history, but rather in its record of the evolution and development of Jewish religion, which Christ inherited, and out of which Christianity grew.

The religion of the Hebrews, from the time when Moses delivered them from their Egyptian bondage (probably about 1300 B.C.) to the time of the prophet Elijah (about 850 B.C.), was not strictly speaking monotheism. They worshipped Jehovah or Jahveh, the god of Moses, but apparently did not deny the existence of other gods. Thus Solomon, in addition to the Temple of Jehovah, built temples in Jerusalem for Moloch, the god of the Ammonites, and Chemosh, the god of the Moabites. Under Ahab, who ruled the northern kingdom from 876 to 854 B.C., the worship of Jehovah was dominated by the worship of Baal, the divinity of Tyre whence Ahab's wife, Jezebel, had come. It was this which provoked the opposition of Elijah, the forerunner of the great prophets. He taught that Jehovah was the only god. This was monotheism, for it implied that all other gods were not only false but non-existent. Elijah also represented Jehovah as one who delighted in righteousness, and who would punish wickedness. Thus Ahab was reproved for the judicial murder of Naboth, whose vineyard he had coveted. Similarly, during the reign of David, the prophet Nathan had denounced the king for his share in the death of Uriah the Hittite. This marks a distinct advance in the conception of deity. Most of the Semitic tribes, and indeed most early peoples, thought of their gods as keenly interested in the political and military welfare of those who did them honour, and ever ready to punish disrespect or neglect of religious ceremonies; but, generally speaking, they took no interest in the personal morality of their worshippers unless it affected the efficiency of the tribe or nation to which they belonged.

About a hundred years after Elijah's day the period of the great Hebrew prophets begins. At this time there was much wealth and also considerable poverty in the kingdom of

Israel. 'There were palaces of ivory in Samaria, and houses of hewn stone without number, castles and forts, horses and chariots, pomp and power, splendour and riches wherever one might turn. The rich lay on couches of ivory with damask cushions; daily they slew the fatted calf, drank the most costly wines, and anointed themselves with precious oils.'[1] On the other hand, the poor were scandalously oppressed, and it was obvious to any but the most partial observer that the whole system of society was unsound. The moment was ripe for the appearance of some one to denounce the luxury and corruption of the age, and he came in the person of Amos of Tekoa, a rough unkempt herdsman who startled those present at an official festival to Jehovah held at Bethel (about 750 B.C.) by declaring that God took no delight in feast days and solemn sacrifices, but that his joy was rather in right conduct and justice, and that he would punish Israel by using their enemies as an instrument to overthrow them. Thirty years later the kingdom of Israel was conquered by the Assyrians and disappeared for ever from human history. Nevertheless, most of those who listened to Amos must have regarded his words as the ravings of a madman. That God should desert his own people and join their enemies was inconceivable. Amos, however, was proclaiming a new doctrine, that Jehovah was God not of Israel only, but was the righteous ruler of the whole world. The same idea pervades the teaching of the prophets who succeeded Amos. The book called after Isaiah says 'Israel shall be the third with Egypt and with Assyria ... whom the Lord of hosts shall bless, saying, Blessed be Egypt my people, and Assyria the work of my hands, and Israel mine inheritance' (Isaiah xix. 24–5). Yet at a later date Isaiah discouraged alliance with Egypt against Assyria, because he was convinced that Assyria was an instrument in the hand of God. He makes Jehovah say, 'Ho, Assyrian, rod of mine anger,' and

[1] Cornill, *The Prophets of Israel*.

he believed that Assyria's triumphs could never have been accomplished if it had not been the will of God. But when in 701 B.C. Sennacherib, King of Assyria, attacked Jerusalem, Isaiah was the life and soul of the resistance to him, because while he might be convinced that it was God's will that Judah should lose its political independence, he was equally convinced that it was not his will that the Holy City should be destroyed, and its religious life obliterated.

The idea of the universality of God gained further strength from the Jewish captivity in Babylon. The very fact of the exile proved that God could not dwell in Palestine alone, and that he was the righteous ruler of all the nations. Thus the Jews became entirely monotheists, denying the existence of any god but their own. A marked change in the character of God is also noticeable. This will readily be perceived by comparing the god of Moses with the god of Isaiah or Hosea. The former was a somewhat fierce national god, 'visiting the sins of the fathers upon the children unto the third and fourth generations'; the latter is a god of mercy and kindness, just to all and especially beneficent towards the poor and needy and such as are oppressed and down-trodden. Hosea compares the relationship of God and of Israel with that of marriage. A husband has married a wife who is faithless to him, and he is almost inclined to let her go her way to ruin without any effort to save her. But he cannot, although he has been so cruelly wronged. He remembers that she was once his wife and that she once loved him. Therefore he takes her back to his house, and when she has proved that she is trully repentant for her sins he will restore her to her former position in his affection and confidence. Similarly God is ever ready to pardon the repentant sinner as exemplified by His erring people Israel, and to forgive injuries which He has suffered.

Another feature which is noticeable in the teaching of the Hebrew prophets is what is known as the Messianic Hope.

The Jews, unlike the Greeks, always pictured their Golden Age in the future. Jehovah promised Abraham descendants 'like the sands of the sea in multitude', 'in whom all the families of the earth shall be blessed'. In the writings of the prophets this promise is recalled and emphasized as the reward of those who will survive the national calamity which is coming as a punishment for Israel's lack of faith. The Jews are once more to come into close contact with God; the blessings of material prosperity and political supremacy will be theirs; and the worship of Jehovah will spread over the whole earth. Later writers, such as the authors of the Book of Daniel and the uncanonical Book of Enoch, came to the conclusion that the Kingdom was too vast a conception to be staged in this imperfect world. The End of the World must first come, but before this God would send his Messiah to prepare men for the Last Judgement. This is the 'Divine King' whom Isaiah described as 'Wonderful, Counsellor, the Mighty God, The Everlasting Father, the Prince of Peace'. There can be no doubt that many of the Jews expected him to display all the characteristics, but on a much more magnificent scale, of an earthly monarch; to shatter unrighteous rulers; and to free his chosen people from bondage to Rome. When the Pharisees were in alliance with the Maccabees against Antiochus Epiphanes, they expected a prince of that line to prove himself Messiah.

The belief that the Kingdom of God was beyond the End of the World was responsible for the growth and development among the Jews of a belief in a Future Life, which the Pharisees accepted and the Sadducees rejected. The idea is absent in the writings of the Old Testament, or is, at best, but dimly foreshadowed there (e.g. Job), except in the Book of Daniel and in one or two Psalms of late date. The grave was pictured as a place 'where the wicked cease from troubling and the weary are at rest', and relationship with ghosts was condemned as immoral, as in the case of Saul, who induced the Witch of Endor to call up the spirit of Samuel. The Sheol of the Jews was as shadowy and unreal as the Hades of the Greeks. But the idea of a Kingdom of God beyond the End of the World implied a life of bliss for those alive on earth at the time of the Last Judgement, and it was inevitable to assume from this that those already dead would rise from their graves.

Jesus Christ did not at first openly proclaim himself as the Messiah, although his followers regarded him as such. The record of his life and teaching is contained in the first four books of the New Testament. These were not written until many years after the death of Jesus. At first his followers were content with a mere verbal record of what he had said and done. Eventually, however, probably with the object of prosecuting a more active propaganda, perhaps because there was danger lest he might lose his historical character and become 'as vague and unsubstantial a figure as any pagan deity',[1] the Four Gospels were written (A.D. 70 to 110).

The teachings of Christ were acceptable neither to the Scribes nor to the Sadducees. The latter regarded them as an attack upon the temporal authority of Rome which they supported; the former could hardly be expected to relish his indictment of their laws and traditions, which had grown considerably since the time of Ezra and which in some respects had become a mere travesty of their original. Moreover, those who looked for the establishment of a Kingdom of God on earth were disappointed with a religion which taught that the Kingdom of God was not a political kingdom nor one in another world, although it extended beyond the grave. It was a moral kingdom whose test of membership was the possession of such virtues as meekness, righteousness, love of peace, and readiness to undergo persecution and misrepresentation for the truth. It was a kingdom where wealth conferred no privileges; where social position did not exist; where love

[1] *A Short History of Our Religion* (Somervell), pub. Bell.

of God was synonymous with love of Man ; and where the Brotherhood of Man was an accomplished fact. In short, the gospel of Jesus was a call to a new way of life. It implied so vast a breaking with the traditions and conceptions of the past that it is not surprising that his attempt to ennoble the world ended in apparent failure.

There is nothing in the history of the world more remarkable than the recovery of the Christian Church after the confusion caused by the death of its founder. This was accomplished within the space of thirty years. At the beginning of the period (A.D. 29), the Christian Church was merely a small handful of Jews differing from the rest of their fellow countrymen only in that they believed that the Messiah expected by all had actually come. At the end (A.D. 59) it was a European institution, predominantly Gentile in character. Christian communities had been established at Antioch, at Philippi, at Ephesus, at Rome, and at many other places. Christianity was a vigorous and thriving religion, destined to become one of the great creeds of the world. The Christian apologist would naturally regard this as a result primarily and perhaps entirely due to the innate qualities of the religion itself. But there were many other circumstances which contributed, at least, towards the spread of Christianity, of which perhaps the chief were the zeal of the early Christians ; the austere purity of their lives, contrasting vividly with the corruption and licentiousness of the world which they strove to convert ; the existence, among those to whom they preached, of aspirations after higher morals and better modes of life ; and last, but by no means least, the influence of St. Paul.

The zeal of the early Christians is abundantly testified by their uncompromising fidelity to their beliefs ; 'their invincible valour, which disdained to capitulate with the enemy whom they were resolved to vanquish';[1] their readiness to endure all things—dangerous voyages by land and sea,

[1] Gibbon, *Decline and Fall of the Roman Empire*, Chap. XV.

A model of the Jewish synagogue at Capernaum, where our Lord preached

personal obloquy and abuse, scourgings, even death itself in the service of what they conceived to be eternal truth. The historian Tacitus, in a famous passage in the *Annals*, has accused them of a 'general hatred to mankind', an accusation which perhaps has its origin in a belief in the imminent Second Coming of Christ, which was widespread in the early Church—'when the country of the Scipios and Caesars should be consumed by a flame from Heaven, and the city of the seven hills, with her palaces, her temples, and her triumphal arches should be buried in a vast lake of fire and brimstone.'[1] This belief, according to Gibbon, was one of the chief causes of the growth of Christianity, for while the most awful calamities were predicted for unbelievers, the disciples of Jesus were promised 'a joyful Sabbath of a thousand years' when 'Christ with the triumphant band of the saints and the elect who had escaped death, or who had been miraculously revived, would reign upon earth till the time appointed for the last and general resurrection'.[1]

But the great moral appeal which the new religion made had a far more lasting effect than the belief in a millennium. It is not only Christian writers like St. Paul[2] and Cyprian who call particular attention to the moral depravity of the age into which Christianity was born. The Stoic Philosopher Seneca declared that the world was filled with crimes and vices, and that wickedness had become so widespread that innocence was nowhere to be found.[3] The rich were mean and servile, passionately devoted to money-making and caring little how they made it. The poor were brutal and bloodthirsty, callously indifferent to human suffering, their minds enervated and their finer feelings destroyed by the cruel sports of the amphitheatre. The most degrading features of the pagan religions were openly practised.

[1] Gibbon, *Decline and Fall of the Roman Empire*, Chap. XV.
[2] Romans i. 21-32.
[3] 'On Anger' (probably written during Caligula's reign, A.D. 37-41)

'The priests of Astarte roamed from village to village, carrying their sacred image on an ass's back, and at every halt attracted the gaping rustics with the strains of their flutes, danced in a circle round the goddess with their hair dripping with unguents, cut themselves with knives and swords, and dashed their own blood around them, handing finally a cap from rank to rank for the pence, figs, or crusts of the admiring spectators.'[1]

It is not easy to estimate the part played by Christianity in checking such practices as these, and in combating and arresting the worst evils of the times. The early Christian missionaries may have owed something to the prior influence of the Stoic philosophy, which had done much to undermine the most foolish errors of paganism, and to sow in men's minds feelings of doubt and apprehension regarding the truth of many of the doctrines to which they had been accustomed to yield the most implicit belief.[2] But the Stoic philosophy made its chief appeal to educated people; it had little influence on the poor, among whom Christianity made great headway.

In Greece, the writings of Euripides, Plato, Aristotle and others had shaken the old polytheistic religion to its very foundations. Indeed, it would hardly be an exaggeration to say that it had been almost killed by the ridicule of the philosophers, but no adequate substitute had taken its place; Philosophy appealed only to the intellectual few; Judaism was too racial and exclusive; Christianity was saved from the possibility of such a fate by the genius of Paul (or Saul), a Jew of Tarsus in Cilicia, probably the greatest missionary who has ever lived.

Paul so adapted and explained the Christian religion that it seemed to include the essentials of all the religions with which it came into contact, in addition to certain peculiar

[1] *History of the Romans under the Empire* (Merivale), pub. Longmans.

[2] Thus Seneca wrote that God does not dwell in temples of wood or stone, that He is no respecter of rank or condition, that He does not delight in the blood of victims, and that to serve Him truly is to be like unto Him.

merits of its own, such as the respect which it accorded to women and the certainty of freedom beyond the grave which it offered to slaves. Thus, as he himself says, he became 'all things to all men, that perchance he might gain some'. To disciples of the philosophers

'St. Paul would show that the Unknown God who figured as a dim shadow in their philosophical treatises, the Omnipotent Being who loved Righteousness, was in very truth the God he had come to preach to them. Others would perhaps be initiates in the mysteries of Isis or Cybele. To such St. Paul would offer mysteries or, to use our own word, sacraments, far more impressive and convincing than their own. In place of the vague and shadowy man-god Horus, a being without place, time, or character, on whose resurrection they pinned the hope of their own resurrection and future salvation, he could offer Christ who had lived and died within their own lifetimes; whose resurrection had been acclaimed by his followers immediately after his death ; whose life and character was the evidence of his divinity and the pattern for his followers.'[1]

Paul was a man of tireless activities, which took him not only to the cities of Asia Minor—Antioch, where the Gentile Church was born, and Ephesus, where was a famous temple to the goddess Diana—but also to the wilder and more barbarous regions—to Phrygia, Pamphylia, and Galatia—then across the Hellespont to Philippi, Thessalonica, Macedonia, Athens, and Corinth, and finally to Rome itself, where, according to a tradition which cannot be substantiated, he was one of the martyrs who suffered during the persecution initiated by the Emperor Nero. That his lot was often a hard and difficult one we know from the terse and graphic account which he has himself given us :

'Of the Jews five times received I forty stripes save one. Thrice was I beaten with rods, once was I stoned, thrice I suffered shipwreck, a night and a day I have been in the deep ; in journey-

[1] *A Short History of Our Religion* (Somervell).

ings often, in perils of waters, in perils of robbers, in perils by mine own countrymen, in perils by the heathen, in perils in the city, in perils in the wilderness, in perils in the sea, in perils among false brethren; in weariness and painfulness, in watchings often, in hunger and thirst, in fastings often, in cold and nakedness.'[1]

One of the most brilliant Christian writers of the present century writes:

'To the historian there must always be something astounding in the magnitude of the task he set himself, and in his enormous success. The future history of the civilized world for two thousand years, perhaps for all time, was determined by his missionary journeys and his hurried writings. It is impossible to guess what would have become of Christianity if he had never lived; we cannot even be sure that the religion of Europe would be called by the name of Christ. That stupendous achievement seems to have been due to an almost unique practical insight into the essential factors of a very complex and difficult situation. We watch him with breathless interest steering the vessel which carried the Christian Church and its fortunes through a narrow channel full of sunken rocks and shoals. With unerring instinct he avoids them all and brings the ship, not into smooth water, but into the open sea, out of that perilous strait.'[2]

It is interesting to compare the theology which Paul eventually led the Church to adopt with that of Peter, the other great apostle of the early Christian Church. Peter thought of the Crucifixion of Jesus as a defeat, wiped out by the great victory of the Resurrection. Paul spoke and wrote of it as an example of redemption through sacrifice. God had endured the pains of death so that he might triumph over death, not for himself alone but for all humanity. Such an interpretation would appeal to those who believed in the mysteries of Isis, a pagan cult which succeeded for a time in maintaining itself against Christianity. One of the chief

[1] 2 Corinthians, xi. 24–7.
[2] Dean Inge, *Outspoken Essays* (First Series).

features in the mysteries was the resurrection of the slain god Osiris, the husband of Isis.

Although Christianity was in origin a Jewish religion, its spread was fatal to the position of Jews in Christian countries. Not a single Christian people has kept itself free from the reproach of inhumanity to the Jews. The Christian emperors of Rome and of the Eastern Empire adopted methods of repression against them. Marriages between Jews and Christians were prohibited under pain of death; the number of synagogues was curtailed; and in A.D. 537 Justinian declared Jews to be absolutely ineligible for any honour whatsoever. In the Middle Ages they were persecuted in every Christian country where they settled. This was partly because Jews were lenders of money, a trade which was the only one permitted to them by their Christian rulers. The lending of money, now universally performed by banks, was and is an economic necessity, but the doctrines of the Church forbade it to Christians, though it was forced upon the Jews. Partly also the continual persecution of the Jews was due to a widespread conviction that descendants of those who crucified Christ must be monsters of cruelty and moral depravity. This view is clearly expressed by Shakespeare in the character of Shylock in *The Merchant of Venice*. In modern times there have been Jewish 'pogroms' in Russia and Poland and in all the lands that the Nazis controlled between 1933 and 1945. But despite persecution the Jewish race has persisted, and the debt of civilization to its members is very great. Jews had a large share in the restoration of learning and in the cultivation of science during the Renascence. Through them many Greek writers, who had been translated into Arabic, were retranslated into various European languages and made accessible to the universities of the West. Through them medicine was revived, to become the parent of physical science in general. Their schools at Montpellier in France, Salerno in Italy, and Toledo, Cordova, and

TO THE JEWS

Seville in Spain abounded in men of learning and skill. In most of the civilized countries of to-day, Jews have risen to high position. Every department of learning, science, and philosophy has had Jews among its most eminent exponents. England, France, and Italy have all had prominent statesmen of Jewish origin (e.g. Disraeli, Crèmieux, Luzatti.) One of the persons mainly responsible for the overthrow of the Russian Empire, the last great power to persecute them, was a Jew;[1] so too was the first High Commissioner of Palestine,[2] where Hebrew along with English and Arabic has been declared an official language.

'It is the marvel of history that this little people, beset and despised by all the earth for ages, maintains its solidarity unimpaired. Unique among all the peoples of the earth, it has come undoubtedly to the present day from the most distant antiquity. Forty, perhaps fifty, centuries rest upon this venerable contemporary of Egypt, Chaldea, and Troy. The Hebrew defied the Pharaohs ; with the sword of Gideon he smote the Midianite ; in Jephthah the children of Ammon. The purple chariot bands of Assyria went back from his gates humbled and diminished. Babylon, indeed, tore him from his ancient seats and led him captive by strange waters, but not for long. He saw the Hellenic flower bud, bloom, and wither upon the soil of Greece. He saw the wolf of Rome suckled upon the banks of the Tiber, then prowl, ravenous for dominion, to the ends of the earth, until paralysis and death laid hold upon his savage sinews. At last Israel was scattered over the length and breadth of the earth. In every kingdom of the modern world there has been a Jewish element.'[3]

[1] i.e. Trotsky.
[2] Sir Herbert Samuel (High Commissioner, 1920–5).
[3] *The Jews* (Hosmer), Story of the Nations Series, Fisher Unwin.

APPENDIX I

Some important dates in Ancient History

B.C.

3400 [1] Menes united Upper and Lower Egypt and founded the First Egyptian Dynasty.

3000–2500 [1] The Pyramid Age in Egypt.

2750 [1] The Sumerian Empire overthrown by Sargon I.

2100 [1] Hammurabi conquered Babylon and founded an Amorite Empire.

2000 Copper in general use in Europe.

1750 The Shang Dynasty founded in China.

1600 Cretan civilization at its zenith.

1600–1150 (approx.) The period of the Egyptian Empire.

1375–1358 Akhnaton, the world's first idealist, ruler of Egypt.

1400–1200 Settlement of Palestine by the Jews.

1200–800 (approx.) Probable date of the Rigveda.

1125 The Shang succeeded by the Chu Dynasty in China.

1000 The Palace of Cnossos destroyed, probably by the Greeks.
The Greeks firmly established in Greece, Asia Minor, and the Aegean Islands.
(approx.) Zoroaster founded his religion.

814 The building of Carthage.

753 Traditional date for the founding of Rome.

745 Tiglath Pileser III founded the Assyrian Empire.

722 The kingdom of Israel conquered by the Assyrians.

700 (approx.) The Homeric songs collected into a cycle and committed to writing.

670 Egypt conquered by the Assyrians.

624 Draco codified the Laws of Athens.

612 The Assyrian Empire overthrown by the Chaldeans.

600–500 (approx.) The Age of the Tyrants in Greece.

594 The Laws of Solon.

586 Nebuchadnezzar destroyed Jerusalem and carried the people away captive to Babylon.

550 (approx.) Buddha and Confucius lived.

539 The Chaldean Empire overthrown and the Persian Empire founded by Cyrus the Great.

525 The Persians conquered Egypt.

[1] Approximate dates, on which there is disagreement among experts.

APPENDIX I

B.C.
- 490 The battle of Marathon.
- 490–226 Conquest of Italy by the Romans.
- 480–479 The defeat of the great Persian invasion of Greece under Xerxes. Thermopylae (480).
- 460–430 (approx.) The Age of Pericles.
- 431–404 The Peloponnesian War.
- 404–371 The Ascendancy of Sparta.
- 338 The Macedonians under Philip overthrew the Greeks at Chaeronea.
- 334–323 The conquests of Alexander the Great.
- 264 The First Punic War began.
- 264–227 King Asoka reigned in India.
- 246–210 Shi-Hwang-ti reigned in China.
- 218–202 The Second Punic War (The Hannibalic War).
- 146 The destruction of Carthage and of Corinth by the Romans.
- 133 Death of Tiberius Gracchus.
- 121 Death of Caius Gracchus.
- 89 ALL Italians became Roman citizens.
- 58–50 Julius Caesar conquered Gaul.
- 48 Caesar defeated Pompey at Pharsalus.
- 44 Julius Caesar assassinated.
- 31 Mark Antony defeated by Octavius Caesar at Actium.
- 27 Octavius Caesar (Augustus) made 'princeps'.

A.D.
- 117 Death of the Emperor Trajan. Roman Empire at its greatest extent.
- 180 Death of Marcus Aurelius followed by unrest and disorder in the Roman Empire.
- 313 Constantine announced that Christianity was to be tolerated everywhere throughout the Roman Empire.
- 395 The Empire divided between the two sons of Theodosius.
- 410 Rome sacked by the Visigoths under Alaric.
- 445–453 The invasions of the Huns under Attila.
- 455 Rome sacked by the Vandals.
- 476 The end of the Roman Empire.

PART II
FROM THE BEGINNING OF THE MIDDLE AGES TO THE PRESENT DAY

THE INTERIOR OF SANTA SOPHIA AT CONSTANTINOPLE

XVI

EUROPE AFTER THE FALL OF ROME

WITH the fall of Rome and the break-up of the Empire, civilization enters upon a period lasting for about a thousand years to which the term Middle Ages is generally applied. It is a period marked in Europe by the operation of certain great forces, of which the chief are feudalism (from the ninth to the fourteenth century) ; the development from the tenth century onwards of town life, which had been seriously retarded by the fall of Rome ; increased intercourse with the East ; and the conception of a common superior whose decisions should be binding upon states. At the beginning of the ninth century there was an attempted revival of the Roman Empire under the Frankish king Charles the Great, who claimed that universal supremacy which the Romans had at one time imposed, and which to most medieval minds was quite a reasonable proposition. The weakness of Charlemagne's successors and the rising power of the Christian Church gave the Popes an opportunity to assert a rival claim to world dominion, which was strikingly manifested in such events as the Crusades, the control of learning, and the international character of the Roman Catholic religion. Belief in the theory of universal supremacy was, however, rudely dispelled by the Reformation, which became a great international conflict in which popes and temporal princes took rival sides, and the power of the Emperor was exposed in all its futility and ineffectiveness. The Reformation also, together with the Renascence and the further stimulus given to men's minds by the great geographical discoveries of the fifteenth and sixteenth centuries, created or revived a sense of individual liberty, which helped to promote the growth of national consciousness. But for centuries after the fall of Rome there were few, if any, indications of that important event being anything other than an unmitigated evil. The period of chaos to which it gave rise gave the world an excellent opportunity of learning by practical experience the good points of Roman civilization at its best. For some years, however, the evil days were averted, mainly because of the influence of Theodoric, King of the East Goths, who succeeded to the overlordship of Italy after he had defeated and killed Odoacer in the year 493. Theodoric was one of the greatest of the barbarian chieftains. He had spent ten years of his life at Constantinople, and he greatly admired Roman laws and institutions, which he did his best to preserve. He employed both Romans and Goths, caused many beautiful buildings to be erected in Ravenna, which was his capital, and encouraged learning. He put the name of the Emperor at Constantinople on the coins which he issued, and did all in his power to placate that ruler, even though he was not really subordinate to him.

At this time the Franks were establishing themselves in Gaul, and the West Goths in Spain; the Burgundians in the Rhone valley, and the Vandals in North Africa appeared to be fairly secure. Marriage alliances were concluded between the various reigning houses, and it seemed as if Europe was really settling down after the turmoil and stress of the barbarian invasions. But appearances were deceptive. Western Europe was just about entering upon a period which is known as the Dark Ages, a period of constant warfare, and one in which learning sank to a very low ebb. One of the most distinguished of the counsellors of Theodoric was Cassiodorus, who lived from 490 to 585. He certainly laboured incessantly in the cause of learning, even though some of his work is disfigured by incorrectness. He established two monasteries on his ancestral estate at Squillace in the South of Italy, where learning could be acquired, profane as well as sacred, and whence it might be transmitted to subsequent generations. He collected valuable manuscripts which his

JUSTINIAN

monks had to copy, and superintended the translation of many Greek works into Latin. He also wrote a sort of encyclopaedia of sacred and profane literature, part of which dealt with the seven liberal arts—grammar, arithmetic, logic, geometry, rhetoric, music, and astronomy. The world certainly owes Cassiodorus much for saving many of the great writings of the ancient Greeks and Romans at a time when they were in danger of being swept away by a tide of barbarism. Another sixth-century writer who deserves to be remembered is Gregory of Tours (538 to 594), the historian of the Franks. He had an intimate knowledge of contemporary events, and although not always successful he does try to be impartial. He is certainly inclined to excuse the crimes of kings like Clovis, who protected the Church, and his grammar is often bad, but in spite of his shortcomings he is an attractive writer. He neither conceals nor invents anything, and his narrative powers have earned for him the title of 'the Herodotus of the barbarians'.

In the meantime the Eastern Empire had been experiencing a period of prosperity under Justinian, one of its greatest rulers, who began to rule the year after Theodoric died (527), and did not die until 565. There were at this time great architects in the Byzantine [1] Empire, and Justinian used them to build the magnificent church of St. Sophia in Constantinople. Architects still build churches in the Byzantine style. An example is the Roman Catholic cathedral at Westminster. Justinian also reconquered North Africa from the Vandals and Italy from the Goths, founded a university, and codified the law. Historians are generally agreed that the great contribution of Rome to mankind is the idea of society founded on law. When Justinian became Emperor the condition of the laws was not what it should be. They had never been collected and thoroughly sifted, and there were many inconsistencies and contradictions among them; consequently

[1] So called after Byzantium, the ancient name of Constantinople.

262 EUROPE AFTER THE FALL OF ROME

the administration of justice was very difficult. To remedy this, Justinian appointed a commission to collect, harmonize, and arrange the laws of the Empire. The opinions, explanations, and decisions of famous judges and lawyers were also collected, so as to guide those who administered the law, and a treatise on the principles of Roman law was compiled for the use of students.

Justinian's expulsion of the Goths from Italy was hardly a good thing for that country. Immediately after his death it was overrun by the Lombards, the last of the great German tribes to establish themselves within the former Roman Empire. The Lombards were a savage race, much inferior to the Goths, and a considerable number of them were still pagan. They first occupied the region north of the river Po (Lombardy) and then extended their conquests southward, pillaging and massacring as they went, but they were never able to conquer the whole of Italy. Rome, Ravenna, and Sicily continued to be imperial territory. The Lombards eventually lost their wildness and adopted the language and customs of those whom they conquered; their kingdom lasted for more than two hundred years, from 568 to 774, when it was overthrown by Charlemagne.

More important and more extensive than the conquests of any other German people were those of the Franks. Probably this was due to the fact that the Franks, unlike the Goths, the Vandals, and the Lombards, did not sever their connexion with Germany when they proceeded in their search for new territory. Their plan was to conquer by degrees the lands around them, and however far they went they remained in constant touch with their fellow barbarians behind them. Thus they retained the warlike vigour which was lost by those tribes who allowed themselves to be enervated by the luxuries of Roman civilization. In 486, under their great king Clovis,[1] they defeated a Roman force which

---

[1] This name ultimately grew into Louis.

THE FRANKISH CONQUESTS

was sent against them, and they soon extended their control over Gaul as far as the Pyrenees. Clovis also enlarged his empire on the east by the conquest of the Alemanni, a German tribe who lived in the region of the Black Forest, and on the south-east by the conquest of the Burgundians, another German people. The battle in which the Alemanni were defeated is notable because it was responsible for the conversion of Clovis to Christianity. At a time during the fighting when the day seemed to be going against the Franks, the king, whose wife was already a Christian, swore that he would also become a Christian if Jesus Christ would help his arms to victory. The successful issue of the battle was regarded as an answer to his prayer, and accordingly Clovis and three thousand of his warriors were baptized. Gregory of Tours henceforward writes of him as God's chosen instrument for the support and promulgation of the Christian faith —a somewhat remarkable instrument, for Clovis was cruel and unscrupulous to a high degree. He died in Paris in 511, and his four sons divided his possessions among themselves. For over a hundred years from this time the history of the Franks is a record of constant wars, fratricidal strifes, and many murders—but even these did not stop the expansion of their territories. The kings who followed Clovis were successful in asserting their authority over practically all the lands which are now known as France, Belgium, and Holland, as well as over a considerable part of Western Germany. The people who settled in the country which is to-day called France gradually adopted the language of the conquered, a conversational form of Latin much simpler than book Latin. The same process was going on in Spain and Italy, with similar divergences from written Latin—and so we get the formation of the French, Spanish, Portuguese, and Italian languages. The northern Franks who did not penetrate far into the Empire, the Germans who remained in Germany, and also those who settled in Scandinavia and in England did not give up their native tongues. Accordingly, while French, Spanish, Portuguese, and Italian are in their origin Latin languages, Dutch, German, Danish, Swedish, and English are Germanic.

One great body or institution—the Christian Church—derived undoubted benefit from the unsettled condition of Europe after the fall of the Roman Empire. Even before this the power of the Church had been considerable. St. Ambrose had made the Emperor Theodosius do public penance in the cathedral of Milan, and ever since the time when Leo the Great had persuaded Attila the Hun to withdraw his armies from the very gates of Rome many began to look to the Bishop of Rome as their natural protector against the violence of the barbarians, for even the barbarians feared and respected the power of the Church. Undoubtedly one of the chief reasons for this was the Christian doctrine of the life after death. The educated Greeks and Romans of the classical period, when they thought of the next life at all, thought of it as a shadowy uninteresting kind of existence, where there was no possibility of pleasure. It was therefore to every one's interest to make the best of this world, to enjoy the good things of earth, and to avoid excess and everything which endangered happiness. Christianity, on the other hand, taught that man's brief existence on earth was infinitely less important, and, for the good, infinitely less happy than the life after death. With some, this belief became so intense that they shut themselves up in monasteries so as to render themselves more fit for the life which was to come, or escape some of the punishments which their sins had merited. The barbarians were taught that their fate in the next world depended upon the Church. Its ministers were never weary of pointing out that one of two alternatives faced everybody after death—eternal bliss in heaven, or eternal torment in hell. Only those who had been baptized into the Christian faith could hope to reach heaven. But baptism washed away

GROWTH OF CHURCH INFLUENCE

only past sins ; it did not prevent a relapse into new sins. In order to avoid that, constant communion with the Church, respect and honour for its ministers, and gifts and alms according to each man's means were recommended. The continued increase of such gifts and the growing weakness of the temporal rulers enormously increased the power of the Church. Churchmen submitted with good grace to the dictates of an emperor like Constantine, who had made Christianity the state religion, and who had, since his conversion, shown a commendable zeal in stamping out paganism. But they entertained feelings neither of respect nor of gratitude towards the new rulers who sprang up when the Roman Empire fell to pieces. Consequently they began to claim immunity from government control, and then to assume the functions of government themselves when the weakness of the kings had caused many of these functions to fall into abeyance. Thus the Church was, by means of threats or persuasion, frequently able to preserve order when no one else could. It saw that contracts were kept, the wills of the dead carried out, and marriage obligations observed. It dispensed charity, protected widows and orphans, and promoted what little education there was.

The early Christian church buildings were constructed on the model of the basilicas or public halls of the Romans. These buildings were to be found near the market-place in every Roman city of any consequence, and in them townspeople used to meet to transact business, or judges to hear cases. Their roofs were generally supported by long rows of columns, and there were sometimes two rows on each side of the main row, forming a sort of nave and two side aisles. The early Christian churches were constructed in the same fashion, and were actually called basilicas. They were generally plain and unattractive on the outside, although frequently very beautiful within. The church of Santa Maria Maggiore in Rome, built about a century after the time of Constantine the Great, gives one an excellent idea of a Christian basilica, with its fine rows of columns and its exquisite mosaic decorations.

Almost from the beginning of the Christian era, the Bishop of Rome was regarded as the most important of the Christian bishops. The majesty of Rome, the fact that it was the capital of the world, had something to do with this belief, but there was also the connexion of Peter and Paul, the greatest of the Christian missionaries, with the city. The New Testament has references to Paul's presence in Rome, and there were few Christians who did not believe that Peter was the first Bishop of Rome. He too was the apostle who was entrusted with the keys of the kingdom of heaven, and there were many, like the English king Oswiu, who embraced the Roman Catholic form of the Christian religion lest when they reached the gates of heaven Peter should refuse them admission. It was not, however, until the time of Leo the Great (440–61) that the supremacy of the Bishop of Rome over all other bishops was definitely declared. In 445 the Emperor Valentinian, at Leo's suggestion, made such a declaration, and commanded that all bishops throughout the West should accept as law all that the Bishop of Rome approved, and that any bishop refusing to obey a summons to Rome should be forced to do so by the imperial governor. Six years later, a council which met at Chalcedon asserted that new Rome on the Bosphorus (Constantinople) should have equal privileges with old Rome on the Tiber, the second rank among the patriarchates, and patriarchal jurisdiction over Pontus, Asia, and Thrace. The Western Church never admitted this canon, and the Eastern or Greek Church gradually separated from the Western or Roman Church.

The title 'pope' was originally given to all bishops and even to priests. Gregory VII (1073–85) was the first to declare explicitly that in future the name should be used for the Bishop of Rome alone. Of the early popes probably

THE RULE OF ST. BENEDICT 267

the greatest was Gregory the Great (590-604), who is of particular interest to English people because it was he who sent Augustine to convert their ancestors to Christianity. Gregory was the son of a rich Roman senator, and like Gautama Buddha and Francis of Assisi, while yet a young man he abandoned his rich ways of living and became an ascetic. With his considerable fortune he founded seven monasteries, and over one of them he presided himself. He was the first monk to become Pope; he ruled in Rome like an independent king, organizing armies and making treaties, and he was chiefly responsible for keeping the Lombards out of Central Italy. But his greatest work was, perhaps, his fostering of missionary enterprise. He recovered Spain and England for the Roman Catholic Church and prepared the way for the subsequent conversion of Germany. 'When he died, in 604, he left the Roman See exalted to a pitch of greatness which it had never before known, revered by all the Teutonic peoples of Europe, and half freed from its allegiance to the rulers of Constantinople.'[1]

In his work of converting the heathen Gregory relied chiefly upon monks. At this time the monasteries were beginning to exercise that influence which makes them so prominent a feature of the life of the Middle Ages. They first developed on a large scale in the South of Egypt during the fourth century, whence the idea quickly spread to Asia Minor and Europe. In the sixth century there were so many monks in Western Europe that it became necessary to establish definite rules and obligations which should regulate their activities. The constitution which Benedict drew up for the monastery of Monte Cassino, of which he was head, was so wise and so adapted to the needs of the time that it was rapidly accepted by other monasteries, and gradually became the 'rule' according to which all the Western monks lived. St. Benedict is one of the central figures in the history of

[1] Oman, *The Dark Ages* (published by Rivington).

monasticism. In some respects his career recalls that of Gautama Buddha. Like Buddha he was a young man of good family, who started his religious career by a life of austerity and fasting, but eventually he, too, realized the futility of such conduct, and when many years later he heard of a recluse who had chained himself to a rock in a narrow cave, his message to him was: 'Break thy chain, for the true servant of God is chained not to rocks by iron, but to righteousness by Christ.' When he first went to Monte Cassino, which is half way between Rome and Naples, he found a temple of Apollo there, and a sacred grove where the people of the countryside were wont to do honour to the pagan god. It was with difficulty that he persuaded the peasants to destroy the temple and cut down the grove. Benedict did not found an order in the same sense as Dominic and Francis of Assisi afterwards founded orders, but those monks who followed his rule are from the thirteenth century onwards commonly spoken of as belonging to the Benedictine Order.

The Rule of St. Benedict is as important as a State constitution. It provided for the government of monasteries and also for the kind of life which the monks were to lead. At the head of each monastery there was to be an abbot who was to be elected by the brethren, and who was to be obeyed without question [1] by all the monks when obedience did not involve the committing of sin. Before any one was allowed to become a monk he had to undergo a period of probation, called the novitiate, so as to establish his fitness for the monastic life. All monks were expected to practise poverty, chastity, and obedience, which later became formal vows. They were not allowed to marry, and they were to possess no personal property. Benedict was a strong believer in

[1] The abbot was, however, to consult *all* the monks, even the youngest, on matters of great importance to the monastery. On minor matters he was bidden to consult a few of the elder monks. But in neither case was he obliged to follow the advice given.

ST. BENEDICT

In the margin a beggar with wooden leg and crutch

the value of hard work. His monks were not to live in idleness. In addition to frequent prayer, they were expected to do the cooking and washing of the monastery, and to raise such grain and vegetables as were necessary. They also had to find time for reading and teaching, and the weaklings among them were probably employed in copying books.

The monastery or abbey in which the monks lived was built around a central court, on all four sides of which was a covered walk known as the cloisters. On the north side was the church, which always faced west; on the south, opposite the church, was the refectory or dining-room, near which was a lavatory where the monks could wash their hands before meals; on the west were store-rooms for provisions; and on the east the dormitory where the monks slept. This always adjoined the church, for the Benedictine monks had seven services a day to attend, and one of them was in the early hours of the morning—sometime between 1.30 and 3 o'clock, when it would be necessary for them to leave their beds for a short time. This was not so great a hardship as it might appear, for the monks had already had seven or eight hours unbroken slumber, unless it happened to be very hot weather, when they were allowed a siesta after the midday meal as a compensation for being kept a little later than usual at their daily tasks before being allowed to retire for the evening. The rule of St. Benedict was not harsh. The monks were allowed proper clothes, and sufficient food and sleep. The fact that they were denied flesh meat, whatever it might be in northern countries, was certainly no hardship in the South of Europe. The Benedictine monasteries were as far as possible self-supporting. Consequently, just outside the buildings surrounding the cloisters, there would be found a garden, an orchard, a mill, a fish-pond, and fields for raising grain. There were also a hospital for the sick, a guest-house for the reception of pilgrims and poor people, and in the greater

THE CLOISTERS, GLOUCESTER CATHEDRAL
Showing the lavatorium where the monks washed

monasteries special quarters where kings or great nobles could be entertained.

The influence of the Benedictine monks upon the history of Europe is so great as to be incalculable. Twenty-four popes are claimed to have been chosen from their ranks, and nearly five thousand archbishops and bishops. They have produced thousands of writers, some of them of very great distinction. Their work as missionaries was of the utmost value to the Roman Catholic Church—St. Augustine and his monks were Benedictines, and, after Christianity had been firmly established in England, English Benedictines—Wilfrid, Willibrord, and others—evangelized Friesland and Holland, and another, Winfrid or Boniface, founded and organized the German Church and became Archbishop of Mayence. Other Benedictine missionaries went still farther afield to the Scandinavian countries and to Poland and Prussia. The monasteries which sprang up on the scenes of the labours of all these monks became centres of civilization on account of the object lessons which they presented in organized work, in farming, and in such industries as masonry and glass-making. They were also seats of learning at a time when learning was little if at all valued by the mass of the people. One of the greatest of the early Benedictine scholars was an Englishman named Baeda, often called the Venerable Bede (673–735), a monk of Jarrow, in Northumbria, who wrote an admirable history of the English Church—our chief source of information about the period with which it deals. It was a period of unrest and general insecurity throughout Western Europe, and the monasteries were almost the only places where literature could be written, where ancient manuscripts were preserved, and where there was reasonable assurance of a humane and well-ordered life.

XVII

THE RISE AND SPREAD OF ISLAM

THE religion of Islam originated in Arabia, a country which from time immemorial has been inhabited by nomadic tribes, over whom at various times a somewhat shadowy authority has been exerted by Egypt, Persia, Macedonia, and Rome. This country is, for the most part, sparsely populated and thinly cultivated. Among its important towns are Medina and Mecca, both of them on the main caravan route from Syria. Mecca, from early times, has been a holy city containing a temple called the Kaaba, the most important part of which is a black meteoric stone, which was at one time regarded as the chief of the many gods whom the Arabs worshipped. During certain months of the year all the tribes of Arabia observed a truce from the struggles for power in which they frequently indulged, and then pilgrims flocked to Mecca, and after their religious ceremonies had been duly performed it was their custom to hold contests of musical and literary skill, a practice which resembles the Olympic festivals of the ancient Greeks.

It was in the holy city of Mecca that Mohammed, the Prophet, was born in the year 570. Mohammed was the son of very poor parents. His mother died soon after his birth and he was brought up first by his grandfather and then by his uncle who was a merchant in Mecca. When he was about twenty-four years old he entered the service of a certain Khadija, the widow of a rich merchant, and eventually married her. It is probable that he accompanied her caravans to Syria and Palestine, and so became acquainted with the monotheistic beliefs of the Jews and the Christians. As a young man he turned away from the idolatry practised by his fellow Arabs and spent a great deal of his time in contemplation. But it was not until he was forty years of age that a new religion, which meant the worship of one god, was revealed to him in a vision by the archangel Gabriel. At first his only converts were his wife Khadija, his adopted son Ali, his friend Abu Bakr, and a slave named Zeid, and the authorities at Mecca treated him with indulgent contempt, but when the number of his disciples began to increase they became alarmed. The city was so sacred that no blood could be shed in it, and other methods, such as confiscation of property and the boycott, had to be adopted against the Muslims. When the people of Medina heard of this persecution of the Muslims in Mecca, they invited the Prophet and his followers to come to Medina and settle there. At first he sent some of his followers to do the work of missionizing, and did not follow himself until his enemies in Mecca, alarmed at the conversion of Medina, decided to violate the sanctity of their city and kill the Prophet. Mohammed's flight to Medina is known as the Hijira. It took place on 24 September 622, and was taken by his followers as the beginning of a new era, the Year One as all true Muslims reckon time.

Mohammed was enthusiastically received by the people of Medina, and there immediately followed a series of wars, or rather skirmishes, between them and the people of Mecca, ending in 630 in the complete victory of Mohammed, who entered the town of Mecca as its master after a treaty with its inhabitants which involved a little compromise, such as returning the sacred stone of the Kaaba to its hereditary keepers. When pilgrims go to Mecca today they still walk round the Kaaba seven times, and on each occasion they kiss the black stone, which is fixed in the outside wall at the south-east corner. After the fall of Mecca the power of Mohammed was extended, until when he died in 632 he was the master of the whole of Arabia. Mohammed never claimed divinity. He was merely the Prophet of Allah, the divinely chosen interpreter of his will, and because of that he demanded

THE KORAN

unswerving obedience from his followers, and from all who became subject to his authority. He showed great courage and enlightenment in his curbing of blood feuds in Arabia, and in his suppression of the long established practice of infanticide. His teachings and his precepts are to be found in the Holy Koran, the Sacred Book of Islam. It has 114 suras or chapters of varying length. Each chapter save one starts with the words, 'In the name of Allah, the Compassionate, the Merciful'. It is unquestionably one of the most widely read and most influential books in the world. All good Muslims regard its authority as absolute.

The Holy Koran is, for the most part, a collection of the sayings of Mohammed, written down by his disciples as they heard them from his lips, and collected into a volume shortly after his death. Unlike the New Testament of which many versions exist, there is only one version of the Holy Koran. The original Arabic text has been carefully preserved and all true Muslims believe that it consists of the very words of God as revealed to his Prophet. It contains the chief beliefs of the new religion as well as the rules which are to regulate the lives of all good Muslims. The Holy Koran teaches reverence for one God, 'the lord of the worlds, the merciful and compassionate', and admits that Abraham, Moses, and Jesus were great prophets (but none of them as great as Mohammed, the last Prophet, to whom a complete revelation had been made); it enjoins honour to parents, charity towards the poor and afflicted, and justice towards all men; and it bids men abstain from strong drink altogether. Like the Christian religion, it speaks confidently of a life after death and of a last judgement, when all men shall receive the reward of their earthly actions.

Islam was a much simpler religion than the religion of the Christian Church of the Middle Ages; it was easily understood and it contained no doctrines likely to confuse and perplex men's minds. It permitted every man to have four wives provided he was able to support them. It did not provide for a priesthood and it was not obscured and overcast by a multitude of ceremonies. The Muslim mosque is a house of prayer and a place for reading the Holy Koran; it has no altars and no images or pictures of any kind; its walls are adorned with passages from the Holy Koran, and rich rugs cover the floors. Many of the mosques are very beautiful, with colonnaded courtyards, exquisite mosaic work, and lovely stained-glass windows. They have one or more minarets, from which an official called the muezzin calls the people to prayer five times a day, for every true Muslim is expected to pray just before sunrise, just after noon, just before and after sunset, and when the day has closed. In addition there are four other things which he is expected to do. He must recite daily the simple creed, 'There is no god but God (Allah), and Mohammed is His Prophet'; he must give alms to the poor; he must make the pilgrimage to Mecca at least once during his lifetime; and he must fast during the month Ramadan, when he is allowed neither to eat nor drink from sunrise to sunset, for it was in this month that the archangel Gabriel came down from heaven to reveal the Holy Koran to Mohammed. A Muslim must also always be prepared to fight for his faith and for God. If *Jihad* (holy war) is declared he cannot refuse to fight for Islam.

When Mohammed died his place as the leader of Islam was taken by Abu Bakr. There were some who thought that Ali, the adopted son and son-in-law of the Prophet, should succeed, but the elective principle ultimately prevailed, and the most capable man was chosen. Abu Bakr had good organizing ability, and considerable strength of character. He took the title of Caliph, which means successor, and one of his first exploits was to dispatch the expeditions which led to the defeat of the Byzantine armies and the conquest of Syria for Islam. Then, with a faith which is extraordinary, he deliberately set himself the task of converting the world to Islam.

MOSLEM ARCHITECTURE. The great mosque in Kairouan, North Africa
Photograph by Sir Alan Cobham

Abu Bakr died in 634, but the work which he had begun was worthily carried on by his successor Omar, the brother-in-law of Mohammed. It was under Omar that the chief conquests of the Muslims took place. Before he died in 643 Syria, Mesopotamia, all the Euphrates valley, Babylon, Assyria, Persia, and Egypt had been conquered. These astonishing successes, while mainly due to the resolution and efficiency of the Muslim armies, could never have been achieved had it not been for the weakness and futility of the powers they opposed. Wherever the Muslims went they invariably offered their foes a choice of three courses: conversion, tribute, or the sword. Jerusalem was given special terms. There Christians were to be tolerated so long as they paid a poll-tax, and all the churches and relics were left in their possession. After his armies had overrun North Africa as far as Tripoli, Omar thought that they had conquered enough, but his efforts to put a limit to the spread of Islam failed. Under his successors it was carried to the confines of India and the river Oxus; the Turkish tribes in Central Asia were reached and converted; early in the eighth century Muslim armies conquered the whole of North Africa and crossed over into Spain, which rapidly became theirs; and France would almost certainly have followed suit had it not been for a defeat at the hands of Charles Martel, the chief minister of the Frankish king, at Tours in 732. It is doubtful whether the victory of Charles and his barbarous soldiers is such a good thing as many historians are apt to imagine. If the Muslims had been allowed to settle in Southern France, they would almost certainly have developed science and art much more rapidly than did the Franks. The kingdom which they established and developed in Spain was far greater and more prosperous than the Christian kingdoms to the north of them. Some of the buildings which they erected soon after their arrival still stand, such as the mosque at Cordova, which is now a Roman Catholic cathedral. They built beautiful palaces, laid out

MOORISH ARCHITECTURE IN SPAIN
A corner of the 'Courtyard of the Lions'
in the Alhambra at Granada

charming gardens, and founded a university at Cordova to which even Christians went for instruction. One of their palaces, the Alhambra at Granada, is one of the architectural glories of the world.

Many of the Muslim conquests were achieved despite a certain amount of internal disunion. After the death of Omar, a Meccan named Othman was appointed as his successor. Ali, the son-in-law of the Prophet, was particularly displeased at this election, and he was supported by the men of Medina; in 656 Othman, who was then an old man of eighty, was stoned by a mob in the streets of Medina, chased to his house, and murdered. Ali then became Caliph, only to be himself murdered five years later. The Omayyad dynasty, to which Othman had belonged, was then restored and the capital was moved to Damascus in Syria. In 749 the last of the Omayyad Caliphs was overthrown, and a new dynasty, the Abbasid, so called because its members were descended from Abbas, the uncle of the Prophet, came into power. About ten years later the capital was again shifted, this time to the city of Bagdad on the river Tigris. This probably helped to hasten the political dissolution of the Muslim empire. The religious supremacy of the Caliph of Bagdad was hardly questioned, but it was impossible to rule Africa and Spain from a city so far east. These provinces gradually broke away, until in the tenth century two additional caliphates were established, one at Cairo in Egypt, and the other at Cordova in Spain. The Egyptian Caliphs claimed descent from Fatima, the Prophet's daughter. The Caliphate of Bagdad reached its height under Harun al Rashid (786–809), the hero or villain of many imaginative works.[1] Outwardly his empire was extremely prosperous. Bagdad was a wealthy and beautiful city where schools and colleges abounded; it

---

[1] He is the Harun al Rashid of the *Arabian Nights*. Tennyson wrote a poem about him, and he is one of the chief characters in James Elroy Flecker's play *Hassan*.

STREET SCENE IN OLD BAGDAD

was the centre of a vast commercial traffic; and it attracted poets, philosophers, theologians, doctors, and students from all parts of the civilized world. The army was efficient and loyal, the ministers of state and provincial governors industrious and trustworthy, and the various departments of government clearly defined and well regulated. But there were some distinct elements of weakness. The Caliph had lost the simplicity and directness of the early holders of the office. He had become an Eastern potentate, revelling in luxury, and surrounded by guards, spies, jesters, poets, and dwarfs. The wealthier classes had become irreligious; speculative philosophy was taking the place of the Holy Koran; and so the bond which had held the empire together, the sternness and plainness of the Muslim faith, was visibly weakening. 'For a moment', writes Sir Mark Sykes, 'we stand amazed at the greatness of the Abbasid dominion; then suddenly we realize that it is but as a fair husk enclosing the dust and ashes of dead civilizations.'[1] It began to fall to pieces very soon after the death of Harun al Rashid. The emirs or governors of provinces began to make themselves independent of the Caliph and to rule as kings; in this way Persia, Mesopotamia, Chorassan, and Syria detached themselves, and the Caliph was forced to establish a standing army of mercenaries composed largely of Turks, who were not slow to take advantage of the weakness of their employers. The Seljuk Turks made themselves masters of the eastern provinces, and in 1058 the Caliph summoned their leader to Bagdad, surrendered all his temporal power to him, and made him Sultan of the Muslim world. The Caliph became merely a religious officer; the political power passed entirely into the hands of the Turks.[2]

During the five centuries following the death of the Prophet

[1] *The Caliph's Last Heritage.*
[2] This arrangement lasted until 1258, when the son of the great conqueror Jenghiz Khan put to death the last Caliph of Bagdad.

The Extent of the
MOHAMMEDAN EMPIRE
in 750 A.D.

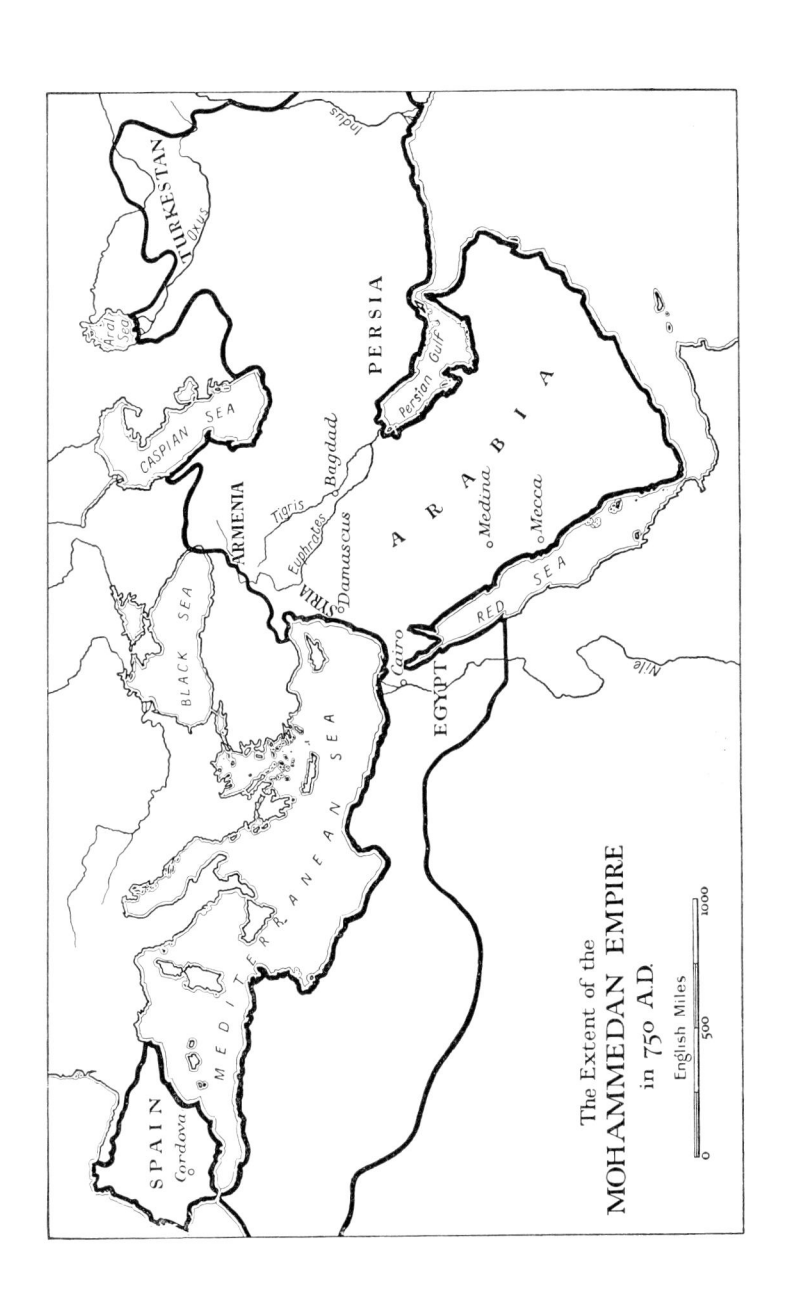

English Miles
0 500 1000

284 THE RISE AND SPREAD OF ISLAM

Mohammed his followers evolved a civilization much superior to anything which existed in Europe at the time. For it they were undoubtedly greatly indebted to the civilizations of Greece and Persia, and perhaps India as well, but they added something of their own to what they received from these sources. The Caliphs owed a very great deal to the wisdom which led them to employ the skilled officials, architects, and scholars of the Byzantine Empire. They were great *patrons* of learning rather than creative geniuses; the debt of subsequent generations to them is hardly the less on that account. They had well-ordered systems of government and good schemes of taxation. They restored the old Roman roads and constructed many new ones so that their empire should be closely knit together. An effective postal system was in operation among them, they made canals and aqueducts, and they developed a beautiful style of architecture characterized by the round arch, the dome, graceful minarets, and rich ornamentation. They founded great universities, which excelled those of Christian Europe for several centuries. The Universities of Bagdad, Cairo, and Cordova were particularly famous. The University of Cairo had as many as twelve thousand students. Great libraries were formed, some containing over a hundred thousand volumes, and all the books were properly catalogued and arranged. The many Christians who studied in the University of Cordova carried culture and learning into the countries from which they came, and the influence of the Spanish universities upon the Universities of Paris, Oxford, and those which were established in Northern Italy must have been considerable. One of the most famous of the Christian students at the University of Cordova was Gerbert, afterwards Pope Silvester II, who did much to introduce the science of mathematics into Europe.

The scientific world owes a great deal to the Muslims. They probably invented the so-called Arabic numerals; algebra is practically their creation; they developed trigonometry, optics, and astronomy; they invented the pendulum; and in medicine they made very remarkable progress. They studied physiology and hygiene; they performed some of the most difficult operations known; they knew how to use anaesthetics; and some of their methods of treating patients are still in use to-day. At a time when in Europe the practice of medicine was practically forbidden by the Church, when religious rites such as exorcizing imaginary devils were regarded as cures for diseases, and when quacks and charlatans abounded, the Muslims had a real science of medicine. One of their greatest physicians was Avicenna (980–1037), who was born near Bokhara, in Turkestan. In literature too the Arabs made important contributions to the world's thought. They had a special fondness for poetry, but their most enduring production is the *Thousand and One Nights* or the *Arabian Nights Entertainments*, which contains many of the most famous stories of all time, such as Ali Baba and the Forty Thieves, Sinbad the Sailor, and Aladdin and the Wonderful Lamp. This collection was got together in Egypt, probably as late as the fifteenth century, but many of the stories are very much older, and were translated into Arabic from Persian when the Caliphs of Bagdad were at the height of their power. They give a vivid idea of Muslim manners and customs. Another important contribution which the Muslims made to the intellectual life of mankind was the art of manufacturing paper. They certainly did not discover this for themselves (they probably learnt it from the Chinese), but they were undoubtedly the means of its introduction into Europe. Before this time books had to be written on papyrus or parchment, but after the Arab conquest of Egypt Europe was cut off from the papyrus supply. Until paper became fairly abundant printing was of very little use, and anything like a widespread system of education was impossible.

The Muslims also showed much skill in matters appertaining to trade and commerce.

286   THE RISE AND SPREAD OF ISLAM

'In manufactures they surpassed the world in variety and beauty of design and perfection of workmanship. They worked in all the metals—gold, silver, copper, bronze, iron, and steel. In textile fabrics they have never been surpassed. They made glass and pottery of the finest quality. They knew the secrets of dyeing. They had many processes of dressing leather and their work was famous throughout Europe. They made tinctures, essences, and syrups. They made sugar from the cane and grew many fine kinds of wine. They practised farming in a scientific way. They had good systems of irrigation. They knew the value of fertilizers. They fitted their crops to the quality of the ground. They excelled in horticulture. They knew how to graft and were able to produce some new varieties of fruits and flowers. They introduced into the West many trees and plants from the East.'[1]

Their commerce was considerable, extending to China and the Indies, to Africa and Russia, and even to the countries around the Baltic Sea. Their caravans went from one end of their empire to the other, and their ships were to be seen on all the known seas of the world. The great fairs which they held at such places as Bagdad, Bokhara, and Samarcand were visited by merchants from all parts of Europe and Asia. The conquests of the Turks were fatal to this fine civilization. The Turks were ignorant fanatics, hostile to science because they thought that it was injurious to religion, and they so effectively destroyed the Arabic civilization in those places where they came into contact with it that 'lands which were once like gardens are now almost like a desert'.[2] Spain was far beyond the orbit of Turkish influence; consequently the Moorish civilization which had taken such firm root there maintained its vigour and power for centuries longer.

[1] *Europe in the Middle Age* (Thatcher and Schwill), pub. Murray.
[2] Ibid.

XVIII

THE EMPIRE OF CHARLES THE GREAT

AT the beginning of the eighth century the King of the Franks had become so weak that most of his important functions were carried out by his chief minister, who was known as the Mayor of the Palace. Twenty years after the Battle of Tours, Pippin the Short, the son and successor of Charles Martel, decided to end this ridiculous arrangement.

A silver denarius of Charlemagne

He therefore deposed the last king of what is known as the Merovingian dynasty, and founded the Carolingian dynasty with himself as its first representative. Before doing so he obtained the consent and approval of the Pope, and he was subsequently anointed king by the Pope's representative, Boniface, Archbishop of Mayence, and afterwards by the Pope himself. Henceforward it became a religious as well as a political duty for the Franks to obey their king. He was God's representative on earth; and so we have the origin of the 'Divine Right of Kings', a theory which was destined to exercise much influence upon the subsequent history of the world. Its influence can be traced among the causes which precipitated the great French Revolution; its exercise by the Stuart kings of England had much to do with the founding of the United States of America.

In 771 Pippin's son Charles became sole king of the Franks. (For the three preceding years he had ruled jointly with his brother Carloman). He is generally known as Charlemagne or Charles the Great, and he figures prominently in romantic literature. He and his knights are almost as famous as Arthur and his Knights of the Round Table. Lancelot and Galahad are hardly more familiar figures than Roland and Oliver. But, unlike Arthur, the historical Charlemagne is much more important than the legendary Charlemagne. He is one of the greatest men of the Middle Ages, the first historical personage among the German peoples of whom we have any really satisfactory knowledge. We know that he was a tall man of commanding presence, a friend of the Church, and a patron of learning and art. He never became a scholar himself, but he loved to be surrounded by learned men. He founded a school for young nobles in his palace, and at its head was an Englishman, Alcuin of York. He also realized the importance of elementary education, and gave expression to this conviction in 789, when he ordered the clergy to gather together the children of both freemen and serfs in their neighbourhood, and establish schools in which they should be taught to read. He planned the great cathedral at Aachen (Aix-la-Chapelle); commenced two palaces, one near Mayence, and the other at Nimwegen in Holland; and caused a long bridge to be erected across the Rhine at Mayence.

His great political ideal was to bring all the German people together into a Christian Empire, an ideal which he had undoubtedly got from St. Augustine's *City of God*, in which the perfect emperor is pictured as holding his sceptre as a gift that God had given and might take away, and conquering his enemies that he might lead them to greater knowledge and prosperity. When Charlemagne became King of the Franks, nothing like the whole of modern Germany was included in his kingdom. Frisia and Bavaria were semi-independent, Christian states which admitted the Frankish overlordship. Saxony, which lay between them, was wholly independent.

Church and State in the days of Charlemagne

St. Peter giving the stole to Pope Leo III, and the banner of Rome to Charlemagne

The Saxons were pagans, in much the same condition as the Germans whom Tacitus describes; they had no towns or roads; and they were extremely difficult to conquer, for when an enemy advanced they retreated to their forests and swamps, from which, until the time of Charlemagne, they could not be dislodged. Their conquest was a task which took many years to accomplish; it is easily the greatest of Charlemagne's military exploits, and it is significant that, when they had been conquered, he should insist that they should all become Christians. He believed that their conversion, forcible though it might be, was so necessary that he decreed that those who refused to be baptized should be put to death. Heavy fines were imposed upon those who continued to make vows in the pagan fashion, and Christian monasteries were built in various parts of the country. Men would naturally settle around these, and so town life began in Saxony. The chief of the towns was Bremen, which is still one of the greatest German ports.

Charlemagne also conquered the Lombards; he made a successful expedition against the Slavs who had settled to the north and east of Saxony; he forced the Bohemians to pay tribute to him; and he drove the Muslims back from the Pyrenees as far as Barcelona. Thus he began the gradual expulsion of the Muslims from Spain which was finally achieved in 1492 with the conquest of Granada. On Christmas Day 800 he was crowned Emperor by the Pope in the Church of St. Peter at Rome. Thus after a lapse of more than three centuries the Western Empire overthrown by Odoacer was revived. In its new form it is generally known as the Holy Roman Empire, and it lasted for more than a thousand years, until it was finally overthrown by Napoleon in 1806. The reasons for the Pope's action appear to have been that the name of Emperor had at the time ceased among the Greeks, inasmuch as they were ruled by a woman (the Empress Irene), and Charlemagne 'held Rome itself, where the ancient Caesars had always dwelt, in addition to all his other possessions in Italy, Gaul, and Germany. Wherefore, as God had granted him all these dominions, it seemed just to all that he should take the title of Emperor, too, when it was offered to him at the wish of all Christendom.'[1] Even though the empire thus founded or re-established might be regarded as a continuation of the old Roman Empire of Augustus and Trajan, the claim was in many respects, especially after the death of Charlemagne, nothing more than a pleasant fiction. Despite the fact that in 812 Byzantine envoys formally acknowledged Charlemagne as Emperor and Augustus, the Eastern Empire continued to lead a separate existence, and most of Charlemagne's successors had the utmost difficulty in maintaining their authority in Germany alone ; even that task was frequently too much for them. The revival of the Western Empire seriously retarded German unity. It led German kings upon whom the somewhat visionary title of Emperor was conferred to make attempts to assert their authority in Italy, when it would have been far more to their interest to consolidate their position in Germany, where most of the princes claimed and carried on the right of private war, and did purely nominal allegiance to the Emperor.

'The medieval emperor was perpetually finding himself overtopped by one or other of his nominal vassals, and history has few more pitiable spectacles than some that were presented by the Holy Roman Empire—men bearing the great names of Caesar and Augustus—tossed helplessly to and fro on the waves of European politics, the laughing stock of their own barons and marquises, and often unable to provide for the ordinary expenses of their households.'[2]

The task of governing his empire was one of such difficulty that it caused much anxiety even to so able a man as Charlemagne. This was chiefly due to a scanty royal revenue and

[1] *The Chronicles of Lorsch* (a Frankish history).
[2] *Charles the Great* (Thomas Hodgkin), pub. Macmillan.

officials who were often too powerful, and apt to neglect the commands and interests of their sovereign. There existed no system of general taxation such as there had been in the Roman Empire. Charlemagne's income, like that of all medieval rulers, came mostly from the royal estates, and if these were not well looked after the Emperor would probably find himself in serious financial difficulties. The officials upon whom the Frankish kings were forced to place most reliance were the counts, who were expected to maintain order in their districts, see that justice was done, and supply troops when the King wanted them. There was no regular standing army. On the frontiers were estates known as Marks (marches) over which were officials known as margraves (marquises) who had special privileges (and therefore special chances of making themselves independent of the central authority) on account of the arduous nature of their duty : they were expected to keep out invaders such as the Slavs. It was Charlemagne's custom to hold assemblies of the nobles and bishops of his empire every spring or summer, so that he might have their advice on matters relating to the general welfare. With their approval he issued an extraordinary series of laws, called capitularies, a number of which have been preserved. Some of them are retrograde in character, such as those which advocate the use of the ordeal as a means of deciding guilt or innocence ; others deal with the prompt and impartial administration of justice, and the rights of widows and orphans, and are wholly admirable. Charlemagne was not, however, a great codifier of the laws like Justinian. His general policy was to leave the peoples whom he conquered under their own laws and institutions so long as they were loyal and obedient to the central government. In modern society, if a citizen of one country goes to live in another, he becomes subject to the laws of the country where he has settled. This was not the case under Charles the Great and his successors in the ninth century.

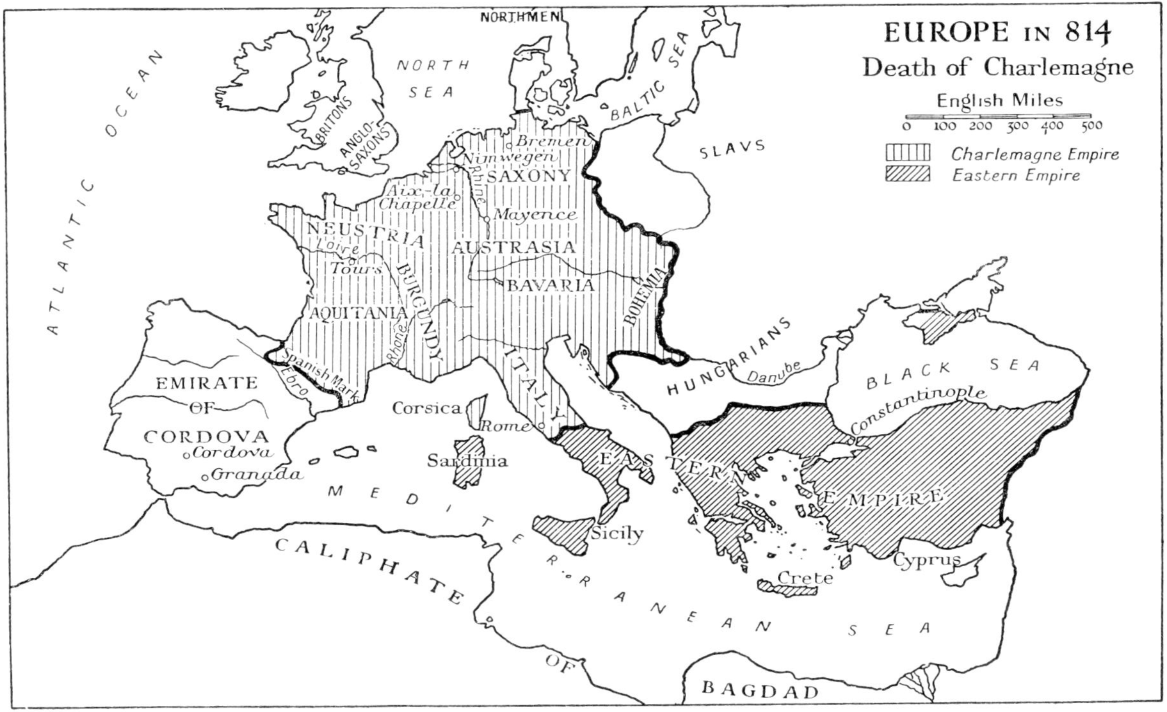
EUROPE IN 814
Death of Charlemagne
English Miles
0 100 200 300 400 500
Charlemagne Empire
Eastern Empire
NORTHMEN
NORTH SEA
BALTIC SEA
SLAVS
ATLANTIC OCEAN
BRITONS
ANGLO-SAXONS
Bremen
Nimwegen
SAXONY
Rhine
Aix-la-Chapelle
Mayence
NEUSTRIA
AUSTRASIA
Loire
Tours
BURGUNDY
BAVARIA
BOHEMIA
AQUITANIA
Rhone
Spanish Mark
Ebro
EMIRATE OF CORDOVA
Cordova
Granada
HUNGARIANS
Danube
BLACK SEA
Constantinople
ITALY
Corsica
Rome
Sardinia
EASTERN EMPIRE
Sicily
Cyprus
Crete
MEDITERRANEAN SEA
CALIPHATE OF BAGDAD

In those days every man carried his own legal atmosphere about with him. A Lombard, a Frank, a Bavarian, or a Roman resident in a foreign land could always claim to be tried according to the law of his native country. 'So great was the diversity of laws that you would often meet with it, not only in countries or cities, but even in single houses. For it would often happen that five men would be sitting or walking together, not one of whom would have the same law with any other.'[1] This was apt to lead to much confusion and difficulty, and Charlemagne had schemes for improving and harmonizing the many national codes which he found in existence, but these schemes were never properly realized. The laws of which he was himself the author are a curious mixture of German, Roman, and Biblical elements. Since his empire was to be pre-eminently Christian, the Bible was to be the highest authority, and he sought to make his laws conform to it.

One of the most interesting and characteristic of Charlemagne's innovations was the institution of a special class of officials known as 'missi dominici',[2] royal messengers whose duty it was to inquire into the conduct of all officials, to see that justice was done, to hear appeals, to enforce the rights of the royal treasury, to hunt down robbers, to report upon the morals of bishops, and to see that monks lived according to the rule of their order. Their choice depended upon the nature of the work which they had to do. A soldier would be chosen to command an army, a clergyman to inspect monasteries. In Charlemagne's time the counts, although men of wealth and great local influence, had not succeeded in making their offices hereditary : the strong hand of the central government prevented this, and the institution of 'missi dominici' was undoubtedly one of the modes of prevention. But it was a method that might easily fail under a weak

[1] *Charles the Great* (Thomas Hodgkin), pub. Macmillan.
[2] Cf. the itinerant justices of the English kings Henry I and Henry II.

ENCOURAGEMENT OF LEARNING

emperor, and, although it worked well under the robust rule of Charlemagne, it became more and more ineffective under his incompetent sons and grandsons. The 'missi' became worse oppressors of the common people than the counts whom they were appointed to superintend. Admirable instructions for their guidance were sent to them from headquarters, but they were persistently disregarded, and there was no means of enforcing them.

Probably Charlemagne's surest claim to fame rests upon his encouragement of learning.

'Herein he takes a foremost place among the benefactors of humanity, as a man who, himself imperfectly educated, knew how to value education in others ; as one who, amid the manifold harassing cares of government and of war, could find leisure for that friendly intercourse with learned men which far more than his generous material gifts cheered them on in their arduous and difficult work ; and as the ruler to whom perhaps more than to any other single individual we owe the fact that the precious literary inheritance of Greece and Rome has not been altogether lost to the human race. Every student of the history of the texts of the classical authors knows how many of our best manuscripts date from the ninth century, the result unquestionably of the impulse given by Charles and his learned courtiers to classical studies.'[1]

A monk of the monastery of St. Gall, writing two generations after the death of Charlemagne, has given us an interesting story illustrating the importance which the Emperor attached to learning. Charles had persuaded an Irish scholar named Clement to settle in Gaul, and had sent him a number of boys, sons of nobles, middle-class people, and peasants, to be educated by him at the royal expense. After a time he visited Gaul, and ordered that the boys should be brought before him with the letters and poems which they had composed. The middle-class and lower-class boys submitted compositions which were 'beyond all expectation sweetened

[1] *Charles the Great* (Thomas Hodgkin).

with the seasoning of wisdom ', but the compositions of the young nobles were ' tepid and absolutely idiotic ', whereupon the King set the industrious boys on his right hand and the idlers on his left. He addressed the former with words of commendation, ' I thank you, my sons, for the zeal with which you have attended to my commands. Only go on as you have begun, and I will give you splendid bishoprics and abbacies, and you shall be ever honourable in my eyes.' But to those on his left hand he said:

'You young nobles, you dainty and beautiful youths, who have presumed upon your birth and your possessions to despise mine orders, and have taken no care for my renown ; you have neglected the study of literature, while you have given yourselves over to luxury and idleness, or to games and foolish athletics. By the King of Heaven, I care nothing for your noble birth and your handsome faces, let others prize them as they may. Know this for certain, that unless ye give earnest heed to your studies, and recover the ground lost by your negligence, ye shall never receive any favour at the hand of King Charles.'

Charlemagne's great empire did not survive his death in 814. Eight years before, the great Emperor, who does not seem to have expected that it would hold together, had made a formal division of his dominions between his three sons, but two of them died before their father, so that Louis, called the Pious, his only surviving son; succeeded to the whole of the Frankish domains in 814, and two years later was crowned Emperor by the Pope at Rheims. Louis proved a very feeble ruler, and tried to calm his unruly sons by dividing various parts of his dominions among them. But he did not succeed in winning either their respect or their gratitude. On one occasion they even went so far as to depose him, and when he died in 840 there followed a dreary period of struggle for territory between his sons and grandsons. In 843, by the Treaty of Verdun, the Frankish dominions were divided into three separate states under three of Louis's sons. a West Frankish

DISINTEGRATION

kingdom which corresponds roughly with modern France and Belgium, an Eastern Frankish kingdom which included much of modern Germany, and a kingdom which comprised about half of Italy, and a strip of territory stretching from the mouth of the Rhone to the mouth of the Rhine, including Provence, the greater part of Burgundy, and the cities of Rome and Aachen. When Lothair, the king of this latter kingdom, died, his three sons divided his territory among them, one taking the Italian part, another Burgundy, and the third the northern part, which was subsequently called Lotharingia after him. When he died, his uncles fell upon his lands like birds of prey, and divided them by what is known as the Treaty of Mersen, which only patched up matters for a little while. It was soon followed by centuries of disorder, and Western Europe sank once more to a condition of apathy comparable to that from which it had been rescued by the genius of Charlemagne.

The general weakness of the kings was aggravated by a series of invasions which the Christian states did well to survive. The Muslims got control of the island of Sicily, and terrorized Italy and Southern France; the Slavs and Hungarians caused endless trouble on the east; and more formidable than any were the Northmen, Danes, or Vikings. These were pirates who came from Denmark, Norway, and Sweden; they came in long black galleys, making little use of sails ; from the fifth to the ninth centuries they had been perfecting themselves in the arts of seamanship ; they had braved the terrors of the Arctic in their little vessels, and had even got across the Atlantic to the continent which afterwards became known as America ; when fighting they were utterly careless of their own lives, for to be killed in battle was, in their opinion, the greatest of all boons, since it would be followed by entry into Valhalla, a paradise where they would spend their time in alternate warfare and feastings. In the tenth and eleventh centuries many of their sagas began to be written down in Iceland. One of the greatest of them is the Volsunga Saga, the story of Sigurd the Volsung. It is a tale which has been told in other lands besides Iceland. We read part of it in the Old English poem of Beowulf, and in Germany it was subsequently made into a great poem called the Nibelungenlied. The musician Wagner has set it to music in a famous series of operas called The Ring of the Nibelungs, and the English writer William Morris has written one of the greatest of his poems on the subject. The story is in every way typical of its original authors : It is full of valiant adventures, fierce loves, gigantic feastings, and that spirit of reckless daring which once led the Church to insert a special clause in its litany—'From the fury of the fierce Northmen, good Lord deliver us.' The Vikings, when they first began to make their marauding expeditions, were particularly bitter in their animosity to the Christian Church ; they delighted to destroy monasteries and nunneries and slaughter their inmates ; perhaps they remembered the treatment which Charlemagne, in the name of Christianity, had meted out to their pagan brethren, the Saxons. Later on they lost much of their fierceness and were baptized into the Christian religion. One of the most important of their conquests was Normandy (Northmandy—the place of the Northmen). The change which came over them in the course of a couple of centuries can be well realized by comparing the cultured Normans of the twelfth century with their barbaric ancestors of 912, whose settlement in his dominions the King of France was powerless to prevent.

The general insecurity of life in Western Europe during the couple of centuries that followed the death of Charlemagne and the weakness of kings favoured the development of what is known as Feudalism. This was an organization of society through the medium of land tenure. Kings granted land to powerful lords or barons, and they in turn sublet it to numerous tenants, the title upon which the land was held in all cases

CAPTURE OF SYRACUSE BY SARACENS IN THE NINTH CENTURY

From the fourteenth-century manuscript of Skylitzes at Madrid

Photograph, G. Millet, Collection des Hautes Études, Sorbonne, Paris

being some form of personal service, usually military. The great noble would be expected to supply the King with a certain number of soldiers when he went to war, and the obligations of the subtenants to their lords would be similar—but, generally speaking, a vassal need not serve for more than forty days at his own expense. There were other obligations too, such as the payment of a sum of money called a 'relief' by a tenant when he succeeded to an estate, and 'aids' which were payable on three occasions—to ransom the lord from captivity, to provide a marriage dowry for his eldest daughter, and when his eldest son received the honour of knighthood.

All tenants did allegiance (homage) for their holdings (fiefs), the tenants-in-chief to the King, the subtenants to their immediate lord. This might and did in many cases lead to great abuses. Thus, if the Duke of Normandy chose to break his feudal vows and fight against the King of France, it would be the duty of Norman landowners to follow their duke. This sort of thing had a most disruptive effect; it was absolutely fatal to the growth and development of a powerful nation. The first of the Norman dukes to become King of England, probably with this in mind, made all English landowning men swear fealty to him,[1] so that it might be impressed upon them that their duty to the King took precedence of all other duties. But even in England feudal lords were apt to forget such obligations, and under a weak king like Stephen they did practically as they wished.

The Feudal System was of very gradual growth; it did not owe its origin to any royal decree or to the genius or imagination of any one man or body of men; it was a mutual product of the times during which it flourished. It existed long before the time of Charlemagne, and one of the capitularies which he issued just before his death contains a very clear allusion to the feudalization of society. It ordains that no man shall be allowed to renounce his dependence on a

[1] Oath of Salisbury, 1086.

feudal superior after he has received any benefit from him, except in one of four cases—if the lord has tried to kill his vassal, or if he has struck him with a stick, or if he has endeavoured to dishonour his wife or daughter, or tried to take away his inheritance. A feudal fief was hereditary in the family of the vassal and passed down to the eldest son from one generation to the other. So long as the conditions upon which it had been originally granted were faithfully observed, neither the lord nor his heirs could rightfully regain possession of the land.

One of the circumstances which contributed most to the development of feudalism was the practice of 'commendation'. During the times of confusion and universal insecurity which followed the death of Charlemagne, small landowners were forced by an instinct of self-defence to 'commend' themselves to some powerful lord. They would give up their lands to him, and receive it back again as his tenants, and he would agree to protect them against all foes. Commendations were frequent during the period of the Danish invasions. But although a desire for security on the part of ordinary people was a powerful factor in the development of feudalism, that system did not prove a panacea for their ills. The feudal lord often claimed and exercised two rights which were detrimental to the interests of the community—the right of private jurisdiction, and the right of private war. A strong king like the English Henry II would curtail the former, and absolutely forbid and prevent the latter; but few of the kings of Western Europe during the early Middle Ages were strong enough to curb the rebellious instincts of their barons. The condition of affairs in England during the reign of the good-natured and weak Stephen (1135–54) illustrates what the lack of an effective central authority meant. The chronicler William of Newbury writes: 'Castles rose in great numbers in the several districts, and there were in England, so to speak, as many kings or rather tyrants as lords of castles. Individuals took the right of coining their private money, and of private jurisdiction.' The Anglo-Saxon Chronicle is still more explicit:

'When the traitors perceived that Stephen was a mild man, and soft and good, and did no justice, then did all wonder. They had done homage to him and sworn oaths, but held no faith; for every powerful man made his castles and held them against him, and they filled the land full of castles. . . . Many thousands they killed with hunger; I neither can nor may tell all the wounds, or all the tortures which they inflicted on wretched men in this land; and that lasted the nineteen winters while Stephen was king, and ever it was worse and worse.'

It is hardly an exaggeration to say that war was the law of the feudal world. Brother frequently fought against brother and sons against their father.[1] The jousts or tournaments which form so picturesque a feature of medieval life were military exercises designed to occupy the tiresome periods between wars, and to keep knights in good trim for them when they came. The Church did a little to check or rather limit this warlike spirit by demanding special immunity for priests, merchants, peasants at their ploughs, women, and pilgrims, and by the institution early in the eleventh century of what was called a Truce of God, according to which all were to refrain from fighting during the season of Lent and on Thursday, Friday, Saturday, and Sunday of each week. Failure to comply with the truce would lay the defaulter open to the terrors of excommunication. He would be denied the consolation of the services of the Church; he would be allowed to die unshriven; he would be buried in unhallowed ground; and he would be excluded from the joys of paradise. But all the influence that the Church could exercise, and all the threats that it could make

[1] e.g. the sons of the Emperor Louis the Pious rebelled against their father, and the English kings William I and Henry II both had similar experiences.

A TOURNAMENT

From a carved ivory panel of the thirteenth century

and enforce, were not sufficient to deter many of the feudal lords, and the truce was frequently broken. The great bishops were generally feudal lords themselves, and some of them, like Odo, Bishop of Bayeux, the half-brother of William I of England, were as fond of war and martial exercises as any of the lay barons.

The condition of the lower classes of the people under feudalism was very far from being a happy one. The estates of the lords were tilled by peasants, generally serfs who did not own their own fields. These were known as villeins[1] and they held their land in long strips which were not necessarily contiguous. In return for them they had certain definite duties to perform; they had to work for two or three days in the week on the portion of the manorial land which the lord reserved for his own use: during harvest time they might be expected to work for as many as five days a week. In addition a villein might have to give the lord payments in kind such as wheat, oats, or a fixed number of hens at Easter and Michaelmas. Thus the time that he would be able to devote to the cultivation of his own holding would be very severely limited, and in order to make a bare living for himself and his family he would have to be content with much work and very little rest. Generally speaking, so long as he did the lord's work satisfactorily and paid his dues, he was secure in the possession of his strips of land, but he had no legal remedy against a lord who chose to dispossess him. It was illegal for a lord to maim or kill his serf, but he could do almost anything else to him with impunity, and the serf had to put up with many irksome restrictions of his personal liberty. Thus he could not sell his ox or his horse, neither could he give his daughter in marriage, without the consent of his lord. He could, however, obtain his freedom by running away to a town and remaining there undetected for a year and a day. It was the labour of the villeins which made

[1] i.e. belonging to the *villa* or *manor* (Lat. *villanus*).

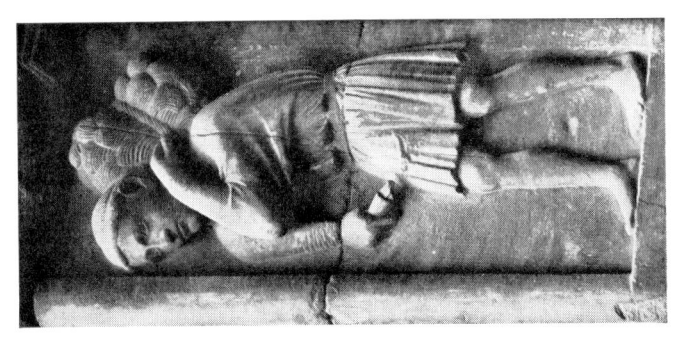

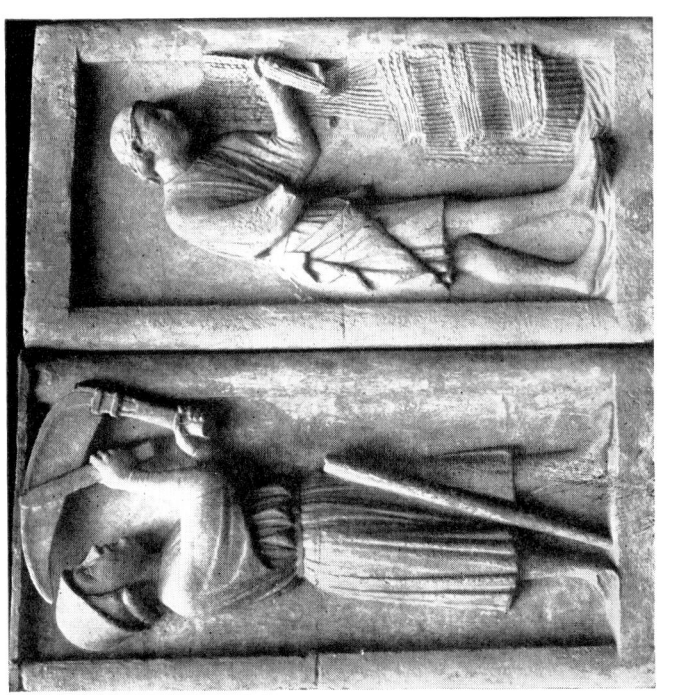

THE LABOURER IN THE MIDDLE AGES
From reliefs on Notre-Dame in Paris

it possible for the feudal lords to indulge their passion for fighting; it relieved them from the responsibility of looking after their estates and left them free to spend their energies upon other and more congenial pursuits.

The increased use of money during the twelfth and thirteenth centuries led to the decay of villeinage. The habit of trading one commodity against another without the intervention of money began to disappear; villeins sold the products of their labour for money in neighbouring towns; and lords found it to their interest to accept money payments from their serfs instead of the labour services which they had previously demanded. Thus the villein became a free man, and his position approximated more and more to that of the tenant farmer of to-day who pays rent to a landowner for his holding.

XIX

THE POWER OF THE MEDIEVAL CHURCH

THE condition of Rome in the tenth century almost baffles description. The decay of Charlemagne's empire left the Pope without a protector, threatened by the Muslims from Southern Italy and exposed to the caprices of the unruly nobles of Rome, who made and unmade popes pretty well as they liked. Thus a certain Marozia, a woman of noble birth, in 928 deposed Pope John the Tenth and replaced him by her own illegitimate son. Her grandson, John the Twelfth, also became Pope. His vices seem to have been as lurid and shameless as those of some of the better known popes of the Renascence period.[1] But he is chiefly notable as the Pope who invited Otto the Great, King of the Saxons, to come to Italy to be crowned Emperor in 962. Otto had already shown his ability by maintaining a fair amount of order among his turbulent nobles and by finally driving the

[1] e.g. Alexander VI (father of Cesare Borgia).

Hungarians out of Germany; his intervention in Italian politics was an act of doubtful statesmanship. He would probably have been much wiser if he had occupied his time in making his hold upon Germany more secure. He set an example which his successors followed with consequences which were often disastrous. Instead of confining their attentions wholly to German affairs, they conceived it their duty to keep a hold upon their Italian kingdom, and, with that end in view, to make journeys into Italy in order to secure the election of friendly popes or the deposition of unfriendly ones. Thus they became involved in a long struggle with the Papacy which brought them many humiliations and few gains, and which considerably diminished the power and prestige of the Empire.

The condition of the Roman Catholic Church during the two centuries which followed the death of Charlemagne had little in it to suggest the great power which it afterwards attained. It seemed, on the contrary, to be losing its strength and dignity and to be falling apart just like the Frankish empire. The great bishops and abbots were feudal nobles who held extensive fiefs for which they did homage and swore fealty just like other vassals. In theory a bishop was chosen by the clergy of his diocese and his choice then ratified by the people, while an abbot was elected by the members of the monastery over which he was to preside. But there was a wide gulf between theory and practice. Although the outward forms of an election might be observed, the kings and nobles really chose both bishops and abbots. If their nominees were not chosen they would refuse to hand over the lands attached to the bishopric or abbey. After his appointment the bishop (or abbot) would do homage to his lord, and not infrequently also receive from him the ring and staff which were the symbols of his spiritual office.[1] There

[1] The ring signified that the bishop was wedded to his diocese; the staff was a symbol of his spiritual rule.

THE POWER OF THE MEDIEVAL CHURCH

were many who thought this a disgraceful procedure, for the feudal lord was often a rough soldier to whom religion was merely a matter of convenience. Some went so far as to declare that the Church should have the full right not only to control its own elections, but also to dispose of its property, and that it owed no allegiance to any lay authority. This was an impossible doctrine for a king or a great noble to admit, because the clergy were in possession of very extensive lands, and if they did no homage for them, they would be perfectly free to rebel against the King and endanger the well-being of the country in which their estates were situated. Hence when they put forward their claim for immunity from secular control, there followed a long and bitter struggle, which could only end in a compromise. This is generally known as the Investiture struggle.

The nature of royal and baronial control was not the only danger which threatened the wealth and power of the Church during the ninth and tenth centuries. There were also some dangers from within. The law forbidding the clergy to marry seems to have been widely disregarded in England, France, Germany, and Italy; if this had been allowed to go on unchecked, bishops and abbots might have founded families, their estates would have become hereditary, and Church property would to all intents and purposes have become private property. Another source of weakness was the evil known as simony,[1] the sale of Church offices, which had reached alarming proportions. Kings and nobles sold bishoprics and abbacies, bishops recouped themselves at the expense of the priests whom it was their duty to appoint, and the priests got their money back by charging exorbitant fees for baptizing or burying their parishioners, and for conducting marriage ceremonies.

---

[1] So called after Simon Magus, who offered the Apostle Peter money if he would confer upon him the gift of imparting the Holy Spirit to those on whom he laid his hands (Acts viii, verses 18-24).

Thus it was obvious that the popes had much to do if they were to make the Church a great international organization, greater than any monarchy and capable of controlling princes. The first important step towards this end was taken by Pope Nicholas II, who in 1059 issued a decree taking the election of the Pope definitely out of the hands of the emperors and the people of Rome and transferring it to a college of cardinals representing the Roman clergy.[1] In 1073 Gregory VII became Pope, and the twelve years of his rule are among the most important in the history of the Papacy. One of his writings, the *Dictatus*, gives a brief list of the powers which he thought the popes should possess: The Pope has the right to depose or reinstate other bishops; he can dethrone emperors and absolve subjects from allegiance to an unjust ruler; his decrees cannot be annulled, but he can annul the decrees of all other earthly powers; no one may pass judgement upon his acts; and no one should have the presumption to condemn any one who makes an appeal to the Pope. Moreover, the Church of which he is the head upon earth is infallible: it has never erred, and it will never err to all eternity. Gregory at once acted up to this lofty and somewhat arrogant conception of his office. He warned the King of France that if he did not give up the practice of simony he would excommunicate him and absolve his subjects from their oaths of allegiance; and he explained to William I of England that the papal power and the kingly power were both established by God as the greatest of earthly powers, just as the sun and the moon are the greatest of the heavenly bodies. But just as the sun is greater than the moon, so the papal power is greater than the kingly power, for it is responsible for it. This made little impression on William. He refused to acknowledge that he held England as a fief of Rome, and he defined in the clearest of terms what his relations to the Papacy were. No Pope was to be acknowledged in

[1] The College of Cardinals still elects the Pope.

310 THE POWER OF THE MEDIEVAL CHURCH

England without his approval; no papal letters received in the country or sent out without his express sanction; no laws or canons enacted by the clergy without his consent; and none of his barons excommunicated or otherwise proceeded against without his permission. Gregory was helpless against such determined opposition, but he was more fortunate in his dealings with the Emperor Henry IV. In 1075 the Pope declared that the clergy were not to receive investiture from laymen. Henry and the German bishops generally disregarded this injunction, and the Emperor continued to appoint bishops and abbots in direct opposition to the Pope's wishes, and to place reliance upon counsellors who had been excommunicated. Whereupon Gregory sent envoys or legates to Germany to reprove Henry for his wicked conduct, which was said to merit 'the permanent loss of all his royal honours'. The Emperor replied by holding a great council at Worms which was attended by two-thirds of the German bishops, who publicly declared that Gregory had ceased to be their pope. But the allegiance of the bishops was not backed up by similar loyalty on the part of the nobles. When the Pope absolved Henry's subjects from their oaths to him and forbade 'any one to serve him as king', many of his vassals hailed it as a good opportunity for getting rid of a ruler who was beginning to become a little obnoxious[1] to them, and the Pope was invited to visit Augsburg to consult with the nobles as to whether Henry was to remain King of Germany or whether he was to be deposed. The Emperor became thoroughly alarmed, so much so that he decided to anticipate Gregory's arrival in Germany and do full submission to him. He hastened across the Alps in midwinter until he reached the castle of Canossa in Northern Italy, where the Pope was

[1] The Saxons were particularly incensed against the Emperor. They had rebelled against him because they resented the castles which he had built in their land, full, so they said, of rough soldiers who preyed upon the people. The Pope sympathized with the Saxons and had reproved Henry for his conduct towards them.

The castle of Carcassonne in France, a typical medieval stronghold

resting on his way to Augsburg. Nothing could exceed the humiliation of Henry. For three days, barefooted and in the coarse garments of a pilgrim, he waited outside the closed doors of the castle, and when at length the Pope consented to receive him his submission was as abject as it could possibly be. The pardon which he received did not please some of the German princes. They elected another king, and three years of struggle between the adherents of the rival kings followed. The Pope remained neutral until 1080, when he again deposed Henry. But on this occasion he had overreached himself. Henry showed amazing energy in replying to the papal challenge, his friends rallied strongly to him, the bishops once more renounced their allegiance to the Pope, he defeated and slew his rival, and at last was able to invade Italy itself with the double purpose of being crowned Emperor and deposing the Pope who had caused him so much trouble. He was crowned Emperor by Clement III, whom the German bishops had elected as their pope when they had thrown over Gregory, and in 1085 he drove Gregory from Rome. Shortly afterwards the Pope died. His last words were: 'I have loved justice and hated iniquity, therefore I die an exile.' His death did not put an end to Henry's troubles, nor did it settle the Investiture dispute. It was not until 1122 that the settlement known as the Concordat of Worms was effected. The Emperor admitted the right of the Church to elect its bishops and abbots, and to invest bishops with the ring and the staff. But the elections were to be held in the royal courts, in the presence of the King or his representative, and the new bishop or abbot was afterwards to be formally invested with his fief by the King and do homage to him.[1]

Thirty years after the Concordat of Worms one of the most famous of the German emperors began his reign. This was Frederick the First, commonly called Frederick Barbarossa

[1] Henry I of England and Anselm, Archbishop of Canterbury, had settled their Investiture Quarrel in a similar way fifteen years earlier (1107).

on account of his red beard. It was his ambition to restore the old Roman Empire to its former magnificence, and he regarded himself as the successor not merely of Charlemagne and Otto the Great but also of the Caesars. After the German princes had acknowledged him as Emperor he informed the Pope that the imperial dignity had been conferred upon him by God. He did not ask for papal approval like his predecessors. Naturally therefore the struggle for dominion between Empire and Papacy entered upon another of its acute stages. Frederick had also to combat the force of Italian nationality. He believed that Northern Italy was an integral part of his empire, and in his efforts to assert this he was brought up against an opposition which had not troubled his predecessors—the opposition of the towns Milan, Cremona, Mantua, Ferrara, Verona, Padua, Parma, Bologna, and Venice. Some of these towns were practically independent states. They were constantly fighting among themselves, but still they contrived to become very wealthy. Their trade was flourishing and in later times they were to become centres of culture comparable to the cities of ancient Greece. If they had remained isolated they would not have been a very great hindrance to the success of Frederick's policy, but the idea of paying taxes to a German king awakened their national prejudices, and they formed what is known as the Lombard League to resist him. Ultimately the Emperor had to be content with an acknowledgement of his overlordship at the price of allowing the cities to manage their own affairs, and even to determine the important questions of peace and war. The towns in their opposition to the Emperor could always rely upon the approval if not the active support of the Papacy. They did more than any other agency to shatter Frederick's dream of a restoration of the Roman Empire. His intervention in Italian affairs, far from strengthening the position of himself and his empire, really weakened it, for Frederick created a new difficulty for his descendants.

Undeterred by his lack of success in Northern Italy, he tried to secure Southern Italy by arranging a marriage between his son Henry and Constance, heiress of Naples and Sicily. The Pope was the feudal overlord of these territories, and he disapproved strongly of the Emperor exercising any control over dominions to the south as well as to the north of the papal lands. When Frederick II, the son of Henry and Constance, who had succeeded in the natural course of events to his mother's possessions, was offered the imperial crown of Germany in 1211, he secured the support of Pope Innocent III by agreeing, if he were elected, to relinquish his lands in Sicily and Southern Italy, to put down heresy in Germany, and to free the clergy from lay jurisdiction and taxation. Frederick kept none of these promises, and in the course of the struggle which ensued all the weapons which the Papacy could use were employed against him. He was excommunicated on more than one occasion, and in 1245 Pope Innocent IV declared his deposition. After five years of gallant combat against his troubles, Frederick died in 1250. His sons maintained themselves in their Sicilian kingdom for a short time longer, until they were driven out by Charles of Anjou, the brother of the King of France, who had been offered Southern Italy by the Pope. Frederick II was one of the most enlightened of the medieval emperors. He was a patron of learning, and a man of some tolerance in an age of almost universal intolerance. He welcomed Jewish and Mohammedan as well as Christian philosophers to his Sicilian court ; he was responsible for the introduction of Arabic numerals and algebra among Christian students ; he was one of the first to write Italian verse (it has been claimed that Italian poetry was born at his court) ; and in a sense it may be said that he foreshadowed the Reformation. In a letter denouncing the pretensions of Pope Innocent IV, he condemned the wealth and irreligion of the clergy, and proposed to his fellow rulers a general confiscation of Church property

THE CRUSADES

for the spiritual benefit of the Church. After him the Empire became an almost exclusively German institution. The electors [1] were German princes, and most of those whom they elected confined their attentions to purely German matters. Few attempted to assert their rights in Italy, and few took the trouble to go to Rome to be crowned by the Pope. The ambition to revive the glories of Rome was never again a serious menace to the peace of Europe, but a curious incident happened in 1347, when the romantic Cola di Rienzi made an abortive attempt to establish a 'Holy Roman Republic' on the model of the famous republic of ancient times.

The events known as the Crusades illustrate no less clearly than the struggle with the Empire the power of the Medieval Church, its immense influence over men's minds, and its failure to inculcate a religion of charity and goodwill. Throughout the Middle Ages pilgrimages to shrines of saints were regarded as among the most effectual ways of atoning for past misdeeds, and pilgrimages to the Holy Land, to those places which were for ever consecrated by association with the earthly life and activities of Christ, were considered to be particularly effectual. They could be undertaken in comparative safety when the Roman Empire was an effective force, and subsequently too under the mild rule of the Caliph Omar and his successors. A stately mosque, the Mosque of Omar, was erected on the site of the Temple at Jerusalem, but the custody of the Holy Sepulchre and of the other Holy Places was given to the Christians. With the break up of the caliphate, however, the lot of the pilgrims became a dangerous one, especially so after the conquest of Jerusalem by the Seljuk Turks in 1076. These were Muslims

[1] In 1356 the Emperor Charles IV issued his famous Golden Bull, which, among other things, fixed the number of electors at seven—the Archbishops of Mainz, Koln (Cologne), and Trier, the King of Bohemia, the Count Palatine of the Rhine, the Duke of Saxony, and the Margrave of Brandenburg.

like the Arabs, but they were fiercely intolerant; and they soon showed what respect they had for the Christians when they dragged the Patriarch of Jerusalem through the streets by his hair, threw him into prison, and kept him there until he had paid a heavy ransom. Pilgrims flocked back to Europe with harrowing tales of their cruelty, among them a hermit of Amiens in France, named Peter, whose rude eloquence had much to do with the First Crusade.

'He preached to innumerable crowds in the churches, the streets, and the highways; the Hermit entered with equal confidence the palace and the cottage; and the people were impetuously moved by his call to repentance and to arms. When he painted the sufferings of the natives and the pilgrims of Palestine, every heart was melted to compassion; every breast glowed with indignation when he challenged the warriors of the age to defend their brethren and rescue their Saviour.'[1]

But the stories of pilgrims, although they did much to rouse European indignation against the Turks, were not the real causes of the Crusades. It was hoped that they would not only result in the deliverance of the Holy Land from the Turks, but that they would also be the means whereby an end would be put to the divisions among the Catholic princes of Europe, and so the power and influence of the Papacy would be increased. Accordingly, when the Eastern Emperor Alexius appealed to Urban II for help against the Turks, whose advance threatened the security of his throne, the Pope called a great Council at Clermont in France, where he preached with such power and eloquence that thousands pledged themselves to take part in a Holy War. Urban promised all who responded to his appeal remission of the penances which they had incurred by their sins, and with his own hands he distributed crosses, which were henceforward to be the badges of the warriors, and which gave them their name of Crusaders.

[1] *Decline and Fall of the Roman Empire*, vol. vi, chap. lviii.

A PILGRIMAGE

The Earl of Warwick embarking for the Holy Land, *c.* 1475

The First Crusade (1096-9) was the most successful of them all, despite lack of unity among the Crusaders and much conduct which was distinctly un-Christian. No kings took part, but many feudal barons of high rank, such as Godfrey of Bouillon, Raymond of Toulouse, and Bohemund of Otranto, led armies to the East. Preceding them were disorganized bands of poorer people under the leadership of Peter the Hermit and a knight called Walter the Penniless. These fared very badly. They had to pass through Hungary, which had recently been converted to Christianity, and food being short—probably they had nothing to give in exchange for it—they began to plunder the inhabitants, who took up arms against them and killed many of them. Those who eventually fought against the Turks were hopelessly beaten, and many, faced with the alternative of death or conversion to Islam, chose the latter. The feudal levies were more successful, and, after first capturing Antioch, they achieved the object of their expedition by the conquest of Jerusalem, where a Christian state was at once established. Godfrey of Bouillon was chosen as its first ruler, with the title of Baron and Advocate of the Holy Sepulchre, since he refused to wear a crown of gold in the city where his Saviour had worn a crown of thorns. Three dependent states were also established: Tripoli, Edessa, and Antioch. These were constantly at war with one another and with the kingdom of Jerusalem, and it is not surprising that in 1144 Edessa was recaptured by the Turks, an event which led to the Second Crusade (1147), which accomplished nothing; indeed it probably weakened the position of the Christians of Palestine, and in 1187 Jerusalem fell once more into Muslim hands, when it was conquered by the Saracens under Saladin. A Third Crusade followed, in which the Emperor Frederick Barbarossa, Philip II of France, and Richard I, King of England, all took part. The Emperor was accidentally drowned before reaching Palestine, and his army encountered the

A crusader's castle above Antioch, built across the old Seleucid Wall

Saracens with the most disastrous consequences; for years afterwards German slaves are said to have been very plentiful and very cheap in the markets of Syria. Philip of France and Richard of England, who set out later with their armies, got on so badly together that shortly after the capture of Acre from the Saracens Philip returned home, leaving to Richard the task of winning Jerusalem. The English king performed prodigies of valour in the fighting which followed; his fame as a warrior was great in Palestine many years after his departure from that country; but the task of conquering Jerusalem proved too much for him, his difficulties being considerably increased by the ravages of fever among his troops. Richard on one occasion was within sight of Jerusalem, but he refused to look upon it, declaring that he, who was unworthy to recover the Holy City, was unworthy to behold it.

The Fourth Crusade (1202–4) was a particularly mean and sordid affair. The Crusaders—drawn mainly from Flanders, Champagne, and Venice—never got farther than Constantinople. Instead of fighting Muslims, they turned their arms, first against their Christian brethren of Hungary, whose port of Zara the Venetians coveted, and then against Constantinople, which they conquered and subjected to three days of plunder and rapine. Even the churches were pillaged, and many priceless art treasures were ruthlessly destroyed. A Latin empire was founded with Baldwin, Count of Flanders, as its head. This had an even shorter life than the Latin kingdom of Jerusalem. In 1261 the Greek emperors were back in Constantinople once more, but with their power so weakened that it is remarkable that almost two centuries elapsed before they were conquered by the Turks.

There were four more Crusades, in addition to a singular movement known as The Children's Crusade (1212) which shows that in the thirteenth century the emotions of the poorer classes could be stirred just as easily as they had been by Peter the Hermit at the end of the eleventh century. A

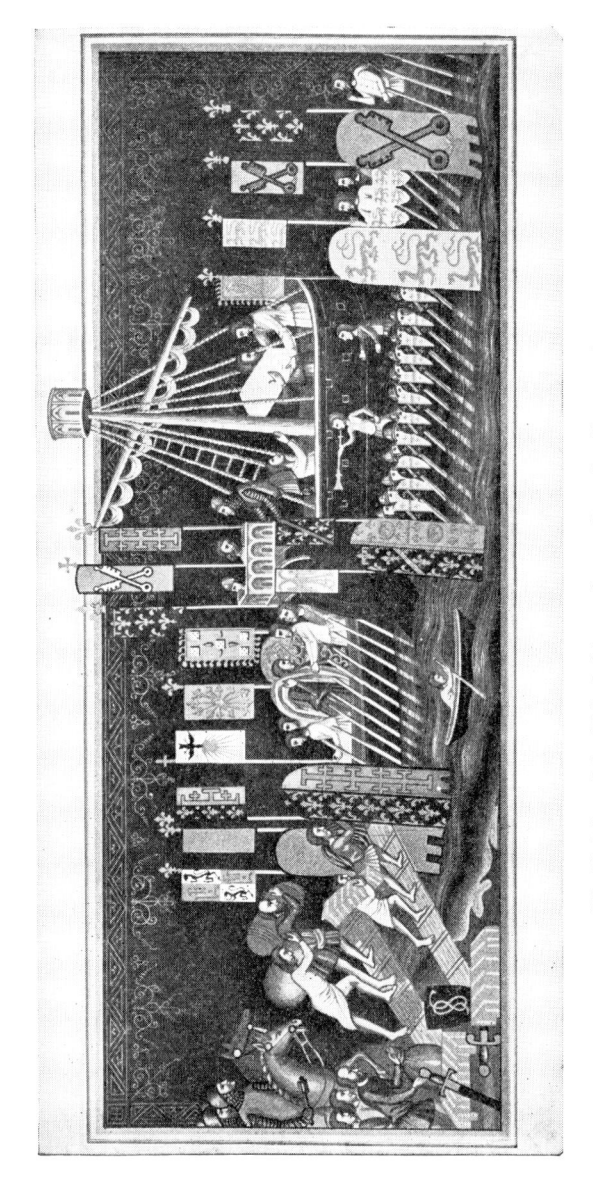

The Knights of the Holy Spirit starting on Crusade. Fourteenth century

large number of boys, peasants, and women assembled in France under the leadership of a youth named Stephen, marched to Marseilles, and were there embarked by two rascally merchants on ships which took them, not to Syria, but to the slave markets of Northern Africa. There was a similar movement in Germany. Thousands of German youths made their way into Italy, many died during their journey through the Alps, and those who subsequently reached Brindisi were wisely persuaded by the bishop of that city to go home. Very few, however, saw Germany again. Pope Innocent III is reputed to have said of this Children's Crusade: 'These children shame us. While we are asleep, they march forth joyously to conquer the Holy Land.'

The spirit which Innocent desired was hard to arouse in the thirteenth century among any but the very poorest, and when Jerusalem was recovered in 1229 it was by the sceptical Emperor Frederick II, who was at the time under the papal ban.[1] This was the last notable success of the Crusaders, and it was not of very long duration. In 1244 Jerusalem was lost again,[2] and the subsequent attempts to recover it—the Seventh and Eighth Crusades—are chiefly remarkable for the part played in them by Louis IX, King of France (St. Louis), whose motives were actuated by genuine piety, and by no selfish considerations. Louis died of fever during the Eighth Crusade, which is also notable because one of the leaders was the English prince Edward (afterwards Edward the First), one of the greatest warriors of the Middle Ages. Edward conquered Nazareth (1271), but returned to England in the following year to take possession of his kingdom. After his departure the Christians of Palestine quarrelled so much among themselves that any hope of making headway against their enemies was futile. Even in Acre, the one

[1] See p. 314.
[2] It remained a Muslim possession until 1917, when it was captured by a mixed force of British, French, and Indians under General Allenby.

WHAT THE CRUSADES ACHIEVED

important town still held by the Crusaders, so much fighting went on between the Christian inhabitants that a considerable part of the city was destroyed. In 1291 it was conquered by the Saracens, who thus took possession of the last remnant of the kingdom of Jerusalem, founded with much pride and enthusiasm nearly two centuries before.

The failure of the Crusaders was due chiefly to their own shortcomings. St. Bernard of Clairvaux, whose eloquence was mainly responsible for the Second Crusade, gives a most unflattering description of those who hearkened to his appeal: 'In that countless multitude you will find few except the utterly wicked and impious, the sacrilegious, homicides, and perjurers, whose departure is a double gain. Europe rejoices to lose them and Palestine to gain them; they are useful in both ways, in their absence from here and their presence there.' One of the most remarkable features of the Third Crusade was that while many of the Christian leaders hated one another and did not hesitate to show it, Christians and Muslims grew to respect each other. The relations of the King of England and the King of France were distinctly unfriendly, while those of Richard and Saladin, the Muslim leader, were almost cordial. The failure of the Christians to retain their hold upon Jerusalem is therefore not to be wondered at. But even though the Crusaders won no permanent military successes, their expeditions were fruitful of good results in other directions. They helped to destroy feudalism, because the lords often sold their lands and feudal rights in order to get money to go on a crusade; they diminished the number of feudal subjects of the lower class and so created a demand for labourers which helped to bring about the emancipation of the serfs; and they gave a tremendous impetus to trade and commerce. They created a demand for ships and so stimulated the shipbuilding industry, and they were responsible for the introduction into Europe of many new articles of merchandise.

'The Crusades created and supplied a large demand in the West for wines, sugar, cotton, silk, all kinds of textile fabrics, rugs, pottery, glass-ware, spices, medicines, perfumes, colouring substances, incense, various kinds of oil, mastic, dates, grain, and many other things. It would not be too much to say that the Crusades made Europe rich.'[1] The cities, particularly those of Northern Italy, such as Venice, Genoa, and Pisa, benefited greatly from this commerce, and it is not surprising that merchants provided the financial backing for more than one of the Crusades. But perhaps the greatest effect which they had upon the European world was that they gave Christians the opportunity of travelling in foreign lands which had finer civilizations than their own, and so they took the place of a liberal education.

'Life in the West was still very rude. The houses lacked all luxuries and comforts, and most of those things which are now regarded even as necessities. The European, whose experiences had been very limited indeed, entered into a new world when he set out on a crusade. He found new climates, new natural products, strange dress, houses, and customs. The features of the landscape, and even the skies above him, were different. In the houses he found many new objects of comfort and luxury, such as divans, sofas, alcoves, mattresses, carafes, jars, and precious stones. Talisman, amulet, carat, and the names of many stones are Arabic. The geographical knowledge of the West was very limited, but the Crusades brought experience in travel and a practical knowledge of large territories. Great interest was aroused in the study of geography. A good knowledge of the Mediterranean and large parts of Asia and Africa was acquired. The curiosity awakened by the new regions, together with the mercenary and commercial interests in many quarters, led Europeans to undertake long journeys of discovery. One of the most famous of the travellers of the Middle Ages was Marco Polo,[2] who traversed Central Asia, visiting all the peoples of that region, and finally

[1] *Europe in the Middle Age* (Thatcher and Schwill).
[2] See Chap. XXII, pp. 372-4.

POPE INNOCENT III

reaching even the Pacific. Other travellers only a little less famous are Plan Carpin and Andrew of Longjumeau. The accounts of their travels, which they published, were very widely read, and while adding information they increased the interest of Europe in foreign lands. The influence of the Crusades in this direction can hardly be overestimated. Without them the Renascence could not have been what it was.'[1]

It would, however, be wrong to suppose that all this progress would not have taken place if there had never been any Crusades. Contact with the Eastern Empire and with the Muslims of Spain and Sicily would have had the same ultimate effect. During the eleventh century, before Pope Urban made his memorable appeal, trade and commerce were extending in Europe, towns were increasing in importance, universities were being founded, and the East was helping to mould the civilization of the West through the influence of the cultured Moors of Spain. The Crusades accelerated a process which had already begun to work.

Probably the Roman Church reached the height of its power under Innocent III (1198-1216). He was the Pope who used the three great weapons of interdict, excommunication, and deposition against John, King of England, and so humbled him that he surrendered his crown to the papal legate Pandulph, receiving it back again as the vassal of the Pope. The Church at this time was something far more than a religious body. It was a State, a great international monarchy, with an elaborate system of law and courts of its own, where cases were tried which are now settled in the ordinary civil courts, such as matters relating to wills, contracts, usury, and blasphemy. The existence of Church courts caused kings an infinite amount of trouble.[2] Murderers who

---

[1] *Europe in the Middle Age* (Thatcher and Schwill).

[2] In England, Henry II's attempts to make clergy who were charged with criminal offences subject to the ordinary jurisdiction of the land led to a famous quarrel with Thomas Becket, Archbishop of Canterbury. The subsequent murder of Becket forced Henry to give up his attempt.

could show that they were clerks (clergymen) frequently escaped with very light penalties, such as being unfrocked—and ability to read a single line was often taken as sufficient proof that an offender was a clergyman, for it was assumed that no one unconnected with the Church could read at all. For six or seven centuries after the fall of the Roman Empire very few apart from the clergy ever took the trouble to study, or even to learn how to read and write. Thus almost all the books that appeared were written by clerics; it was they who formed and directed public opinion; and kings were obliged to entrust the most important functions of government to them.

The Church had a universal language—Latin—in which its services were conducted everywhere and all official communications written. It also claimed the universal adherence of Western Europe to its doctrines and teachings. To question them was a crime punishable by death. Yet there were some who thought that the Medieval Church with its great wealth, its powerful organization, its insistence upon a complicated ritual, and its arrogant claim of infallibility had departed far from the true spirit of Christianity. To hold such beliefs and to profess them openly required an immense degree of courage, but in the twelfth and thirteenth centuries two sects, the Waldenses and the Albigenses, who questioned the teachings of the Church and proposed to cast off its authority, attracted many members. The Waldenses were the followers of a man called Peter Waldo of Lyons. They gave up all their property and lived lives of apostolic poverty, but they were obnoxious to the Church because they denounced the riches and luxury of the clergy, and because they translated the Scriptures from Latin into the language of the people. The Albigenses derived their name from the town of Albi in Southern France, where they were very numerous. They went still farther in their criticism of the Roman Church. They believed, like the Zoroastrians of Ancient

THE MURDER OF BECKET; from an ivory

Persia, that two great principles, Good and Evil, were constantly striving for mastery in the world. The Jehovah of the Old Testament they denounced as the power of evil, against whose cruelty they maintained that Jesus Christ was a rebel. They were among the most peaceful of the subjects of the King of France; the lives of most of them were conspicuously virtuous in an age of violence and licentiousness. But that availed them little; to question the authority of the Church, to doubt the soundness of its interpretation of the Bible, were sins which only death could wipe out. Innocent III preached a crusade against them which did not end until the heresy had been effectually crushed and the South of France reduced to a pitiable condition by the mixed force of devout Catholics and adventurous scoundrels of whom the crusading army was composed. The Waldenses were more mercifully treated. Their founder, it is true, was excommunicated by Pope Lucius III in 1184, but 'the wise policy of later Popes allowed the more moderate to combine their own way of thinking with acceptance of the Church's authority, and they remained for the most part humble quietists, whose highest aspiration was to live in peace.'[1]

The vigour and strength of the Albigensian heresy led to the establishment in 1215 of a kind of permanent court of defence against the spread of similar errors in the future. This was the so-called Holy Inquisition, which existed to ferret out cases of unbelief and lack of orthodoxy, and to see that fitting examples were made of the offenders. A heretic who persisted in his heresy was handed over to 'the secular arm' to be burned alive without any further trial.[2] The Church did not punish him itself because its law forbade it to shed blood. There can be little doubt that many of the

---

[1] *The Empire and the Papacy* (Tout), published Rivingtons.
[2] If a heretic confessed his errors and abjured his heresy, he was forgiven and received back into the Church, but sentenced to life imprisonment as penance for his sin.

AUTO-DA-FÉ. From a painting of about 1500
(For description see page 328)

inquisitors were sincere men honestly convinced that their actions were in accordance with the will of God, but their methods, the gross unfairness of the trials which they conducted, their use of torture, and their attempts to make accused persons implicate others, have made the very word Inquisition into a synonym for intolerance and cruelty.

Much more to the credit of Roman Catholicism was the work of the two great orders of friars, the Dominicans and the Franciscans, whose founding in the early part of the thirteenth century does much to relieve the gloom cast by persecuting popes, and priests whose ambitions led them to neglect their religious duties. The Dominicans are so called after the name of their founder, the Spaniard St. Dominic, while the Franciscans owed their origin to the piety and love for humanity of St. Francis, a native of Assisi in Central Italy, and one of the most unselfish and lovable figures in all history. Both Francis and Dominic were well aware that, whatever might be the outward condition of the Church, it was really beginning to lose its hold over men's minds, on account of the negligence and misdeeds of the clergy, and so each of them founded an order of mendicants, or begging friars, who were to lead lives of self-sacrifice and awaken people by their examples and precepts to a better religious life. They were to hold no property and were to depend for their very subsistence upon the generosity of those to whom they ministered. Both orders were officially recognized by Pope Innocent III after some years of hesitation, and both defended the Church against the attacks of heretics, but whilst Dominic was appalled by the ignorance of mankind and the spread of heterodoxy, it was the misery of mankind which especially impressed the mystical and enthusiastic St. Francis. He even forbade worldly studies among his followers, an injunction which was not carried out—fortunately for the cause of learning, for some of the greatest scholars of the

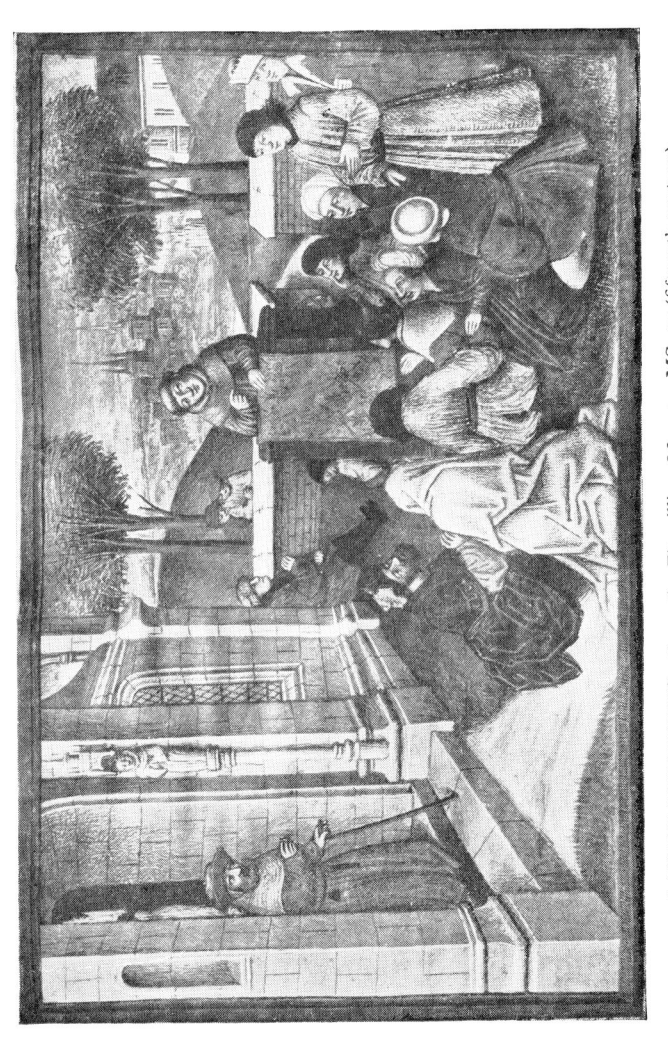

A FRIAR PREACHING. From the Fitzwilliam Museum MS. 22 (fifteenth century)

Middle Ages were friars. Thomas Aquinas was a Dominican and Roger Bacon a Franciscan.

The early friars were perhaps, above all things, the apostles of a social mission. The monastic orders had done their chief work in the country districts. The mendicants were the missionaries of the towns. For the towns their coming was a religious revolution. During the twelfth and thirteenth centuries there was a great development of municipal life. Nevertheless, a vast amount of squalor, wretchedness, ignorance, and poverty existed in the towns without any adequate means for counteraction. Improvement could not keep pace with the rapid increase of population. Fever and plague were the inevitable results of the narrowness of the streets and the inferior sanitary arrangements. Outside the walls which surrounded all medieval towns there herded masses of men and women, neglected and outcast, looked upon with despair or disgust by the parish priest. 'Burgher and artisan were left to spell out what religious instruction they might from the gorgeous ceremonies of the Church's ritual or the scriptural pictures and sculptures which were graven on the walls of its minsters.'[1] The advent of the mendicants was hailed with an enthusiasm which is hardly to be wondered at when we reflect that their poverty kept them on a par with the masses among whom they laboured, many of them outcasts among whom the foul plague of leprosy stalked like a remorseless demon. This disease set at defiance the skill and philosophy of the age: the utmost men could do was to banish it, to drive the leper from home, occupation, family, and township. St. Francis and his followers set nobler examples by devoting themselves to lighten the burdens of these pariahs of the social world. All Franciscan novices were made to undergo a period of training in leper hospitals as a preparation for the work which was before them. From their labours came a great impetus towards the study of

[1] *A Short History of the English People* (J. R. Green).

The western doorway of the Benedictine Abbey of Ripoll in Spain (about A.D. 1150) showing Old Testament scenes that were probably copied from miniatures in a Spanish illuminated manuscript bible

334 THE POWER OF THE MEDIEVAL CHURCH

medicine, and the good they did in the mitigation of some of the worst forms of human suffering is incalculable.

In later times the friars deteriorated sadly: worldliness and wealth sapped the vigour and sincerity which had made them so potent an influence for good, until by the time of the great English poet Geoffrey Chaucer (1340–1400),[1] there was little to distinguish them from the monks whose lax ways and love of riches they had reproved as much by their example as by their preaching. St. Francis apparently foresaw the danger when he wrote : 'I, little brother Francis, desire to follow the life and the poverty of Jesus Christ, persevering therein until the end ; and I beg you all and exhort you to persevere always in this most holy life of poverty, and take good care never to depart from it upon the advice and teachings of any one whomsoever.' After his death there were some who wished to follow his precepts literally ; there were others who argued that it was right that they should accept the gifts that people might be disposed to give them, and that, while individual friars should remain poor, there was no reason why the Order should not have monasteries and beautiful churches. In Assisi itself a stately monastery was constructed, and two churches, one to receive the remains of St. Francis, who in life had been quite content to live in a deserted hovel. Hardly less marked was the effect of increasing wealth and influence upon the Dominicans. They became arrogant and tyrannical, the apostles of rigid orthodoxy in matters of religion : some of the most powerful of the Inquisitors were Dominicans. This perhaps is not remarkable. Even Dominic had lost his temper with heretics who had not been convinced by his arguments. In his last sermon he told them :

'I have exhorted you in vain, with gentleness, preaching, praying, and weeping. But according to the proverb of my country,

[1] See the description of the Friar in the Prologue to the *Canterbury Tales*.

POPE BONIFACE VIII

" where blessing can accomplish nothing, blows may avail ". We shall rouse against you princes and prelates, who, alas, will arm nations and kingdoms against this land . . . and thus blows will avail where blessings and gentleness have been powerless.'[1]

The rise of the mendicant orders undoubtedly strengthened the Roman Church at a time when the deficiencies of many of its clergy were beginning to weaken its influence. But the friars, even if they had remained true to the ideals of St. Francis and St. Dominic, could not have prevented the ultimate disaster which inevitably resulted from the Pope's arrogant assumption of the right to dictate to kings how they should order the government of their states. There must come a time when the claims of the Papacy would be carried too far. It came in 1296, when Pope Boniface VIII forbade the clergy to pay taxes to laymen. This immediately brought him up against two strong kings—Edward I of England and Philip IV of France. Edward replied by outlawing the clergy, which meant that they could not expect the protection of the civil power which they affected to despise ; to kill a clergyman ceased to be an offence in the eyes of the law. The King of France took somewhat different action, but it was quite as effective. He forbade the exportation of gold and silver from his country; this meant that the Pope was deprived of the contributions of the French Church, a very fruitful source of revenue. Boniface, therefore, thought it wise to withdraw his injunction. The Papacy had received a severe blow, yet a few years later its prestige seemed outwardly as high as ever. In the year 1300 Boniface held a great religious festival at Rome to celebrate the opening of the new century. Pilgrims assembled from all parts of the Christian world; the Pope had two swords carried before him as signs that he possessed both spiritual and temporal power ; and the influx of money into the papal treasury was so great that two assistants were kept busy with rakes collecting the offerings

[1] *Encyclopaedia Britannica.*

336 THE POWER OF THE MEDIEVAL CHURCH

as they were deposited at the tomb of St. Peter. Meanwhile the Pope's relations with the King of France were getting worse rather than better. The Pope told Philip that he must not consider himself above papal control : only a fool or an infidel would think that : a list of the King's misdeeds was drawn up, and he was told that he might have to answer for them before a Church Council. Philip answered arrogance with arrogance: he dispatched troops to Anagni,[1] where Boniface was residing, and for three days the Pope was kept a prisoner in his palace while some of the French soldiers heaped insults upon him. The shock to his pride was so great that he died a few weeks later (1303). Philip now determined that he would have no more trouble with popes. He secured the election of a Frenchman in place of Boniface, and the transference of the Papacy itself from Rome to Avignon in France. Then followed a period of seventy-two years (1305-77) when the popes were exiled from their capital city ; they were all Frenchmen, and so much under the influence of the King of France that their efforts to raise revenue and assert their authority met with considerable opposition in countries like England which were politically hostile to France.

There were some whose criticism took a more dangerous form : they began to attack the Church for its intrinsic weaknesses quite apart from its political connexions. Of these the greatest was the English priest John Wycliffe (1320-84). He declared that the popes had no authority except in so far as they acted according to the Scriptures ; he condemned the sale of pardons for sins ; and he said that it was quite right for people to refuse to contribute to the upkeep of priests who led sinful lives. Wycliffe had many disciples, of whom the most distinguished was a learned Czech, a professor in the University of Prague, named John Huss, whose teachings made such headway in Bohemia that he was excommunicated

[1] In Italy, about forty miles from Rome.

THE PALACE OF THE POPES, AVIGNON

by the Church and afterwards inveigled by a safe conduct to Constance and there burnt as a heretic (1415). For thirty-seven years prior to this date the Church had offered a humiliating spectacle to the world by the existence of two popes at the same time, each claiming to be the true head of the Church, one at Rome and the other at Avignon. It was chiefly in order to put an end to this impossible state of affairs, and to secure the undivided allegiance of Roman Catholics to one Pope who should reside at Rome, that the Council of Constance was called. It succeeded in its task, but its attempts to destroy heresy by burning Huss and ordering a similar fate for the bones of Wycliffe completely failed. The death of their leader did not dismay the followers of Huss, nor did the series of crusades which the Papacy organized against them. The Lollards, as the English followers of Wycliffe were called, suffered a period of persecution, but the eclipse of the ideas for which they stood was only temporary. They were subsequently to revive in a form which was destined to rend the Church in twain. Wycliffe is the precursor of Luther, and he has been well termed 'The Morning Star of the Reformation.'

XX

THE GROWTH AND DEVELOPMENT OF TOWNS DURING THE MIDDLE AGES

TOWNS have at all times been the chief centres of culture and civilization, because men and women must always live closely together in fairly considerable numbers before they can erect imposing buildings, carry on trade with foreign countries, found schools and universities, and feel the need for museums and art galleries and whatever else contributes to the development of the human mind. One of the most striking characteristics of the five or six centuries following the downfall of the Roman Empire was the absence

EARLY MEDIEVAL TOWNS 339

of large towns in Western Europe, and this fact in itself is sufficient to explain why there was so little progress during the period. The barbarian invasions resulted in the disappearance of many towns, and those which survived were apparently of slight importance. The gradual revival of town life from the tenth century onwards is symbolical of the gradual emergence of society from the confusion of the Dark Ages to a more orderly and settled condition of affairs.

Many of the medieval towns grew up around the castle of a feudal lord or around a monastery; others originated as market centres because they were easy of access, or were situated at cross roads or on the banks of navigable streams, or at a place where it happened to be easy to ford an important river;[1] still others grew up on the sites of old Roman cities which had been allowed to fall into ruins.[2] They were all surrounded by walls to protect them against the attacks of enemies, and were generally very crowded and compact, not to be compared with their Roman predecessors. They had no amphitheatres or public baths and the streets were extremely dark and narrow, with the jutting stories of houses on opposite sides of the road almost meeting.[3] During the eleventh and twelfth centuries most towns outside Italy, with some notable exceptions such as Cologne, Mainz, Troyes, Reims, London, Bristol, and Norwich, were very small; in size they were no bigger than a modern village. They had little intercourse with the outside world. They produced most things which their inhabitants needed, and they were usually under the absolute control of the lord upon whose estate their lands were situated. Thus the townspeople were not much better off than serfs, with many irksome payments to make to the lord, such as *passage*, a payment on goods passing through a manor; *stallage*, a payment for the privilege of setting up a stall in the

[1] e.g. Oxford.
[2] e.g. Colchester, which was built on the site of the Roman city of Camulodunum.   [3] e.g. The street called 'the Shambles'.

market-place; and *pontage*, a payment for taking goods across a bridge. But as trade grew wealth grew, and the towns had opportunities of buying their freedom. Kings, lords, and prelates needed money to build castles, to carry on private wars, and above all to go on Crusades, and they frequently obtained that money by selling their rights over towns. When freedom had been thus obtained, the townspeople were very anxious to prevent outsiders from sharing the privileges for which they had had to pay; they were equally anxious to prevent any encroachments upon their rights by any one whatsoever, and so they formed protective unions which are known as gilds. Before the end of the eleventh century merchant gilds had become a feature of town life. These gilds controlled all the buying and selling within the town, except the trade in food, which was left free of tolls and charges; they prevented illegal transactions, such as buying up all the goods in a market in order to sell them again at a higher price, or holding goods back in the expectation of a rise in prices; and they did not forget social duties. Important meetings were preceded or followed by feasting and drinking, and members who were ill or who had suffered serious loss through fire or some other mischance received grants from the gild chest in order to tide them over their difficulties. In course of time the gilds became so important that their chief officers were almost invariably the chief officers of the town as well, and the Gild Hall, where the business of the gild was transacted, became the Town Hall from which the government of the municipality was carried on. In some towns the merchant gilds were not of long duration. As trade grew, each of the greater crafts, such as the weavers, the bakers, the butchers, the fishmongers, the armourers, and the fullers formed a gild of its own. For a time there appears to have been no distinct dividing line between the merchant gilds and the craft gilds. A member of one might be a member of the other. Craftsmen were freely admitted to the merchant gild,

'Medieval towns were all surrounded by walls to protect them against the attacks of enemies

THE CITY WALLS OF AVILA IN SPAIN

342 GROWTH AND DEVELOPMENT OF TOWNS

for the craftsmen were also traders or merchants who bought the raw material of their particular industry and sold the finished product in their shops. It has been suggested that the origin of the craft gilds is to be found in the exclusion of craftsmen from the merchant gilds by the more prosperous merchants, but although this happened in some cases, it was probably quite exceptional. There was no reason why there should be rivalry between the two types of gild. The merchant gild looked after the general trade of the town, the craft gild protected the interests of workers in a particular industry. In many cases the craft gilds came into existence as branches of the merchant gild, but eventually they replaced the merchant gild by a general gild in which all the craft unions were represented. The life of a town centred in its craft gilds, and the earliest way to obtain the borough franchise was by becoming a member of one of them. In the gilds were masters, journeymen, and apprentices. No one took up a trade without long and careful training in it. An apprentice lived in the house of a master workman, but received no pay. The years of apprenticeship varied, three in the case of the simpler crafts, as many as ten in the goldsmith's craft. When they were over, the apprentice became a journeyman wage earner,[1] and if he proved successful at this he ultimately became a master. Sometimes he had to go through a kind of examination and submit a sample of his work called a 'masterpiece'. Everything in the life of a craftsman seems to have been regulated by the rules of his gild. They fixed his hours of labour, the quality of the commodity which he would be expected to produce, and the price which he was to ask for it. Cheats and profiteers received exemplary punishments. Thus a baker who gave short weight would be drawn through the streets on a hurdle with his loaves tied round his neck, while the seller of bad ale or wine might be compelled to drink part of it, and the remainder

[1] i.e. he worked for master workmen and not directly for the public.

THE MEDIEVAL CRAFTSMAN. A Mason and a Carpenter
proving their skill before a Gild Warden

was then poured over him. But the craft gilds did not confine their activities to craftsmanship and craft products. Like the merchants gilds, they also performed certain social and benevolent functions. They gave money to the sick and the old, they provided pensions for widows and funeral expenses for poor members, they paid for masses for the souls of dead members, and they did much to cultivate the spirit of good fellowship. Thus, if a man fell ill in the middle of a task, he could be certain that his fellow gildsmen would finish his work so that he would not lose his profit from what he had done. Some gilds maintained schools, and they also provided the play acting of the Middle Ages, so that they made a definite contribution to the development of the drama, which, since the days of the great Greek dramatists, had fallen upon very lean times.

The twelfth and thirteenth centuries witnessed a tremendous development of trade throughout Western Europe. Consequently there was a corresponding increase in the prosperity of the towns. So long as the manor system prevailed, and men were content merely to produce what was needed by those who lived on the particular estate where they worked, there was nothing to send abroad and nothing to exchange for luxuries, but when merchants began to bring tempting articles into the towns, and particularly when the products of the East began to arrive, the townsfolk were encouraged to produce more than was sufficient for their own requirements, so that they could exchange their surplus products for others which they desired, such as Indian spices or Chinese silks. The Muslim invasions and the Crusades both had stimulating effects upon trade and commerce.[1] Barcelona and the towns of Southern France entered into commercial relations with the Muslims of North Africa; the Italian cities established trading stations in the East itself, and carried on a direct traffic with the caravans which brought

[1] See Chap. XIX, p. 324.

to Syria and Palestine the products of Arabia, Persia, India, and the Spice Islands. The two great centres of the Eastern trade in Europe were Venice and Genoa. At one time Genoa had practically the monopoly of the Black Sea trade.[1] By the fifteenth century, however, Venice had become the chief centre of the Eastern trade. The riches of the East—cottons, silks, precious metals, precious stones, pearls, gold, frankincense, and myrrh, ivory, cloves, pepper, ginger, and aromatic spices—came to Venice from Beyrout or Jaffa, Alexandria or Constantinople, and from Venice much of it would be sent by land through the Brenner Pass to Central Europe or through the Valley of the Po to the cities of Italy, or it would be carried by sea, for Venice had a great fleet of more than three hundred vessels, the property of the state, but hired out to the merchant princes and capable of conversion into warships at need. Once a year a large fleet was sent on a trading voyage, carrying the products of the East and the wines and currants of the Greek Islands to the ports of Spain, Portugal, France, England, and Belgium, and bringing back some of the products of those countries. In the South of Germany towns like Augsburg and Nuremberg became important and prosperous because they were situated on the trade route between Venice and the North, and could therefore operate as distributing centres or markets for the wares of the East. Cologne on the Rhine was, during the twelfth and thirteenth centuries, the centre of English trade with Germany. The towns of Hamburg, Bremen, and Lubeck also carried on an active trade with England and with the countries on the Baltic Sea, while the Flemish towns of Bruges and Ghent were important as centres of the trade in woollen cloths for which Flanders was famous.

The briskness of trade during the later Middle Ages is all the more remarkable when the harassing restrictions and

[1] Some of the Eastern trade came to Europe by way of the Black Sea and Constantinople.

346 GROWTH AND DEVELOPMENT OF TOWNS

annoyances which merchants had to endure are taken into consideration. Money was scarce and the coins often debased by needy monarchs or clipped by people who could not resist the temptation to take advantage of their rough and irregular edges ; usury was forbidden by the laws of the Church, so that money-lending, which is necessary to all commercial and industrial ventures of any magnitude, was left to the Jews from whom Christian conduct was not expected ;[1] the system of tolls impeded the prompt dispatch of goods both by land and by river ; and the dangers of sea traffic were enhanced by pirates, who were numerous in the North Sea and the Mediterranean, so that towns were obliged to form associations for mutual defence. The most famous of these unions was that of the cities of North Germany, known as the Hanseatic League (German *hansa* = a union), which at the height of its influence included more than eighty cities, of which the chief were Lubeck, Cologne, Brunswick, Wisby, and Danzig. In its most vigorous period (1350–1450) all the important coast and inland cities of North Germany were members of the league, and it had factories in Denmark, Sweden, Russia, and England. Novgorod in Russia was the eastern and London[2] the western limit of its influence. It practically monopolized the trade of the Baltic and the North Sea ; it made successful war on piracy and did much to lessen the dangers of commerce ; it had great fleets like Venice, and on one occasion (1370) it went to war with the kingdom of Denmark, which was threatening its interests, and extorted a promise that in future it was to accept no ruler without the previous sanction of the league.

The increasing wealth of the merchants could not fail to

[1] In the thirteenth century Italians or Lombards began to act as bankers. They lent money free of interest, but exacted damages for delay in repayment, which seemed perfectly fair even to those who condemned usury. Their name survives in Lombard Street, London, still an important banking centre.

[2] Its factory was near London Bridge and was known as the Steelyard.

VENICE. The Grand Canal to-day

bring about social and political changes, even in places which were not as directly controlled by them as Venice and the towns of the Hanseatic League. The clergy began to lose their old monopoly of learning, since the merchants were keen upon giving their sons good educations, and even in countries like England and France, where the towns were not as yet so important a factor of the national life as they were in Germany and Italy, the kings summoned representatives of the cities and boroughs to their councils. The gradual rise of the trading and commercial classes to a position not inferior in dignity and influence to that of the older orders of clergy and nobility is one of the most remarkable features of history from the thirteenth century onwards, and it is no exaggeration to say that the more civilized the country the more rapid was the process. It cannot be too often insisted that the towns with their skilful craftsmen, their democratic spirit, their civic love of law, were the centres of culture during the Middle Ages. A comparison of the cities of Germany with the states and principalities of that country affords a striking illustration of this. The Emperor was frequently unable to exercise any real control over the turbulent princes and bishops, and they in turn could not preserve order within their own dominions and put an end to the desolating private warfare which was draining the resources of the country. In the towns, on the other hand, although disorderly scenes were by no means unknown, their influence was not strong enough to prevent progress or impede seriously the acquisition of wealth. An examination of the buildings of the period reveals originality of mind as well as material prosperity. Few modern buildings can compare in beauty and grandeur with the cathedrals and town halls which were constructed in the cities of England, France, Italy, Spain, and Germany during the twelfth, thirteenth, and fourteenth centuries. Up to the twelfth century churches were built in what is called the Romanesque or Roman-like style of architecture because

AMIENS CATHEDRAL, one of the finest examples of
Gothic Architecture

350 GROWTH AND DEVELOPMENT OF TOWNS

they resembled the old Roman basilicas.[1] These churches usually had stone ceilings supported by very thick and solid walls. In the centre of the building was a main aisle called the nave, and on each side a narrower aisle separated from the nave by massive stone pillars which also helped to hold up the ceiling, and which were connected to one another by round arches[2] of stone. In the twelfth century French architects invented a new style of architecture which is known as the Gothic. Its main features are the use of buttresses instead of thick walls to support the ceiling, the replacement of the round by the pointed arch, the construction of large windows, most of them filled with stained glass of the most exquisite beauty, and the profusion of carving in stone. In the fourteenth and fifteenth centuries many Gothic buildings other than churches were built. The town halls of Louvain and Malines in Belgium and the belfry of Ghent are as good examples of this style of architecture as the cathedrals of Rheims or Salisbury. In the German cities the influence of Gothic was very pronounced. What is best in the town halls and churches of Nuremberg, Augsburg, and Strasburg dates from this period. The main part of Cologne cathedral was built between 1248 and 1322. The nave of Strasburg, which is pure Gothic, dates from 1275, and in 1377 the building of Ulm cathedral was begun. Market-places were adorned with beautifully sculptured fountains, and the inside of churches with magnificent paintings. In the fifteenth century John Gutenberg, of the city of Mainz, discovered or learned the art of printing by the use of movable types, and the arts of engraving and wood-cutting were widely practised in most of the German cities, whose wealth and prosperity so impressed the writer Aeneas Silvius (afterwards Pope Pius II) that he wrote: 'No people in Europe has cleaner cities. Their appear-

[1] See Chap. XVI, pp. 265-6.
[2] Called in England Norman Arches, after the people who were chiefly responsible for building them.

THE INVENTION OF PRINTING
A page of the Mainz Bible (*c.* 1455), reduced

ance is as new as if they had been built yesterday. They pile up riches. At meals the citizens drink out of silver beakers, and there is no burgher's wife without her jewelry.'

Still more remarkable were the wealth and culture of the cities of Italy during the fourteenth and fifteenth centuries. These cities were of two kinds—some, like Rome, Pisa, and Milan, had been famous in classical times; others, like Venice, Florence, and Genoa, first became really important during the period of the Crusades. Venice and Genoa were maritime republics, both competitors for the Eastern trade, and therefore bitter rivals until Venice won the final victory. Venice, during the later Middle Ages, occupied a position of power and influence. Originally built on some sandy islets in the Adriatic Sea, a place of refuge for fishermen and others whom the stress of the barbarian invasions had driven from the mainland, its development had been so marked that by the fifteenth century its inhabitants numbered over two hundred thousand, and its fleet was the most powerful on the seas. Nominally its government was democratic, but actually it was an oligarchy, controlled by the famous Council of Ten, a sort of committee of public safety chosen by the senate and acting as a bulwark for the Venetian aristocracy against any disposition that there might be among the poorer classes to rebel against their authority.[1] The nominal head of the republic was called the Doge. His power varied considerably. Some of the doges had much; others very little. It was not until the fifteenth century that Venice began to take any real interest in Italian affairs. Then, the growth of the power of Milan and the necessity of securing some control over the Alpine passes through which their goods went to the towns of Northern and Central Europe forced the Venetians to transfer part of the attention which they had hitherto concentrated on the Eastern trade

[1] In the sixteenth century the government of Venice became still more oligarchical, when the Ten delegated their functions to a sub-committee, the Council of Three.

FLORENCE 353

to matters nearer home. The connexion with the East was apparent in many ways besides the commercial activities of Venice. It even affected the appearance of the city. Many of its buildings were distinctly Oriental in character. The domes, the coloured marble columns, and the rich mosaics of the celebrated church of St. Mark suggest Constantinople rather than Italy. In some ways Venice was hardly an Italian city at all, and when the spread of Turkish power and the great geographical discoveries of the fifteenth and sixteenth centuries ruined her Eastern trade her greatness was at an end.

The history of medieval Florence in many ways recalls that of Athens during the Age of Pericles. There was the same restless energy both physical and mental, the same democratic fervour, the same frequent outbursts of factiousness, but despite it all a remarkable development of the human mind resulting in the works of some of the greatest of the world's creative artists, such as the poets Dante, Petrarch, and Boccaccio, the architect Brunellesci, the painter Fra Filippo Lippi, and the sculptor Donatello. The parallel does not end here. Florence, like Athens, experienced a period when the city was ruled by tyrants or despots—the great Medici family—who, despite the fact that they were not distinguished by any title, were as obviously the rulers of Florence from 1434 to 1494 as if they called themselves dukes or counts. The most famous members of the family were Cosimo, who died in 1464, and his grandson Lorenzo, who died twenty-eight years later, after a rule which lasted for twenty-three years, during which the city reached the height of its prosperity. The Medicis owed their power to the great wealth which they amassed as bankers. They based it entirely upon popular support; they had no military force behind them, nor any of the ordinary securities upon which a despotism generally depends for its continuance. The Florentines supported them because they conciliated the interests of most of the citizens, and because they maintained the credit and influence of the state in Italy and

354 GROWTH AND DEVELOPMENT OF TOWNS

Europe. When Piero de Medici, the son and successor of Lorenzo, by conduct which was at once arrogant and impolitic, gave the citizens the impression that he was attacking their interests, they expelled him and restored republican independence for a few troubled years.[1] Cosimo and Lorenzo were great patrons of art and literature, particularly Lorenzo, who richly deserves his title of 'The Magnificent'. Among those whom he employed to add lustre and beauty to Florence were Leonardo da Vinci, Michelangelo, Verrocchio, and Botticelli, four of the greatest artists of all time. He was also a great builder and a patron of music and poetry, and he succeeded in inspiring others by his example, so that the powerful families of the city, the magistrates, and the trade gilds vied with one another in showing their zeal for culture by such buildings as the Pitti Palace, the Palazzo Vecchio, and the Baptistery. Another Italian city where the influence of tyrants was productive of some good results was Milan, which from 1312 to 1450 was dominated by the Visconti family. The Visconti were more cruel and domineering than the Medici, they were less regardful of popular rights, but they showed similar partiality for artists and learned men, they strove to make their city beautiful, and the greatest of them, Gian Galeazzo Visconti, might, if he had not been carried off prematurely by plague in 1402, have extended his rule over the greater part of Italy and so achieved Italian Unity four and a half centuries before it was effected by the teachings of Mazzini, the diplomacy of Cavour, and the arms of Garibaldi.

The city of Rome, when the popes returned after their seventy years' residence in Avignon, was half in ruins from desertion and neglect, but a number of energetic rulers like Nicholas V, Pius II, and Julius II so improved it that some of its former glory was revived. The ancient basilica of

[1] Subsequently the Medici were restored and they succeeded in maintaining their authority, with some fluctuations of fortune, until 1737.

THE AGE OF THE GREAT ITALIAN TYRANTS
Equestrian statue on a tomb of the Scaligers,
the great family who ruled Verona

St. Peter's was taken down and the magnificent church of the same name erected in its stead. Its building was begun about 1450, but it was not ready for consecration until 1626, and several great architects were employed in the work, the most famous being Bramante, Raphael, and Michelangelo. The old palace of the Lateran, which had been the seat of papal authority for more than a thousand years, was deserted, and the imposing new palace of the Vatican[1] built in its place. Nicholas V founded the Vatican Library, which has the most valuable collection of manuscripts in the world. Even worldly and debauched popes like Leo X, the son of Lorenzo de Medici, and Alexander VI (1498–1503), were patrons of art and literature. So too was the infamous Cesare Borgia, the illegitimate son of Alexander, who was employed by his father to establish a papal despotism over the States of the Church. Cesare was one of the patrons of the great Leonardo da Vinci, who is regarded by many as the greatest of the world's painters, but his patronage of Leonardo is not as well remembered as the fact that it was the example and successes of Cesare which inspired the Florentine historian Machiavelli to write *The Prince*, a practical and cold-blooded manual for the despots of the time. The author discusses the way in which usurpers may best retain their authority over a town which they have captured, he tells them how many of its inhabitants they may advantageously kill, he considers the extent to which it is expedient for princes to keep their promises, and he concludes that those who have not observed their engagements very scrupulously and who have not hesitated to remove political rivals have fared better than those who have been influenced by moral or ethical considerations. It is a devastating doctrine which has been followed by many rulers

---

[1] The Vatican has a thousand rooms, many of them adorned by paintings by some of the greatest of Italian artists, and ancient statuary of priceless value.

WARFARE IN ITALY. Part of a picture of an army besieging Florence, by the painter Vasari

and diplomats since the days of Machiavelli, generally with disastrous results for the peace and well-being of humanity.[1]

The great defect of the Italian cities of the Renascence, as the period from the fourteenth to the sixteenth century which witnessed such a remarkable rebirth of literature and art is called, was their mutual antagonism. Like the cities of ancient Greece, they were continually fighting among themselves. There was no such thing as national consciousness. They often employed hired troops or condottieri to carry on these wars, and it sometimes happened that the leader of these condottieri turned against his employers and seized authority for himself. This happened in Milan in 1450, when Francesco Sforza, after helping the Milanese to defeat the Venetians, forced the people to acknowledge him as duke. The Sforzas, like the Visconti, were patrons of art, and one of them, Ludovico, the son of Francesco, was the patron of Leonardo da Vinci for many years, during which time the great artist painted 'The Last Supper', one of the most famous of the world's pictures, on the wall of the refectory of the convent of Santa Maria della Grazie, and executed his almost equally famous equestrian statue of Francesco Sforza, which was shortly afterwards destroyed by the French when the disunion of the cities and actual invitations from some of their inhabitants resulted in their invasion of Northern Italy and the temporary occupation of Florence and Milan. The political weakness which made this possible was to last for nearly four hundred years more. In the meantime Italy was to act as a battleground for the rival ambitions of Spaniards, Germans, and French, and the idea of an Italian nation was to get little beyond the speculations of philosophers. Town life undoubtedly impeded the growth of nationality, but it is

[1] Machiavelli does, however, admit that of the two ways of contending, by law and by force, the former is proper to men, the latter to beasts—but he goes on to say that the former is often insufficient, so a prince must study both so as to know 'when to make use of the rational, and when of the brutal way' (*The Prince*, Chap. XVIII).

TOWNS AND NATIONAL UNITY

doubtful whether the glorious Italian genius of the fourteenth, fifteenth, and sixteenth centuries would have come to bloom in any atmosphere other than that of the cities.

XXI

THE GROWTH OF NATIONALITY DURING THE MIDDLE AGES

THE development of town life during the Middle Ages was not conducive to national unity, because, generally speaking, the towns aimed at a species of independence which would be quite foreign to national ideas. The citizen of another town in the same country would be quite as much of a foreigner in a town to which he did not belong as the inhabitant of another country. This feeling of exclusiveness was particularly marked in Italy and Germany, where were the finest and wealthiest of the medieval cities, and it had much to do with the fact that in both these countries there was nothing approaching a strong national government during the Middle Ages. German nationality and Italian nationality were, indeed, not achieved until the latter half of the nineteenth century. In most of the other great European countries, however, towns were not allowed to develop their local rivalries in such a way as to endanger the unity of the country, and before the end of the Middle Ages nations whose members were bound together by kindred interests had come into being. One reason for this was the triumph of the kings in their long struggles against the attempts of the feudal lords to build up independent principalities for themselves. In Germany the Emperor failed to establish any effective authority over his powerful vassals. In England and France the kings succeeded. The result was an English Nation and a French Nation centuries before the idea of nationality even presented itself as a possibility to the minds of the German people.

THE GROWTH OF NATIONALITY

England, or rather Britain, was, during Roman times, regarded as an outlandish country inhabited by savages and separated from the real world by a sea which it was an adventure to cross. When the Roman occupation ended, the country was invaded by swarms of German tribesmen—Angles, Saxons, and Jutes—who drove the Britons into Cornwall, Wales, Strathclyde,[1] and Scotland, and settled themselves in South, East, and Central England, and also in that part of Northern England which is now covered by the counties of Yorkshire, Durham, and Northumberland. One of these tribes—the Angles, gave their name to the country, which became known as Angleland (England). For the ensuing two or three centuries the various tribes struggled among themselves for overlordship, until about the year 830, when Egbert, King of the West Saxons, achieved it. It was not, however, until the reign of Edgar (959-75) that the whole of England was really united under the leadership of Wessex. In the meantime the country had been invaded by the Danes, and Alfred the Great, the West Saxon king who at this time emerges as a sort of national leader, could do no better than divide England with them (878). Early in the eleventh century they were still more successful, and a Dane named Canute became King of all England. He was also King of Denmark, Norway, and part of Sweden, so that England formed part of a great Northern Empire. The Danes ruled England for less than thirty years, then, after a short interval in which there were English kings again, the country fell under the rule of another batch of foreigners—the Normans—who were themselves of Danish ancestry, but greatly superior in culture and refinement to the Danes of England. Indeed, the Norman Conquest proved a blessing in disguise. It marks the beginning of the consolidation of England, although many centuries were to elapse before the union of England with Wales, Scotland, and Ireland was effected. At first

[1] Cumberland, Westmoreland, and part of Lancashire.

Knocking down acorns for swine. Treading grapes

Harrowing, sowing, and digging

Weeding and picking flowers (?)

COUNTRY LIFE IN MEDIEVAL ENGLAND

the Normans treated the English with a contempt which they made no effort to disguise. They seized their land, oppressed them in various ways, and even degraded the language which they spoke. Latin became the speech of learned men, French the speech of polite society, while English was the speech of the common people. Gradually, however, this feeling of contempt disappeared. Marriages between Normans and English began to take place;[1] and English and Norman French combined to form the English language much as we know it to-day. Chaucer, the first great English poet, used the new language for his *Canterbury Tales*, which give a lively picture of fourteenth-century England, and Wycliffe translated the Bible into the same language. The loss of Normandy during John's reign (1204) forced the barons who held land in both England and Normandy to decide between allegiance to the King of England or to the King of France. Henceforward the English barons became closely identified with English interests, and a national feeling began to arise, the strength of which was clearly shown in the following reign by the opposition to papal exactions and to the King's foreign favourites, and also by experiments in representative government. The towns and counties as well as the great nobles and churchmen were invited to send representatives to the national assembly or parliament. This principle was carried out much more fully by the next king (Edward I), who also reflected the growing spirit of nationalism by checking feudalism, increasing the national control over the Church, expelling the Jews from the country because they were aliens, conquering Wales, and embarking upon an attempt, which was only frustrated by death, to conquer Scotland as well, and thus put the whole of Great Britain under one government. From 1338 to 1453 England was intermittently engaged in the great struggle with France which is known as the Hundred Years' War. Much of the

[1] Henry I, the third of the Norman kings, married an English princess.

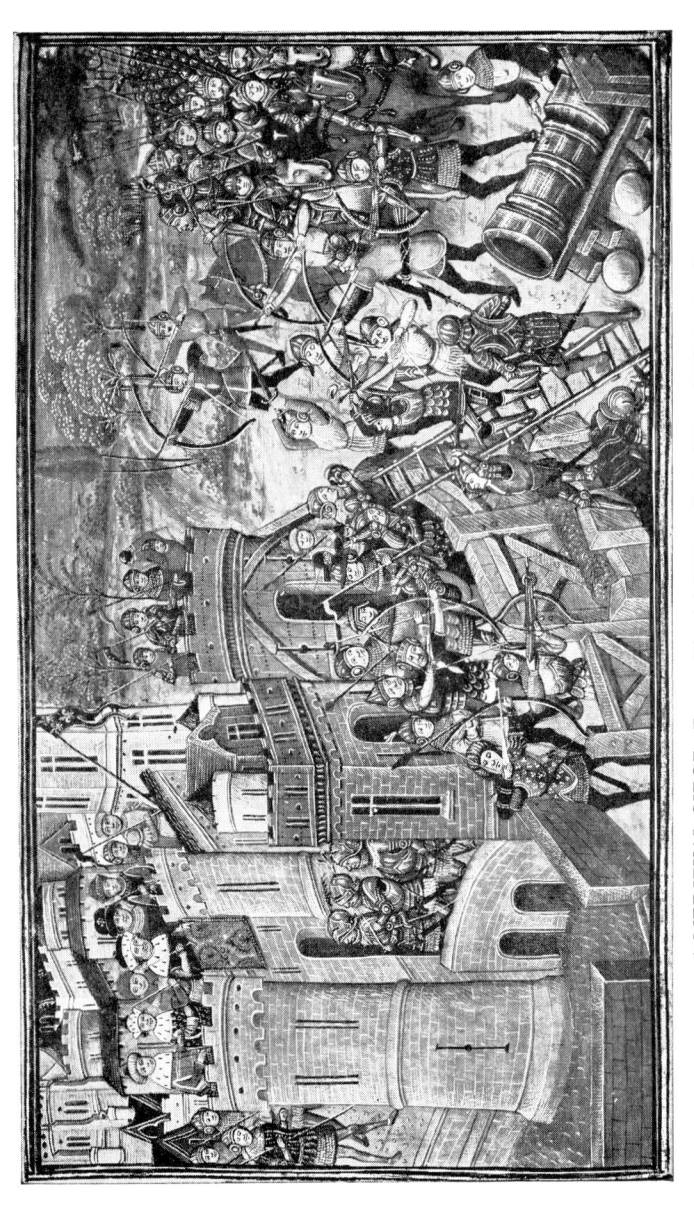

A MEDIEVAL SIEGE. From a Flemish MS. made for Edward IV about 1480

THE GROWTH OF NATIONALITY

early enthusiasm for that war was due to the fact that national feeling was inflamed by the somewhat spectacular victories which Edward III and his son, the Black Prince, won over the French, and when, later on, another king, Henry V, wished to strengthen a weak claim to the throne, he adopted the most effective method by repeating with much success the victories of the Black Prince. When the Hundred Years' War had ended in the expulsion of the English from France, it was followed by a civil war which was mainly confined to the nobles and their retainers, and which is known as the Wars of the Roses. It is interesting because it gave the death-blow to feudalism in England, already weakened by the Hundred Years War and by the loss of about a third of the population by the Black Death (plague, 1343-9). It crippled the power of the nobles, many of whom were killed, and prepared the way for the strong monarchical government of the Tudors (1485-1603), during which time the Church was completely nationalized, the trading and commercial classes raised to power and affluence, Wales began to be really settled and content to be part of England,[1] and the spirit of nationalism reached its zenith in the exploits of the great seamen and literary men of the Age of Elizabeth. Men gloried in the fact that they were Englishmen, as Shakespeare showed when he wrote:

> This royal throne of kings, this sceptr'd isle,
> This earth of majesty, this seat of Mars,
> This other Eden, demi-paradise,
> This fortress built by Nature for herself
> Against infection and the hand of war,
> This happy breed of men, this little world,
> This precious stone set in the silver sea,
> Which serves it in the office of a wall,
> Or as a moat defensive to a house,
> Against the envy of less happier lands,
> This blessed plot, this earth, this realm, this England.[2]

[1] The Tudors were themselves of Welsh descent.
[2] *Richard II*, Act II, Sc. i.

FRANCE A NATION

It was not until the end of the twelfth century that France first really began to be a nation. When Philip Augustus came to the throne in 1180 he had little more power than some of his barons, and a foreign prince, the King of England, actually owned more of France than he did himself. But before he died in 1223 Philip had proved himself superior to all his vassals, and had extended his influence to the remotest parts of France. He had defeated a conspiracy of some of his most dangerous subjects, headed by the Count of Flanders and the Duke of Burgundy, and had compelled them to surrender several rich districts to him ; and he had forced the English king, John, to cede Normandy, Touraine, Anjou, and Poitou. Philip had more than doubled the domains of the Crown, and had become the largest landowner in the country. For the first time in the history of France, the King was more powerful than any of his feudal subjects. The next three centuries of French history witness a process of national consolidation, and the gradual establishment of an absolute power centred in the Crown. One after another the great feudatories were reduced to submission, and their territories incorporated in the royal domain. Louis IX (1226-70), by encouraging the towns, secured powerful support for the Crown against the nobility, whom he treated with great firmness and skill, forcing them to submit to the jurisdiction of his own royal officers and to his own court as a final court of appeal. Thus the superiority of royal justice over all forms of local jurisdiction was established. Louis's reputation for goodness and justice, which earned for him the title of St. Louis, probably made the nobles less reluctant to entrust their interests to him than they would have been if they had to do with an ordinary king. Philip IV (1285-1314) enhanced the prestige of the French monarchy considerably by the successful outcome of his quarrel with Pope Boniface VIII and by bringing about the removal of the Papacy from Rome to Avignon. But a temporary check was given to

French unification during this reign by the revolt of Flanders from French overlordship. However, so many of Philip's nobles were killed in the Flemish campaign that the King's feudal strength was greatly increased, just as the Wars of the Roses increased the power of the King in England. The Hundred Years' War with the English, although it caused France much suffering, finally led to a remarkable outburst of national feeling, and the expulsion of the English from all their French possessions with the exception of Calais, which they held until 1558. Early in this war France seemed for a time to be progressing towards representative government. In 1357, the year after the Black Prince had won one of his most notable victories at Poitiers, the Parisians, led by a man named Étienne Marcel, and supported by many of the clergy, demanded redress of grievances before they should be required to contribute money for the continuance of the war. They asked that the national assembly or States General should levy taxes, and not the King. There were risings in Paris, and also various peasant outbreaks against the nobles in the country. Both were eventually suppressed, and nothing more was heard for centuries of popular control of the monarchy. The power of the French king was practically absolute until the great revolution of 1789, and before the end of the fifteenth century the unification of the country had been completed. Louis XI (1461–83), by cunning diplomacy rather than by any striking military successes, thwarted the forces of disintegration and won a great victory for centralization. His most dangerous opponent was Charles the Bold, Duke of Burgundy, whom the King finally circumvented by stirring up the Swiss against him. Charles was killed, and shortly afterwards Louis annexed much of his territory. When he died in 1483 the only great fief which had not been incorporated was Brittany, but that was soon effected by the marriage of Louis's son and successor, Charles VIII, with the heiress of Brittany.

SPAIN, PORTUGAL, SWITZERLAND

Other countries which achieved unity before the end of the fifteenth century were Spain, Portugal, and Switzerland. By 1238 the Muslims or Moors of Spain had been driven into their last stronghold, the kingdom of Granada. At that time there were three Christian kingdoms in the Peninsula— Aragon, Castile, and Portugal. Portugal had originally been a vassal state of Castile, but in 1140 its count had declared himself independent, and taken the title of king. Castile and Aragon were constantly at war with one another and with the Moors of Granada, but in 1479 the marriage of Ferdinand of Aragon with Isabella, the heiress of Castile, effected the union of the two provinces, and when Granada was conquered in 1492 the whole of the country had been brought under one ruler and Spain had become one nation. Within a few decades she rose to be one of the most powerful countries in Europe, but before the end of the sixteenth century she was already beginning to show signs of decay. This was due partly to the revival of France after the Civil Wars of the second half of the sixteenth century, but more to the revolt of the Netherlands (the richest of her European possessions) provoked by over-centralizing the government, and by Spain's pursuit of foreign policies far beyond the capacity of her resources.

The story of how Switzerland became a nation forms one of the most heroic episodes in the history of Europe. 'It is a story of the banding together of sturdy mountaineers, in the days when simple country-folk were held of little account, who, strong in their longing for freedom and in the love of their mountain home, were able to oppose successfully kings, nobles, and trained armies, and to form an independent government which has held its own down to the present day.'[1] In the thirteenth century there was no such country as Switzerland. The land which we call by that name then formed part of the Duchy of Swabia, which was part of the

[1] *The End of the Middle Age* (Eleanor Lodge), pub. Methuen.

Empire and divided among various feudal lords. The most powerful of these were the Austrian Habsburgs, who were the overlords of the three cantons or districts of Uri, Schwyz, and Unterwalden, who in 1291 laid the foundation of the Swiss nation by forming a league of mutual defence. The Habsburgs viewed the league with some apprehension, but their attempt to crush it was frustrated by a Swiss victory at Morgarten in 1315. Other districts hastened to join the confederacy, and by 1353 the original three cantons had increased to eight. Thirty-three years later they were powerful enough to defeat a great army of nobles and mercenaries from Germany, Italy, and France, led by Leopold of Habsburg, at Sempach, about ten miles to the north of Lucerne. By the close of the fifteenth century the Swiss had secured complete independence even of the Empire, although the fact was not officially recognized until 1648.

Although the growth of nationalism forms one of the most striking features of European history from the thirteenth to the end of the sixteenth century, it hardly made itself felt at all in the Empire. In the countries which are now known as Germany and Austria there were a few hundred more or less independent authorities, nominally subject to the Emperor, but most of them quite beyond his control. Some were ruled by dukes; others by counts, archbishops, bishops, or abbots; there were many cities like Nuremberg and Cologne, which were as independent as great duchies like Saxony and Bavaria; and there were also knights, who often exercised control over no more than a castle and a village which had grown up around it, yet they too aimed at as much immunity from outside control as they could get. Their lands were generally too small to support them in comfort, and they frequently took to robbery, and were a great nuisance to merchants and traders. The Emperor could not suppress them. He was almost always short of money and soldiers, and much less powerful than his great vassals. There was a national

THE EMPEROR CHARLES V

assembly known as the Diet, which met at irregular intervals in various places, for there was no capital city. The towns were not allowed to send representatives until 1487, and the knights and minor nobles were not represented at all. Consequently they did not always consider themselves bound by its decisions. In the first half of the sixteenth century there was a sort of temporary revival of the outward glories of the Empire. Charles V, who was Emperor from 1520 to 1556, also ruled over Spain, the Netherlands, Sardinia, the kingdom of Naples and Sicily, Milan, and the rich Spanish possessions in the New World. But despite his vast realms, and the great wealth which he had at his disposal, he did not succeed in establishing order or harmony in the Empire. He failed to crush the German protestants or to eradicate the doctrines of Luther; his well-meant efforts to achieve religious unity resulted in civil war; his efforts to check the westward advance of the Turks were hampered so much by the difficulty of getting the princes to combine even against these formidable foes that Charles was obliged to buy them off by the payment of an annual tribute; finally in 1556, weary of the cares and responsibilities of his position, the Emperor abdicated and retired to a Spanish monastery, where he lived a life of ease and luxury until his death two years later. He was succeeded in the Empire by his brother Ferdinand, while the rest of his dominions went to his son Philip II, the king who sent the great Armada to England and lost the Netherlands.

XXII

THE MONGOLS AND THE TURKS

TOWARDS the close of the twelfth century the people known as the Mongols first began to figure in history. They were nomads who made their initial appearance in the country to the north of China, the land of origin of the Huns and the Turks, to whom they were probably related by race. All the great nomadic races of history seem to have this in common—that they appear when civilization seems to be growing effete, clogged up, as it were, by too much wealth and luxury. Then it is that the nomads make their invasions; they bring with them something of the clean air of the desert or the open spaces whence they have come, and exercise a stimulating influence even upon the civilizations which they appear to overthrow. It was so with the Semitic invaders of ancient Sumeria, with the Arabs who conquered Persia and shook the Eastern Empire to its foundations, and with the Mongols who, under their great leader Jenghiz Khan, in the early part of the thirteenth century achieved their conquests with an ease and thoroughness which astounded the world.

The time for their appearance was particularly opportune. The great Muslim Empire had broken up into a number of separate states whose relations with one another were by no means consistently friendly. Egypt, Palestine, and Syria formed one state under the successors of Saladin, the leader of the forces which opposed the Christians in the Third Crusade; there was another caliphate in Bagdad; the Seljuk Turks ruled over Asia Minor; while the country between the Ganges and the Tigris was under the authority of another band of Turks and was known as the Kharismian Empire. The Chinese Empire was in a similar state of disintegration and decline. The southern part was under a native dynasty called the Sung; in the north the Huns had formed what is known as the Kin Empire with its capital at Pekin. Jenghiz

Khan started his career of conquest at their expense by attacking them and taking Pekin in the year 1214. He then turned his arms against the Kharismian government, which had taken the incredibly foolish step of putting to death envoys whom Jenghiz had sent to them. In a very short space of time the Mongol horsemen swept through Turkestan and Persia, and after taking Samarcand, the capital, made themselves masters of the whole of the Kharismian Empire. They even got as far west as the Black Sea, defeated all the Russian armies which were sent against them, and so frightened the Greeks of Constantinople that they at once began to strengthen their fortifications. When Jenghiz died in 1227 his dominions extended from the Pacific Ocean to the river Dnieper in Russia.

Under his son and successor, Ogdai Khan, this empire was considerably enlarged. Practically the whole of Russia became tributary to the Mongols, Poland was ravaged, and in 1241 a mixed force of Poles and Germans was literally cut to pieces at the battle of Liegnitz in Silesia. But the victors advanced no farther westwards. They were getting into hilly and wooded country which did not suit them, and they were preparing to settle in the great Hungarian plain when Ogdai Khan died, disputes arose as to who should succeed him, the undefeated Mongols trooped back to the East, and by a lucky stroke of chance Europe was saved from further humiliations. Tibet was overrun and Bagdad captured, but by 1260 the main force of the Mongol attack had spent itself, and when in that year Kubla Khan was elected Great Khan he succeeded to a divided empire. His authority was only really effective in China and Mongolia; Persia, Syria, and Asia Minor formed a virtually independent state under his brother; the Mongols of Russia were another practically separate group; and there was still another independent state in Turkestan. Kubla shifted his capital from Karakorum in Mongolia to Pekin, and founded a Chinese dynasty, the Yuan, which lasted until 1368.

His main interest for Europeans probably springs from his connexion with the Polos, and his eagerness to adopt Christian religion if it could be demonstrated that it was in fact as good as its exponents claimed that it was. So in 1269 he entrusted two Venetian gentlemen, Nicolo Polo and Mafeo Polo, who had been travelling in his dominions, with a mission to the Pope, asking him to send a hundred men of learning and ability to his court, so that they might prove to his satisfaction that the 'Law of Christ' was superior to all others. Unfortunately, the request came at a time when there was no pope. Disputes had arisen as to who should be head of the Church, and for two years there was no pope at all. When one was ultimately appointed, he sent two Dominican friars to convert the greatest of the Asiatic powers to his rule. They were appalled at the magnitude of their task, and soon found an excuse to turn back. The two Polos and Marco, the son of Nicolo, who accompanied the friars, however, went on, and many years later (1298) Marco Polo, who had been captured during a sea-fight between his native city of Venice and Genoa, beguiled the tedium of his captivity by relating to a writer named Rusticiano an account of his adventures in the East. The result was *The Travels of Marco Polo*, one of the most famous travel-books ever written, a book which directly inspired Christopher Columbus to discover America. Marco Polo had written of Japan, which he described as a country fabulously rich in gold, and Columbus imagined that by sailing across the Atlantic Ocean, in the direction of what we now know as Mexico, he would reach Japan. The Polos stayed in China for more than sixteen years, and Marco so pleased the Great Khan that he made him the governor of a province, and employed him on several diplomatic missions. So it was that he got his knowledge of such places as Burma with its hundreds of elephants, Japan with its gold, and Prester John, or John the Priest, who was reputed to be the king of a Christian

MARCO POLO'S TRAVELS

A ship sailing from Venice, from a MS. illustration of the
early fourteenth century

people somewhere in China—a story which was the inspiration of one of the most famous of the legends of the Middle Ages. The Polos returned to Venice in 1295, and it is related that they were dressed in Tartar garb and so unrecognizable that it was with difficulty that they obtained admission to their own house. Then they gave a great feast, in the midst of which they sent for their old padded suits, which they ripped open, whereupon there fell out before the eyes of the astonished observers a remarkable collection of 'rubies, sapphires, carbuncles, emeralds, and diamonds'. Much more remarkable, however, was the effect which the experiences of the Polos had upon those who, while not privileged to behold their riches, could yet be stirred by the records of their adventures. *The Travels* inspired many other explorers less famous than Columbus, and they stimulated that intercourse with the East which was to affect the civilizations of the West profoundly by the introduction of such important inventions as printing, gunpowder, and the mariner's compass.

It was unfortunate that the request of Kubla Khan for Christian missionaries should have met with so feeble a response. The Roman Church lost an opportunity which never recurred. When at last it had recovered from the schisms of the Middle Ages and the severe blow of the Reformation, and when in the persons of the Jesuits it had the most effective missionary organization that the world had ever known, the great opportunity of bringing about a moral unification of East and West was irrevocably lost. The Mongols in China and Central Asia had become Buddhist; in South Russia, Syria, Persia, Mesopotamia, and Western Turkestan they had embraced the doctrines of Islam.

The history of the divided Mongol Empire after 1260 is of more than ordinary interest. In China the successors of Kubla Khan became more and more Chinese, and ruled until 1368, when a nationalist rebellion resulted in the establishment of the cultured and artistic Ming Dynasty, which maintained its authority until it was overthrown in 1644 by the Manchus,[1] who ruled until the republican government of 1912 was proclaimed. In Turkestan the people fell back to the old tribal and nomadic ways of life from which they had been rescued by Jenghiz Khan, and an antipathy sprang up between the town dwellers and the nomads which has lasted to the present day. Tibet became a home of Buddhism. In South Russia, as in Turkestan, there were considerable numbers of nomads who roamed over very large areas, and also towns where people settled down to a more ordered condition of life. In cities like Kieff and Moscow, town life went on under Russian dukes or Tartar governors who collected the tribute which was exacted by the nomad Khan, the Khan of the Golden Horde. The Grand Duke of Moscow appears to have gained the special confidence of the Khan, and consequently to have obtained a sort of ascendancy over many of the other payers of tribute. In the fifteenth century, under Ivan the Great (1462–1505), the city threw off its allegiance to the Mongols altogether, and refused to pay tribute any longer; it succeeded in subjugating the trading republic of Novgorod; and Ivan the Terrible[2] (1533–84), the grandson of Ivan the Great, took the imperial title of Czar (Caesar). Thus the foundation of the Russian Empire of modern times was laid, but until the time of Peter the Great (1689–1725) it was almost entirely Asiatic in character. In Persia, Syria, and Mesopotamia there was a very marked return to nomadic ways of life. The Mongols in these regions seem to have adopted the attitude that the settled life of towns rendered men weak and vicious, besides being an unwarrantable encroachment upon good pasture land. The result was the almost complete disappearance of city life; even the

[1] The Manchus were of Hun origin and closely related to the Kin, whose empire Jenghiz Khan had overthrown.
[2] So called because of the cruelties which he perpetrated.

irrigation system which had endured for at least eight thousand years was destroyed; and Mesopotamia, which from very early times had been renowned for its fertility, became a land of malarious swamps and ruins. The same fate would probably have overtaken Egypt had not the Turks prevented the Mongol power from extending there. In the fifteenth century there was a still more destructive outbreak of the nomadic spirit in Western Turkestan, under the leadership of a certain Tamerlane or Timur the Lame, a descendant of Jenghiz Khan. He made Samarcand his capital, and extended his authority to South Russia, Siberia, and southward as far as the river Indus. He called himself Great Khan, and was very anxious to restore the empire of Jenghiz Khan, a project which it was beyond his power to effect. He is chiefly known because of the methods which he adopted in order to achieve his purposes. Like the ancient Assyrians, he appears to have taken an insane delight in the prospect of a pyramid of skulls, and after the storming of the city of Ispahan he is said to have made one of seventy thousand. He devastated the Punjab and massacred the inhabitants of Delhi, after they had surrendered to him, and when he died in 1405 he left behind him a name for fiendish terrorism, countries in ruins and desolation, and a dynasty which only survived for fifty years.

In pleasing contrast to the deeds of this lunatic are those of another Mongol chieftain, Akbar the Great (1556–1605), who ruled over Afghanistan and Northern India.[1] All the other administrations of the descendants of Jenghiz Khan have long since given place to different forms of government, but some of Akbar's work survives in India to the present day. He was a man of a singularly tolerant and generous disposition, and he showed the qualities of a true statesman when he set himself the task of using every kind of able man, whatever his race or religion, whether he were Muslim or Mongol,

[1] His great-grandson Aurungzebe was master of practically the whole of India, and was known as the Great Mogul (Mongol).

AKBAR THE GREAT 377

Aryan or Dravidian, high or low caste, for the public work of the community. In religious matters he was himself a Muslim, but there was no Koran, tribute, or sword about the policy which he pursued. There was perfect toleration for those whose opinions were different from his own—and this at a time when the Holy Inquisition was persecuting Protestants in some of the civilized countries of Europe, and Roman Catholics and Puritans were being persecuted in England. In battle Akbar is reputed to have shown the greatest bravery, and after victory he always displayed humanity to the conquered, and would never countenance any exhibition of cruelty. But his greatest qualities were revealed in the work of peace. He endeavoured by every means to develop commerce; he levied taxes equitably, and gave the strictest instructions that extortion on the part of tax gatherers was to be stopped; he forbade such barbarous rites as trial by ordeal and the burning of widows after the deaths of their husbands; and he was a munificent patron of literature. He established schools throughout his empire for the education of both Hindus and Muslims; and at Fatehpur-Sikri,[1] his capital, he gathered round him men of literary talent who translated a number of Sanskrit scientific works into Persian. It is even said that he employed a Jesuit missionary, Jerome Xavier, to translate the Four Christian Gospels into the same language.

One possible result of the Mongol conquests was the appearance in Europe early in the fourteenth century of a curious Eastern people who had been forced to leave their original homes, possibly on account of the invasion of Jenghiz Khan. At one time it was believed that they came from Egypt. Hence their name of Egyptians or Gipsies. They have also been known by various other names, such as

[1] Near Delhi. The city is now deserted, and although many of Akbar's buildings still stand, they are empty and desolate, and wild beasts roam through the silent streets.

Romanies, Hungarians, and Bohemians. They still retain their nomadic habits, and they have still a peculiar language, which contains many North Indian words, and some of Persian and Armenian origin.

A more important and much more certain dislodgement was that of the Ottoman Turks, who fled in a south-westerly direction when Jenghiz Khan invaded Western Turkestan. For many years they wandered about from place to place until they at last found a resting-place in the country which is now known as Anatolia, and congenial neighbours in their kinsmen, the Seljuk Turks. They increased in importance as the years went on, and when the Seljuk empire split up into various small principalities, that of the Ottoman Turks obtained a sort of ascendancy over the others. For many years before they attacked Constantinople they made encroachments upon the Eastern Empire. They crossed over into Europe by the old route of Xerxes at the Dardanelles, and gradually occupied Macedonia, Epirus, Illyria, Serbia, and Bulgaria. They converted as many of the conquered populations as they thought advisable to Islam; those who desired to remain Christian were allowed to do so on condition that they paid tribute for the privilege. Early in the fourteenth century the Sultan Orchan introduced the innovation of exacting this tribute not only in money or goods, but also in children. Every Christian village was compelled to furnish every year a fixed number of the strongest and most promising boys of about the age of eight years. These were brought up in the Muslim faith and educated with the most scrupulous care both for their bodies and their minds. As they grew older they were drafted into the army or into the civil administration. The civil servants formed a body which for efficiency compared favourably with anything of a similar nature in any other country of the time, while the soldiers constituted the famous Janissaries, who for two centuries were unsurpassed

THE BULAND DARWAZA AT FATEHPUR SIKRI, AKBAR'S CAPITAL
The city is now uninhabited

by any military force. Thus the most famous victories of the Muslim Turks over the Christians were won by the children of Christians.

For many years before the fall of Constantinople the relations between the Turks and the Byzantine Empire were singular in the extreme. Intermarriage was fairly common;

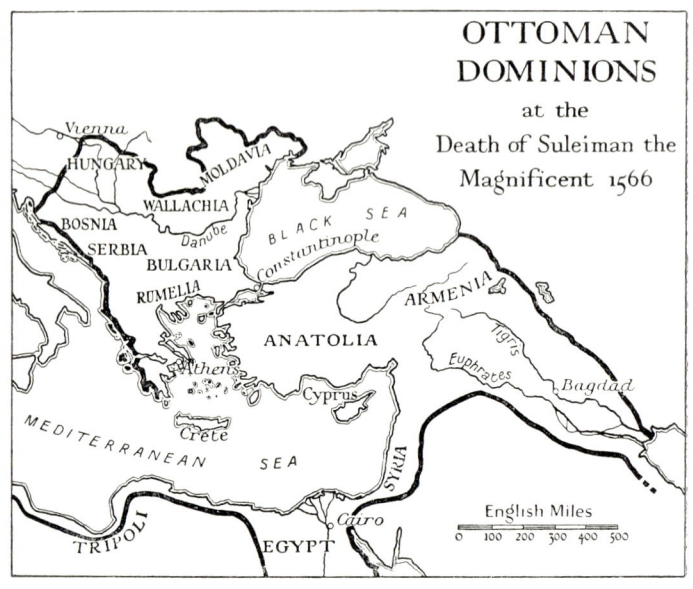

OTTOMAN DOMINIONS at the Death of Suleiman the Magnificent 1566

Turkish troops had been lent to the Emperor on frequent occasions; Byzantine princes and statesmen had accompanied Turkish armies on the field of war; and yet the Ottomans never ceased to annex imperial cities both in Asia Minor and in Thrace. It was an impossible situation, and it was ended in the inevitable way in 1453 when the Sultan Mohammed II attacked Constantinople itself, and after a memorable siege made himself master of the city. The last of the Greek emperors was killed in battle, and much looting and massacre followed the victory of the Turks. The famous church of

SULEIMAN THE MAGNIFICENT

St. Sophia was robbed of its treasures and turned immediately into a Muslim mosque. An era of Turkish conquest followed. Mohammed II was not satisfied with his success at Constantinople; he also aspired to conquer Italy and establish his authority over the imperial city of Rome. He captured and looted Otranto in Southern Italy, and it is probable that he would have achieved his ambition and entered Rome itself in triumph if death had not checked his career of victory in 1481. His successors extended the Ottoman power over Armenia and Egypt, and under one of them, Suleiman the Magnificent (1520-66), Bagdad, Algiers, and the greater part of Hungary were conquered, and the Sultan was acknowledged as the Caliph of all Islam.

The fall of Constantinople marks an epoch in the history of the world. The Eastern Empire came to an end, and Turkey started her career as a European state. As soon as the first effects of the ardour of his victorious soldiers had worn off, Mohammed II did his best to remedy the damage which his success entailed. He adopted an attitude of conciliation towards the Greeks, and did his best to ensure that Constantinople should continue to be a home of culture and a great centre of commerce. But the task proved too difficult. Its markets dwindled away; its culture and civilization fled; but all the bad features of the later Byzantine rule remained—espionage, bribery, and the evils which spring from corruption and the existence of too many officials. The Christian states of Europe regarded the fall of the city with feelings of undisguised apprehension, and there was some talk of a crusade to drive the Turks out of Europe. But the days of crusades were over, and indirectly the Turkish conquests were to have results of a most far-reaching and beneficial character. It is not true that the fall of Constantinople was responsible for the study of Greek in the West: scholars, especially in Italy, were already teaching the Greek language and literature, but after 1453 the number of such scholars increased; fugitives from the conquered regions made their ways to the Christian states where they would not be subject to the blighting influence of the Turks, and among them were many scholars of distinction. The study of Greek became more systematic and widespread, and, by helping to remove the restrictions which the Roman Church had placed upon freedom of thought, it contributed materially towards ending that phase of the world's progress to which we give the name 'medieval'. The year 1453 is, accordingly, taken sometimes as a convenient date to mark the beginning of modern times. It is sometimes claimed that the Turkish conquests also stimulated the efforts of mariners to find a sea route to India, so that the trade route with the Far East should not have to depend on the old land routes which the Ottoman conquests had rendered unsafe. But in fact the old land route was not affected until the Ottoman conquest of Egypt in 1517, and by that date the Portuguese had established their all-sea route to the Spice Islands of the Far East. Furthermore, the Ottoman Turks were as keen as anyone else to share in the profits of the lucrative spice trade.

XXIII

THE BEGINNING OF MODERN TIMES

IT is quite impossible to draw a hard-and-fast line of demarcation between the Middle Ages and Modern Times. Many European countries were in some respects medieval as late as a hundred and fifty years ago. Feudalism existed in France until the great revolution of 1789, serfdom was not abolished in Prussia until the early years of the nineteenth century, while in Russia it existed until 1861. But historians are, nevertheless, in general agreement that three great events, the Renascence, the geographical discoveries of the fifteenth and sixteenth centuries, and the Reformation, mark a definite transition from the Middle Ages to a state of affairs which can, with a reasonable degree of accuracy, be called modern.

The word Renascence signifies the rebirth of the freedom-loving, adventurous thought of man, which, during the Middle Ages, had been fettered and imprisoned by religious authority. The influence of the Church was paramount both in the schools and in the universities which had been founded at such places as Paris, Oxford, Cambridge, Naples, Prague, Cologne, Heidelberg, and Vienna, and no encouragement was given to a spirit of inquiry. The curriculum included grammar, rhetoric, logic, and some mathematics; no attention was given to the important subject of history, nor was Greek taught, although considerable deference was paid to the philosophy of Aristotle, who was practically regarded as the ultimate authority on almost every branch of knowledge. Instruction was given in Latin, and all important books were written in that language, but curiously enough little time was spent in studying the great classics of Rome such as the works of Virgil and Horace. Scholars of an original turn of mind like Peter Abelard and the Englishman Roger Bacon were extremely uncommon. Abelard, who taught in the University of Paris between 1110 and 1140, declared that a doctrine was not to be believed 'because God has said it, but because we are convinced by reason that it is so'. This was pure rationalism, and it so alarmed the Church that Abelard was tried for heterodoxy, and forced to recant his opinions. Roger Bacon (1214-94) suffered from the disadvantage of holding beliefs which were at least two centuries ahead of his time; he accordingly spent some years of his life in the prisons of the Church. His career has been well described as an intellectual tragedy. The blind and unreasoning acceptation of the teachings of Aristotle simply because of the fame of their author seemed wrong to him; and he made a bold and vigorous appeal for a freer use of the powers of

A RENASCENCE SCHOOLMASTER AND HIS PUPILS
A sculptured relief from Giotto's Campanile at Florence

the human mind. The modernity of his spirit is particularly noticeable in his predications of what to expect when the mind is allowed to work freely :

'Machines for navigating are possible without rowers, so that great ships suited to river or ocean, guided by one man, may be borne with greater speed than if they were full of men. Likewise cars may be made so that without a draught animal they may be moved cum impetu inestimabili, as we deem the scythed chariots to have been from which antiquity fought. And flying machines are possible, so that a man may sit in the middle turning some device by which artificial wings may beat the air in the manner of a flying bird.'

Roger Bacon was, unfortunately, only a lonely scholar, and the forces arrayed against him were too powerful. If it were not for the fear of prison and perhaps worse, his speculations might have been still bolder and more revolutionary in character, and the Renascence might have achieved its results more quickly. Actually it was a very gradual process, which took two or three centuries to reach its culminating point. It is generally regarded as having started in Italy at the beginning of the fourteenth century with the publication of *The Divine Comedy* by the Italian poet Dante. This great work departed from precedent inasmuch as it was not written in Latin, but in Italian, the language of the common people, and so it assumed that other people besides scholars had minds. Its subject—the pilgrimage of Dante through Hell, Purgatory, and Heaven—was certainly religious, showing that its author belonged in part to the Middle Ages when religion was the chief mental interest. But it abounds with many other interests—human love, love of country, interest in natural phenomena, and even the desire for a free and united Italian nation. After Dante came Petrarch (1304-74) and Boccaccio (1313-75). Petrarch was a great lover of classical Latin, and he did much to interest men anew in the works of Virgil, Cicero, Livy, and other famous Roman writers.

Boccaccio is chiefly noted for his *Decameron*, a book which recounts the stories which certain fine ladies and fine gentlemen are reputed to have told one another in a country-house outside Florence, whence they had been driven by plague. The English poet Chaucer was inspired by this writer's example to compose his famous *Canterbury Tales*. Boccaccio is also notable because he set an example to his contemporaries by learning Greek, and the study of Greek had consequences far greater than those which usually come from learning a foreign language, for the Greek writers were men of singular originality and boldness of intellect. Their historians were real historians; their men of science endeavoured to probe deeply into the mysteries of the universe, and refused to accept the traditional beliefs of their age without qualification or question; their philosophers were earnest students of how human happiness could be best secured; and their poets and dramatists had shown the joys and griefs of life with an imaginative insight which had never since been equalled. The capture of Constantinople by the Turks was responsible for the spread over Western Europe of numbers of teachers of Greek, but for many years before that time the study of Greek had been pursued with enthusiasm, particularly in Italy; Plato, Euripides, and Herodotus had been found to be as worthy of attention as Aristotle; and the minds of men were quickened in such a way that they began again to produce masterpieces which make the Age of the Renascence comparable with the Age of Pericles.

A striking example of the new spirit is to be found in the school which the Italian Vittorino da Feltre began in 1423. Philip of Macedon gloried in the fact that it was possible for him to employ Aristotle as his son's tutor. Similarly in the Italy of the Renascence a great schoolmaster was very highly esteemed by the more enlightened princes. Francesco Gonzaga, Marquis of Mantua, gave Vittorino a house in his park where he might hold his school. It was a beautiful house set amid the most beautiful surroundings, for Vittorino was a firm believer in the influence of beauty in moulding the impressionable minds of youth. He believed in the right of every one to be properly educated, and he bestowed equal care on the sons of noblemen and the sons of peasants. He paid particular attention to the health of his pupils, and, besides Latin, Greek, and Mathematics, he provided instruction for them in swimming, riding, fencing, archery, tennis, and gymnastics.

The revival of learning was enormously helped by the appearance of printed books. Probably the first European printer was Gutenberg of Mainz, who is generally supposed to have printed 'The Indulgence of Nicholas V', which was issued to obtain assistance for John II, King of Cyprus, against the Turks. It is thirty-one lines in length; copies of it are preserved in various European libraries; and it bears the date 1454. There were printers in Italy about twenty years later, and Caxton set up the first English printing press at Westminster in 1477. By this time it had become possible to manufacture paper in fair abundance and at a reasonable price, so that there naturally followed a great increase of books in the world. Moreover, printed books were much easier to read than manuscripts which had been copied by hand, and education ceased to be the monopoly of the Church.

Besides a rebirth of learning, the Renascence also resulted in a rebirth of art. During the Middle Ages pictures had been painted and sculptures carved always with the object of teaching religion. Even the colours which painters could use were regulated. Any departure from recognized rules was regarded as impious. The result was stiff and lifeless representations of madonnas and saints, which, whatever their value as pictures, are not true art. The saints frequently have unnaturally long necks so as to show that they are straining towards heaven. The Renascence was a revolt

'THE REBIRTH OF ART IN THE RENASCENCE'

The Loggia dei Lanzi at Florence, itself a fine example of Renascence architecture, and containing a marvellous collection of masterpieces of Renascence sculpture

against the bondage of medieval rules and traditions, and nowhere is this more noticeable than in the domain of art. The great artists and sculptors, like the Greeks whom they admired so much, painted portraits and carved statues to approach nature as nearly as possible, and with so much success that their work has never been equalled since. The study of anatomy became necessary for a painter, and new artistic methods such as frescoes for wall pictures, oil colours, and woodcuts were tried and perfected. It is true that the painters still devoted their talents mainly to the illustration of religious subjects, but they treated these subjects in a human and secular spirit, and by so doing they helped to effect a change in the very character of religion itself. It ceased to be a superstitious reverence for something unearthly and inhuman; it was brought into closer touch with the ordinary life of humanity. The revived study of antiquity probably had greater effect upon sculpture than upon either painting or architecture. The works of the great painters of ancient Greece had all perished. It was therefore only the Greek spirit which influenced painting; direct imitation was impossible. Classical influence was no new thing in architecture. The Romanesque style of the early Middle Ages was directly based upon ancient models, and even in the Gothic cathedrals it is possible to trace the influence of the ancient Greeks. But sculpture had almost become a lost art, and its revival was due to the discovery and imitation of some of the great masterpieces of Greece and Rome, many of which had been buried in various parts of Italy at a time when the statues of pagan deities were regarded as dangerous and likely to lead men away from the true religion. Some of these statues were so perfect that it was impossible to surpass them, and there were sculptors who copied ancient originals with almost servile fidelity. But there were some, like Michelangelo and Benvenuto Cellini, who showed skill rivalling that of the Greeks themselves, and there was Lorenzo Ghiberti, who

ONE OF THE CARVED PANELS OF THE 'GATES OF PARADISE', BY LORENZO GHIBERTI
Baptistery of St. John, Florence

carved the gates for the Baptistery in Florence with such exquisite art that Michelangelo declared that they were worthy to be the gates of Paradise.

The art of the Renascence reached its highest development during the sixteenth century, and among all the great artists of the time three stand out above their fellows: Michelangelo, Raphael, and Leonardo da Vinci. Michelangelo and Leonardo achieved distinction as painters, sculptors, and architects, and Leonardo also typifies the new spirit of scientific inquiry which is typical of the age. He was a man of astonishing versatility—a naturalist, an anatomist, an engineer, as well as a very great artist, and his note-books show that he was convinced of the practicability of mechanical flight. He is one of the earliest in a splendid galaxy of scientific men whose discoveries during the sixteenth, seventeenth, and eighteenth centuries were destined to revolutionize men's ideas of the universe. After him came Copernicus, a Pole (1473-1543), who suggested that the earth moves round the sun; then Tycho Brahe, a Dane; Kepler, a German; Galileo, an Italian; and the Englishman Sir Isaac Newton (1642-1727), the discoverer of the law of gravitation. The work of Galileo (1564-1642) was considerably hampered by the attentions of the Church, which still exercised much authority over the opinions which men might express. Galileo reasserted the theory of Copernicus that the sun is the centre of the solar system, and that the earth moves around it. The Church decided that this was a dangerous doctrine, implying, since the earth was made inferior to the sun, that Christianity and man were of little account, and considerably lessening the importance of the Pope. Galileo was accordingly made to recant his opinions, and pretend that he believed that the earth was the immovable centre of the universe.

From Italy the Renascence spirit spread to other European countries. In Flanders the brothers Van Eyck painted pictures which were as good as those of the Italian artists of their day, and discovered a new way of mixing colours superior to that employed in Italy, while Rubens and Antony Van Dyck carried the Flemish school to the zenith of its achievement. In Holland[1] Rembrandt; in Spain Velasquez; and the Germans Albrecht Durer and Holbein produced work which entitles them to be regarded as among the greatest of the world's artists. In France and England the effect of the Renascence is chiefly noticeable in the development of national literatures. France, in the person of François Rabelais (c. 1490-1553), produced a writer whose *Gargantua and Pantagruel* is a sort of epitome of the Renascence:

'the tremendous vitality, the enormous erudition, the dazzling optimism, the courage, the inventiveness, the humanity, of that extraordinary age. . . . Alike in the giant hero, Pantagruel, in his father Gargantua, and in his follower and boon companion, Panurge, one can discern the spirit of the Renaissance—expansive, humorous, powerful, and above all else alive, Rabelais' book is the incarnation of the great reaction of his epoch against the superstitious gloom and the narrow ascetism of the Middle Ages. He proclaims, in his rich re-echoing voice, a new conception of the world ; he denies that it is the vale of sorrows envisioned by the teachers of the past ; he declares that it is abounding in glorious energy, abounding in splendid hope, and by its very nature, good. With a generous hatred of stupidity, he flies full tilt at the pedantic education of the monasteries, and asserts the highest ideals of science and humanity.'[2]

In England the influence of the new learning is to be seen in the founding of good schools ; the study of Greek ; the *Utopia* of Sir Thomas More, a book which, though written in Latin, is far too bold and original to be regarded as a typical product of the Middle Ages ; but above all in the development of English poetry, particularly that branch of it which

[1] Holland also produced one of the greatest scholars of the Renascence in the person of Desiderius Erasmus of Rotterdam.
[2] *Landmarks in French Literature* (Strachey), O.U.P. Home University Library.

we know as the drama. The Renascence spirit is clearly discernible in the daring imagination of Christopher Marlowe, the many-sidedness of Shakespeare, the wit of Ben Jonson, and the zeal for personal liberty which is frequently expressed in the majestic poetry and prose of John Milton. Shakespeare (1564–1616) has never been excelled as a writer of plays. He is the only dramatist who challenges comparison with the great tragedians of ancient Athens—Aeschylus, Sophocles, and Euripides—and most critics agree that he is the greatest dramatist that the world has ever known.

In still another way did the men of the Renascence show their adventurous spirit. They sailed into unknown seas, and established contact with parts of the world whose very existence had not been previously known. Some time before the end of the thirteenth century the mariner's compass was introduced into Europe. This was an invention of supreme importance, since it enabled long voyages to be made out of sight of land. Portugal at first led the way in the work of exploration, discovering the Canaries, Madeira, and the Azores. In 1442 sailors sent out by Prince Henry the Navigator reached the Guinea Coast of Africa, and in 1486 Bartholomew Diaz rounded the Cape of Good Hope. The huge profits gained by Venice and Genoa from their monopoly of trade between Europe and the Far East were a permanent incentive to other states to break this monopoly, and European navigators were induced to try every possible way to reach the East by sea—by sailing round Africa; by going west in the hope of getting to the Indies, for most intelligent people at this time believed that the world was round; and, after America had been discovered, by sailing round it to the north or south. There can be little doubt that the desire for spices was one of the chief motives which prompted these voyages. Spices were at that time used to preserve food, and to make spoiled food more palatable. The possibilities of ice as a preservative were not realized.

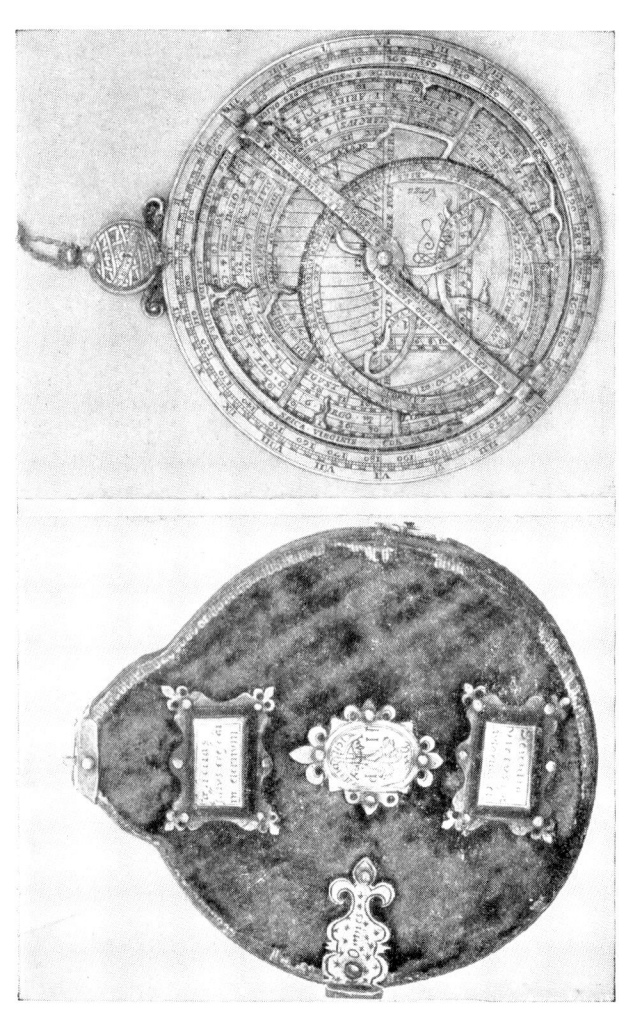

The Quadrant and the Astrolabe were the chief instruments of medieval navigation
An astrolabe of 1574

THE BEGINNING OF MODERN TIMES

The most famous of the explorers of the period were Christopher Columbus, Vasco da Gama, and Ferdinand Magellan. Columbus was a Genoese sailor originally in the employ of Portugal, in whose ships he made voyages to the Guinea Coast and to Iceland, so that he had had practical experience of the Atlantic Ocean from the Arctic regions to the Equator, before he set out upon the voyage which has made him famous. But the idea which eventually led to it came to him from books, particularly the voyages of Marco Polo and the writings of a Florentine geographer named Toscanelli, who maintained that the best way to reach the Indies was by sailing westwards. Columbus made his first proposal for such a voyage, naturally enough, to the King of Portugal, and just as naturally it was refused, since at this time the Portuguese had nearly accomplished the circumnavigation of Africa, and it would be far easier to monopolize such a route to the East than one across the Atlantic. Columbus next tried Genoa, his native place, and then Venice, but both republics were more interested in the maintenance of the old overland routes than in the discovery of a new route by sea. It was clear, therefore, that the only hope of support lay in some power on the western coast of Europe who had no vested interest in maintaining the old channels of commerce, and for whom the discovery of the new route would open up new sources of wealth. England, Spain, and France were such powers, and Columbus decided to make a simultaneous appeal to the two former. He sent his brother Bartholomew to England while he himself went to Spain. One morning he was found in a state of semi-starvation outside a Franciscan convent in that country. The friars treated him well, and also secured for him an introduction to the court of Castile. There he encountered some opposition and much support, but years were spent in fruitless discussions, and it became obvious that neither Ferdinand nor Isabella, the Spanish sovereigns, would support him until the Moors had been conquered and the whole of Spain made into a Christian State. In 1492 this was accomplished. The great Moorish stronghold of Granada fell ; Jews were expelled from the country ; and Columbus realized that his opportunity had at last come. He painted in glowing colours to the Spanish monarchs the wealth which would result from an expedition westwards to discover the East. He would bring back sufficient slaves to pay all expenses and sufficient gold to reconquer Palestine. In return he asked for the dignities of Admiral of the Atlantic and Viceroy in the lands which he should discover. Eventually Ferdinand and Isabella gave their consent, but only after an offer to finance the expedition had been made by an Aragonese official named Santaguel, who probably hoped by such an action to save himself from any disagreeable consequences which might otherwise result from his Jewish descent.

On 3rd August 1492 Columbus sailed from the harbour of Palos near Cadiz with three small ships: the *Santa Maria*, his flagship, the *Pinta*, and the *Nina*. He first sailed southwards to the Canary Islands, where he made a short stay in order to repair the rudder of the *Pinta*, and the real voyage started when he left the Canaries and struck westwards on September 6th. The ships lost sight of land on the second day and did not again see it for five weeks. Those were for the admiral days of apprehension and anxiety. Faced with the superstitious terrors of his crews, most of whom believed that they would never see Spain again, he had to make use of every device that presented itself to his fertile mind in order to retain their loyalty. He cajoled them ; he threatened them ; he compared favourable weather to April nights in Andalusia, wanting only the melody of nightingales ; he kept two logs, one a true one, and the other deliberately falsified so that the sailors might not realize how far away from their homes they were ; and he was continually calling their attention to signs which made it obvious that land was near, birds which never sleep at sea, pelicans, floating river weed, crabs, and whales. On 7 October the course was changed in order to follow the flight of birds, 'knowing also that the Portuguese had discovered most of the islands they possessed by attending to the flight of birds',[1] and five days later Columbus and his men landed on one of the Bahama Islands. During the next few months they visited Cuba and Haiti, and gained a good general knowledge of the West Indian archipelago. In negotiating the shoals and currents of those seas they were much aided by nautical instruments made in Nuremberg, much more so than Columbus ever admitted. He declared that his success was due more to a study of the prophet Isaiah than to science. Columbus never realized the magnitude of his discovery. He thought that the island where he landed after his voyage across the Atlantic was in the East Indies; he believed Cuba to be part of the mainland of Asia; and he mistook Haiti for Zipangu, the golden land of Marco Polo.

When he returned to Palos in the *Nina*—the *Santa Maria* having been shipwrecked, and the *Pinta* arriving later—he was most enthusiastically received. The very people who had execrated and cursed him when he started on his great expedition into the unknown, seven and a half months earlier, were now the loudest in their praises, and his journey to Barcelona, where the King and the Queen were, has been likened to a Roman triumphal procession. Ferdinand and Isabella showered favours upon him; regarded with interest the six Indians, the rare plants, and the stuffed birds which he had brought with him as proofs of the truth of his story; and listened eagerly to his tales of lands of unlimited extent and boundless wealth. A fleet of seventeen ships was fitted out for another voyage, which was undertaken before the end of the year (1493), but no great cargo-loads of gold came back to Spain; the Spanish colonists got on badly with the

[1] *The Journal of Columbus' First Voyage to America* (pub. Jarrold).

Of Potatoes of Virginia. Chap. 335

Battata Virginiana siue Virginianorum, & Pappus.
Potatoes of Virginia.

Virgin
holi
trail
three squa
kneed in f
distances,
commeth
made of d
ler, & oth
vpon a fa
of a swart
to rednes.
bling thos
at the firs
ward shar
from the b
come foo
footstalks
faire and
of one ent
folded or
fort, that i
made of fi
which car
except the
The colou
expresse.
light purp
the middl

with a light shew of yellownes, as though purple and yellow were mixed
of the flower thrusteth foorth a thicke fat pointell, yellow as golde, wi
pricke or point in the middest thereof. The fruite succeedeth the flowers
bignes of a little bulleffe or wilde Plum, greene at the first, and blacke wh

The introduction of the potato to the Old World. An illustration from
Gerarde's *Herball*, 1597

400 THE BEGINNING OF MODERN TIMES

Indians; Columbus proved a poor administrator; the slaves whom he dispatched to the markets of Seville to make up for the lack of gold were of little value; Spaniards returned from the New World poor and fever-stricken; and in 1500 an official named Bobadilla was sent from Spain to hold an inquiry into Columbus's government. He sent the great sailor in irons to Spain, an act which so outraged public opinion that Bobadilla was recalled and Columbus put in command of another small expedition which sailed in 1503 but accomplished little. In 1506 Columbus died. He had added to the map of the world the West Indian Islands, and the coasts of Honduras, Nicaragua, Costa Rica, Darien, and Para in Venezuela. In half the time which he took to do this, had his abilities been suitably employed, he might have discovered the whole of the American coastline. A few years after his death his name was almost forgotten, and the continent was named after Amerigo Vespucci, a native of Florence who visited the New World and wrote accounts of his voyages, and whom an ignorant people associated with Columbus's great achievement.

Meanwhile, in 1498, a Portuguese sailor, Vasco da Gama, had succeeded in discovering an actual sea route to India. He sailed round the Cape of Good Hope, then in a northerly direction beyond Zanzibar, and then with the assistance of an Arab pilot straight across the Indian Ocean until he reached Calicut. But much more wonderful was the voyage undertaken by Magellan, who was also Portuguese, although, like Columbus, he was employed by the King of Spain. In 1519 he sailed from Spain to the south of South America and, steering his course through the straits which now bear his name, came into the Pacific Ocean, which had already been sighted many years before by Spanish explorers from the Isthmus of Panama. Then followed a terrible voyage of eighty-nine days across unknown and apparently limitless seas. During the whole of that time only two small desert islands

Columbus's fleet reaching America. From a woodcut of 1494

Magellan's ship *Victoria* (*Vittoria*)

THE GREAT EXPLORERS

were sighted, and the crews of Magellan's ships were reduced to such a state that they were obliged to eat rats, sawdust, and even cowhide in order to allay the pangs of hunger. In this condition they arrived at the Ladrone Islands, and thence they sailed to the Philippines, where Magellan and some of his captains were killed by the natives. Five ships and two hundred and eighty men had left Seville in 1519. Three years later, one of them—the *Vittoria*—with eighteen Europeans and four black men aboard, returned with the distinction of being the first ship that ever sailed round the world.

The coast of North America was explored chiefly by English mariners, who for more than a hundred years made vain attempts to discover a North-West route to India. Two of the most famous of these—John Davis and Martin Frobisher, are immortalized in the straits which bear their names. But England, like France and Holland, came late into the adventure of exploration. Both in America and in the East, Spain and Portugal had a good half-century's start over all other countries, and in 1493 Pope Alexander VI endeavoured to regulate colonization by a generous division of what did not belong to him. He said that everything west of a line 370 leagues west of the Cape Verde Islands was to belong to Spain, while everything to the east of the line was to belong to Portugal. Fortified by this award, the Spaniards began to build up an empire in the New World with a zeal which rose superior to all obstacles. In 1519, under a leader named Cortez, they overthrew the Aztec Empire of Mexico, and in 1530, under Pizarro, they conquered Peru. Both Mexico and Peru were rich in treasure, and a steady stream of gold and silver began to flow across the Atlantic to Spain. The achievement of national unity by the conquest of the Moors came just in time for Spain to concentrate upon the building up of an empire in America, and it was the wealth coming from her possessions in the New World which, more than anything else, was responsible for the position of importance

EXPLOITATION OF THE NEW WORLD

which she occupied in the sixteenth century. When her colonial supremacy began to be seriously challenged by other nations, the power of Spain visibly declined, and her economy, undermined by inflation and by the tasks thrust upon her during her brief period of greatness, has never since recovered. Before the end of the sixteenth century the district along the northern coast of South America, which is known as the Spanish Main, was much frequented by adventurous seamen who carried on a flourishing if somewhat hazardous trade with the colonists, and did not always refrain from plundering Spanish treasure-ships and attacking Spanish treasure-houses. Many of these were Englishmen, the most famous being Sir Francis Drake.[1] Judged by ordinary standards they were pirates, for they did most of their work when their countries were at peace with Spain, but there can be no doubt that England owes the beginning of her commercial greatness and her great colonial empire to them. It is significant that Queen Elizabeth knighted Drake and showed no reluctance to share in his spoils, but she made it quite clear to him that if he were clumsy enough to fall into the hands of the Spaniards he must not expect her to intervene on his behalf.

The Europeans frequently behaved in a cruel manner towards the people with whom they came into contact in the New World, and showed little regard for their rights. The Spaniards showed much brutality and injustice towards the Indians of Mexico and Peru, and early in the sixteenth century the practice of kidnapping negro slaves in West Africa and importing them to the Spanish colonies began. One of the most successful of those who carried on this nefarious practice was the Englishman John Hawkins. However, the luckless natives of South America who had been dispossessed did find some champions, even among the nation which oppressed them. Friars of the orders of St. Dominic

[1] The first Englishman to sail round the world.

and St. Francis called attention to their wrongs and denounced the tyranny of the planters; so too did a certain secular priest named Las Casas, who, until his conscience smote him, had himself been a planter and slave-owner in Cuba; and from about the middle of the sixteenth century onwards the natives had new champions among the Jesuit priests, who found South America a good field for their missionary activities.

Closely connected with the Renascence is the great religious movement which is known as the Reformation, for the Renascence, by emancipating thought, helped men to realize that the Roman Church was not what it should be, and that there were certain abuses which could not be explained away by any such doctrine as that of papal supremacy. The great Dutch scholar Erasmus, one of the foremost advocates of the New Learning, a man whose influence extended beyond his own country to England, France, Germany, and Italy, in 1519 published a book called *The Praise of Folly*, of which it has been said that 'the jokes of Erasmus did the Pope more harm than the anger of Luther'. Folly, he wrote, is the chief source of happiness. It rules the world, and particularly the Church. It is responsible for spreading belief in the miraculous power of images of saints, belief in indulgences, and belief that ignorance and dirt are forms of piety. Erasmus hoped that he would be able to effect the reforms which he desired in the Church by a direct appeal to the reason of humanity. He abhorred war of every description, and the violent methods of some of those who rebelled against the tyranny of Rome were as hateful to him as the causes which produced them.

The character of the great German reformer Martin Luther was by no means so gentle. Luther was the son of a poor Saxon miner; he was born at Eisleben in 1483, and after receiving a village education he went to the University of Erfurt. Subsequently he became a monk and a professor of

Inside the silver-mines of Potosi. From an eighteenth-century engraving

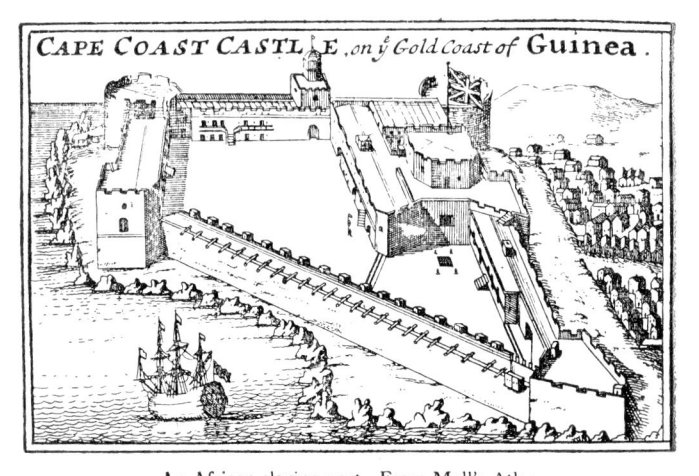

An African slaving post. From Moll's Atlas

SPAIN IN THE NEW WORLD AND THE GROWTH OF SLAVERY

philosophy at the University of Wittenberg. While he was there, a certain man named Tetzel came round selling indulgences, with the object of getting money for the new church of St. Peter at Rome, which was nearing completion. An indulgence secured for its purchaser some mitigation of the sufferings which he would have to endure in purgatory before he would be considered fit enough to enjoy the blessings of heaven. Luther thought the system irrational, and he accordingly nailed a protest on the door of the church at Wittenberg (1517). He argued that, while an indulgence might excuse a penance imposed by the Church, it could not excuse a punishment imposed by God after death ; still less could it remove the guilt of sin. There was nothing new in this argument ; Erasmus and others had said exactly the same thing. But there was something in the way in which Luther delivered his appeal, and in his vigorous personality, which seriously alarmed the Pope, and he summoned him to Rome, where he would probably have been burnt, but Frederick, Elector of Saxony, whose subject Luther was, refused to let him go. In 1520 the reformer was excommunicated, and a year later the ban of the Emperor Charles V was pronounced against him. But papal excommunication and imperial ban were alike ineffective ; Luther could count upon the support of the North German princes, particularly the rulers of Saxony and Brandenburg, and the enthusiastic adherence of thousands of the peasants. Some of them interpreted his teachings so literally as to bring down upon themselves his fierce denunciation. Luther had preached the equality of all men in the eyes of God, and the peasants argued that if they were equal to their masters in the eyes of God, the inequalities of their positions in the world were quite irrational, and contrary to the teachings of Scripture. Accordingly in 1525 they rose in rebellion, demanding the abolition of serfdom, 'because Christ redeemed us and made us free'. Luther realized that if he gave them his support he would lose the support of the princes, and of others who would assume that the Reformation meant anarchy and revolution. He therefore published a pamphlet against 'the murdering, thieving hordes of peasants', urging the princes to 'knock down, strangle, and stab' them, and even going so far as to assert that 'in such times a prince can merit heaven better by bloodshed than by prayer'. It was a most unfortunate pamphlet; it lost Luther the support of the masses; it showed that his genius was destructive rather than constructive; and from this date the character of the German Reformation degenerates. About half of the princes of Germany threw off the authority of Rome. Some of them did so from religious motives, but far the greater number did so for political reasons, as did Henry VIII of England. They foresaw an increase of authority if they were acknowledged as the heads of their respective states in matters spiritual as well as temporal; they wanted an opportunity and an excuse to confiscate the wealth of the monasteries; but they had no intention of allowing their subjects to exercise their judgements freely in religious questions. Their ideal was a national Church dependent upon the throne, and they did not scruple to persecute those who opposed their settlements.

The revolt against the authority of Rome was by no means confined to Germany. A year after Luther's denunciation of Tetzel the new doctrines were preached at Zurich in Switzerland by Zwingli, and eighteen years later the French Reformer John Calvin began his connexion with the city of Geneva, which was to last, except for the interruption of a brief exile, until he died (1536–64). During that time Calvin was the real ruler of the city, the director and controller not only of the religious opinions of the inhabitants, but also of such secular matters as education, sanitation, and trade. His rule, though efficient, was somewhat harsh. Public worship was compulsory; gay clothes and dancing were made punishable offences; and immorality was sometimes punished with death. Heretics were burnt, and there is one instance of a child being beheaded for having struck his parents. The religion which Calvin established was gloomy beyond measure; it has inspired no art; it destroyed individual liberty; and its main doctrine, that of predestination, is one of the most terrible ever postulated. It declares that all are predestined at birth either to everlasting happiness after death, or to everlasting damnation. Nothing that a man may do in life can apparently change his fate. Such a belief might well paralyse human effort, if logically followed.

'But few sane men have ever believed themselves to be eternally reprobate, or acted as if they disbelieved in free will. The practical results of Calvinism have therefore been to produce a type of men like the founder himself, John Knox,[1] and Theodore Beza,[2] men of remarkable strength of will, extraordinary devotion, and indomitable energy, and to furnish a creed for the most uncompromising opponents of Rome.'[3]

The peoples who adopted Calvinism—the Scots, the Dutch, the French Huguenots, the English Puritans—were all distinguished for their sturdy self-reliance, their industry, their strength and vigour of character.

The spread of Protestantism caused the Roman Church to make a determined attempt to reform itself from within, and thus we have what is known as the Counter Reformation, which drew its vigour from Spain, for its success in winning back to the Catholic faith districts which had become Protestant was mainly due to the Order of Jesus, which was founded in 1540 by a Spaniard who is known as Ignatius Loyola. Loyola had started his career as a soldier, but a wound having incapacitated him for further service, he determined to become a soldier of Jesus like his great fellow countryman St. Dominic. The Jesuits were unlike any other

[1] The great leader of the Scottish Calvinists.
[2] The successor to Calvin's position at Geneva.
[3] *Europe in the Sixteenth Century* (Johnson), pub. Rivingtons.

THE REFORMATION. Preaching at St. Paul's Cross

religious order that had ever existed. They had no special dress, no special homes, no special religious duties, and they did not believe in the efficacy of fasting. But, like the older orders, they rendered implicit obedience to their superior or general. They gave themselves freely and entirely to be used by the Church, and their influence upon the subsequent course of Roman Catholic Christianity is very considerable. They were the dominant spirits in the great Council of Trent (1545-63), when the doctrines of the Church were clearly stated, and the authority of the Pope was declared to be paramount in matters of religion; they won back large parts of Germany to the orthodox faith; they did not hesitate to proclaim their beliefs even in countries like England which had absolutely discarded the authority of the Pope; there was no limit, physical or geographical, to the dangers which they were prepared to face in the execution of what they considered to be their duty; they carried Christianity to China, to India, and to North and South America. The fact that, in spite of their good work and their self-sacrificing zeal, they have a reputation which does not always do them justice, is probably due to the doctrine of casuistry which is often associated with them. This doctrine attempts to justify sin if the end aimed at is laudable, and there is no doubt that during the great religious wars of the sixteenth and seventeenth centuries some Jesuits definitely encouraged the assassination of Protestant sovereigns. Their greatest work was done in education. Their schools became the best schools in Europe, even earning the praise of such a confirmed Protestant as the English writer and statesman Francis Bacon.

The Reformation and the Counter Reformation had one most regrettable result. They ushered in a period of religious wars and persecutions which were a disgrace to Christendom. Between 1560 and 1600 the Calvinist Dutch won their independence from the Catholic Philip of Spain, and the Huguenots of France secured toleration everywhere except

RELIGIOUS INTOLERANCE

within five miles of Paris, but in both cases only after fierce struggles which were marred by such atrocities as the massacre of St. Bartholomew in France, and the barbaric methods of Philip's representative, the Duke of Alva, in the Netherlands. In Germany, from 1618 to 1648, was fought what is known as the Thirty Years' War, when the Emperor Ferdinand II made a determined attempt to stamp out Calvinism and possibly Lutheranism as well. The Lutheran King of Sweden, Gustavus Adolphus, came to the assistance of the Protestants, and the war ended with Germany split up as before between Catholics, Lutherans, and Calvinists, and each prince free to determine the religion of his own territories. This war too was frequently fought with a ferocity which reflects severely upon the Christianity of the combatants, and the decline of Germany started by the opening of the oceans to European trade was confirmed. Depopulation set in; there was a complete decline of maritime and a partial decline of river commerce; universities ceased to be founded; and learning suffered a very serious set-back. In England religious persecution resulted in emigrations to America, and it had much to do with the Great Civil War (1642–9), which ended in the execution of a king, the partial eclipse of the established religion, and a period of eleven years of republican government. In 1685 King Louis XIV revoked the edict[1] of his grandfather, which had granted toleration to French Protestants, and by so doing drove some of the most desirable of his subjects into exile, and seriously injured the commerce of his country. Nor was this spirit of religious bigotry confined to Catholics; it is quite as noticeable among Protestant communities. Even the English Puritans who left their native land on account of persecution and founded new homes for themselves across the Atlantic did not scruple to persecute those who differed from them on religious matters. Toleration was not acknowledged as a principle in the world

[1] Edict of Nantes.

until intolerance in all its forms had been tried and found ineffective. For centuries men laboured under the illusion that uniformity was the surest road to unity. The old persecuting spirit took a long time to die. In England Roman Catholics could not sit in Parliament until 1830, Jews not until 1858, and Atheists not until 1886.

XXIV

GRAND MONARCHY IN THE SEVENTEENTH AND EIGHTEENTH CENTURIES

THE decline of the Empire and of the Papacy and the growth of separate nations inevitably led to the formation of strong monarchies in many of the countries of Europe. Kings aimed at making themselves absolute, and they were frequently successful. At the end of the sixteenth century France was rapidly approaching a position in which the King could do practically as he liked ; Spain was ruled autocratically, so too were many of the Italian principalities ; and the English monarchy had reached the zenith of its power. During the seventeenth and eighteenth centuries the rulers of France, Prussia, Austria, and Russia succeeded in enhancing considerably the strength and the outward grandeur of their positions, but in England attempts to establish absolute monarchy ended in failure. There the trading and commercial classes were prepared to tolerate royal pretensions so long as they did not seriously interfere with their own interests, but when the dignity of royalty demanded arbitrary taxation, and the control of people's consciences, they preferred rebellion to compliance with a state of affairs which struck at the very root of personal liberty.

In England the Tudors, partly in order to humiliate the nobility and strengthen the Crown, had encouraged and fostered the development of the middle classes, and although they aimed at making Parliament subservient to themselves,

SEVENTEENTH & EIGHTEENTH CENTURIES

they did not succeed in utterly crushing the spirit of individuality among its members. This was very obvious when the Tudor dynasty came to an end and its place was taken by that of the Stuarts. The first of the Stuart kings, James I, had very exalted views as to the nature and scope of the royal authority. He declared that as it was blasphemy on the part of men to question what God could do, so it was high presumption on the part of subjects to question what the King could do. He considered himself to be above the law, and once went so far as to levy customs duties in defiance of the principle, already centuries old, that there should be no taxation without consent of Parliament. Moreover, James desired uniformity in religious matters, and saw no reason why liberty of conscience should be granted to those who would not conform to the established religion of the state. His son, Charles I, followed the bad precedents set by his father, and after a troubled reign of eighteen years, during which arbitrary taxation, illegal imprisonment of political opponents, and religious intolerance had almost become features of the national life, the Puritans and those who believed in the supremacy of Parliament rebelled against the King, and a civil war of seven years' duration ended with the execution of Charles and eleven years of republican government. Oliver Cromwell, the chief leader of the opposition to the King, became Lord Protector, and under his strong rule the name of England was feared and respected abroad, the commercial supremacy of the Dutch was undermined, and an important step taken in the development of the British Empire by the conquest of the West Indian island of Jamaica. But the English people had no liking for the republic which Cromwell gave them, and less than two years after his death they invited Charles, the son of the late king, to restore the monarchy. That young man, who had been spending his time in profitless exile, was only too glad to accept the invitation. He would have liked to govern as an absolute monarch like his friend and example, Louis XIV of France, and he did go some distance in that direction, but he was careful not to go too far, for he was determined above all things not to set out on his travels again. His brother, James II, who succeeded him, had none of this caution, and after three years of almost incredibly foolish government, during which he overrode laws in the most deliberate manner and contrived to alienate almost everybody in the country except the Roman Catholics whom he favoured, his subjects decided that they could not put up with him any longer. He was accordingly deposed, and the crown conferred upon the Dutch prince, William of Orange, and his wife, Mary, who was James's daughter. The deposition of James was a great triumph for law and constitutionalism. It was almost immediately followed by the Bill of Rights, which defined the position of the sovereign and the rights of his subjects. It inaugurated a period lasting about a hundred and fifty years, when England was virtually ruled by the landed gentry. It was a period marked by distinct progress in many directions—in religious toleration, in freedom of speech, in the evolution of newspapers, and in the growing control of government by ministers responsible to a majority in Parliament. But the great mass of the people had, as yet, little or no control over public affairs. The right to vote for members of Parliament was practically confined to the propertied classes, and there were all sorts of anomalies in the system of representation. Before the passing of the Reform Act of 1832, great towns like Manchester and Birmingham returned no members to Parliament, while places like Old Sarum in Wiltshire, which consisted of a mound and a few houses, and Dunwich on the East Coast, which was nothing more than a ruined sea wall, returned two members apiece. The government of England from 1688 to 1832 was distinctly aristocratic in character; it was better than absolute monarchy, but it was far removed from democracy. It was really a form of benevolent despotism—all for the people and

INTERIOR OF THE HOUSE OF COMMONS IN 1742

nothing by the people—but controlled, not by a king who was a law unto himself, but by an oligarchy who clung to power partly because they liked it, and partly because they believed that the destinies of the country could be safely entrusted to no one but themselves.

There was one other European country where absolute monarchy failed to take root, and where its overthrow resulted, as in England, in an aristocratical form of government. This was the country which we now know as Holland. Holland was the northern part of the Netherlands, which formed part of the extensive dominions of the Emperor Charles V. It was early affected by the doctrines of the Protestant Reformation, particularly by Calvinism, and the determined efforts of Charles V to eradicate it by persecution failed. His son and successor, Philip II, pursued the same policy of repression with practically the same results. He further exasperated the Netherlanders by taxing them heavily in order that he might have money to carry on a war with France. The result was that by 1570 the whole of the Netherlands, South as well as North, was in revolt. The South, which to-day forms the kingdom of Belgium, was ultimately subdued, and at the end of the struggle remained Spanish and Roman Catholic, but the North, under their great leader William the Silent, Prince of Orange, broke away altogether, and by 1609 had succeeded in forming an independent republic [1] under the headship of the Prince of Orange, who took the title of Stadholder and held the supreme military and executive power in the state. His authority was, however, limited by the existence of the States-General, which made laws like the English Parliament, and which was even less representative of the mass of the people.

In England and Holland Grand Monarchy failed to establish itself. Elsewhere it was more successful, particularly in France, where the kings not only reached a position

[1] Its independence was not fully recognized until 1648.

of almost unbridled power and grandeur, but furnished an example which inspired the kings of other European countries. In France, although the landowning and the merchant classes frequently found their interests threatened by the pretensions of royalty, they were not able to resist them so effectively as the landowners and merchants of England. The French States-General had nothing approaching the influence of the English Parliament. Its meetings were very irregular; kings had occasionally summoned it when they needed money, but merely in order that its approbation of new taxes might make their collection easier. They never admitted that they had not the right, if they chose to exercise it, to levy taxes without consulting their subjects at all. When the States-General met in 1789, the first year of the great Revolution, it was actually assembling for the first time since 1614. Thus opposition to royal demands could not be effectively made in the States-General. Those who thought that the power of the King should be curbed had to fall back upon the device of forming leagues against him, which generally lacked unity and constructive purpose. The most famous of these leagues was that known as the Fronde, which was contemporary with the later stages of the English Civil War, to which it bears some resemblances. They were both protests against absolute monarchy, and just as Charles I had to pay the reckoning for the deeds of his father James I, so Cardinal Mazarin, who really ruled France[1] when the Wars of the Fronde were waged, had to pay for carrying on the policy of his great master and predecessor, Cardinal Richelieu, the policy of building up a strong and ruthless absolutism, which would make the King (or his chief minister) the undisputed master of France. But the English Rebellion was successful; the Fronde was not, and one of the chief causes of its failure was the lack of seriousness among many of those who took part in it, and the selfish ambitions of others. The Frondeurs, unlike the Parliamentarians

[1] Louis XIV, the King, was a minor.

of England, did not have religion to animate them and nerve them to overthrow the whole edifice of irresponsible government. Indeed their very name, Frondeurs, signifies how desultory and irresolute they were. It was given to them because of their resemblance to the schoolboys who slung stones in the moats of Paris and ran away when the authorities appeared. In 1652 they were conclusively beaten, and after that date the King and his courtiers dominated French life. From this time until the Revolution of 1789 the government of France was as autocratic as it could well be. Taxes were imposed in the most arbitrary manner, and in such a way that they fell principally upon the poorer classes, who were least able to pay them; people were committed to prison and kept there for years without any charge being specified against them;[1] wars were made in order to gratify personal ambitions and increase the grandeur of royalty; and the King definitely took up the attitude that he held his authority direct from God, and that he was answerable to nobody else.

Grand Monarchy reached its climax under Louis XIV, 'The Sun King' (1643-1715). Louis was an exceptionally ambitious man. He wished to extend the boundaries of France to the Rhine and the Pyrenees, and to absorb the Spanish Netherlands. In the former of these objects he partially succeeded; in the latter he was thwarted by the opposition of England and Holland. He also appears to have had some sort of idea of eventually attaining a position comparable to that of Charlemagne, and, when his grandson was offered the throne of Spain, he accepted it for him and grandiloquently declared that the Pyrenees had ceased to exist. The result was the War of the Spanish Succession, in which Louis was defeated by the combined forces of England, Austria, and

[1] Such occurrences enable us to realize the importance of the Great Charter which the English king John was forced to sign in 1215, and which was considered binding upon his successors. One clause states that no freeman shall be imprisoned except by lawful judgement of his equals and according to the law of the land.

THE GRAND MONARCHY. GROUNDS OF LOUIS XIV'S PALACE AT VERSAILLES

Holland, his pleasant dreams shattered, and France brought to the verge of bankruptcy. It was not only by wars of aggression that Louis XIV spent the hard-earned money of the French people. Splendour was almost a craze with him; his court became proverbial for its lavish display of wealth; and his palace at Versailles, with its salons, its mirrors, its parks, and its fountains, became the envy and admiration of the world. His patronage of art and literary men was part of the same policy, but a more excellent part. In this he set a worthier example for monarchs to follow. Some of the greatest figures in French literature—the dramatists Molière and Racine, the chronicler Saint-Simon,[1] and Madame de Sévigné, one of the greatest letter-writers of all time—lived during the reign of Louis XIV, and the favour shown to them by the King is perhaps the best thing which he did for his country. One of the worst was the renewed persecution of the Huguenots, who, ever since the time of Henry IV, had been allowed to follow their occupations and practise their religion without interference from the Government. Louis, however, revoked the edict which secured toleration for them, and by so doing drove some of the most valuable of his subjects abroad. What was France's loss was the gain of other countries. Thus the silk manufacture of England was founded by Protestant exiles from France at this time.

Louis XIV was succeeded by his great-grandson, Louis XV, during whose reign money was spent lavishly on wars and on various worthless mistresses who ministered to the King's pleasures, and France was plunged deeper and deeper into the morass of bankruptcy. During this reign lived the great writer Voltaire, who employed his caustic wit to call attention to the more flagrant and absurd characteristics of Grand Monarchy as it was practised in France. He was particularly scornful of the attitude of mind which considered

[1] Saint-Simon's *Memoirs* give a vivid description of the French Court and society during the reign of Louis XIV.

it beneath the dignity of a nobleman to engage in trade. He declared that the merchant who enriches his country contributes far more to the happiness of the globe than 'the thickly powdered lord who knows exactly what time the King rises and what time he goes to bed, and gives himself mighty airs of greatness while he plays the part of a slave in the minister's anteroom'. Voltaire, when he was quite a young man, visited England, and, among other things, he was impressed by the freedom of the people as compared with those of France; by the hatred of war manifested by the small religious sect known as the Quakers; and by the achievements of Sir Isaac Newton, whom Voltaire regarded as a much greater man than either Alexander the Great or Julius Caesar. 'It is', he wrote, 'to him who masters our minds by the force of truth, not to those who enslave men by violence; it is to him who understands the universe, not to those who disfigure it, that we owe our reverence.' There were many Frenchmen who admired Voltaire and welcomed his teachings. Among them was Denis Diderot, who persuaded many scholars to co-operate with him in writing a French *Encyclopédie*, which was ultimately completed in seventeen volumes, despite the opposition of the Government and the Church. The *Encyclopédie*, in its articles on such subjects as slavery, taxation, the criminal law, and the question of tolerance in religious matters, attacked some of the chief abuses of the time. It emphasized the value of commerce, and the interdependence of nations upon one another. Lord Morley, in his admirable study of Diderot and the Encyclopaedists, writes that ' it was this band of writers, organized by a harassed man of letters, and not the nobles swarming around Louis XV, nor the churchmen singing masses, who first grasped the great principle of modern society, the honour that is owed to productive industry. They were vehement for the glories of peace and passionate against the brazen glories of war.' Bolder even than the speculations of Voltaire, Diderot, and the Encyclopaedists were those of Jean-Jacques Rousseau, who believed that society was over-civilized, and advocated a return to simpler and more natural ways of living. In his book, *Le Contrat social*, he declared that men owed all their miseries to priests and rulers, and that sovereignty should really be exercised by the people. Even though they should appoint a single person such as a king to manage their government for them, they should themselves make the laws since it is they who have to obey them. *Le Contrat social* is one of the most influential books ever written, pointing forward through the Jacobin dictatorship during the French Revolution to the totalitarian democracies of Lenin, Mussolini, and Hitler in the present century.[1]

Outside France Grand Monarchy was most successful in Prussia and Russia. Prussia was ruled by a dynasty, the Hohenzollern, which was not overthrown until 1918. Its rise, from the comparatively small duchy of Brandenburg to a kingdom which eventually covered nearly two-thirds of Germany, is one of the most striking features of modern history. The first of its rulers to give some indication that a formidable power was arising was the Elector Frederick William, known as the Great Elector (1640–88), who succeeded in creating an absolute monarchy. His son, Frederick I, was the first to take the title of King of Prussia. His grandson, King Frederick William I, a rough and boorish king, increased his army from twenty-seven thousand to eighty-four thousand men, and by careful management and miserly economy left a well-filled treasury as well for his son and successor, Frederick II, who is generally called Frederick the Great. Under him the Prussian kingdom made marvellous progress, despite two long and exhausting wars. It was considerably enlarged by the acquisition of Austrian Silesia and part of

[1] See J. L. Talmon, *The Origins of Totalitarian Democracy* (Secker and Warburg, 1952).

Poland ; its population was trebled ; its army, two hundred thousand strong, was the most efficient in the world ; and Frederick could have declared, with perfect truth, that the state was himself. In some respects he aped Louis XIV. He built a great palace at Potsdam, and a park, the Park of Sans Souci, whose fountains, avenues, and statuary copied the glories of Versailles. He patronized literary men, and entertained Voltaire, an experiment which was not a success. But Frederick did not follow the example of Louis by persecuting those whose religious opinions did not coincide with his own. All the great rulers of Prussia, from the Great Elector downwards, permitted religious freedom to a remarkable degree. Although the state religion was Protestant, Catholics were eligible for office, and the Huguenots whom Louis XIV drove from France were openly welcomed in Prussia.

Russia, until the accession of Peter the Great in 1689, was an Asiatic state with no seaport, no ships, and an army which it would have been almost ludicrous to oppose to the well-disciplined troops of Western Europe. Peter spared no effort to make his country into a European power. He visited Germany, Holland, and England so as to investigate the arts and sciences of the West; he brought back with him skilled artisans, architects, ships' captains, and scientific men to aid in the development of Russia ; he forced his subjects to abandon many of their Oriental habits, such as their custom of growing long beards ; he remodelled the government according to Western ideas ; he built a navy and made the army more efficient ; and he conquered from Sweden lands such as Livonia and Esthonia, which lay between Russia and the Baltic Sea. Not content with the old capital, Moscow, which clung somewhat tenaciously to its ancient habits, he built a new capital, St. Petersburg,[1] and (eighteen miles away) like Frederick the Great of Prussia, he built an imitation

[1] Its name was changed to Petrograd in 1914, and to Leningrad in 1924.

Versailles, the Peterhof—with a park, fountains, cascades, and picture galleries. Almost the only feature of the old régime which he was content to retain was its despotic nature. The Czar must remain the absolute master of all his subjects, and there are frequent instances of Peter punishing those who dared to resist his authority, with a barbarity which was more Oriental than Western. He is reputed to have himself executed many nobles and churchmen who rebelled against the introduction of European customs, and there is a strong suspicion that he killed his own son Alexis for not living up to the ideal which he expected of him, and for resisting the paternal authority. After Peter's death in 1725 Russia was governed by various incompetent rulers until the accession of Catherine II, a German princess, in 1762. She ascended the throne after arranging the murder of her husband, the Czar, in true Oriental fashion, but she afterwards ruled in a manner which was almost wholly Western, and ever since her time Russia has been a force to be reckoned with in the affairs of Europe and the world.

While the Hohenzollerns of Prussia from their capital of Berlin had been extending their authority over Northern Germany, another family, the Habsburgs, from their capital of Vienna had been gradually building up the Austrian Empire, the vast realm over which they ruled until 1918. From 1438 until 1806, although the old form of election was still maintained, all but one of the Emperors were Habsburgs, and in 1806, when Napoleon brought the Holy Roman Empire to an end, they took the less pretentious but far more practical title of Emperor of Austria. When Maria Theresa succeeded her father in 1740, the Austrian dominions included Austria, Moravia, Hungary, Bohemia, Silesia, Styria, Carinthia, Tyrol, the Austrian Netherlands (Belgium), and Milan. Silesia was soon conquered by Frederick of Prussia, but the Empress secured some compensation by the acquisition of Galician Poland. The task of ruling these extensive territories was a particularly difficult one, because of the numerous and diverse races who inhabited them. The people of Austria were Germans ; there was an admixture of Slavs and Germans in Moravia ; Magyars in Hungary ; Italians in Milan ; and Flemings in the Austrian Netherlands. When Maria Theresa died after a reign of forty years she was succeeded by her son Joseph II, a man of considerable enlightenment, whose great ambition was to consolidate all his dominions into one homogeneous whole, to break down the barriers of nationality, ' to raise the mass of the community to legal equality with their former masters, to constitute a uniform level of democratic simplicity under his own absolute sway.'[1] His intentions were, generally speaking, admirable, and if he had had to deal with an enlightened or a united people they would have been welcomed. But Joseph, when he set himself the task of forming a well-organized central state, like that formed by Frederick the Great in Prussia, apparently failed to grasp the peculiar difficulties of his position. He had to carry through his policy in a state composed of the most diverse elements in Europe, only held together by the personal tie of sovereignty and the influence of the Church, which he alienated by an attack upon its privileges. National prejudices were too strong for him, he was regarded with suspicion on all hands, insurrections broke out in the Netherlands and other places, and, despite his utmost efforts, Austria remained a ramshackle empire until its final dissolution in 1918.

The Greek philosopher Aristotle once wrote that the best of all possible governments was the government of the perfectly just tyrant. But a perfectly just tyrant is practically an impossibility. Tyrants are generally men of great ambition, who may do some good, but usually because it helps them to realize their own selfish desires. All the absolute monarchs of the seventeenth and eighteenth centuries would answer

[1] *Historical Studies* (Herman Merivale).

to this description with the possible exception of Joseph II of Austria. The regard which they had for the welfare of their subjects is illustrated by the wars which they fought, wars which often gratified their thirst for glory, but which meant for the common people death, wounds, and taxation so heavy as to make their lives a burden to them. Diplomacy and international relations were conducted in a manner which would have earned the warm approval of Machiavelli. The public career of Frederick the Great of Prussia is an illuminating commentary upon the morals of the age. His first act as king was to seize Silesia, a province which belonged to Austria, and to which his claims were so slight that he cynically remarked that he first sent his troops to occupy the province, and then relied upon his lawyers to find a claim. Two wars followed, the War of the Austrian Succession, which lasted for eight years (1740-8), and the Seven Years' War (1756-63). Both were fought on exactly the same issue—whether Frederick should be allowed to retain Silesia or not; but in the Austrian Succession War Great Britain supported Austria and France supported Prussia, while in the Seven Years' War British troops fought for Frederick while the French were the allies of Austria. Great Britain had no real interest in the Silesian question at all, but it served as a convenient excuse for a war with France, which was really fought on grounds of colonial rivalry. England got practically nothing out of the Austrian Succession War, but her policy of subsidizing Frederick so as to keep the French occupied in Europe during the Seven Years' War proved extraordinarily successful. It enabled English troops to defeat the French in North America, thus adding Canada to the British Empire, and to lay the foundations of British control over India. In 1763 Maria Theresa had to resign herself to the loss of Silesia. She might well declaim against the treachery and bad faith of Frederick which had deprived her of it, but not many years later she associated herself with the King of Prussia and

The Defeat of the French in North America and the Acquisition of Canada. Wolfe capturing Quebec

Catherine II of Russia in one of the most flagrant acts of international perfidy ever perpetrated—the partition of Poland. Poland was a sort of aristocratic republic ruled by a king whose position was elective, not hereditary. Its inhabitants, noble as well as others, were extremely poor, and it had no trade or commerce to speak of. It had a Diet of four hundred members, but any one member could veto any proposal which came before it—and the King could do nothing without the consent of the Diet. Thus the government was practically an anarchy, and its weakness proved a temptation which the rulers of Austria, Russia, and Prussia could not resist, and so they shamelessly proceeded to annex the country. There were three partitions. In 1772 about a third of Poland was divided among the spoilers, another third in 1793, and the remainder two years later. After 1772 the Poles did their best to avoid a further loss of territory. They abolished the individual veto, they set up a Parliament on the British model, and they made the Crown hereditary in the hope of saving their country from foreign intrigues. There was also a considerable development of literature, art, and education—but nothing that they could do could save them from the cupidity of the rulers of Austria, Russia, and Prussia, and after 1795 Poland ceased to be a nation until her nationality was restored after the World War of 1914-18. The partitions of Poland aroused little indignation anywhere else in Europe, and of those who actually participated in it the only one who appears to have had any qualms of conscience was the Empress Maria Theresa. It is said that when she heard of the first partition she wept, an action which called from Frederick the Great the cynical but well-justified remark: 'Elle pleure, mais elle prend.'[1]

'She weeps, but she takes.'

XXV

THE AMERICAN AND FRENCH REVOLUTIONS

BEFORE the eighteenth century ended there were two rebellions: the American Revolution of 1775-83, and the French Revolution of 1789-95—which were both of them severe blows to the theory of absolute monarchy, and which were destined to have a considerable effect upon the subsequent history of the human race.

The American Revolution, or the War of American Independence, as it is sometimes called, was a revolt against the autocracy of England, which at this time was ruled by a well-meaning but obstinate king, George III, who had a desire to revive the personal power of the Crown. The Revolution was a direct consequence of England's intervention in the Seven Years' War, and of the ideas which prevailed throughout Western Europe at that time as to the proper way of governing colonies. It was thought that colonies were part of the parent country, and that they should be administered not primarily for the benefit of the colonists, but for the benefit of the country from which the colonists had originally come. In accordance with this principle, England had on two occasions in the seventeenth century passed laws known as Navigation Acts, which enacted that colonial produce was to be exported only in British ships; some commodities were to be sent to no country but Great Britain; and some were to be shipped to Great Britain first, and thence to other parts of the world, the reshipping very naturally forcing up prices. There were also laws passed restricting or prohibiting the manufacture of certain articles in the colonies, such as cloth—the idea being that if their manufacture were allowed, English industries of vital importance to the prosperity of the country would be seriously affected. On the other hand, English people were not allowed to engage in industries of which it was considered right that the colonists should have a monopoly. Thus tobacco growing in England was absolutely forbidden, and troops were repeatedly sent to the counties of Gloucestershire, Warwickshire, and Herefordshire to destroy crops of it. Judged from the standpoint of the age, Great Britain's treatment of her colonies in the eighteenth century was not illiberal. The Spanish, French, and Portuguese colonists fared much worse, but they did not have the sense of freedom, the jealous regard for their own personal liberties, which made it politic to placate and not to coerce the British colonists.

The Seven Years' War secured Canada for Great Britain. Montcalm, Wolfe's opponent at Quebec, predicted that this very success would mean the loss of her other colonies in North America, and his prediction was verified less than a quarter of a century after his death. These colonies were fourteen in number, and they varied much in character and in the ways in which they had been acquired. The Southern colonies—Virginia, the Carolinas, and Georgia—contained large estates growing tobacco and cotton, worked by slave labour. There, to a certain extent, the lives of the English squires were reproduced on American soil.[1] The northern or New England colonies—Connecticut, Rhode Island, New Hampshire, and Massachusetts—had been founded by Puritans, men discontented with the Anglican Church, and not disposed to tolerate the tyranny of James I or Charles I. They were a hardy population of farmers, well educated, with fine colleges at Harvard and at Yale. In the centre there were the remains of the old Dutch settlements ceded in the reign of Charles II, and a colony once distinctly Roman Catholic named Maryland. There was also Pennsylvania, colonized by a somewhat unique branch of the English Puritans, the Friends or Quakers, who, as a body, had an especial hatred

[1] Thackeray's novel, *The Virginians*, gives an admirable description of their lives.

'THE SMOAKING CLUB' by Bunbury, about 1780

Cotton-growing in the Mississippi Valley. A woodcut from
The Illustrated London News, Sept. 1881

of war and of methods of violence generally. Each colony stood by itself. Each had its own governor, appointed by the Home Government; and each had a legislative assembly, which passed local acts and voted the governor's salary. Thus they enjoyed a considerable degree of self-government, which had the effect of making them long for more. They wished their assemblies to have equal rights with the British Parliament; they thought that they should be allowed to levy their own taxes, and contribute in their own way, if at all, to the expenses of the Imperial Government; and they objected to being taxed by a body sitting thousands of miles away, and in which they were not represented. They had little sentimental affection for or patriotic loyalty to the Home Government. Their distance from England, the difficulties of transport and communication, the English practice of regulating their trade in the interests of the mother country, political and religious differences, had all tended to dull the sense of kinship and to make the colonists dream of complete independence. This feeling of aloofness had been frequently apparent during the Seven Years' War when the colonial assemblies voted inadequate supplies and did not co-operate with the mother country in the way which was expected of them. The English conquest of Canada precipitated matters. The removal of all danger from the French made the colonies more rebellious and less disposed than ever to submit to the dictatorship of England, while the English Government felt that, since the conquest of Canada had rendered the Americans more secure, and since the expenses of the war had been great, it was but just that the colonists should pay part of them. The method adopted was to impose certain duties on articles used by the Americans. It was first proposed that they should maintain a force of ten thousand men, part of the cost to be defrayed by a stamp-tax on legal documents. This provoked so much opposition in America that the whole scheme was abandoned, to be revived

DECLARATION OF INDEPENDENCE

in another form a year later, when taxes were imposed on certain American imports. Again there was determined opposition, and all the taxes were repealed except one—a tax on tea —which was retained as an assertion that the British Parliament had a *right* to tax the colonies directly as well as indirectly. This the colonists refused to admit, and, after further misunderstandings, war broke out. Nova Scotia, the most northerly of the fourteen colonies did not join in the rebellion.

At first the colonists fared badly, but gradually they gained the upper hand. Their ultimate success was due to a variety of causes; their superior knowledge of the country where the war was fought, the good generalship of their leader George Washington, the great distance of the English from their own country, the incompetence of the English Government, and the assistance which the French gave to the rebels. The most momentous event of the war was the American Declaration of Independence on 4 July 1776. This important document, which may be fittingly described as the birth certificate of the United States of America, was drawn up by a Virginian named Thomas Jefferson, but his original draft suffered some modifications before it was finally accepted by Congress. Thus he had denounced slavery and the slave trade fiercely, and wished to see them abolished, but most of the colonists differed from him and refused to accept his recommendations on the matter. The slave trade was prohibited in 1807, but many more years were to elapse before the slaves of America were set free, even though the Declaration of Independence asserted that all men were born equal. There were, however, difficulties in the way of emancipation. There were many in Virginia who wished to set the slaves free, but they thought that those who had been set free must under no circumstances remain in Virginia. The prospect of the rise of a free black community was too appalling to contemplate, and so it was thought better to keep the black population under control as slaves rather than risk the safety and well-being of the whole community.

Great Britain acknowledged the independence of the United States in 1783, seven years after the Declaration of Independence. The community which thus came into being was quite a new phenomenon in the history of the world. Its head was a president elected from among the people and holding office for four years. It was fitting that the first holder of the office should be George Washington. There was no state religion; no princes, dukes, counts, or hereditary titles of any description; and a strong central government was evolved and made effective in a space of time whose shortness is amazing when compared with the centuries of slow and gradual development which have been the rule of most other countries. In 1783 the central government of the United States was a very feeble body, a Congress in which every state had one vote, and which had practically no jurisdiction over individual citizens. It had, for example, no control over the foreign trade of each state, and it could not coin money or levy taxes by its own authority. It had no power of compelling the obedience either of states or of individuals. Six years later, however, a new constitution had been drawn up, through the efforts of Alexander Hamilton and others, and, what is more remarkable, accepted by the thirteen states. This constitution made the American people a nation; previously they had been a mere league of states. It defined clearly what powers the provincial governments should continue to exercise, and separated these powers from those which were to be under the direct control of the central government, such as the control of the army and navy, the making of war and peace, the post office, and the currency. Hamilton and his associates were not innovators. They were practical politicians, eager to copy the best features of the governments with which they were familiar. They preferred to walk in old paths, as far as circumstances per-

THE AMERICAN CONSTITUTION

mitted, rather than adopt methods which had not been justified by experience, and they were especially indebted to the example of the British Constitution.

'They held England to be the freest and best governed country in the world, but were resolved to avoid the weak points which had enabled King George III to play the tyrant, and which rendered English liberty, as they thought, far inferior to that which the constitutions of their own States secured. With this venerable mother and these children, better in their judgment than the mother, before their eyes, they created an executive magistrate, the President, on the model of the State Governor, and of the British Crown. They created a legislature of two Houses, Congress, on the model of the two Houses of their State legislatures, and of the British Parliament. And following the precedent of the British judges, irremovable except by the Crown and Parliament combined, they created a judiciary appointed for life, and irremovable save by impeachment.'[1]

The valuable assistance which the French gave to the American colonists was largely the result of a desire to revenge themselves upon England for the loss of Canada, but it was a vengeance for which a heavy price had to be paid. The financial assistance which France gave to the Americans was such as she could not really afford, and the volunteers who crossed the Atlantic to fight for the colonists returned with ideas of individual liberty which made them very intolerant of the restrictions and absurdities of Grand Monarchy. At this time the finances of France were in a hopeless state; the poorer classes were still the most heavily taxed; the nobles and higher clergy hesitated to come forward and save the state (and had they but known it, their own positions as well), by voluntarily resigning their claims to immunity from certain taxes; and matters were further complicated by the extravagance of the court and the sheer incompetence of the King, Louis XVI.

[1] *The American Commonwealth* (Lord Bryce), pub. Macmillan.

Much has been written on the misery of the French peasants of the period. Carlyle in his picturesque way has said that 'one-third of them had nothing but third-rate potatoes to eat for one-third of the year', and that they had often to be content with meals of husks and boiled grass. Two shrewd observers, the American Thomas Jefferson and the English writer Arthur Young, who travelled in France just prior to the Revolution, were somewhat differently impressed. Young, although he came across some scenes of rural happiness, was apparently more impressed with scenes of misery and destitution, which afterwards led him to write that 'the dispensations of Providence seem to have permitted the human race to exist only as the prey of tyrants, as it has made pigeons for the prey of hawks.'[1] In another passage he declared that 'kings and ministers, and parliaments, and States' had much 'to answer for their prejudices, seeing millions of hands that would be industrious idle and starving through the execrable maxims of despotism, or the equally detestable prejudices of a feudal nobility'.[1] But even Arthur Young admitted that the government of France was 'the mildest government of any considerable country in Europe, our own excepted'.[1] Thomas Jefferson, expecting to find physical discomfort and misery among the peasants, found instead a degree of prosperity and contentment which amazed him.[2] He certainly does not give us the impression of a people who have reached such a state of desperation that they can bear their burdens no longer. Undoubtedly the French peasants had various petty inconveniences and restrictions to endure, which might easily develop into flagrant abuses. The last relics of serfdom had not yet disappeared from their lives. Lords still claimed and enjoyed certain feudal dues, such as the right to impose the use of certain things on their lands (e.g. ovens where all were obliged to

---

[1] *Travels in France* (1792).
[2] Letter from Nice, 11 April 1787.

bake bread, and pay for so doing); the right of levying a toll on sheep and cattle driven past the manor house; and the privilege of hunting and preserving game. Many of the manors had great pigeon-houses, in which a couple of thousand pigeons were kept, and the peasants were not allowed to protect themselves against these pests, even though they spread over their fields devouring the newly sown seed. But, with all these things, the French peasants were much better off than the peasants of Prussia, Russia, Austria, Italy, or Spain. In almost all the countries of Europe, with the exception of England, the peasants were still serfs; they had to work on certain days in the week for their lords; and they could not marry, or dispose of their lands, without his permission.

The reason why France was the first country on the continent of Europe to do away with the irritating survivals of feudalism was not that the French people were oppressed above all others, but because they were sufficiently enlightened to realize the evils and absurdities of the system of government under which they suffered. The writings of Voltaire and the Encyclopaedists had been widely read and their teachings accepted with enthusiasm, so that there was a general disposition to regard kings and lords as oppressors who had no real right to the tyrannical powers which they claimed. The number of people who read Rousseau, however, was comparatively small, and the influence of his doctrines was not much felt until the later stages of the Revolution. In much the same way, the Russian Bolsheviks, inspired by the revolutionary ideas of the German Socialist writer Karl Marx, achieved the revolution of 1917 which gave them the control over the government and destinies of Russia. In each case we have a strong and determined minority imposing their wills upon a majority who had been oppressed for centuries, and who were therefore in the best mood to accept changes which might improve and which, they believed, could hardly make worse their material conditions. They apprehended nothing but ultimate good from the forcible destruction of systems which exalted dynastic or class interests at the expense of the general interests of the community.

The French Revolution began with the meeting of the States-General in May of 1789, and the destruction of the Bastille, the great prison of the city of Paris, in July of the same year. At first, despite occasional excesses like risings of the Paris mob and château-burning in the provinces, it proceeded along right lines. The representatives of the people, or the Third Estate, early got an ascendancy in the States-General, which constituted itself into a National Assembly and passed some very useful and necessary measures. Before the end of the year 1789 the survivals of feudalism had been abolished; the tithes of the Church had been done away with; exemptions from the payments of taxes had been abolished for ever; it had been declared that 'all citizens, without distinction of birth, are eligible to any office or dignity'; and the Declaration of the Rights of Man had been drawn up and made into law. This was a most important document, comparable with the English Bill of Rights, although its influence has been greater, for it served as a model for similar declarations in many other parts of the world. It asserted that all men have equal rights; that law must be the expression of the will of the people and that it should be the same for all; that no one should be arrested or imprisoned except in accordance with the law; that no person should suffer on account of his opinions, provided that the expression of them did not imperil the peace and well-being of the community; and that 'all citizens have a right to decide, either personally or by their representative, as to the necessity of the public contribution, to grant this freely, to know to what uses it is put, and to fix the proportion, the mode of assessment and of collection, and the duration of the taxes'. The King, naturally, showed reluctance to ratify the Declaration, and there were

OPENING OF THE STATES-GENERAL, 5 MAY 1789

rumours that he was secretly getting together an army to overthrow what the revolutionists had done. These things, together with the scarcity of food on account of poor crops, aroused the excitable populace of Paris, and several thousand women and some armed men marched out to the palace of Versailles and forced the King and the royal family to return with them to Paris. They imagined that their very presence among them would solve the problem of scarcity and ensure plenty. The King, the Queen, and the Dauphin were conducted to the palace of the Tuileries, where they were kept in a condition practically the same as captivity.

In 1791 they tried to escape, but were stopped at Varennes, a few miles from the north-eastern border of France, and brought back to Paris. Louis's idea appears to have been to reach certain French troops upon whose loyalty he could rely, and then with their help and that of the Emperor Leopold II, who was the brother of Marie Antoinette, his queen, he would be able to march on Paris and recover his former power once again. When the news of his arrest at Varennes and his unwilling return to Paris reached the Emperor, he invited the rulers of Russia, England, Prussia, Spain, Naples, and Sardinia to co-operate with him in re-establishing 'the liberty and honour of the most Christian king and his family, and place a check upon the dangerous excesses of the French Revolution, the fatal example of which it behoves every government to repress'. The response was disappointing; the King of Prussia was practically the only ruler who thought it worth his while to interfere in the internal affairs of France. His troops joined those of the Austrians, and with the assistance of some emigrant nobles invaded the country. The French army, having lost many of its officers by emigration, at this time was perilously insubordinate; but at Valmy, in the Argonne, it contrived to stay the advance of the invaders, and then in an astonishingly short space of time suddenly transformed itself into a force whose

STORMING OF THE TUILERIES, 10 AUGUST 1792

vigour and revolutionary enthusiasm carried it from victory to victory. It invaded Germany and took several towns on the Rhine, including Mayence, and it also occupied the Austrian Netherlands and Savoy. So intoxicated did the French become with their successes that they offered their assistance to any country which wished to establish its freedom by throwing off the yoke of monarchy, and early in 1793 they declared war upon England.

In the meantime the Revolution had changed considerably in character. The danger of foreign invasion,[1] the assistance given to the invaders by French noblemen, and the ill-concealed eagerness with which the King awaited the reversal of the Revolution caused panic in various parts of France, particularly in Paris, and extremists who wished to depose the King and take drastic measures against those who impeded the Revolution gradually gained the upper hand. For the next few years the history of France reads like the incidents of some terrifying nightmare. On 10 August the palace of the Tuileries was stormed and the royal family sent to prison; on the 2nd and 3rd of September 1792 hundreds of men and women suspected of counter-revolutionary tendencies were ruthlessly massacred in the streets of Paris; before the end of the month the King had been deposed and the first French republic proclaimed; in January of the next year the luckless Louis was tried for high treason, found guilty, and executed; in June the Girondins, or moderate revolutionaries, who had really been opposed to the execution of the King (although some of them had voted for it), were overthrown and their leaders guillotined; in October the Queen, Marie Antoinette, was executed. From June of 1793 to July of 1794 there was a veritable Reign of Terror in France. The government was

[1] There are many who believe that the bloody character of the Russian Bolshevik Revolution should be attributed to a similar cause, namely, the panic caused by the invasions of Russia by counter-revolutionary armies aided by foreign volunteers and subsidized by foreign money.

A

LIST OF PERSONS

CONSPICUOUS IN THE

FRENCH REVOLUTION,

And their Fate. to 1795

N. B. Those names with the initials M. C. were Members of the Convention, who voted for the death of Louis XVI.
Those with an X did not vote for the death of the King, yet became eminent in the Revolution.
G. General of their Republican Army.

A.

Achille Duchaffelet	G	Died in prison.
Albert Rouë	G	Guillotined.
Amiral	X	Ditto.
Anacharsis Cloots	M C	Ditto.
Antiboul		X Ditto.

B.

Baily, first Mayor of Paris	X.	Guillotined.
Barnave	X	Ditto.
	H	Bar-

(86)

Chatelet (Duke of)	X	Ditto.
Chomette	X	Ditto.
Chambon	M C	Maffacred by the mob.
Champford	X	Killed himself with a razor.
Chancel	G	Guillotined.
Chapui	G	Prisoner.
Claviere	X	Killed himself.
Collet d'Herbois	M C	Banished to Guyenne, South America.
Coutard	X	Guillotined.
Couthon	M C	Ditto.
Cuftine	G	Ditto.
Cuftine (his son)	X	Ditto.
Cuffy	X	Ditto.

D.

Dampiere	G	Died of his wounds.
Danton	M C	Guillotined.
Daoult	G	Ditto.
Dagobert	G	Died in his army
Davesnes	G	Guillotined.
Deftaing (Admiral)		Ditto.
Delaunay	M C	Ditto.
Delatre	G	Ditto.
Deverges	G	Ditto.
Deflers	G	Ditto.
Dillon, Arthur	G	Ditto.
Delaporte	X	Ditto.
Dortoman	G	Ditto.
Donadieu	G	Ditto.
Duc d'Orleans	M C	Ditto.
Drouet	M C	Prisoner of war.
Ducos	M C	Guillotined.
	H 2	Du

(89)

L.

Lanne (Joseph)		Guillotined.
La Source	M C	Ditto.
La Borde	X	Ditto.
La Cafe	X	Ditto.
La Croix	M C	Ditto.
Lamarliere	G	Ditto.
Lavalette	G	Ditto.
Launay (P. F. G,)	X	Ditto.
Laurent	X	Ditto.
Le Bas	M C	Killed himself.
Le Brun	X	Guillotined.
Lechelle	G	Poisoned himself.
Lezard	X	Guillotined.
L'Huillier	X	Killed himself with a razor.
Le Pelletier	M C	Killed by a Royalist.
Le Roy (pierre)	X	Guillotined
Le Hardy	X	Ditto.
Leftanduere	G	Ditto.
Luckner	G	Ditto.
Latude (Baron)	X	Ditto.
Louis (claude chatelet)	X	Ditto.
Louis (Jean)	X	Ditto.
Lochefer	X	Ditto.

M.

Mainville	X	Guillotined.
Marat	M C	Killed by Charlotte Cordé.
Manuel	X	Guillotined.
Marcé	G	Ditto.
Maziasly	G	Ditto.
		Mi-

(90)

Milanois	X	Guillotined.
Mirabel	G	Killed before Bellegarde.
Momoro	X	Guillotined.
Moulin	G	Shot himself with a pistol.
Monaco, Prince	X	Guillotined.

N.

| Nion | M C | Guillotined. |
| Noel | X | Ditto. |

O.

| Omoran | G | Guillotined. |
| Orleans (Duke of) | M C | Ditto. |

P.

Philipeaux	M C	Guillotined.
Populus	X	Ditto.
Pommier	X	Ditto.
Payan, C. F.	X	Ditto.

Q.

| Quetiniau | G | Ditto. |

R.

Rabaut Pommier	M C	Guillotined.
Rabaut de St. Etienne	X	Ditto.
Rabaud the younger	X	Ditto.
Rebecky	M C	Drowned himself.
Roberspierre	M C	Guillotined.
Roberspierre, jun.	M C	Ditto.

THE REIGN OF TERROR. Pages taken from an alphabetical list compiled about 1795; out of these eighty-five persons, all but sixteen were guillotined, and seven of these sixteen committed suicide.

in the hands of a Committee of Public Safety of nine members, of whom the chief was a provincial lawyer named Maximilien Robespierre, who had once resigned a judgeship rather than sentence a man to death. He recognized no such compunctions when it fell to him to direct the Revolution. He considered it his patriotic duty to take the most drastic measures against all who might in any conceivable way endanger its permanence. The Revolutionary Tribunal was never idle, and thousands of suspects were guillotined. No one was safe. Even Danton, member of an earlier Committee of Public Safety, whose popularity was second only to that of Robespierre, was accused of treason, and after a mere mockery of a trial executed. His great crime was that he had become tired of bloodshed, and had had the temerity to advocate moderation. A few months later a coalition was formed against Robespierre by colleagues who feared that he would demand their heads next. The city of Paris was roused against him, and he was arrested, tried, and executed. After his death the Reign of Terror ended. Some of those who had been most prominent in doing its cruel work, such as the public prosecutor of Paris, were themselves sent to the guillotine, but otherwise the Revolutionary Tribunal convicted very few of those who were brought before it. The Jacobin Club at Paris, to which most of the extreme revolutionists had belonged, was closed, and a new constitution drawn up for the French Republic. It was enacted that the power of making the laws should be vested in an assembly consisting of two houses, while the executive powers of the state were put in the hands of a Directory of five persons, to be chosen by the assembly.

The French Revolution is one of the most important events in modern history. It marks the definite entry into continental politics of a new force, the force of the People or the Third Estate. It was a great triumph for the idea of Democracy, even though it left much to be achieved in this direction, for it was in many ways essentially a middle-class revolu-

GROWTH OF DEMOCRACY

tion. It did not at once bring about the complete enfranchisement of the great masses of the people. The history of the nineteenth century was one of gradual but very definite advance towards the sovereignty of the people, and a great deal of the progress which was made can be traced directly or indirectly to the influence of the French Revolution. Thus, in England, those who had for years been advocating a wider and more democratic franchise were so inspired by what the French had done that they made greater and more sustained efforts to achieve their purpose, and were not deterred by imprisonment, transportation, social ostracism, or any other punishments which the governments of the day might inflict upon them. They made no progress during the years of peril from Revolutionary France, but seventeen years later the middle class won political power in England.

The idea that government exists for the security and protection of the governed was fully grasped in the eighteenth century, but it was believed—in countries like England almost as much as in countries like Russia, which were only just emerging from barbarism—that the people should certainly not be allowed to govern themselves. There is no political idea in the modern world which finds more general acceptance than the idea that government should be directed by the people through their own representatives, and that it is better for a nation to make mistakes in self-government rather than be ruled by irresponsible monarchs, however benevolent and wise they may be. This doctrine was energetically propounded in France during the Revolution, and when French armies marched into the Netherlands, Western Germany, and Northern Italy they carried their revolutionary ideas with them and did much to ensure the ultimate triumph of popular government in those countries.

The opposition of governing classes generally to the Revolution, and the attacks which the rulers of Austria and Prussia made upon it, were dictated by something of far greater consequence than the wrongs of Louis XVI or the indignities to which Marie Antoinette had been subjected. The opponents of the Revolution realized that the revolutionary spirit is very infectious, particularly among people who are in any way oppressed, and therefore, in order to prevent it from spreading to their own countries, they did their utmost to stamp it out in France. The fall of the French monarchy, with its record of eight centuries of unbroken succession and its tradition of magnificence, the spoliation of the Church, and the extinction of the nobility were to them ominous portents which it would be suicidal to treat with indifference. But the opposition of despotic kings and autocratic ministers was never a source of real danger to the Revolution, for they represented an expiring medieval order whose day was obviously over. What was infinitely more dangerous was the way in which the opinions of moderate men were alienated by the excesses of the Reign of Terror.

'To the advanced thinkers of the Continent the destruction of feudalism in its Bourbon citadel had presented itself as an omen of the deliverance of the whole of Europe from the effete institutions of the Middle Ages. But everywhere eager sympathy had given place to horror and loathing as control of the revolutionary movement had passed from the hands of reasonable men and had been secured by gang after gang of murderous fanatics, each more extreme, unbalanced, and sanguinary than its predecessor.'[1]

In England the Revolution was at first very popular. The ideals of the revolutionists—Liberty, Equality, and Fraternity —were admirable, and it was felt that the French were doing exactly the same as the English had done in 1688, when they had got rid of a despotic king, James II, and remodelled their government on more rational principles. The poet Wordsworth wrote of the early days of the French Revolution:

>Bliss was it in that dawn to be alive
>But to be young was very heaven.

[1] *Main Currents of European History* (Hearnshaw), pub. Macmillan.

The politician Fox spoke of the fall of the Bastille as the greatest and the best event that had ever happened in the world ; and some enthusiasts, among them the poets Coleridge and Southey, projected the founding of a colony on the banks of the river Susquehanna in America, where they would be able to live in strict accordance with revolutionary ideals. But terrorism produced a reaction which was quite as remarkable as this early enthusiasm. Even Wordsworth became conservative and anti-revolutionary, and reformers who expressed the mildest of progressive sentiments laid themselves open to legal penalties, whose frequent barbarity illustrates the alarm with which the governing classes regarded the spread of anything approximating to revolutionary ideas. Thus in 1793 two Scottish gentlemen, Muir and Palmer, were transported to Botany Bay [1] for advocating parliamentary reform, and Lord Braxfield,[2] the judge who sentenced them, declared from the bench that 'the landed interest alone has a right to representation'. It is a somewhat remarkable fact that the writer Edmund Burke, who had been the foremost English advocate of the rights of the American colonists who rebelled against Great Britain, was from the beginning distinctly hostile to the French Revolution. 'He saw only the glare of hell in the light which others took to be the dawn of the millennium', and predicted that it would be followed by a military despotism in France, and that it would, if not checked, destroy the very foundations of civilization. He was right about the despotism, wrong in his other prediction.

The Revolution was followed by the despotism of Napoleon Buonaparte, which was, in some respects, more absolute than that of Louis XIV; but it lasted for less than twenty years, and, even while it lasted, the main achievements

[1] In those days Australia, whose history as a British colony was just beginning, was mainly used as a place to which the worst convicts could be sent.

[2] Lord Braxfield figures as Weir of Hermiston in R. L. Stevenson's story of that name.

of the Revolution were not lost sight of. Uniformity of laws was enforced throughout France ; legal and class privileges were suppressed ; religious disabilities vanished ; large estates which had formerly belonged to the Crown and the nobility were broken up and sold cheaply to men of the middle and lower classes ; commerce was encouraged ; men were taxed according to their means ; and every calling and profession was made free to all French citizens. It was because Napoleon gave practical expression to the achievements of the Revolution, and preserved the order necessary for their continuance, that the French people endured for so long the sacrifices which his policy entailed. Meanwhile his armies, by spreading revolutionary doctrines and at the same time oppressing the peoples upon whom they were quartered, did much to develop that feeling of nationality which is one of the chief features of nineteenth-century history. This was rather a curious result of the French Revolution, which, in theory at least, was distinctly anti-national. The idea of fraternity recognizes no national barriers ; it regards all men as brothers ; and the French were acting in strict accordance with the principle when they issued their famous appeal to the oppressed and down-trodden of all countries to rise against their governments and join the new French Republic in a federation of the free. But as the number and importance of their military successes increased these generous sentiments lost their power, and those who had formerly proclaimed them began to look upon themselves as a nation apart from and superior to all others. The old evil lust for conquest and world dominion took hold upon their minds, and instead of a world animated by liberty, fraternity, and equality their thoughts turned more and more to the idea of a vast empire of subjugated nations dominated and controlled by France. Some of Napoleon's early successes were largely due to the half-hearted nature of the opposition to him. The people of the countries which he invaded had little interest in resisting

PERMANENT EFFECTS

the French soldiers. They had been driven unwillingly, by governments which they hated, to fight against foes whose revolutionary sentiments they admired, and whom many of them were disposed to welcome as deliverers rather than resist as invaders. But when the French began to show that their devotion to the ideals which they professed did not get beyond mere lip service, and when they began to behave with the insolence and arrogance of typical conquerors, a great passion of patriotic feeling was aroused against them, and the ultimate downfall of Napoleon and of French Imperialism was chiefly due to this. The war against him, which began as a war of dynasts, ended as a war of peoples.

The French Revolution is one of the most important events in the history of the world.

'Herder compared it to the Reformation and the rise of Christianity; and it deserves to be ranked with those two great moments in history, because like them it destroyed the landmarks of the world in which generations of men had passed their lives, because it was a movement towards a completer humanity, and because it too was a religion, with its doctrines, its apostles, and its martyrs. It brought on the stage of human affairs forces which have moulded the thoughts and actions of men ever since, and have taken a permanent place among the formative influences of civilization. As Christianity taught man that he was a spiritual being, and the Reformation proclaimed that nothing need stand between the soul and God, so the Revolution asserted the equality of man, conceiving individuals as partakers of a common nature and declaring each one of them, regardless of birth, colour, or religion, to be possessed of certain inalienable rights.'[1]

Practically all the great revolutions of the nineteenth century are traceable to its influence. The Revolution inaugurated a new epoch in the history of the human race; it gave the death-blow to feudalism, which, although it had long ceased to govern the relations between kings and nobles, still continued

[1] *Cambridge Modern History*, vol. viii. Article on 'Europe and the French Revolution' (G. P. Gooch).

in France and elsewhere to regulate the relations of nobles and peasants; and by giving feudalism a mortal blow and proclaiming in its place the doctrine of equality it prepared the way for notable triumphs in the cause of individual liberty. The conception of equality could not fail to strengthen and promote such movements as those for the removal of religious restrictions, and for the abolition of slavery. 'It is to the Revolution, to Mirabeau and Grégoire, to the march of the French armies, that the Jews look back as the signal for their emancipation,'[1] and although religion had much to do with the abolition of slavery, particularly in the British dominions, the movement received great support from the widespread acceptance of French ideas.

XXVI

NAPOLEON BUONAPARTE

THE astonishing career of Napoleon Buonaparte would have been impossible if there had been no French Revolution. Under the old régime he would probably have had little opportunity of displaying his great military qualities, and he would certainly not have risen to a position of eminence in the state.

Napoleon was hardly a Frenchman by birth. He was born in 1769 in the island of Corsica, which had only been a French possession for a year; his ancestors were Italian; his native language was Italian, and he always spoke French with a foreign accent; in his youth his great ambition was to free Corsica from French control; and in some respects his career is a repetition on a very large scale of that of the Italian condottierri of the Middle Ages. He was educated at the military schools of Brienne and Paris, where his relations with his fellow students were not happy. They despised him

[1] *Cambridge Modern History*, vol. viii. Article on 'Europe and the French Revolution' (G. P. Gooch).

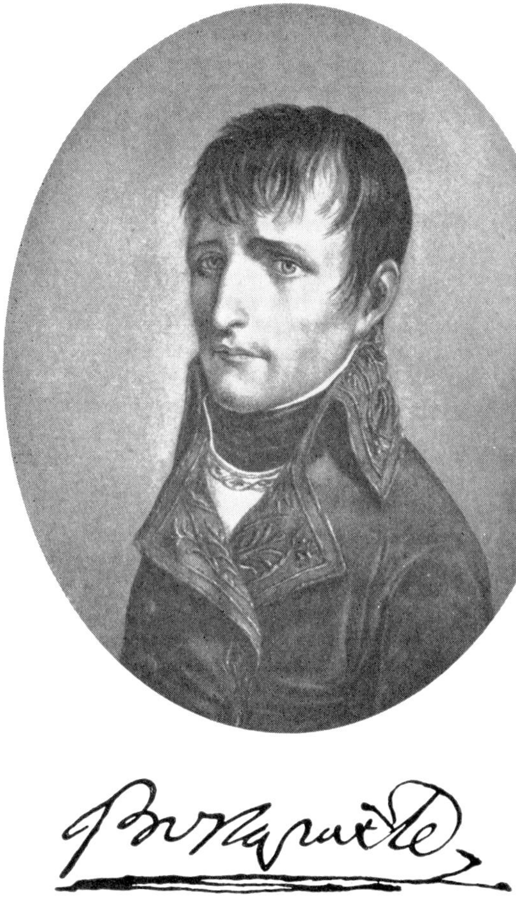

for his reserved, sulky ways, and perhaps also for his poverty, and he thought that they were all inferior to himself in 'noble sentiments'. In course of time he entered the army as an artillery officer, and became a Jacobin and an ardent supporter of the French Revolution. He was befriended by the brother of Maximilien Robespierre, a fact that nearly cost him his life when that leader fell from power. Napoleon was thrown into prison and for a little time there existed some doubt in the minds of the authorities as to whether he should be guillotined or not. He was eventually released, and during the next couple of years so impressed the Directory with his military skill that in 1796, at the early age of twenty-seven, he was made commander-in-chief of their army in Northern Italy. He very soon justified the confidence which had been reposed in him. Within a year the Austrians, with whom the French were still at war, had been driven out of those parts, and a Cisalpine republic carved out of the smaller states of Northern Italy. This new state included Milan, Modena, some of the papal dominions, and part of the possessions of the republic of Venice. The other part, including Venice itself, was given as a sort of indemnity to Austria, who formally ceded the Austrian Netherlands to France.

Napoleon, thus early in his career, gave clear indications of the qualities which were afterwards to make him such a menace to the peace of the world. He told the Italians that the French had come to break their chains, but he did not scruple to tax them heavily in order that his army and the somewhat costly court which he maintained should be supported, and he took away the liberties of Venice without the slightest compunction. He was perfectly clear in his own mind that he had not won his victories in order to advance 'the lawyers of the Directory', and that the French people needed above all else 'a head who is rendered illustrious by glory and not by theories of government, fine phrases, or the talk of idealists'. He was equally clear that this head could be no one but himself. But, after the successful conclusion of his Italian campaign, he was faced with rather an awkward situation. The time was not ripe for him to return to France and impose his authority upon the people ; on the other hand, if he resigned his command and simply returned to live the life of an ordinary person, he would lose so much prestige as to jeopardize seriously his designs for the future. He accordingly persuaded the Directory that it was in the best interests of France that England should be ruined, and that the most effective way of doing that was to deprive her of her Eastern possessions. And so he was allowed to take his army to Egypt [1] and thence across the desert of Sinai towards the East. But he never reached India; probably he never expected to do so. When he was besieging Acre in Syria, a French newspaper was sent to him from which he discovered that, in his absence, the affairs of France had not been prospering. The Directory had proved itself hopelessly incompetent, and the Austrians had recovered most of what the French had won in Northern Italy. Napoleon had probably been expecting such news for some time. The way was now clear for him to return to France and make a definite bid for power. Leaving his army, and accompanied only by some of his best officers, he made his way thither by sea with the utmost dispatch, and before the end of the year 1799 his intrigues had been so far successful that the Directory had been superseded by a government of Three Consuls, with Napoleon holding the title of First Consul, and practically all the power. A plebiscite was at once taken of the people, and they voted by over three million votes to less than sixteen hundred in favour of the new government. It was almost universally believed that the rule of Napoleon was bound to be a great improvement upon those which had preceded it,

[1] The French invasion of Egypt led to the discovery by a French engineer at the Rosetta mouth of the Nile of the famous Rosetta Stone, which has made the reading of ancient Egyptian possible.

and there were many who thought that it would give France the peace which she desired above all other things.

They were soon to be disillusioned. Napoleon quickly recovered Northern Italy from the Austrians, and in 1801 and 1802 he made peace with all the powers with whom France had been at war—Austria, Naples, Turkey, Russia, and England. But he never intended this peace to be anything other than a truce. In 1802 he told his Council of State that

'France needs glorious deeds and hence war. She must be the first among the states or she is lost. I shall keep the peace as long as our neighbours keep it, but I shall regard it as an advantage if they force me to take up my arms again before they are rusted. ... I regard myself as destined while I fill my present office to fight almost without intermission.'

His ideal was that the whole of Europe should be subject to one Emperor, namely himself, and that he should be able to reward the most able and devoted of his officers with kingships over the various countries of which the continent was composed. After 1803, when war was resumed, he set himself resolutely to the task of bringing this about. He planned a great invasion of England, which never came to anything, although he succeeded in alarming the English people pretty thoroughly, particularly those who lived on the south coast. He made himself King of Italy, dissolved the Holy Roman Empire, occupied Vienna, defeated the combined armies of Austria and Russia in the terrible Battle of Austerlitz, which the English Prime Minister William Pitt regarded as of such significance that he declared, with prophetic accuracy, 'Roll up that map (of Europe), it will not be wanted these ten years'; and utterly humiliated the Prussians, whose lands he occupied. In 1802 he had got the French to make him First Consul for life, and in 1804 he received the title of Emperor. He was probably at the zenith of his power between the years 1808 and 1810. He had so far succeeded in his king-making ambitions that he had made

NAPOLEON'S PLAN FOR THE INVASION OF ENGLAND

A fanciful print of 1798 contemplating invasion by air, sea, and a Channel tunnel

his brother Louis King of Holland, another brother Joseph King of Naples, while still another brother Jerome became the first and last King of Westphalia, a new German state which Napoleon carved out of territory which he had conquered from the Prussians and the Hanoverians. When in

1808 he made Joseph King of Spain, he transferred the rule over Naples to Murat, one of his marshals. Another of his marshals, Bernadotte, subsequently became King of Sweden. In 1810 the French Empire had reached its maximum extent (see map), and in the same year Napoleon, who had divorced his wife Josephine, married Marie Louise, the daughter of the Emperor of Austria, and so gained admission into the Habsburg family, one of the oldest and proudest of the reigning families of Europe.

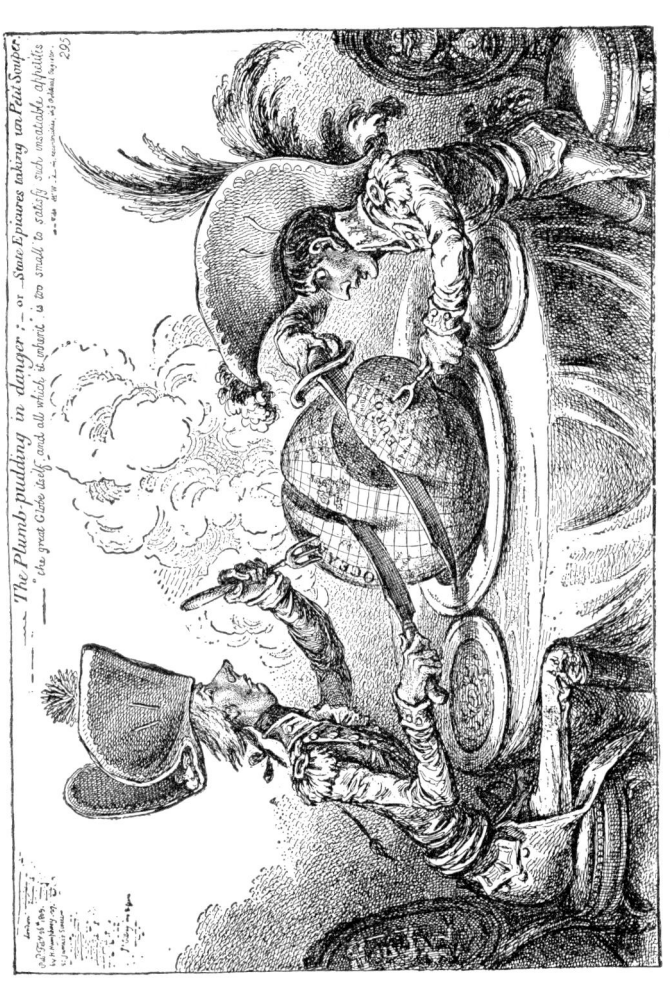

Napoleon and the growth of the French Empire. A cartoon of 1805 by Gillray; Napoleon helps himself to Europe, while Pitt holds the sea for England.

After 1810 his power gradually declined, and his downfall four years later must be attributed to three main causes : the opposition of England and particularly the strength of the British fleet ; the fact that the war against him became a war of peoples ; and the disastrous issue of his Russian campaign of 1812. From the beginning the British fleet had been a tremendous barrier in the way of the complete realization of Napoleon's ambitions. The great victory which the English admiral Nelson had won over the combined French and Spanish fleets off Cape Trafalgar in 1805 had been quite as decisive as Napoleon's land victory of Austerlitz. It meant that the French navy ceased to count as an effective instrument, and so made it quite impossible for the Emperor to blockade England and prevent foreign ships from trading with English ports. On the other hand, the English navy was able to do much damage to French trade, and to prevent articles of foreign or colonial commerce from entering France or any of the countries which formed part of the French Empire or were allied to Napoleon. It was this fact which caused Russia, allied to France since 1807, to break that alliance. Napoleon was furious at what he chose to regard as inexcusable perfidy on the part of the Czar, and in 1812, with an army of six hundred thousand men, he invaded Russia. Six months later he entered Poland on his homeward journey with scarcely more than twenty thousand of them left. The Russians, after one great defeat, had persistently refused to fight pitched battles against the invaders ; instead, they had hung upon the flanks and the rear of the French army, harassing them as much as they could ; they had abandoned towns and villages through which the invaders would pass, and had removed supplies of food, so that when the French reached Moscow their bodies were half-famished and their spirits thoroughly depressed by the severe trials of the advance—the sultry heat of midsummer, bad roads, burning villages, and one great battle at Borodino, in which

MOSCOW. A general view of the Kremlin in 1913
Photograph by Mr. Louis Cahen

the French, though victorious, had lost as many men as their foes. There was nothing but retreat left for them, particularly since, before they got to Moscow, a considerable part of the town had been set on fire, and during their stay there mysterious conflagrations broke out in various parts of the city. The return journey was much worse than the advance, since the soldiers were then exposed to the rigours of a very severe winter, accentuated by scarcity of food and fuel and remorseless attacks by the Russian troops. Napoleon hastened back to Paris before the tattered remnants of his army could arrive, making light of the disaster, and before the year 1813 was over he had got together another army of six hundred thousand men, largely recruited of old men and boys.

Meantime the character of the struggle against him had changed. The English statesman George Canning had predicted that Napoleon would eventually be defeated by a war of nations, and that this war of nations would start in Spain. His prediction was amply verified. The Spaniards resented Napoleon's attempt to foist his brother Joseph upon them as their king, and with the assistance of English troops under General Wellesley, who afterwards became Duke of Wellington, they fought a long war, the Peninsular War, which has been graphically described as a running sore in the side of France, and which resulted in the deposition of Joseph and the expulsion of the French armies from Spain. Meanwhile, in Germany, the exactions of Napoleon, the arrogance of his soldiers, and the patriotic appeals of philosophers like Fichte had led to an astonishing outburst of national feeling. In Prussia particularly, the government had been overhauled, serfdom had been abolished, and the army made into a really effective fighting force. Thus when Napoleon marched into Germany in 1813 he had to face an opposition which was more dangerous than anything which he had previously encountered. The Russians, the Prussians, and the Austrians had at last learned the necessity of combining against their common

HIS FALL

enemy, and the struggle against him had ceased to be merely dynastic. In August he won a victory at Dresden, but less than two months later he was signally defeated at Leipzig in the great Battle of the Nations, and before the end of the year he had been driven back into France.

The allies offered him generous terms. He was to be allowed to keep the crown of France, whose boundaries were fixed at the Rhine, the Alps, and the Pyrenees, and he was also to keep Belgium and Savoy. He hesitated to accept; the allies lost patience with him and invaded France. In 1814 Austrians, Prussians, Russians, and Swedes crossed the Rhine, and British and Spanish troops came into the country through the passes of the Pyrenees. Napoleon fought brilliantly, but the odds against him were too great. Paris fell at the end of March, and a week later he abdicated. The victors then restored the French monarchy in the person of Louis XVIII, the brother of the ill-fated Louis XVI, and Napoleon was exiled to the small island of Elba in the Mediterranean, where he was granted sovereign rights and allowed to retain his imperial title. Such a mockery could hardly have been expected to satisfy a man of his restless and ambitious temperament, and in less than a year he escaped to France and once more persuaded the people to entrust their destinies to him. He promised them individual liberty, freedom of the press, and much else which, in spite of promises, the restored king had not given them, and he renounced war and conquest, declaring his determination to rule as a constitutional sovereign in future. The French people were duped; the allies were not. Vigorous preparations were made to overthrow ' the enemy and destroyer of the world's peace ', and in June of 1815 a force, consisting mainly of British and Prussians; defeated him at Waterloo, in Belgium. A little later he surrendered himself to the captain of an English warship, and was exiled by the allies to the remote island of St. Helena in the South Atlantic, where, until his death in 1821, he busied himself by brooding over his past, writing memoirs to justify it, and quarrelling with the English governor.

Probably more literature has been written about Napoleon than about any other character who has ever lived. His astonishing rise to power, the vast scale of his achievements, the force that lay behind his personality, and the tragedy of his fall have appealed alike to the imaginations of posterity and to those of his contemporaries. He had an opportunity such as comes to very few, and he might, had he been less egotistic, have left behind him the reputation of one of the world's greatest benefactors. He was a man of great mental capacities and extraordinary powers of organization. The fine roads which he constructed across the Alps and along the Rhine; the wide streets, magnificent bridges, and triumphal arches with which he beautified Paris; his work in codifying the laws of France; and his conviction of the importance of education are some indications of what he might have done if personal ambition and the desire for military glory had not warped his judgements and vitiated his whole conception of what a ruler owes to his subjects. Even his domestic achievements were coloured by a desire to exalt himself. The triumphal arches of Paris were meant to prevent the people from forgetting his victories; the central idea of his educational system was that it should turn out loyal subjects of the Emperor, prepared to do his will in all things, particularly military service. When he returned from Elba, and when it was expedient for him to conciliate the French people as much as possible, he promised them a free press, but he had no real sympathy with such an idea; at the very beginning of his administration he suppressed a number of newspapers and forbade the establishment of new ones, and when he became Emperor he adopted the policy of supplying news to the papers, and he gave them strict orders that they were to publish nothing which was 'disadvantageous or disagreeable to France'. His ideal was to suppress all newspapers except one for official purposes.

A great deal has been made by some of his codification of the laws of France, while others have condemned his work as too hurried and superficial. Both the civil and the criminal law were codified, but it is the codification of the civil law—the Code Napoleon—which is the more important, because it served as a model for the legal systems of other countries.[1] It is still used, not only in France, but also, with some modifications, in parts of Germany, Holland, Belgium, Italy, and the state of Louisiana in America. Although some of its provisions, such as the control which it gave a husband over his wife's property, are almost medieval in character, the Code was a good thing inasmuch as it helped to clarify the laws of France, and to secure permanently some of the benefits of the Revolution. It substituted plain statements for legal mysteries and, like all Napoleon's enactments, it made for efficiency. There can be little if any doubt that 'without his driving power it would not have come into existence so soon, and it might not have come into existence at all.'[2] 'He possessed so luxuriant an intellectual nature, so lively a power of concrete vision, so keen an instinct for the large issues of politics, that his contributions to the discussion were a series of splendid surprises, occasionally appropriate and decisive, occasionally involved in the gleaming tissues of a dream, but always stamped with the mark of genius and glowing with the impulses of a fresh and impetuous temperament.'[2] 'To Bonaparte's presence we may ascribe the fact that the civil law of France was codified, not only with more scrupulosity than other portions of French law, but also with a livelier sense of the general interests of the state. What those interests were, Buonaparte knew. They were civil equality, healthy family life, secure bulwarks

[1] Napoleon once said at St. Helena that his winning of forty battles did not redound to his glory so much as the Civil Code.

[2] *Cambridge Modern History*, vol. ix. Article by H. A. L. Fisher on 'The Codes' (Chap. VI).

to property, religious toleration, a government raised above the howls of faction. This is the policy which he stamped upon the Civil Code.'[1]

Napoleon was certainly intoxicated by success. As he grew older his ambitions and his egotism increased, and he became more and more despotic. There seemed to be no limits to his vanity. An author who had written 'A History of Buonaparte' was ordered to change the title to 'A History of the Campaigns of Napoleon the Great'; and in 1806 the Emperor lamented to one of his officers that if he were to pretend to be the Son of God, the veriest fishwife would hiss at him, whereas when Alexander the Great made a similar pretension, all believed him with the exception of his mother, the philosopher Aristotle, and a few Athenian pedants, from which he came to the conclusion that he was not as great a man as Alexander. His desire for glory did find some response in the hearts of the French people. They were proud of his victories, and they made almost unbelievable sacrifices in order to enhance the prestige of France. It is true that they were not heavily taxed, as almost invariably happens to a nation which is at war. Napoleon made the countries which his armies occupied pay for their upkeep. But the French had to pay the price of victory in another and more terrible way. They had to endure the killing and the crippling of their most vigorous manhood. No nation has had a more terrible experience of the evil consequences of militarism. When Napoleon fell in 1815 he was probably regarded with almost universal execration, and there were few, if any, outside his own personal adherents, who regretted his exile to St. Helena. Twenty-five years later, however, his reputation had improved. The dull and often repressive rule of the restored Bourbons had failed to inspire respect either in France or out of it. A new generation had sprung up, oblivious of the ruin

[1] *Cambridge Modern History*, vol. ix. Article by H. A. L. Fisher on 'The Codes' (Chap. VI).

POST-WAR EUROPE

and misery which Napoleon's policy had brought to their country, conscious only of his revolutionary ideas and the fear and awe which his very name had inspired abroad. There was consequently great enthusiasm when, in that year (1840), the body of the Emperor was brought from St. Helena and reinterred with great military splendour in an imposing sarcophagus of red granite beneath the gilded dome of the church of the hospital for old soldiers known as the Invalides. On the pavement around the tomb the names of Napoleon's greatest victories are inscribed, and at the side are colossal statues of victory with about sixty captured banners beside them. The whole structure is apt to give a somewhat false impression, because it does not take into account Waterloo and St. Helena, the inevitable results of the attacks upon the liberties of other nations and the desire to occupy a domineering position in the world, which the captured banners and the statues of victory represent. During his last years of captivity, Napoleon uttered one sentiment which is the best explanation of his fall: 'Brute force has never attained anything durable.'

After Waterloo Europe experienced a somewhat precarious and unstable peace which lasted for nearly forty years. Conferences were held to which the Great Powers, including France, sent representatives, but two things prevented any definite progress towards real international peace, and prepared the way for more fighting as soon as the Continent had recovered from the exhaustion of the Napoleonic Wars. In the first place, the rulers who were restored to their former positions showed that they had learned little from experience, and almost immediately began to aim at absolute power once more. In Spain and Naples there were popular insurrections which were summarily suppressed by the aid of foreign troops, French in one case, Austrian in the other. Europe, during the generation which followed Waterloo, was dominated by the personality and the ideas of the Austrian minister Metternich, and he considered that the Great Powers were acting quite within their rights in putting down promptly any attempt to upset the established order of things in any country which had been at all permeated by revolutionary ideas. The statesmen of Great Britain alone differed from him ; they maintained that every nation has a right to the government which it desires, and that no country should interfere with the internal affairs of another. British resistance was not, however, strong enough to prevent such interferences; but when in 1830 the people of France rose against their king, Charles X, who had endeavoured to make himself absolute, and replaced him by another, Louis Philippe, from whom they expected a more liberal policy, the other continental monarchies, very largely because the revolution was openly approved in Great Britain, wisely refrained from interfering. It was, however, in America that the attempt to revive the spirit of absolutism received its most pronounced check. When Napoleon put his brother Joseph upon the throne of Spain in 1808, the Spanish colonies across the Atlantic, already seething with discontent, had risen in rebellion, and under a leader named Bolivar had started a war for independence which Spain found it so difficult to suppress that in 1823 Metternich, on behalf of Austria, suggested that the other great states of Europe should assist Spain to put down the insurrection. Great Britain at once opposed the idea, but of more significance was the action of President Monroe of the United States, who protested against the claim of the Great Powers of Europe to interfere in the affairs of South America, and declared that any such interference would be regarded by the United States as an unfriendly act. Thus the famous Monroe Doctrine of 'America for the Americans' was enunciated. At the same time Great Britain began to treat with the revolted colonies as with independent states, and within a year or two Colombia, Mexico, Buenos Ayres (the nucleus of the Argentine Republic), Peru, Bolivia, and Chile had completed their emancipation and secured the status of independent republics. About the same time Brazil also proclaimed its independence of Portugal, but accepted the son of the Portuguese king as its ruler.

The second reason why the peace which followed Waterloo was not a lasting peace was because the Congress of Vienna, which drew up the Peace Treaty, did not do its work well. It ignored national aspirations, and in its eagerness to overthrow Napoleonism it overthrew much that was good as well as much that was bad. The diplomats who were responsible for it showed a sad lack of imagination. Their sufferings during the Napoleonic régime had blinded them to the new forces which had been working actively in Europe since the French Revolution, and which Napoleon had done much to encourage. Generally speaking, their ideas of a regenerated Europe did not get beyond the conception of a return to the *status quo ante bellum*. Under Napoleon Italy had been reduced to three political divisions, all dominated by the Emperor. This step towards unity was destroyed in 1815, eight states were set up, and the whole of Northern Italy was handed over to the German-speaking Austrians. Russia was confirmed in her possession of Finland, whose people were entirely alien. Norway and Sweden were united. Germany was organized into a confederation of thirty-eight states, governed by a Diet presided over by Austria. The Dutch Republic was destroyed quite needlessly, and its Protestant inhabitants joined to the French-speaking Catholics of Belgium to form a new kingdom of the Netherlands. A more far-sighted policy might have averted the great wars of the nineteenth century, such as the Italian War of Liberation, and the wars by which Prussia destroyed the power of Austria in Germany and established a new German Empire. The Union of Holland and Belgium came to an end in 1830, and that of Norway and Sweden in 1905. However, although the Vienna Settlement proved a bad one, and although most of its work has been reversed since, those who were responsible for it must not be judged too harshly. Their chief mistake was that they disregarded the principle of nationality; but it must be borne in mind that the most striking illustration of the national spirit which they had witnessed had been in France, and there it had eventually taken the form of a spirit of aggression and self-assertion which they thought it desirable to eradicate. Moreover

'there was little to suggest to political observers of the time that the new passion of national sentiment was more than a passing concomitant of the wars of liberation, and nothing to cause them to realize that it was indeed the new vital and formative principle that was to transmute the old Europe of dynastic states to the new Europe of homogeneous and self-conscious peoples. It would be unjust to condemn the politicians because they were not prophets'.[1]

On the other hand, there is no disguising the fact that these politicians would have made a far better settlement if they had shown less timidity in some things, and more enterprise in others, and if they had been great enough to sink personal feelings and forget personal indignities in a whole-hearted desire for the general welfare of Europe. They gave nothing but moral support to England's appeal against the iniquities of the slave trade, and they refused to deal with the problem of Turkey's oppression of her Christian subjects in Greece and the Balkan Peninsula.

The Napoleonic Wars are important in the history of the development of the British Empire, which received a considerable acquisition of territory in consequence of them. Cape Colony and Ceylon were taken from the Dutch, who were at the time allied to France, and Malta, Mauritius, and the West Indian islands of Trinidad, St. Lucia, and Tobago were conquered from the French. The Congress of Vienna confirmed all these acquisitions, and so helped to demonstrate the fact that Great Britain's most cherished field of activity was ultra-European.

[1] *Main Currents of European History* (Hearnshaw).

XXVII

THE INDUSTRIAL REVOLUTION

WHILE the French Revolution was pursuing its course, and while Napoleon was disturbing the peace of Europe, another revolution, which was destined to affect still more profoundly the history of mankind, was taking place in England. This was the Industrial Revolution, a term which is used to express the change which was responsible for the adoption of the system of making things on a large scale in large factories with the aid of steam-power, as opposed to the old system, which was generally followed up to the middle of the eighteenth century, of making goods in the cottages or shops of the workers. The first feature of the Revolution was the appearance of certain important inventions which entirely revolutionized the cotton industry. They were all made between the year 1760 and the conclusion of the Napoleonic Wars (1815), and their effect was so great that, even amid the storm and stress of war, what had been a very small industry catering mostly for local needs became a vast industry turning out more cloth than was needed for national use. In 1760 England imported about four million pounds of raw cotton; in 1815 over one hundred million pounds; and in 1840, when the world had largely recovered from the Napoleonic cataclysm, she imported nearly five hundred million pounds.

This tremendous increase of trade would have been impossible but for the invention and use of the steam-engine. Hitherto, industries had been obliged to remain at those places where water-power was available, but the discovery of the use of steam made it possible for them to go where they could best obtain their raw materials, their labourers, or their markets. Crude steam-engines had been in use in England for many years before the time of James Watt, but he was the first to make the steam-engine a practical machine for supplying power to the new factories. In 1785 the first experiment was made, and it proved so successful that before the end of the century steam-engines were as common as water-mills in the factories.

The cotton industry was by no means the only one which benefited from the new spirit of invention and enterprise. More effective methods were discovered of manufacturing woollen goods and fabrics of various descriptions; the old method of smelting iron by means of charcoal was abandoned and the coal and iron industries, which had up to this time been of comparatively little importance, made such progress that they eventually became the chief industries of the country; finally, means of communication—roads, canals, and bridges—were improved; in 1804 the first locomotive was made, and in 1830 the first passenger railway, between Liverpool and Manchester, was opened, and Stephenson's engine, 'The Rocket', attained a speed of over thirty miles an hour. After this railways multiplied, and by the middle of the century there was a network of them over Europe as well as England. The steamboat preceded the steam-engine as a means of locomotion. There was a steamboat on the Firth of Clyde Canal in 1802; in 1819 a steamboat crossed the Atlantic from Savannah to Liverpool, taking twenty-five days for the voyage, and after that improvements followed rapidly, so that by 1910 it was possible for a boat propelled by steam to cross from Liverpool to New York in less than five days, a voyage which had at one time taken as many weeks or even months. Still more wonderful, perhaps, were the inventions which arose from the investigations of Faraday and others into the properties and uses of electricity. In 1835 the first electric telegraph came into existence, and sixteen years later the first underseas cable was laid between England and France. In a few years the telegraph system spread throughout the civilized world, and news which had

THE ERA OF STEAM. THE *GREAT EASTERN* OFF THE ISLE OF WIGHT

Launched 1858 with a net tonnage of 13,344

travelled slowly from place to place could be flashed with incredible speed from one end of the earth to the other. The improvements which had originated in England took firm and rapid root in other countries too, until all the great nations of the earth were thoroughly 'industrialized'. In the space of about a hundred years the world had been transformed. If it had been possible for a Roman of the time of the Caesars to come to life in England or in France about the year 1750 he would have found little to surprise him in the industrial methods of the people, but if he had come to life a hundred years later he would have found himself in an altogether unfamiliar world with its busy cities, its factories full of complicated machinery, and its astonishing development of methods of communication. One result of the Industrial Revolution was a great increase of population, and its concentration in places where the new factories were established. The support of this population was rendered possible by agricultural improvements, which are often spoken of as the Agrarian or Agricultural Revolution. Better and more scientific methods of farming were adopted, the old three-field system disappeared, wider areas were put under cultivation, and there were in consequence more corn and meat to satisfy the needs of the increasing town populations.

To some extent the great changes which the Industrial Revolution effected fell on prepared soil. Throughout the eighteenth century there was steady industrial development and great commercial activity in Western Europe, exemplified by the development of banking, the growth of intercourse between nations, improvement in internal means of communication such as roads and canals, and even by factory systems on small scales. Thus in France and Prussia there were factories under state patronage, such as the glass works at Creusot, the chief shareholder in which was Marie Antoinette, and the linen manufacture of Silesia. But most of these industries had very modest capitals, and the number

THE OLD AND THE NEW
A century of progress in the railway engine

of people employed was very small, judged by nineteenth-century standards. In England there were woollen factories as far back as the sixteenth century. Thus John Winchcombe, known as 'Jack of Newbury', is said to have had a hundred looms at work in his own house, and clothing mills were also set up at Malmesbury and Cirencester. But in 1555 this development of capitalist industry was checked by the Weavers Act, which made it impossible for the future for weavers to be collected in large numbers under one roof, by enacting that more than two looms could not be kept in any house. Thus the industry remained in the domestic stage.

The Napoleonic Wars resulted in an enormous increase in the volume of English trade. The supremacy of the British navy, the rigours of the blockade which it imposed, and the fact that England was secure from invasion, had the effect of shutting out raw materials from continental ports and bringing them to those of Britain instead, and this at a time when mechanical inventions made it possible for that country to cope with the increased demand for her manufactured goods. There were few docks in England when she went to war in 1793. During the next thirteen years the East India Docks, the West India Docks, and the London Docks were constructed on the Thames alone, and the Mersey, the Clyde, and the Humber kept pace with the Thames.

On the continent of Europe the wars naturally checked the progress of commerce and industry, but with the coming of peace these revived, and in countries like France, Belgium, Switzerland, and Germany English machines were freely introduced. Some, such as the spinning jenny, had been introduced even before 1789. In 1812 the first steam-engine to be used in a European textile mill was set up in Alsace. During the ensuing thirty years steam came rapidly into use throughout Western Europe. Thus by 1847 France had nearly five thousand steam-engines with a capacity of sixty horse-power, and in cities like Paris, Lyons, Marseilles,

THE FACTORY SYSTEM

Lille, Bordeaux, and Toulouse there were great factories, and whole quarters peopled exclusively by factory labourers.

The wars raised the prestige of London very much. Alone of the great European cities she had been disturbed by no invader, unless it was the foreign capitalist like Nathan Rothschild who found it the best centre for his operations. During the progress of hostilities England had paid subsidies to the allies; during the years following, all nations—France, Prussia, Austria, Russia, even the United States of America, and the South American republics freely after 1820—came to London to borrow. English ideas and implements were borrowed as well as English money, and the early history of the great changes effected by the Industrial Revolution on the continent of Europe contains many English names, such as Cockerill, who helped to found the machine industry of Belgium; Douglas, who made textile machines in France during the Consulate; and the Nottingham men who introduced the bobbin lace machine at Douai shortly after the battle of Waterloo. In some arts and crafts, however, continental nations went ahead of England. Thus Germany became superior in scientific methods of metallurgy, and France in the beauty and design of her textiles.

The Industrial Revolution was not, however, an unmixed blessing. The 'domestic' system of industry which it brought to an end was in many respects more conducive to the happiness of the workers. Artisans usually did their work in their cottages or shops, and in very many cases they were not entirely dependent upon what they earned at their trades for their livelihoods. For instance, in the time of the English poet Chaucer (1340–1400) the cutlers of Sheffield lived in cottages to which plots of land were attached, and in bad times or when they thought that a temporary change of occupation was desirable, they were able to devote their energies to gardening. The Industrial Revolution changed all that. It made it necessary for workmen to live near the factories where they were employed, and long rows of ugly tenement houses with no gardens or even grass plots attached to them were built for their accommodation, and so originated the hideous towns which are still to be seen in many of the industrial districts of the world. The factories were owned by a small class of capitalists, whose main object appeared to be to amass great fortunes for themselves, with little or no regard for the well-being of those who worked for them. Women and children of tender years were employed in large numbers; wages were scandalously low; hours of labour were frequently as high as fifteen or even eighteen in the day; and so inhuman did the system become that governments had to legislate in order to mitigate some of its most obvious cruelties. The factory-owners, naturally, resented these interferences. They contended that industry should be independent of government control, that competition should regulate prices, and that wages and hours of labour should be entirely a matter of supply and demand. If the supply of labour exceeded the demand employers were entitled to take advantage of it and depress wages. The working-classes were at the time unorganized and somewhat incoherent, and therefore almost wholly at the mercy of their masters. Some of them, like the English Chartists, thought that if the franchise were extended, their lot would be improved; others grasped the idea that without organization and unity, no permanent improvement was possible, and so they strove to establish trade unions. In England these unions were at first declared to be illegal, and many of their promoters were imprisoned and transported. In 1824, however, the government legalized them. Since that time they have increased greatly in power and influence, not only in England, but in all the important industrial countries of the world, and they have, undoubtedly, been the means of securing higher wages, fewer hours of labour, and better conditions generally for their members.

Children in a rope factory

English Factory Slaves. Pl.3 Their daily employment.
Cartoon by Robert Cruikshank

CONDITIONS IN THE FACTORIES

Although trade unions have become to some extent socialistic, they have in reality no more connexion with socialism than the fact that both have the same ultimate end in view—the securing of better conditions for the workers. But, whereas trade unions are in the main defensive institutions, socialism is, very definitely, a system of attack. It starts right away with the assumption that the great national services such as the factories, the mines, and the railways should be the property of the state or nation and should not be carried on for the benefit of a few. The earliest Socialists were certainly not revolutionaries, but their ideals and methods have been carried very much farther since their day. Indeed, there are some Socialists who would dispute Robert Owen's claim to be regarded as the founder of modern socialism on the ground that Owen was not a Socialist at all, but rather a benevolent employer of labour like the Levers of Port Sunlight or the Cadburys of Bournville. Owen was a factory-owner of New Lanark in Scotland, and the idea which appealed to him and to most of the other early Socialists was that a concrete appeal to the finer feelings of the factory-owners would not be without good results. If they could be brought to realize that it was possible to conduct a factory on humane lines, even going so far as to give the workers a definite interest in it, and yet make a fair profit, they would readily abandon their old methods of shameless exploitation of the labour of others. At New Lanark Owen reduced the hours of labour ; employed no young children ; made his factory sanitary and pleasant to work in; instituted unemployment pay; shared a certain proportion of his profits with his employees ; and yet was able to make a handsome profit for himself. But although his experiment excited much interest, and he received visits from such exalted personages as the Grand Duke Nicholas [1] of Russia, and the Duke of Kent, the father of Queen Victoria, his example was not followed by his fellow manufacturers,

[1] Afterwards the Czar Nicholas I.

and a new and more aggressive form of socialism soon made its appearance, a socialism which regarded the rich as the natural enemies of the poor, and which claimed that since all wealth is produced by labour, labour was therefore justified in taking what it had produced.

The great teacher of this theory of socialism was a German named Karl Marx, a man of vast learning, particularly in the departments of history, political economy, and philosophy. Marx believed that in just the same way as capitalism had replaced feudalism, so socialism would eventually replace capitalism, and in a manifesto issued in 1848 he made a fervent appeal to the workers of the world to unite, telling them that they had a world to gain and nothing to lose but their chains. Thus he emphasized the international character of labour, and taught the working-classes that their interests were the same the world over, and that national barriers were essentially artificial. But instead of them he erected others, barriers between classes. Even though Marxian socialism might be a force for peace between nations, it is nevertheless a disruptive force within a nation. It has had much effect upon the subsequent course of World History. The revolution which broke out in France in 1848, and which spread from France to Italy, Austria, Bohemia, and Hungary, resulting in each case in the establishment of short-lived democratic constitutions, was largely the work of Socialists, and for a time they exercised a pronounced control over it. Monarchy was overthrown ; national workshops set up, where all who were unemployed could get work or pay ; and strong hopes entertained that France was at last witnessing the end of the reign of capitalism. One agitator wrote : ' We demand the extermination of property and capitalists ; the immediate installation of the proletariat in community of goods ; the proscription of bankers, the rich, the merchants, the bourgeois ; the acceptance of the red flag to signify to society its defeat, to the people its victory ; to Paris the terror to all foreign governments invasion.' But such revolutionary sentiments alarmed the peasantry, whose naturally conservative minds could not but regard with apprehension the 'extermination of property'. Moreover, the national workshops had not been a success. Crowds of idlers had flocked to Paris to be maintained at the public expense, and the thrifty and industrious had been heavily taxed to support them. The result was that when, before the end of the year, a general election took place, the moderates swept the country, and so few Socialists were returned as to make it impossible for them to influence legislation. The new government immediately suppressed the national workshops, those who had been employed in them refused to disband, and for three days there was fierce fighting in the streets of Paris resulting in the deaths of over ten thousand people, more than had perished in the whole of the Reign of Terror. This was followed by the establishment of the Second French Republic, with Louis Napoleon, nephew of the Emperor Napoleon, as its first and only President. Four years later he got himself proclaimed Emperor. When, in 1871, his ambitions had ended in the disastrous defeat of the Franco-German War, another attempt was made to establish a Socialist republic in France. Again Paris was the storm-centre, and again there was furious fighting in the streets: it was only after a very fierce struggle that the revolutionary government was overthrown and the way prepared for the establishment of the Third Republic, which lasted until 1940. Under its régime the Socialists adopted more constitutional methods, and for this and other reasons formed one of the most powerful parties in the French parliament. Some of their leaders, such as Jaurès, whose efforts to prevent war caused him to be assassinated by a fanatic just before the outbreak of the great European struggle of 1914, were men of international reputation.

In Germany, the native country of Karl Marx, socialism made rapid progress after 1850. Bismarck, the chancellor,

DEMOCRATIC LEGISLATION 481

made strenuous efforts to suppress it, first of all by prohibiting meetings and publications, and imprisoning prominent leaders, and then by 'stealing the socialist thunder'. Between 1883 and 1889 he put into operation many of their proposals, such as state insurance against sickness and accident, and old age pensions—but he failed to undermine the power of the Social Democrats, as the followers of Marx called themselves. When William II became Emperor in 1888 they polled less than half a million votes. In 1907 they polled over three million.

But it is in Russia, the least industrialized of all the great countries of Europe, that the principles of Karl Marx have been most thoroughly applied. The Bolshevik government, which has ruled that country since November of 1917, is in both theory and practice a Marxist government, although it had to modify many of its original intentions on account of the hostility of the peasants, who were as much opposed to socialistic experiments as the French peasants were in 1848.

In England the nineteenth century witnessed no revolutions or great political upheavals. Unlike their compatriots on the Continent, the English reformers had not to fight against strongly entrenched despotisms, or governments which were too reactionary to be reformed, and so freedom, in the words of the poet Tennyson, 'broadened slowly down from precedent to precedent'. Successive governments improved the Poor Laws, made the franchise more democratic, did something for education, reformed the criminal law, and it was not until the next century that socialism began to be a force to be seriously reckoned with in political affairs. It was a much less extreme and more practical form of socialism than that expounded by Marx. The first Labour Government of 1924 contained few if any Marxists, and some of its members were not even Socialists.

In the United States of America, despite the existence of

such revolutionary organizations as the Industrial Workers of the World, the forces of capitalism are as yet much too strong for those arrayed against them, partly no doubt because the vast resources of that great country make it possible for workmen to be paid much higher wages than they are paid in the countries of the Old World, and so the most fruitful cause of discontent is to a large extent eliminated, for revolutionary societies naturally thrive where there is discontent and injustice. The Socialist Movement, which has to-day become a world movement, is a standing monument to the fact that among the new class of powerful capitalists whom the Industrial Revolution created, there were few who strove to be the servants of the community like Robert Owen, many who were simply self-seeking oppressive individuals who put their own selfish ambitions before the interests of the community.

XXVIII

THE TRIUMPH OF NATIONALITY IN THE NINETEENTH CENTURY

ONE of the great features of nineteenth-century history is the development of the idea of nationality, despite the attempts of reactionary statesmen to arrest it. Between the years 1822 and 1830, if we include the Spanish American republics and the Portuguese empire of Brazil, about a dozen national states originated. During this period the four great empires of the world were the British, Russian, Austrian, and Turkish, and in each of them national movements exercised a disruptive influence. The Dutch subjects of Great Britain in South Africa and her French subjects in Canada both began to feel British government to be wellnigh intolerable, and most of them would have liked to follow the example set by the rebellious subjects of Spain in South America and found

GREEK WAR OF INDEPENDENCE

separate states. The century was far advanced before British statesmen realized that the real solution of the problem was a federation of states free to govern themselves and bound by the lightest of ties to the mother country. In the Russian Empire, the Finns, who wished to return to Sweden, and the Poles, who desired self-government, were both somewhat turbulent. There was nothing really deserving the name of insurrection in Finland, but the Poles were more enterprising. In 1830 they broke into open revolt, with no other result than to furnish an excuse for the despotic Czar, Nicholas I, to treat them with more rigour and cruelty than ever. Within the Empire of Austria, the Slavs of Croatia and Dalmatia, the Magyars of Hungary, and the Italians of Northern Italy gave frequent expression to their national aspirations.

But it was in the Turkish Empire that nationalism won its most enduring victories during these momentous eight years. First the Serbs succeeded in making themselves practically independent of the Sultan, then Albania and Montenegro defied his authority, and finally the Greeks waged a successful war culminating in the acknowledgement of their independence in 1829. For this result they were much indebted to foreign aid. The glories of the Greek past attracted many volunteers like the English Lord Byron. Their cause was very popular in England and France, and the government of Russia openly sympathized with them. The war which they fought lasted for eight years and it was waged with equal cruelty and baseness by both Greeks and Turks. The Greeks of 1820–30 had few if any of the noble qualities of the Greeks who broke the might of Persia in the fifth century B.C.

Another important national rising of this period was the revolt of the Belgians against the dominance of Holland. The union of Belgium and Holland had not worked well. The Dutch were Protestants, the Belgians were Roman Catholics, but this difficulty might easily have been overcome if it were not for the fact that the Dutch practically monopolized all the important offices in the state. The seat of government was at The Hague; Dutch was declared to be the official language; six-sevenths of the ministers, seven-eighths of the officers of the army, and nearly all the public servants of every description were Dutch. The success of the French revolution of 1830, when the Bourbons were overthrown and the more liberal-minded Louis Philippe made king, encouraged the Belgians to put their fortunes also to the hazard of a rebellion. In less than a year they had achieved their purpose, and their independence had been recognized by the Great Powers of Europe. Russia and Prussia would have preferred to crush them for violating the settlement of Vienna, but the new French government supported them whole-heartedly, and England shrank from the possibility of a European war.

The year 1848, the great year of revolutions, was one of distinct triumph for national ideals, even though the triumph was short-lived. Metternich, the arbiter of Europe, the friend of reaction, the foe of nationality, was forced to leave Vienna in disguise amid the contents of a laundry-cart. Hungary and Bohemia both claimed national autonomy: Milan expelled the Austrians: Venice became an independent republic once more. Charles Albert, King of Sardinia, put himself at the head of an Italian national movement, and declared war upon the Habsburgs. Frederick William IV, King of Prussia, was forced to grant constitutional government to his subjects, and to authorize the summoning of a German National Parliament. In Britain the Chartists made headway, and the Young Ireland Party attempted to make their country a separate nation. But all these movements flattered only to deceive. The national and democratic leaders showed an amazing lack of foresight and prudence, and by stupid quarrels among themselves threw away the fruits of all their efforts. Dissensions among the rebels gave the Austrian reactionaries the opportunity to crush the Bohemian and Austrian movements with much slaughter. The Magyars

The Great Chartist gathering to present the Monster Petition

Police awaiting the procession in Hyde Park

THE CHARTIST MOVEMENT

of Hungary were similarly treated. In this case the Austrian troops received valuable assistance from the Russians and from the Croats, the Slavs of Hungary, to whom the Magyars would not grant the liberties which they desired themselves. In Italy the alliance of the liberal-minded Pope Pius IX, Charles Albert of Sardinia, and the republican advocate Mazzini, whose writings had done much to awaken the national consciousness of his countrymen, was a happy augury of success. But, unfortunately, the alliance broke up, and those who had composed it turned their arms against one another. The Pope was alarmed at the irreligion of the republicans, and he was afraid that his actions might have the effect of estranging Austria from Roman Catholicism. Charles Albert mismanaged his campaigns badly and was defeated at Custozza and Novara, and Mazzini's attempts to establish a republic at Rome failed when French troops were sent against him in defence of the rights of the Pope. In Germany the National Parliament wasted a great deal of its time in the discussion of abstractions, and failed to persuade Frederick William of Prussia to become the head of a German Empire. The result was the restoration of the old ineffective federation of 1815 with Austria as its head. An observer of these events, Otto von Bismarck, remarked at the time: 'Not by speeches and resolutions of majorities are the mighty problems of the age to be solved, but by blood and iron.' In England, the Chartist demonstrations ended in a ludicrous fiasco, and the Young Ireland Movement was easily suppressed.

But the cause of nationality was not lost in either Italy or Germany.

After his defeats, Charles Albert abdicated the throne of Sardinia in favour of his son Victor Emanuel II, under whom the unity of Italy was ultimately to be attained. In 1852 Victor Emanuel made Count Cavour his chief minister. Cavour was a diplomatist of the first order, and henceforth all his gifts were directed to one end—the extension of the kingdom of Sardinia to include the whole of Italy. The abortive risings of 1848-9 had proved that foreign aid was necessary to the achievement of this plan, and there was no

The Divisions of ITALY before the Wars of Independence

country from which assistance could be expected more naturally than from France. The ruler of that country, Napoleon III, prided himself on the fact that he was the nephew of the first Napoleon, and he desired nothing so much as to follow the policy outlined by his great uncle. The Napoleonic régime had not been altogether an evil to the Italians. The country had been divided into three political divisions, all dominated by Napoleon, and thus it had been given some semblance of unity, which was ruthlessly destroyed in 1815, much to the distaste of Italian patriots, who did not relish the return of reactionary Bourbons and alien Habsburgs. So complete was the triumph of reaction that for many years the Nationalists dared not carry on their propaganda in the open. Secret societies came into being, and to the most famous of these, the Carbonari, Napoleon III, when he was a young adventurer with little beyond his dreams to satisfy his romantic temperament, had at one time belonged. There was still another reason why Italian patriots might expect assistance from him. His thirst for glory was almost as great as his uncle's had been, and the Italian adventure seemed to afford an admirable opportunity for satisfying it. Moreover, his model, the great Napoleon, had in the evening of his days at St. Helena, with magnificent disregard for the records of history, announced that the principles which he had tried to realize throughout his career, and which were the foundation stones of his empire, were democracy, peace, religion, and *nationality*. Consequently, Cavour did not find it too difficult a matter to secure the alliance of France, especially since, with an eye to future possibilities, he had sent Italian troops to assist the French during the Crimean War, and so in 1858 it was agreed that Napoleon should aid Sardinia to expel the Austrians from Italy. In the following year the French army of deliverance came into the peninsula, the Austrians were badly beaten at Magenta and Solferino, and then Napoleon, without consulting his allies, made peace with the Austrians, who were to be allowed to retain Venetia. Lombardy and Parma were to be added to Sardinia, but Tuscany and Modena were to remain separate states under the dukes who had formerly ruled them, and the Romagna,

LIBERATION OF ITALY

which had revolted against the authority of the Pope, was to be restored to him again.

Napoleon's desertion of his allies was due to many causes. He had planned the Italian campaign primarily to add lustre to his own name, but most of the glory seemed to have been accorded to Victor Emanuel, who was joyfully hailed as the king of a united Italy. Napoleon did not want to see the whole of the country ruled by the King of Sardinia. The idea which appealed to him was a federation of four states—Sardinia (enlarged by the addition of Lombardy, Venetia, Parma, and Modena), Central Italy, the Papal States, and the Bourbon kingdom of Naples and Sicily, all admitting the overlordship of the Pope. He made peace with the Austrians and allowed them to retain Venetia as soon as he realized that if they were utterly expelled from Italy the whole of the country would be quickly united under Victor Emanuel. But his withdrawal from the campaign did not have quite the effect which he anticipated. The national ardour of the Italians had been thoroughly roused. Tuscany, Modena, and the Romagna refused to return to their former rulers, and France had to agree to their absorption into the kingdom of Victor Emanuel (1860). Then the people of Naples and Sicily rebelled against the inhuman government of the Bourbons, and with the assistance of the great soldier Garibaldi they too achieved their independence, and by an almost unanimous vote decided to become part of the new kingdom of Italy, which before the end of the year 1860 included the whole of the country with the exception of Venetia and a small strip of territory around Rome, which the Pope still retained. After his successes in Naples, Garibaldi was eager to march on to Rome and conquer the papal dominions, but he was prevented by Cavour, who realized that such an action would bring the French into Italy again, but this time probably as the allies of Austria in defence of the rights of the Pope. Thus all the fruits of the War of Liberation would be needlessly thrown away. It was better to wait until favourable opportunities of securing both Rome and Venetia should present themselves. For the final acquisition of these much coveted territories, Prussia was the country to which Italy was indebted.

The unity of Germany was secured by methods which were in many respects very different from those which succeeded in Italy. In both countries a particular state, Sardinia in Italy and Prussia in Germany, put itself at the head of the national movement, and in both countries the kings of these states, Victor Emanuel and William I, had resolute and able chief ministers who were masters of the tortuous and tricky art of diplomacy. In Prussia the role of Cavour was played by that Otto von Bismarck whose contempt for those who sought to solve the problem of German nationality by long speeches in the parliament of 1848 had been so forcibly expressed. In 1862 Bismarck became the chief minister of the King of Prussia. He was no believer in constitutional government like Cavour. The people of Germany were not to be allowed to achieve their unity in their own way. It was to be achieved for them by their rulers by a policy of 'blood and iron'. Shortly before his appointment as the Prussian chief minister, Bismarck, during a visit to London, had made a frank confession of his aims and prospects to the English statesman, Benjamin Disraeli.

'I shall soon', he declared, 'be compelled to undertake the leadership of the Prussian government. My first care will be, with or without the help of parliament, to reorganize the army. The King has rightly set himself this task. He cannot, however, carry it through with his present councillors. When the army has been brought to such a state as to command respect, then I will take the first opportunity to declare war with Austria, burst asunder the German Confederation, bring the middle and smaller states into subjection, and give Germany a national union under the leadership of Prussia.'

HEADQUARTERS OF GARIBALDI, AT THE CONVENT OF SAN SILVESTRE IN ROME

From *The Illustrated London News* of 1848

This was an exact description of the policy which Bismarck actually carried out. He increased the Prussian army and made it the most effective fighting machine in Europe by extending the system of military conscription in a way which was not approved by the elected representatives of the people. He adopted measures of stern repression against Socialists and any others who ventured to oppose or criticize his actions, and then, when he was convinced that his army was sufficiently powerful, he deliberately set to work to isolate Austria diplomatically, and to find an excuse to attack her when isolated. By holding before them the glittering prize of Venetia he secured the promise of Italian assistance in the event of a war with Austria. Russia promised to remain neutral, and so also did France. Napoleon III was so ignorant of the completeness of the Prussian preparations that he believed that there would be a long war in which the combatants would wear one another out. Germany would be more hopelessly divided than ever, and he would be able to interfere and impose what terms he pleased upon both Prussians and Austrians. At this time (1866), Napoleon's prestige was distinctly waning, and something was needed to restore it. In 1863 the Poles had solicited his aid in a rebellion against the Czar. Napoleon had replied with encouraging words which filled them with hopes which were soon falsified, when he sent them no assistance and allowed the rebellion to be crushed in blood. The French Emperor had done nothing beyond estranging the Russian government. Still more unfortunate was his interference in American affairs in the following year. He sent an army across the Atlantic to Mexico to support the claims of Maximilian, the brother of the Austrian Emperor, to the rulership of that country. His action alarmed the government of the United States, who were naturally devoted to the Monroe doctrine of America for the Americans, and Napoleon, to avoid international complications, was obliged to withdraw the French troops and

AT THE GATES!

THE MAN OF IRON

A *Punch* cartoon of Bismarck, 1883

leave Maximilian to the mercy of the Mexicans, who ultimately captured and executed him. Thus when the war between Austria and Prussia broke out Napoleon's reputation needed some rehabilitation. But the result of the war, far from doing this, gave it still another severe blow. In the astonishingly short time of three weeks the Austrian troops were thoroughly defeated and Bismarck was in a position to dictate terms to his foes. The confederation of 1815 was dissolved and Austria ceased to be counted as a German power; Prussia was allowed to annex Schleswig-Holstein, Hanover, Hesse, and other small states which had helped Austria in the late struggle; she was also allowed to organize the states of North Germany into a Confederation under her own headship; and Italy was confirmed in the possession of Venetia.

Nothing now remained for Napoleon III, if he was to recover his lost prestige, but to go to war with Prussia, and nothing suited the plans of Bismarck better. He believed that a war with France would rouse the patriotism of the South German states so that they would unite under Prussia against the common enemy, and afterwards join the North German Confederation. Napoleon, on the other hand, believed that their jealousy of Prussia was so great that they would fight for him. But again he made a bad miscalculation. As Bismarck anticipated, all Germany united against the French. Napoleon was defeated and made prisoner at the battle of Sedan; the victorious Germans even besieged Paris and forced it to capitulate; the Empire was overthrown; and France was obliged to surrender territory and pay a heavy indemnity to the victors. The war, instead of hindering the development of Germany, as the French Emperor had hoped, consummated the work of 1866. The South German states, having sent their troops to fight side by side with the Prussian forces, agreed after their common victory over the French to join the North German Confederation, and in January of 1871, in the palace of Versailles, William I of

Prussia, the president of the Confederation, was proclaimed German Emperor in the presence of the other German princes.

The Franco-German War also completed the unification of Italy. Before it broke out, Bismarck made certain of the alliance of the Italians by holding before them the tempting bait of Rome, which French troops were holding for the Pope. The reverses which he experienced at the hands of the Germans compelled Napoleon III to withdraw the French garrison. A month later the troops of Victor Emanuel entered Rome, the people welcomed them enthusiastically, and the union of Italy was complete. The Pope was allowed to remain in the Vatican, and offered the status of a sovereign prince with the right to receive ambassadors and maintain a guard. He was also offered a liberal annuity. But Pius IX was too much annoyed at the loss of his temporal power to accept these terms. He retired into the Vatican, proclaiming himself a prisoner for conscience' sake, and it was not until 1929 that peace was made with the Italian government, who agreed to pay the Papacy for its loss of earthly power. But it is impossible to resist the conclusion that the loss of its temporal dominions has not been a bad thing for the Papacy. Its spiritual power at the beginning of the present century was probably greater than it had been at any time since the Middle Ages, and this must have been largely due to the fact that the Pope is no longer hampered by the cares and ambitions of an Italian prince.

XXIX

MODERN IMPERIALISM

THE events of the years from 1859 to 1871 virtually destroyed the old Europe of Metternich and the Congress of Vienna, and brought into its place a new Europe based upon nationality. But the settlement of 1815 had one advantage over that of 1871, in that it was international, and not, like the later settlement, imposed to a considerable extent by the dominant will of a victorious power. The Peace of Frankfort which concluded the Franco-German War, was as much an incentive to future strife as the Peace of Vienna. The French were incensed at the loss of the rich provinces of Alsace and Lorraine, which Germany annexed almost as cynically as the Great Powers had divided Poland among themselves in the eighteenth century. The recovery of the lost provinces became almost a national ambition among French people, and the feelings of bitterness which their loss aroused had much to do with the great European War of 1914–18.

Bismarck did his best to allay these feelings by encouraging the French to seek compensation in other directions, particularly in North Africa, where they proceeded to build up a colonial empire for themselves, with as much disregard for the rights of the native inhabitants as the victorious Prussians had shown for French rights in the matter of Alsace and Lorraine. Bismarck never fully realized the value of colonies. This was partly why he encouraged French colonial enterprise. He was also actuated by the belief that it would lead to disputes with Great Britain and Italy, who were also interested in North Africa, and so France would be isolated diplomatically, and be in no position to cause Germany any uneasiness. Algiers had been annexed in 1830 and its development had been one of the main features of the reign of Louis Philippe. In 1881 a French expedition occupied Tunis, to

EXPANSION OF BRITAIN 497

the great displeasure of the Italians, who had been casting longing eyes on the same territory themselves. The result was a period of marked unfriendliness between France and Italy, which lasted for thirty years. Shortly afterwards the French began their so-called 'peaceful penetration' of Morocco, an action which led to acute dissension with Spain.

In 1891 they occupied the Ivory Coast, Dahomey in the following year, and Madagascar in 1895.

In the meantime Great Britain had not been idle. Her territories in South Africa had been much increased by the annexation of Natal and the Transvaal. The latter state had been colonized by Boers, or settlers of Dutch extraction, who won back their independence in 1881, four years after it had been taken away from them. But after the Boer War of 1899-1902 the British government again annexed the Transvaal and also the Orange River Colony, another republic of Boers, who had naturally assisted their kinsfolk in the war. Their period of subjugation was a brief one. In 1907 they were granted the privileges of self-government, and united with Natal and Cape Colony to form a Union of South Africa, very similar to the Dominion of Canada. The first Prime Minister of the Union, Louis Botha, had been the leader of the Boer forces against Great Britain in the late war. In other parts of Africa too the British Empire was considerably extended before the end of the nineteenth century. The Gold Coast colonies, Uganda, Zanzibar, part of East Africa, Nyasaland, and Rhodesia were all either annexed or marked out as definite British spheres of influence. In 1883 Great Britain secured control over Egypt and remained there, despite the fact that technically it was a part of the Turkish Empire. The development of Egypt under British direction was very marked, and in many ways most beneficial to the people; but there was some discontent on the part of Nationalists, who objected to the occupation of their country by a foreign power, however efficient that power might be.

and the path of the British administrator was rendered still more difficult by the fact that it was considered necessary to conquer the Sudan, a tributary state to the south of Egypt, where a Muslim leader, who called himself the Mahdi, was preaching a holy war of liberation. The Mahdi was never conquered, but his successor, the Khalifa, was subsequently defeated and killed, and the conquest of the Sudan achieved, to be followed almost immediately by a dispute with France which might easily have resulted in a European war, and which is an illuminating illustration of how colonial rivalries may easily precipitate international strife. A certain Major Marchand, at the head of a French mission, arrived at Fashoda, on the Upper Nile, and showed a disposition to remain there, although the British declared it to be within their sphere of influence. There were angry recriminations between the two countries, but war was fortunately averted, the French withdrew from Fashoda, and bitter feelings ultimately subsided on both sides.

Germany, mainly on account of Bismarck's ideas on the subject, was somewhat late in the grab for African territory. 'We do not', said Bismarck, 'wish to colonize nor can we do so. We shall never possess a fleet. Nor are our workmen, our lawyers, our retired soldiers worth anything for colonization.' But the commercial instincts of the German people were subsequently too much for him. It became necessary to seek new markets for surplus capital, new sources of raw material. The result was that between the years 1884 and 1890 Germany acquired four considerable areas of African territory: Togoland, the Cameroons, German South-West Africa, and German East Africa. Strenuous attempts were made to develop these regions by building schools and railways and by the liberal expenditure of money upon various schemes of improvement, but wars with the natives and the comparatively poor commercial returns made the value of the experiments somewhat doubtful.

GREAT BRITAIN IN EGYPT. THE BATTLE OF OMDURMAN

The British forces are shown with their backs to the Nile. The gunboats are firing over their heads at the Dervishes in the plain beyond

The Belgians were more fortunate from a purely material point of view. In 1876 King Leopold of Belgium organized a company to explore what is now known as the Belgian Congo, the vast region between German East Africa and the French Congo. It was and is a great rubber-producing country, and the most reprehensible methods were taken to make the wretched natives work. They were forced to labour on railways or to drain swamps for Belgian capitalists, work which was particularly repulsive to them, accustomed as they had been to the free life of the jungle. The chiefs were expected to supply fixed numbers of workmen, and if they did not do so their villages were often burned. The natives were also told that they must supply a certain quantity of rubber every year. Failure to comply meant severe punishments, even torture and maiming. When these methods were exposed there were vigorous protests in both Europe and America, and the force of public opinion became so great that the Belgian ministry was compelled to take over complete charge of the Congo State and see that the natives were treated with more humanity and consideration.

In 1850 Africa was 'The Dark Continent'. Apart from Portuguese settlements on the east and west coasts, Egypt, Cape Colony, Algeria, and a few scattered British, French, and Dutch settlements on the west coast, the continent was one of black mystery, inhabited by native tribes. Then, between the years 1850 and 1880, explorers like Speke, Livingstone, and Stanley braved the terrors of the unknown, torrid heat, terrible diseases, wild beasts, and savages; discovered the sources of the Nile; and made adventurous voyages up the Congo and Zambesi rivers. They brought back with them marvellous stories of scenery of unexampled grandeur, wealth in the form of raw materials which had never been realized or utilized, even remains—at Zimbabwe in Rhodesia—of a vanished civilization. At this time the development of industrialism in Europe and the consequent growth of the population was creating a demand for raw materials of every kind, and that is why the exploration of Africa was followed by such a scramble for territory among the great European

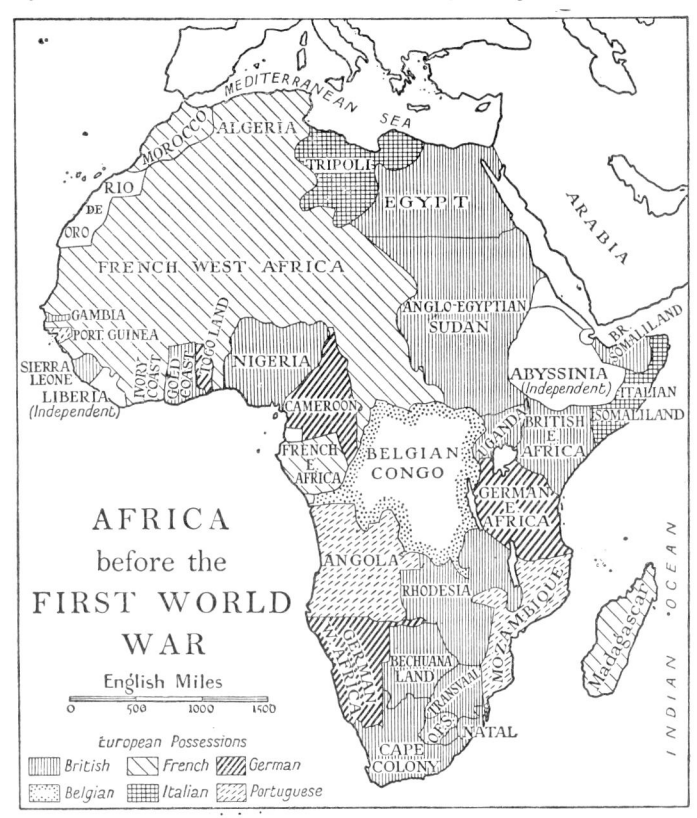

AFRICA
before the
FIRST WORLD
WAR

English Miles

European Possessions
British   French   German
Belgian   Italian   Portuguese

Powers that, by the end of the century, it had been almost completely partitioned. There were only three comparatively small countries unannexed: Liberia; Morocco, which later became a French protectorate; and Abyssinia, which successfully maintained its independence against an Italian army of aggression.

It was not only in Africa that the colonial ambitions of the Great Powers found outlets for themselves. The nineteenth century witnessed an enormous extension of the British Empire in almost all parts of the world. India became entirely British, so too did Australia and New Zealand ; protectorates were established over the Malay States and many of the islands of the Pacific ; and in the Far East Great Britain joined with France, Germany, Russia, and Japan in the economic exploitation of China. The relations of Europe and China go back to ancient history. Some of the Roman emperors, including Marcus Aurelius, sent embassies to the Chinese emperor, and during the Middle Ages China was visited by travellers like the Polos and by missionaries anxious to spread the Christian religion. After Vasco da Gama had discovered the sea route to the East round the Cape of Good Hope, Dutch and English traders made their ways to China, but they received a very cold welcome, and Canton was the only port where they were allowed to embark and disembark their wares. But after 1840 this state of affairs was altered, and China was forced by European powers to open other ports, such as Shanghai and Tientsin; to grant concessions to British, American, French, and German capitalists; and even in some instances to cede territory, such as the island of Hong Kong to Great Britain, Port Arthur to Russia, and Kiau Chau to Germany. Her defenceless condition also exposed her to the aggressive ambitions of her neighbour Japan.

The rise of Japan is one of the most astonishing features of modern history. Until a hundred years ago her world influence was negligible; she was an exclusively oriental power, dominated by such essentially medieval ideas as feudalism and serfdom. During the sixteenth century Dutch and English traders had carried on a little business in Japan, and Christian missionaries had visited the country, but they both became very unpopular and were driven out. Then followed a period when Japan cut herself off almost entirely from the

THE EARLIEST VIEW OF CANTON HARBOUR
From Nienhoff's *Embassy of the Dutch East India Company*, 1655

rest of the world, until in 1853 the United States officer Commodore Perry landed in Yokohama and asked for permission to trade. This was granted, and similar concessions were made to other Powers, but the Japanese were more wary than the Chinese. They realized that they must learn something about European inventions and European ideas if they were to protect themselves against exploitation. The result was the abolition of feudalism, the reorganization of the army and the navy on a European model, the creation of a parliament, the building of factories and railroads, and the emergence of Japan in the course of about fifty or sixty years into the ranks of the Great Powers of the world. The growth of her manufactures had the same effect as the growth of manufactures had in Europe. It made her anxious to extend her trade and seek new markets. The proximity of Korea, and the comparatively defenceless condition of China to whom it belonged, gave her the opportunity which she desired. It was easy to arrange a short war with the Chinese, which the Japanese won (1894–5), and although Korea was not formally annexed until 1910, it had been little better than a Japanese province for the fifteen preceding years. Russia was also interested in Korea; she built forts there, kept troops in the neighbouring province of Manchuria, and leased Port Arthur from China. The result was a war with Japan (1904–5), in which the Russians were so badly beaten that they had to agree to the evacuation of Manchuria and Korea, and give up their rights over Port Arthur to the Japanese.

It would hardly be an exaggeration to say that modern imperialism was a direct result of the Industrial Revolution, which by enabling Europe and the United States of America to produce more goods than they could sell in their own markets, and by furnishing rapid means of transporting these goods from one end of the earth to the other, created keen competition for the control of foreign markets. Sometimes this did not take the form of colonization. For instance, it

THE INFLUENCE OF MISSIONARIES

might confine itself to the investment of money in enterprises such as railways and mines, to develop the resources of backward countries. The investment of German capital in the construction of a railway from Constantinople to Bagdad and the sinking of Russian capital in the Trans-Siberian railway are good examples of this sort of thing. But for the most part the securing of concessions was not deemed sufficient. It was felt that, in order to develop the resources of a country and control its products, the country which was prepared to invest its capital must have some sort of proprietary interest. This might take the form of annexation, sometimes at the wish of the inhabitants, such as the acquisition of the South Sea island of Hawaii by the United States, more often very much against the wishes of the inhabitants, as in the case of the Japanese annexation of Korea. Another class of colony was the protectorate, where native rulers were recognized and where the protecting country agreed to defend the protected from civil wars and from external aggression, and to help them in developing and cultivating their territories. Of such a nature was the British hold over Uganda and Somaliland. A third type of colony was represented by the 'mandated territories', colonies which formerly belonged to Germany or Turkey, defeated nations in the First World War (1914–18), and which were subsequently administered by representatives of the victorious countries under mandate from the League of Nations. Thus Palestine was mandated to Great Britain, Samoa in the South Seas to New Zealand, and German South-West Africa to the Union of South Africa.

No account of the development of modern imperialism would be at all complete without some reference to the part played by Christian missionaries. The British Empire in Africa owed very much to the labours of such men as David Livingstone and Robert Moffat, while in other parts of the world its growth was considerably assisted by the efforts of men like Williams and Chalmers in the South Seas, Grenfell in Labrador, and Marsden among the Maoris. Spain in the sixteenth century was under a similar obligation to the Jesuits. Sir Harry Johnston, one of the greatest authorities on the history of modern Africa, bore striking testimony to the work of Moffat and others among the Bechuana and Matabele tribes, both of whom are now British subjects:

'Nearly all the Bechuana tribes now are Christians and are prosperous and happy, no longer tortured by famine or killing each other in constant quarrels. It must not be forgotten that the missionaries first got a hearing by showing that they were men of their hands, that they could be, if need arose, blacksmiths and carpenters, brickmakers and bricklayers, good shots with the rifle, horsemen and cattle keepers. Not many years elapsed after these episodes, before they had become throughout South Africa, from Cape Colony to the Zambesi, the trusted advisers and allies of the native tribes.'

Another writer [1] declares that the work of the missionaries has

'ennobled South African history by contributing to it an element of the picturesque, a spice of chivalry and romance. Africa became attractive, as a scene of adventure, where among wild beasts and wild men noble lives were lived and sometimes lost. Here, as the world was growing older, there was something to seek, and something to find, something which savoured of the days when, to awakening Europe, the lands beyond the seas seemed bright and young.'

But the work of missionaries has also come in for severe criticism from some quarters. It is claimed that they are but the advance guard who make it easy for soldiers to conquer and traders to exploit the territories of people who are not able to defend themselves with any hope of success against the inroads of the white races. It is, however, hardly fair to blame missionaries for the subsequent actions of unscrupulous traders in lands which have been opened up by their efforts,

[1] Sir Charles Lucas (formerly Under-Secretary at the British Colonial Office).

Livingstone received by an African chief, 1854, in what is now Northern Rhodesia

Peace-making in New Zealand. A mission boat accompanying a war expedition, 1831

and there is no doubt that the greatest obstacle to missionary success has frequently been the low standard of commercial morality shown by such traders. There is no real reason for disagreement with the claim put forward by the World Missionary Conference, which met at Edinburgh in 1910 :

'It would be an impossible task to enumerate the services rendered by Missionaries to Governments. It would, in the first place, be impossible always to draw a dividing line between the aim of the missionary and the aim of the Government. Missions aim not merely at securing the spiritual enlightenment of the individual, but also at promoting the healthy social life of the community. Governments likewise aim at enhancing the welfare of the people. In this field, therefore, Governments have been spared much expense and great care by what Missions have done. Of forms of service lying outside of strictly religious work, in which Missions have done work of a type which Governments appreciate and themselves undertake, we can only make passing mention. In exploration, scores of missionaries have been pioneers ; in sociology, their observations have contributed a mass of material of the highest value. Many languages have been by them reduced to writing, their grammatical principles ascertained and recorded, and development of a literature has been begun. Their study of developed languages has enriched philology and all human culture. Their educational work has been vast and inspiring. In establishing the printing-press and introducing the school-book, the newspaper and healthful literature of all kinds, they have again and again been pioneers. By their medical work they have not only alleviated the sufferings of millions, but have also powerfully promoted the cause of public health, while destroying the malignant influence of pretenders to magical power. By their influence with the people and their dissemination of higher principles of life, they have often made possible the acceptance and enforcement of good laws which without them Governments would have feared to pass, and would have been unable to make effective.'[1]

[1] *Reports of World Missionary Conference* (1910), vol. vii (Missions and Governments).

GOOD AND EVIL CONSEQUENCES

In some respects, the imperialistic activities of modern nations had admirable consequences. In many undeveloped and uncivilized countries efforts were made to improve the people both mentally and materially. Jungles were slowly cleared, prairies cultivated, means of transport enormously improved, and diseases fought and conquered with a courage which is at least as great as that of the soldier in battle. But imperialism has not always developed in this way. It has sometimes led to Congo atrocities, and the conquest by force of unwilling nations followed by shameful exploitation. Not one of the great empire-building countries of the world has a clean record in imperial matters. There are foul pages as well as fair. Even the British Empire was established mainly for commercial reasons, and it would be absurd to imagine that it was ever maintained for purely philanthropic purposes. Many empire builders have been men of unquestionable integrity, brave, unselfish, patriotic in the highest sense. But others have been men bent upon advancing their own individual interests rather than those of their country. While imperialism has undoubtedly been a potent force in the civilizing of backward peoples, it has also been a prolific cause of wars and international discord. In our own century it has been responsible for some minor wars, such as that between Russia and Japan, and it was one of the root causes of the First World War, a greater and more terrible war than any that had preceded it. The ill will between France and Germany was accentuated by colonial rivalry over the matter of Morocco, where France, with the approval of Great Britain, claimed the right to establish a protectorate. Germany disputed French monopoly, and in 1911 almost went to war because France would not consult her in Moroccan matters. Seven years previously, Great Britain had formally recognized the priority of French interests in Morocco in return for a similar recognition by France of British interests in Egypt. Thus the 'entente cordiale' between the two countries originated in the area of colonial rivalry and conflict. Germany's reaction to this unexpected and unwelcome agreement between two Powers whom colonial rivalry had several times brought to the brink of war was increasingly unfriendly and even threatening. As a result Britain and France drew closer together for mutual protection against Germany, which had the effect of bringing the Empire with all its resources to the support of France against Germany when the First World War began in 1914.

XXX

RUSSIA AND THE NEAR EAST IN THE NINETEENTH CENTURY

THE task of making Russia a European country, begun by Peter the Great, was continued after his death, but it was not until the nineteenth century that she became really well known to the other countries of Europe. Her emergence from the isolation of centuries was not entirely due to statesmen and politicians; it was largely the result of the international reputation of Russians like the novelists Tolstoi, Dostoievsky, and Turgeniev, the musician Tchaikovsky, and the scientists Mendelyeev and Metchnikoff.

Russia played a prominent part in the overthrow of Napoleon, and Czar Alexander I was one of the dominant personalities in the Congress of Vienna, and in some of the subsequent attempts to resettle Europe after the Napoleonic upheaval. Alexander, in his younger days, had been a man of liberal ideas, but contact with the Metternich school of politicians and his own observations of the results of the spread of revolutionary principles throughout Europe changed him into a reactionary, impatient of all change. His powers over his subjects were practically unlimited. He could make peace and war; he could commit any one to prison and even order executions without being held answerable to any living being; he could appoint and dismiss ministers as he pleased; and the national church was regarded as being under his personal control. In the years which elapsed between his return from the Congress of Vienna and his death in 1825, he used his vast powers to prevent the influx of progressive ideas into Russia and to keep his people in a state of Oriental subjection. The result was that, when he died, certain revolutionary societies seized the opportunity to start a revolt which was too badly organized to succeed, and which was savagely suppressed by the new Czar, Nicholas I. Five years later an insurrection in Poland was put down with even more harshness and cruelty. Some of the leaders were executed, and forty-five thousand families were forced to leave their native country and settle in the valley of the Don and the Caucasian Mountains.

Nicholas I was one of the most arbitrary and tyrannical rulers with whom a country has ever been afflicted. He believed that autocracy was the only legitimate form of government, and that a ruler should strenuously oppose the spread among his subjects of ideas which were in the least likely to curb his power. From their earliest years children were to be taught that they owed 'worship, fidelity, service, and love' to the Czar, and that they had no claim to liberties other than what he was disposed to grant them. And so the books which came into Russia from foreign countries, even books on science and religion, were rigorously censored, private letters opened and examined to see whether their writers held revolutionary opinions, and any attempt to subvert or reform the government punished by long terms of imprisonment, exile to the mines of Siberia, and even death.

At this time nearly one-half of the Czar's subjects were chattel slaves, worse off than the English serfs of the early

Middle Ages, forced to labour on their lords' lands for certain days in the week, not allowed to marry without his consent, not even secure against personal violence at his hands. Even the best masters occasionally maltreated their serfs;[1] under the worst their condition was wellnigh intolerable, and during the reign of Nicholas I (1825-55) there were more than five hundred serf riots in various parts of Russia. Accordingly, Alexander II, the son and successor of Nicholas, began to think that their emancipation might be an act of sound statesmanship. It was not, however, until 1861 that the edict of freedom was issued, and it was such a half-hearted concession that the benefits which it conferred were far less than they appeared to observers not familiar with the conditions of Russian life. The landowners had to surrender a portion of their estates to the peasants; but they were liberally compensated by the government for what they had lost, and the emancipated serfs were expected to pay back in instalments the money which the government had disbursed. It was more than they could do, and for years they lived absolutely on the edge of starvation, until in 1904 the Czar Nicholas II forgave them the heavy arrears which were still due.

Alexander II freed the serfs, but otherwise his government was little better than his father's had been. Reformers were regarded with the same suspicion; new ideas were treated as if they were deadly crimes; the prisons were filled with political offenders; and a wholesale system of spying upon the private lives of individuals took away the last vestige of personal liberty. Under these circumstances, the more ardent reformers decided upon a new and very hazardous course of action. They resolved to employ against the government the very weapon which the government had used against them, the weapon of intimidation. In 1879 sixteen suspected revolutionaries were hanged, and many more im-

[1] See *Memoirs of a Revolutionary* (Prince Kropotkin).

PEASANTS ON A RUSSIAN ESTATE BEFORE THE FIRST WORLD WAR

prisoned or sent to Siberia. Two years later the reformers retaliated by assassinating the Czar. But methods of terrorism are bound to fail eventually, and even though they have continued in Russia to the present day there can be little doubt that they have retarded rather than promoted progress.

In 1894 Nicholas II succeeded his father Alexander III as Czar of Russia. The new emperor was thought to be favourable to reform, but he soon dispelled all the hopes that had been centred on him by continuing the policy of his predecessors, and particularly by his choice of ministers who were notorious for their reactionary ideas. Jews were persecuted, and in some cases massacred, because they refused to agree to the doctrines of the Russian National Church. Many of them fled from Russia to foreign countries, particularly to the United States of America: it is significant that when the Czardom was finally overthrown Jews figured largely among the destroyers. Another class which suffered under Nicholas II were the literary and scientific men, University professors, writers of distinction, students, all of whom one would naturally expect to be stirred by the ferment of new ideas. Many of them suffered imprisonment and exile for the expression of their opinions, and it was no uncommon thing for literary and scientific meetings to be broken up by the police because they were considered to be disloyal or lacking in respect for the Czar.

This state of affairs could not go on indefinitely, and to the reformers the war between Russia and Japan (1904–5) came as a blessing in disguise, because it exposed the incompetence of the Russian Government, and appreciably weakened its power to continue along the course of unreasonable autocracy which it had marked out for itself. While the Russian forces were fighting in the East, and while Russian money was being squandered in the interests of a few capitalists, the people of Russia were enduring all the torments of famine, and in many cases, driven desperate by their woes, they sacked and burned the houses of the landowners much as the French peasants had done during the great Revolution. On Sunday 22nd January 1905 a great deputation of working men and working women assembled outside the Winter Palace at St. Petersburg to present their grievances to the Czar in person. His reply was to send his troops against them, first with whips, and then, when that did not disperse them, orders to shoot were given; hundreds were killed and thousands wounded. Similar encounters between the people and the military occurred in other parts of the country, and these, together with the failure and bad mismanagement of the Japanese campaign, so incensed the nation that before the year ended the Czar was obliged to consent to the creation of a parliament, called the Duma ; to agree that no law could come into force without its consent ; and to promise the people liberty of speech and the right to hold public meetings. However, he contrived to avoid many of these obligations ; by manipulating the suffrage he kept men of advanced ideas out of the Duma ; he made a practice of dissolving it when it was too critical ; and methods of terrorism were still pursued. During the year 1906 more than nine thousand persons were either killed or wounded for political reasons. Despite all this, the revolutionary societies went on growing in power and influence, and the Duma, crippled as it was, was able to effect some much needed reforms.

When the First World War broke out in 1914 Russia took part on the side of France against Germany and Austria, but the government displayed such an amazing lack of foresight and ordinary efficiency that in 1917 it was overthrown. The Czar was forced to abdicate, and a Coalition Government of advanced Liberals and moderate Socialists came into being. Its failure to give Russia peace made it possible for the extreme Socialists to arrange a *coup d'état*, and in November the Bolshevist Government with a former Russian barrister and political exile, Nikolai Lenin, as its president, was established. It did not immediately succeed in giving Russia peace or stability. In some ways it proved very efficient, notably perhaps in the building up of a strong revolutionary army, which successfully repelled all attempts to restore the old Czarist régime. But personal freedom gained little from the change. The execution of the Czar and other members of the Russian royal family was followed by the murder of thousands of others who had in some way or other expressed their hostility to the new system of government. Critics of the existing order were treated in much the same way as they were under the Czars. The First World War also resulted in a temporary decrease in the size of the Russian Empire. A separate state of Poland was created; Esthonia, Livonia (Latvia), Lithuania, and Finland became independent; and for three years (1918–21) Georgia was also free, after which it became part of Russia again.

Another great empire which experienced a still more remarkable break-up in the century following the Congress of Vienna was the Turkish Empire. For two centuries after their conquest of Constantinople the Turks were a grave menace to the Christian states of Europe, but since the eighteenth century their power has visibly declined. This is due partly to the evolution of Russia as a European power. The inhabitants of that part of the Turkish Empire which became known as the Balkan Peninsula—Bulgaria, Roumania, Serbia, Montenegro—were for the most part Christians who belonged to the same branch of the Church as the Russians. Most of them belonged to the Slavonic race. Russia therefore claimed the right to 'protect' them, and when Turkey conceded this towards the end of the eighteenth century she was giving Russia an excuse for intervening in Turkish affairs, and an opportunity for strengthening her own position in the Near East by stirring up strife among the Christian subjects of the Sultan. The nineteenth century witnessed two processes at work within the Turkish Empire—movements towards independence on the part of the Balkan states with the connivance and sometimes the active assistance of Russia, and a definite policy on the part of the Russian government, if not to exclude Turkey from Europe altogether, at least so to weaken her position there as to force her to visualize her future development as an Asiatic rather than as a European power. Unfortunately for the success of this plan, it was regarded with persistent hostility by the statesmen of England, Austria, and France. England was afraid that Russia might capture Constantinople and so get control of the Dardanelles and the Eastern Mediterranean. Any considerable increase of Russian power was regarded as particularly menacing to the English dominion over India, which the Russians were believed to desire for themselves. Accordingly it became almost an article of faith among the more imperialistic of British politicians that Turkey must at all costs be protected against Russian aggressions. This was the reason why England intervened in the Crimean War, and why in 1878, when the Russian forces had almost overthrown the Turkish Empire in Europe, the English Prime Minister Disraeli, with the active support of Austria, insisted that the victors should stay their hands and submit the whole matter to the arbitration of a general European congress which met at Berlin.

In England, however, sympathy with Turkey was by no means universal. The Liberal school of politicians, under its great leader Gladstone, was more concerned with the sufferings of the Christian subjects of the Sultan than with the possible effect of the Russian conquest of Constantinople upon the British Empire in Asia. The famous English archaeologist, Sir Arthur Evans,[1] has given us a vivid description of the Turkish province of Bosnia in 1875, which can be taken as a truthful account of all the Turkish provinces at that time. He found that, except in the large towns,

[1] The chief discoverer of the remains of the old Cretan civilization at Cnossos.

where they could expect protection from European consuls, the lives of Christians were unsafe because the authorities were violently anti-Christian and pro-Muslim in sympathy. Taxes were levied with little regard for the ability to pay of those upon whom they fell, and outrages were constantly being committed by the Turkish soldiery. No provisions were made against bad harvests; whether the crops were plentiful or whether they failed altogether a fixed quota of taxes had to be paid, and sometimes they were levied in advance before the harvest had been gathered in. In 1874 there was a failure of crops in Bosnia and Herzegovina, and the intolerable conditions which ensued so aggravated the peasants that insurrections broke out which soon spread to other parts of the Balkans. This gave the Turkish government the excuse for perpetrating some of the worst atrocities of which they have ever been guilty. The victims of their lust for blood soon numbered tens of thousands. A wave of horror passed over Western Europe, and frantic appeals for help were made by the oppressed Balkan peoples. In England Mr. Gladstone made the Bulgarian atrocities the text of a series of speeches against the Eastern policy of the government, and insisted that the alliance with 'the unspeakable Turk' should end. But Disraeli, the Prime Minister, still feared Russian designs, and beyond the dispatch of diplomatic notes nothing was done to mitigate Turkey's treatment of her unruly subjects. Under these circumstances Russia decided to act alone, and in 1877 her armies invaded Turkish territory. They met with instant success, and in the following year the Sultan was obliged to agree to the independence of Bulgaria, Serbia, Roumania, and Montenegro. At the time Russian forces were in occupation of the important fortress of Adrianople, about a hundred and fifty miles from Constantinople, and Disraeli, seriously alarmed at future possibilities, made his famous demand for a European congress. This met at Berlin: it confirmed the independence

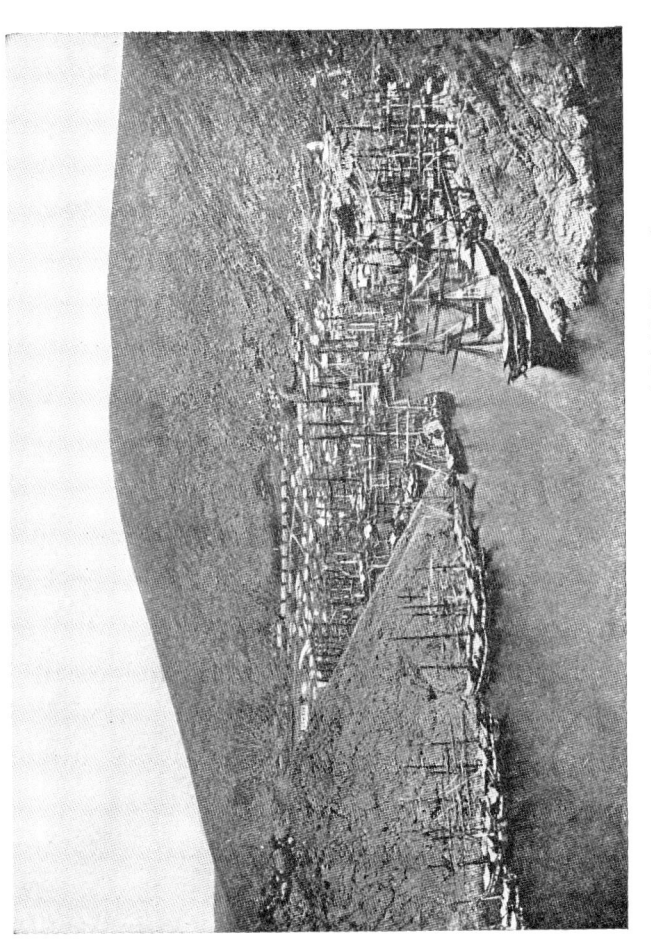

THE CRIMEAN WAR. Balaclava Harbour, with British Fleet and transports
From a photograph taken at the time

of Serbia, Roumania, and Montenegro, and of Bulgaria subject to the payment of an annual tribute to the Turks; and Russia, Great Britain, and Austria were each given some territory which had previously belonged to the Sultan. Great Britain got Cyprus, Russia a tract of land east of the Black Sea, and Austria the right to administer Bosnia and Herzegovina.

Apart from Turkey itself all that was now left of the Turkish Empire in Europe was Macedonia and Albania. The Turkish government realized the importance of retaining supremacy over these regions, but the methods employed were the same as those which had failed in the past: misgovernment, corruption, and sporadic resort to terrorism. It became more and more obvious that if the decline of the Turkish Empire was to be arrested, its methods of government must be radically altered. Gradually a movement developed, particularly among army officers imbued with the excellence of Western ideas, whose object it was to secure for Turkey the benefits of constitutional government instead of the inefficient and stupid autocracy of the Sultan and his officials. This movement was known as 'The Young Turk Movement', and in 1908 it was strong enough to force the Sultan, Abdul Hamid, to grant a constitution and summon a parliament. But the Young Turks had set themselves a tremendous task, and their difficulties were increased by the attitude of other nations towards them. Austria took advantage of the situation to establish full sovereignty over Bosnia and Herzegovina; Italy found an excuse to seize the Turkish province of Tripoli in North Africa; and finally the Greek statesman Venizelos organized a great Balkan League whose object it was to drive the Turks out of the Balkans altogether, and eventually out of Europe as well. In 1912 the Turks found themselves obliged to fight a formidable combination consisting of Greece, Serbia, Bulgaria, and Montenegro, against which they made a very feeble resistance. The victorious

NEUTRALITY UNDER DIFFICULTIES

Dizzy. "*Bulgarian Atrocities! I can't find them in the 'Official Reports'!!!*"

DISRAELI AND THE BULGARIAN ATROCITIES

A cartoon from *Punch*, August 1876

allies advanced as far as Adrianople, which they captured, but then started quarrelling among themselves, and the result was a second Balkan war in 1913, in which Greeks, Serbs, Montenegrins, and eventually Roumanians fought against the Bulgars. This war undoubtedly saved Turkey's position in Europe. Adrianople was recovered, and when peace was concluded at Bucharest, although Turkey had to surrender Macedonia, which was divided up between Greece, Serbia, and Bulgaria, and agree to the independence of Albania, she was allowed to retain Constantinople and a small area to the west including Adrianople.

The Balkan problem had much to do with the World War of 1914–18. It was in Sarajevo, the capital of Bosnia, that the murder of the heir to the Austrian throne, the event which furnished the pretext for the outbreak of hostilities, occurred. Austria held the Serbian government responsible for this; Russia defended the Serbs; Germany came in on the side of Austria, France on the side of Russia, and England on the side of France; and so a comparatively trifling event, in an obscure little town of which most people in the world had never even heard, developed into a prolonged and worldwide war. All the Balkan states, with the exception of Bulgaria, were anti-German. Turkey took some time to decide on which side her interests lay, and finally made the diplomatic mistake of concluding an alliance with Germany. The result was that the Turkish Empire was still further dismembered. Up to this time her losses had been mainly European. There was now little to take in Europe, so she was deprived of control over vast territories in Asia—Syria, Mesopotamia, Palestine, and Arabia including the Hejaz.[1] She also lost her technical sovereignty over Egypt and Cyprus. The

[1] The Hejaz is the name given to a strip of territory stretching for about 700 miles along the eastern coast of the Red Sea and about 200 miles inland. It includes the holy cities of Mecca and Medina, and it is now part of the kingdom of Saudi Arabia.

THE TURKISH REPUBLIC 523

Sultan was allowed to retain his authority over Constantinople and the district around, but the government of the greater part of what was left of the Ottoman dominions in Asia Minor was seized by a body of Turkish nationalists, discontented with the old régime, who styled themselves 'The Government of the Grand National Assembly of Turkey', with their capital at Ankara. In 1922 this government deposed the Sultan and took over the administration of Constantinople, and in the following year Turkey was formally proclaimed a republic with Ankara as its capital, and Mustafa Kemal Pasha, the leader of the nationalists, as its first President.

XXXI

THE UNITED STATES OF AMERICA

NOWHERE did the Industrial Revolution have greater effect than in the United States of America. If it were not for the development of transport, the invention of steam-engines, steamboats, and the electric telegraph, much of the North American continent would still be as sparsely populated as parts of Central Africa ; the Far West would hardly have been colonized at all ; and a state like California would have been as easy to administer from Peking as from Washington. The development of means of transport has had a wonderful effect not only in opening up undeveloped regions but also in bringing together the peoples of the various states which compose the American Union, so that to-day there is less difference between an American of San Francisco and an American of New York than there was in the eighteenth century between a New Englander and a Virginian.

' This great community of the United States ', writes H. G. Wells, ' is an altogether new thing in history. There have been great empires before with populations exceeding a hundred millions, but these were associations of divergent peoples ; there has never been one single people on this scale before. We want a new term for this thing. We call the United States a country just as we call France or Holland a country. But the two things are as different as an automobile and a one-horse shay. They are the creations of different periods and different conditions ; they are going to work at a different pace and in an entirely different way. The United States in scale and possibility is half way between a European state and a United States of all the world.'[1]

The development of methods of transport undoubtedly precipitated the American Civil War of 1861 to 1865, which nearly wrecked the Union, but its final result was to make it very much stronger than it had been. The northern and southern states of the American Union differed widely in interests and modes of life. The southern states were organized on a basis of slavery ; in the northern states all men were free, slavery having been eliminated by 1804, chiefly through the operation of economic law, and as, with the development of transport and the general opening up of the country, new states were created and made parts of the Union, it became a matter of vital importance to determine whether the free institutions of the North or the slave conditions of the South were to prevail in them. In 1833 an anti-slavery society was founded in the North with the object of effecting the complete abolition of slavery throughout the United States, but relations between the North and the South were not really strained until after Texas had become a state of the Union (1845–7). Texas had belonged to Mexico, where slavery was against the law, but its colonists had been largely recruited from the southern states of America, and when they joined the Union, they claimed and, despite strong opposition, won the right to keep slaves. Their victory excited much angry feeling in the North, and it did not completely allay the uneasiness of the South, where the steady stream of European emigrants to

[1] *A Short History of the World.*

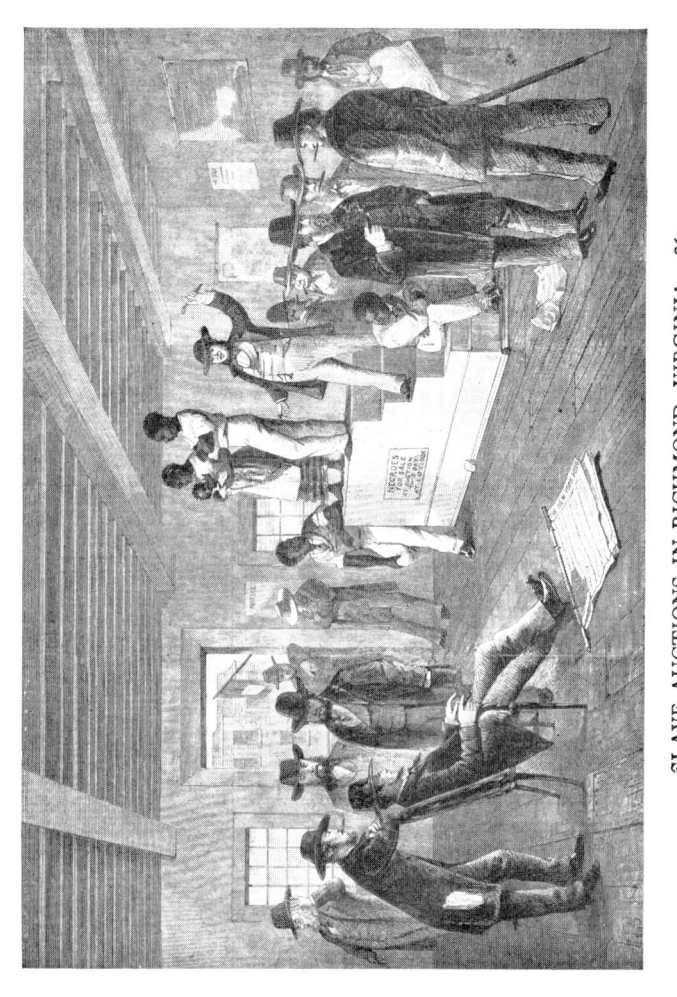

SLAVE AUCTIONS IN RICHMOND, VIRGINIA, 1861

the northern states could not be regarded with anything but apprehension, for it meant the establishment of new states such as Minnesota and Iowa, which were strongly anti-slavery. Thus it appeared probable that the North, which already had a majority in the House of Representatives, would also secure a majority in the Senate and perhaps abolish slavery altogether throughout the Union. In 1860 Abraham Lincoln, a man of much strength of character, who had frequently expressed strong anti-slavery opinions, was elected President, and the southern states—South Carolina, Mississippi, Florida, Alabama, Georgia, Louisiana, and Texas—without waiting for Lincoln's inauguration, decided to secede from the Union and form a Confederation of their own under the presidency of Jefferson Davis. The North disputed their right to secede, and it was upon this issue that the Civil War was fought, not upon the question of slavery, although that naturally came to the front before the contest ended, and Lincoln had made up his mind that, if the North won, slavery should be abolished altogether. But it was not until 1865, the last year of the war, that Congress decided in favour of abolition, and the war had actually ended before this decision was ratified by the states.

At first the result of the conflict was in considerable doubt. The fortunes of the combatants fluctuated in the most bewildering fashion. The northern states were numerically stronger than the southern, and their resources were much greater, but they were handicapped by the lack of good generals and by a considerable amount of disunion, whereas their opponents were led by Robert E. Lee, the greatest military genius of the war. At times Lincoln's difficulties seemed almost insuperable. He had to struggle against dissensions in his own cabinet, defeats in the field, some amount of distrust, considerable war weariness, and even external interference. The French took advantage of the situation to support the Austrian Maximilian's claim to the throne of

ABRAHAM LINCOLN 527

Mexico, thus deliberately flouting the Monroe Doctrine, and the English government did not prevent the agents of the southern states in England from launching three swift cruisers, of which the best known is the *Alabama*, which did an immense amount of damage to the commerce of the northern states.[1] But Lincoln never lost faith in the righteousness and the ultimate triumph of the cause for which he stood. Eventually the North discovered two leaders of the first rank in Generals Grant and Sherman, and on 9 April 1865 the patience and invincible fortitude of the President received their due reward when Lee and his army surrendered to Grant. Within a month all the other secessionist armies had laid down their arms, and the Southern Confederacy was at an end.

Lincoln did not live long to enjoy his triumph. On 14 April, five days after Lee's capitulation, he was assassinated at Ford's Theatre in Washington by an unemployed actor of southern birth, insanely angry at the triumph of the North. His death was a national calamity. The task of reconstruction after a great war is generally even more difficult than the winning of the war. The successful combatants are apt to think more of what they have suffered than of anything else, and they are, on that account, not in a fit state of mind to do justice to their foes. Lincoln was in many ways an extraordinary man, and, if it were possible, he came out of the Civil War a better man than he was when he entered it. He felt no bitterness towards his foes ; he desired above everything that the war should result in 'a new birth of freedom, and that government of the people, by the people, for the people shall not perish from the earth';[2] and in his last public speech, delivered only a few days before his death, he pleaded

[1] A tribunal which met at Geneva (1872) afterwards awarded damages amounting to £3,000,000 against Great Britain for not exercising 'due diligence' in preventing violations of her neutrality, although there was much disagreement amongst jurists as to what she should have done.

[2] Speech at Gettysburg, November 1863.

for reconciliation, tolerance towards former enemies, and the reconstruction of loyal government in the defeated South. He was the one man who could have carried out this humane and far-sighted policy; his death ruined all chances of reconciliation and harmony. It gave the control of national affairs to men who desired only to be just, and who were not inclined, as Lincoln had been, to temper justice with generosity. To them the defeated Southerners were rebels who had forfeited the political rights to which their former slaves had become entitled, and so they enfranchised the negroes and disfranchised their masters. The negroes proved utterly incapable of governing, and the voteless whites took the law into their own hands, so that for many years the southern states were in a most turbulent and unsettled condition, and there was no real peace until the political predominance of the whites had been restored.

At the beginning of the war there was no railway to the Pacific coast. After it railways spread with extraordinary rapidity. Five great lines now link the Atlantic with the Pacific, and there is a total railway mileage throughout the states of more than a quarter of a million miles. There was quite as marked a development of telegraph lines and telephone wires, so that the United States was until the success of the Communist Revolution in Russia the largest real community in the world. After the First World War the development of air lines, radio, and television drew even closer the links binding together great continental areas, such as the U.S.A. and the U.S.S.R., and created a new class of superpowers unknown in the previous history of the world. The United States is a country of very great resources, where the possibilities of producing wealth are far more considerable than in the countries of the Old World. It does not covet colonial possessions, but it has established control over places which are considered necessary for its national safety and prosperity such as Puerto Rico, and the international

AMERICAN INDUSTRIALISM IN THE TWENTIETH CENTURY
A view of Pittsburgh. *Photograph by Ewing Galloway, N.Y.*

waterway known as the Panama Canal, which was opened in 1914 and is governed by a commission with an American as president. Alaska, bought from Russia in 1867, and Hawaii, annexed in 1898, became the 49th and 50th States of the U.S.A. in 1959.

To many the term United States of America will at once suggest big business, industrialism in its most highly developed form, immensely wealthy individuals, and skyscrapers, marvellous products of architectural and engineering genius. But this impression does not do full justice to the American character. Business is, undoubtedly, a dominant interest, a means of self-expression and of advancement in both wealth and power for young people of ambition and talent. Wealth is not, however, worshipped as an end in itself, but rather as a material proof of success, and Americans are remarkably free and generous with their fortunes. The American, while he strives to make the best of the world as it is, is also very much alive to the need for a better world. This latent idealism was admirably expressed by Franklin Roosevelt, in his inaugural Presidential address at Washington in January 1937. He referred to the millions of his fellow citizens who were denied education, recreation, and the opportunities to better the lot of themselves and their children. He declared that one-third of the nation was ill housed, ill clad, and ill nourished, but he made it clear that the picture which he had painted had been painted in the confident hope that the nation was on its way forward to a better state, in which the test of its progress would be 'not an addition to the abundance of those who have much, but the provision of enough for those who have too little'. The elections of President Roosevelt in 1933 and again in 1937 were triumphs for idealism; so, too, was the election in 1913 of Woodrow Wilson, the statesman who will best be remembered for his project of a League of Nations to check wars between civilized peoples. Outside the United States, Americans

THE SKYSCRAPERS OF NEW YORK

Aerofilms Ltd.

have shown a real and a practical interest in the welfare of humanity, such as in their work on behalf of the sufferers in the great Russian Famine of 1921, and in the Marshall Plan to relieve distress and restore the European economy after the Second World War. Their international influence has been, on the whole, decidedly pacific. During the nineteenth century they were involved in only two armed conflicts with European powers: one with Great Britain, between the years 1812 and 1814, and the other with Spain in 1898. The first of these arose from the claim which the British made during the Napoleonic Wars to search neutral ships for contraband of war; it was fought at a time when the relations between the two countries were considerably less cordial than they are to-day; but it has been followed by over a century of unbroken peace, and the frontier between the States and the British Dominion of Canada is absolutely undefended by fort or arsenal of any kind. The war with Spain had reference to the Spanish colony of Cuba, which had been in a state of insurrection for many years. The intervention of the United States was not dictated by any desire for conquest, but mainly by concern for the peace of the American continent, and although Cuba was conquered it was not retained. As soon as the people were fit for it, they were allowed to govern themselves. Cuba became an independent self-governing republic; its subsequent history has been turbulent, with many insurrections, and lately the dictatorship of the Marxist Fidel Castro established in 1959. Puerto Rico and the Philippine Islands were also annexed, much against the wishes of the inhabitants in the latter case; but in 1934 the people of the Philippines were given a constitution by which they were allowed to govern themselves, under the general supervision of a United States High Commissioner, for a period of ten years, after which they were to be completely independent. The Japanese invasion during the Second World

War delayed this, but in 1946 a Philippine Republic was proclaimed. The United States is not keen to annex lands abroad; foreign relations are under public control; and although the President has great powers they are subject to the control of the Senate, which is in its turn responsible to the American people, by whom its members are elected. President Wilson, after the First World War, failed to get the Senate to ratify the terms of peace, and although the Covenant of the League of Nations, for which he was mainly responsible, aroused some enthusiasm in the country, it did not arouse enough to bring victory to his party in the presidential election of 1920.

XXXII

THE TWENTIETH CENTURY

THE twentieth century has been one of great scientific, economic, and political development, but, unfortunately, the pace of moral development has been very much slower. Before the century was half-way through its course, two wars had been fought, which, because of the vast areas which they covered and their almost universal effects, are rightly called World Wars, the first between 1914 and 1918, and the second from 1939 to 1945. The immediate cause of the First World War was the assassination in Sarajevo, a small Bosnian town, of the Archduke Franz Ferdinand, the heir to the throne of Austria, and his wife. This was followed by almost impossible demands by Austria on the Serbian government, which was held to be responsible for the crime. Austria was certain of German support, Russia would not allow the extermination of Serbia, France was the ally of Russia, and Great Britain, bound to France by an *entente*, was finally impelled to go to war because of an unprovoked invasion of Belgium by the Germans. But the crime of Sarajevo was merely the spark which fired a train laid over a period of many years. The real causes of the war were more deep-seated: international rivalries which had existed for at least a quarter of a century before the outbreak of hostilities; competitive armaments; a race for colonies and spheres of influence; the ramifications of high finance; and rankling feelings of discontentment with territorial adjustments which had followed previous wars, such as the cession of Alsace and Lorraine to Germany, and the occupation by Austria of provinces which were claimed to be Italian.

Few, if any, of the war-makers of 1914 could have foreseen its results: the magnitude of operations fought in three continents, and involving the participation of all five; the enormous waste of human life and of human treasure; and the changes in the map of the world which followed the defeat of Germany and her allies. Four empires came to an end, three of them—the German, the Austrian, and the Turkish—as penalties of defeat, the fourth, the Russian, as the result of internal revolution. In 1914 most people expected decisive battles and a comparatively short war; the idea of a world-wide conflict lasting for four years with the killed alone numbering eight millions would have been regarded as fantastic. Germany gained some early and spectacular successes, advancing through Belgium and France almost to the gates of Paris, but when the United States of America, with its great reserves of manpower and its immense industrial resources, entered the war in 1917, the German cause was doomed. Apart from its military significance, this intervention was an event of great historical importance. Europe had failed to save herself, and the New World had again redressed the balance of the Old; the dominance of

THE TREATY OF VERSAILLES 535

Western Europe in world affairs was nearing eclipse. But America, as it transpired, was not yet ready to assume the full responsibilities and obligations of world leadership.

After the war, a conference met at Paris to draw up conditions of peace. Like the Treaty of Vienna of just over a hundred years before, the Treaty of Versailles can easily be criticized. Like its predecessor it was drawn up when passions were still inflamed, and the terms imposed upon Germany were harsh and ungenerous. Stripped of her colonies, her army reduced to negligible proportions, forced to cede Alsace and Lorraine to France, and to agree to the temporary occupation by French troops of the Saar valley, Germany was also compelled to hand over to Poland large parts of the industrial area of Silesia, and asked to pay an impossible sum in reparation for damage done by her troops. These terms gave rise to a strong feeling of injustice, and undoubtedly had much to do with the subsequent success of the Nazi movement. Italy also felt aggrieved. After a period of uncertainty she had entered the war on the side of the victors, and although she was rewarded by the cession of the Trentino and Trieste, she felt that she had been badly treated because Dalmatia, which was claimed to be predominantly Italian, was incorporated in the new state of Yugoslavia. To this the Yugoslavs retorted that the peace treaties had put more than a million of their nationals under Italian rule. On the whole, however, the principle of nationality was not ignored at Paris. New states like Czechoslovakia and Yugoslavia were created, and Poland, Rumania, and Greece were reorganized, with the principle of nationality the predominating consideration in each case; Austria was reduced to the status of a small republic where Teutonic culture prevailed; and frontiers were so drawn that, in the new Europe, only 3 per cent. of the population were subjected to alien rule.

One of the most hopeful features of the settlement was the American President Wilson's insistence upon the formation of a League of Nations, which, he believed, would be a guarantee of future world peace. It was ironical that his policy was not endorsed by his fellow countrymen, and that the United States of America never joined the League, which came to an end in 1946. The essence of the League Covenant was that each member nation should submit disputes and quarrels to the League before resorting to warlike measures; at one time fifty-six nations, including all the great powers except the United States, were members, and it is obvious that, if they had all been sincere in what they professed, the world could have been rid of war. But fierce national and colonial aspirations, and tendencies on the part of strong nations to exploit their strength, rendered much of the League's work ineffective in the difficult years between the two World Wars. It proved very successful in settling minor disputes, and in promoting such humanitarian projects as the regulation of the trade in opium, but it had no success at all in its efforts to curb the aggressiveness of strong powers, or in reducing armaments. It could not stop Japan from seizing Chinese territory in Manchuria in 1931, or Italy from conquering Abyssinia, another member state, in 1936. It was a lamentable fact that in 1937 the armed strength of the great nations of Europe was much greater than it was on the eve of the First World War.

The period between the World Wars (1918–39) was one of ever-recurring turmoil and trouble. Hopes of a freer and happier world received many setbacks, particularly on the continent of Europe, where undermining of authority and weak governments led to the establishment of dictatorships, the negation of democracy. The first of the dictators was the Russian Lenin, who, on the ruins of the Czarist Empire and the ineffective rule of the moderate Socialist Kerensky, founded a Communist or Bolshevist Republic, governed as far as possible in accordance with the principles of Karl Marx. Lenin was a fanatic, a visionary, a fatalist, who had long been

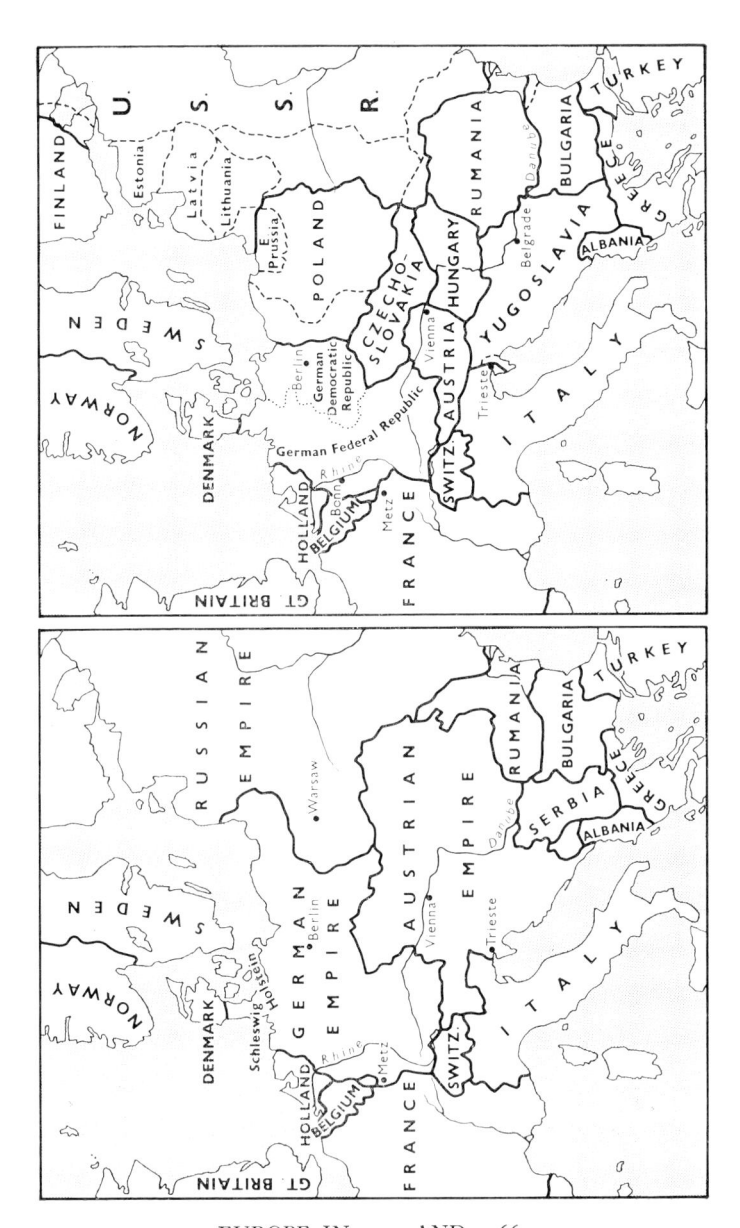

EUROPE IN 1914 AND 1966
(1918 frontiers in broken lines)

obsessed with the idea that it was his destiny to establish the dictatorship of the proletariat in Russia. He retained some of the worst features of Russian imperialism—its secret police, its refusal to tolerate opinions contrary to those of the governing classes, its ruthless removal of people considered to be hostile to the state. But there was also a constructive side to his genius, and under him, and his successor Stalin, Russia became a powerful and well-organized state. Industries were developed and expanded; education, physical training, and public health received intelligent and widespread attention, and the Russian armed forces became far stronger than they had been under the Czars. The Union of Socialist Soviet Republics (U.S.S.R.), the official title of the Russian State, did not always rigidly adhere to Marxist doctrine. Lenin sanctioned private trading in 1921, and both he and Stalin were not averse to the use of foreign capital and foreign skill when it suited them.

The next European country to submit to dictatorship was Italy, where the end of the war was followed by strikes, vigorous anti-German propaganda, and denunciations of patriotism, due to dissatisfaction with Italy's territorial gains, and to high taxes and high prices, which seemed to many to be the chief results of the war. A succession of weak governments failed to improve conditions, to restore public confidence, or even to maintain the semblance of order. Chafing under this state of affairs, a former Socialist, a man of fiery energy and blatant patriotism, Benito Mussolini, the son of a blacksmith, formed a party known as the Fascisti, after the rods or fasces which the lictors bore as symbols of their authority before the Roman Emperors. In 1922 a march on Rome was arranged, and from that time until Mussolini's fall from power in 1943 Italy was a Fascist state. The king was nominally at the head, but the real power was exercised by Mussolini. As in Russia, no opinion was tolerated except that of the state; press, platform, and university were all expected to promulgate the new doctrines; disobedience meant imprisonment or exile to a remote island; but Fascism, unlike Bolshevism, was anti-Communist, even though its leader had at one time been an advanced Socialist. Despite its sinister features, it did some material good in Italy; and the people were made conscious of their high destiny as the heirs of the traditions and culture of Imperial Rome. But the militancy and arrogance of the ancient Roman spirit were also inculcated, with results which were eventually to lead Fascism and the monarchy which supported it to complete disaster.

Among Mussolini's admirers was an Austrian, named Adolf Hitler, a man of humble origin and little education, who had fought in the German army during the war, and had never risen above the rank of lance-corporal. After the war, Germany fell on very evil days. She failed to pay the heavy reparations demanded of her, and depreciation of the currency reduced the value of the mark to such an extent that many Germans became destitute; the strong armies which the French, the Poles, and the Czechs were allowed to maintain on her boundaries caused uneasiness in Germany, and a demand for rearmament; and when in 1929 the statesman Stresemann, who had honestly tried to organize the republic on non-military lines, died, and soon after a great financial crisis in New York led to the withdrawal of American money from Germany, the condition of the country became so serious that the Germans were ready to hail almost anyone as a saviour. This was Hitler's great opportunity. Six years before, his party, the National Socialist or Nazi Party, had failed so completely in an attempt to seize power that few could have expected its revival as a powerful factor in German politics. It was apathy and despair which made Hitler's rise to power possible, but, even so, it could never have been achieved without the support which he got from German capitalists because he preached undeviating opposition to Communism, whose spread they had begun to fear. The government was too weak to suppress the brown-shirted private army which Hitler had gathered around him; in 1933 he became Chancellor, and a year later, after the death of the aged President Hindenburg, the head of the German state. As Chancellor he was responsible for Germany's secession from the League of Nations, and as Führer or Leader, he carried the struggle farther by large-scale rearmament, conscription, reoccupation of prohibited districts in the Rhineland, and repudiation of restrictions imposed by the Treaty of Versailles. His methods were frequently ruthless. Traitors were executed; and Jews and open opponents of the Nazi régime were consistently persecuted. The extent of his influence and the fanatical reverence with which he was regarded by millions of his subjects, are as remarkable as his rise to absolute power from so lowly a beginning. He certainly did much to make the Germans more self-reliant than they had been since their defeat in war, and to improve their physique; but unfortunately all this was for one end. Germany was to be a great military empire again, the dominant power in Europe, and ultimately in the world. Self-reliance turned to arrogance, and to brutal interference in the affairs of other countries. The murder in 1934 of the Austrian Premier, Dr. Dolfuss, who disapproved of Hitler's methods, was contrived by Nazis from Munich; in 1938 German troops occupied Vienna, and Austria and its seven million inhabitants of German race became part of Hitler's empire.

Another country where internal troubles resulted in dictatorship was Spain. In 1923, taking advantage of the weakness of the parliamentary system, General Primo de Rivera seized power and set up a military dictatorship which lasted until 1929. He was an admirer of Fascism and, like Mussolini, brooked no opposition to his will: the king was a mere puppet in his hands; the Press was rigidly censored; intellectuals opposed to the dictatorship were banished from the

DICTATORS

country, and political opponents were thrown into prison. Primo de Rivera died in 1930, and early in the following year a bloodless revolution resulted in the deposition of the king, Alfonso XIII, and the establishment of a republic. But the Republic failed to crush the three pillars of monarchy—nobility, church, and army—or to satisfy extremists, and there followed some years of anarchy culminating in civil war when in July 1936 General Franco led a revolt against a left-wing coalition government. This Civil War spread throughout the peninsula and developed into something far more dangerous than a struggle for power between rival factions. Germany and Italy supplied the rebels with all their bombing and fighting aeroplanes, and with thousands of volunteers, and Russia gave similar assistance to the Spanish government. Great Britain, France, and the United States of America tried to localize the conflict, but with little success, and the war ended in 1939 with victory for Franco, and the establishment of a new dictatorship.

Very different was the dictatorship set up in Turkey in 1923 on the ruins of the old Turkish Empire. The last of the Sultans fled from Constantinople in 1922, and a year later a Turkish Republic was proclaimed with Mustapha Kemal Pasha as its first President. Kemal, who died in 1938, undoubtedly dominated the Turkish National Assembly, and exercised dictatorial powers in carrying out his policy, but it was a policy whose ultimate aim was an efficient, self-governing modern state, free from the taint of connexion with the corrupt and bloodstained government of the Sultans. This was why Constantinople ceased to be the capital; its place has been taken by Ankara (Angora) in the uplands of Anatolia. Kemal was a man of progressive ideas, and under his vigorous direction a remarkable transformation was effected in Turkey. Old restrictions were removed; women were compelled to abandon the veil, men to substitute a rimmed hat for the fez; dervishes, magicians, sellers of charms and amulets and other such relics of the servile and unprogressive past, were decreed out of existence. The Turkish Republic has become a modern state which, while renouncing servitude to the nations of Western Europe, has not hesitated to copy what is best in their culture. Polygamy has been abolished; the laws have been codified and rationalized; careers have been thrown open to women as well as to men; and so great was Kemal's influence that a decree that the Muslim religion should no longer be regarded as the official religion of the state in no way lessened his power or undermined his prestige. After his death democratic progress continued until it was interrupted by a military *coup d'état* in 1961, followed by the trial and execution of Prime Minister Menderes.

In Great Britain, France, and the United States of America war had only a temporary effect upon liberty; democratic institutions were too strong, too firmly embedded, to be permanently destroyed, or even permanently affected. In Great Britain, conscription was discontinued, and although discontent among the labouring classes frequently found expression in demonstrations by unemployed, strikes of different workers, and even in a general strike of nine days in 1926, the good sense of the people always precluded the possibility of an armed rising; doctrines like fascism and communism made little headway; the use of paper led to no catastrophic fall in the value of money, as it did on the continent of Europe; the franchise was widened to include all men and women of adult age; education and the social services were extended; and state insurance against sickness and unemployment helped to alleviate distress. The war strengthened rather than weakened constitutional monarchy. Of this there were two striking illustrations: the widespread rejoicing when King George V attained his Silver Jubilee in 1935, and the peaceful and uneventful accession in December 1936 of George VI, after the abdication of his elder brother, Edward VIII, a popular monarch who chose to renounce his throne rather than a marriage which was strongly opposed by the leaders of Church and State. He realized that, if he were to remain on the throne, it must be as the servant of the people, guided in all matters of importance by the advice of the ministers whom they had put into power. There were important changes in the structure of the British Empire during the inter-war years. In 1921, a new Dominion, the Irish Free State, was created. This was a predominantly Roman Catholic state, and did not include the six Protestant counties of the North, who preferred to remain more closely connected with Great Britain. The new Dominion, like the older Dominions—Canada, South Africa, Australia, and New Zealand—was accorded its own parliament, its own flag, the right to send its own ambassadors to foreign countries, and the right to impose duties on British goods entering the country. In 1931 the Statute of Westminster further increased the prestige of the Dominions, giving them a status equal to that of Great Britain, bound to one another by only one acknowledged obligation, allegiance to the British Crown. Legally this gave them the right to secede if they chose. The accession of a British sovereign not personally acceptable to any one of them might have such an effect, so that the Statute has had a tendency to increase the prestige and responsibility of the Crown. The Irish Free State did secede in 1937, a not very surprising event, when one remembers the embittered relations which had existed between its inhabitants and Great Britain prior to the granting of self-government. But again the northern counties stood aloof. They still remain a very loyal part of the British Commonwealth with a Governor appointed by the British Crown, and representation in the British Parliament, in addition to a parliament of their own.

When the Third French Republic came to birth in September 1870, and indeed for years afterwards, there were many who doubted its continuance for any length of time. In 1875 the historian Hanotaux wrote that 'possibly it would not adapt itself easily to a crisis in which the fate of the country was at stake'. His fears were not justified, but they were not really put to the test until the First World War and the difficult period which ensued. In July 1926 there was a money crisis so grave that the Finance Minister declared that the Public Treasury was at the end of its resources; and in 1934 the country was in a still more dangerous situation as the result of the frauds of a swindler named Stavisky with whom members of the government were widely believed to be connected. In Paris armed force was used against demonstrators, and some of them were killed. In 1936, for the first time in the history of France, Communists and Socialists, brought together by a common fear of Germany, united to form a ministry under M. Léon Blum, and many beneficial social measures were passed: a forty-hour working week was decreed; the school-leaving age was raised; and laws were passed to nationalize the trade in arms and to dissolve Fascist leagues.

When the First World War ended there were many in the United States of America who thought that their country should for the future concentrate on keeping out of European entanglements; this belief, aided by a suspicion that President Wilson was arrogating too much power to himself at Paris, led to a refusal to ratify the peace treaty, and to join the League of Nations. Laws were passed to limit immigration; heavy tariffs were imposed to protect industry from foreign competition; there was much surplus capital to invest abroad; and despite some labour troubles, the policy of internal development appeared to be justified by increased prosperity. Although not a member of the League of Nations the American government did not dissociate itself from international movements to ensure world peace. It figured prominently in the Washington Conference of 1921, the Geneva Conference of 1927, and the Kellogg Proposals of 1928, all of which sought to eliminate causes which might lead to war.

1. Flying. A de Havilland Comet jet airliner

2. Radio. Part of the B.B.C.'s new control room at Broadcasting House, London

TWENTIETH-CENTURY COMMUNICATIONS

Relations with South America, particularly with Mexico, were visibly improved; and a Pan American Congress, held in 1928, condemned war 'as an instrument of national policy', and took steps to ensure the peaceful settlement of all disputes which might arise between American states.

In 1929, American prosperity received a rude shock: the United States government suddenly found itself confronted by a financial crisis of the utmost magnitude—not a mere Wall Street crash, but a nation-wide disaster, affecting all classes. Millions faced starvation, and there was no form of state assistance, as in Great Britain, to alleviate their sufferings. Many believed that unrestrained competition and too much scope for individual enterprise were at the root of the evil, and that state control should be stronger and more extensive. And so, in 1933, Franklin Roosevelt became President, pledged to secure what he called a 'New Deal', which meant that the State was to take over the control of unemployment, to regulate industry, to secure remunerative prices for producers, and to obtain fair wages and good conditions of labour for all workers. The New Deal achieved a large measure of success, and President Roosevelt's re-election in 1937 (and again in 1941 and 1945) testified to the confidence which the American people had in him.

Democratic governments survived the First World War in Belgium (where the victory of the Allies naturally meant the end of German domination, and a return to constitutional monarchy), in Holland, and in the Scandinavian countries—Norway, Sweden, and Denmark—and the new state of Czechoslovakia became a bulwark of democracy in Central Europe under its first President, Thomas Masaryk, one of the greatest men of his time. He declared that 'it is the deliberate and discerning love of a nation that appeals to me, not the indiscriminate love that assumes everything to be right because it bears a national label'. Masaryk's policy was continued by his disciple and successor, Eduard Benes, but,

THE SECOND WORLD WAR 547

unfortunately for him, his country, and the world, Czechoslovakia excited the cupidity of Adolf Hitler. When in March 1938 Austria was added to the German dominions, Czechoslovakia was left exposed; and within six months Hitler, on the false plea that he was concerned at injustices suffered by Germans in the Sudeten territories of Czechoslovakia, induced Great Britain, France, and a reluctant Czechoslovakia to agree at Munich to their surrender to Germany. In March of the following year he seized Prague and the rest of Czechoslovakia. Thoroughly alarmed, Britain and France gave guarantees of protection to Poland, which, it was logical to assume, would be the next of Hitler's victims, and his invasion of Polish territory on 1 September 1939 was followed, two days later, by simultaneous declarations of war against Germany by Great Britain and France. Russia, which had been left out of the Munich discussions, had already made a pact of neutrality with Germany.

The Second World War lasted until 1945. In some respects it followed a pattern remarkably similar to that of the First World War. As in 1914–15, there was an initial German attack of such fury that an overwhelming victory was almost achieved. Poland, Denmark, Norway, Holland, Belgium, and even France were all forced to surrender after incredibly short campaigns, and Britain was for a time left to fight alone in circumstances of utmost peril. In the autumn of 1940 a German invasion from the air was defeated by a small but brilliantly efficient air force. In the following year allies came in: the Russians, whose country Hitler had invaded, and, most important of all, the United States of America, whom the Japanese, the allies of Germany, had brought into the war by a treacherous attack upon the American fleet at Pearl Harbour in Hawaii. As in the First World War, there followed years of great anxiety, defeats alternating with victories, and determined efforts to starve Britain into surrender, until in 1945 Germany suddenly collapsed. With many of her cities in ruins from incessant air attacks, and her territories invaded, she could no longer stand the strain. The industrial might of the United States had again been a decisive factor, and the discovery and use of a new and terrible weapon, the atomic bomb, brought a sudden and fearful end to Japanese resistance.

The scope of the Second World War was even wider than the First. Most of the fighting took place in Europe, but there were also campaigns of great magnitude in Asia and in Africa; there were fights off the American coasts, in the icy Arctic seas, and in the approaches to Australia; and strategy had to be conducted on a world scale, necessitating consultations and conferences between the three great allied leaders, the British Prime Minister Winston Churchill, the American President Franklin Roosevelt, and the Russian dictator Joseph Stalin. One such conference took place at Teheran in Persia in 1943, and another at Yalta in the Crimea in 1945. Proportionately the losses among the armed forces, despite the use of more destructive weapons, were less than in the earlier war, but the civilian losses were very much greater, and material destruction, particularly in Russia and in Germany, was vast and terrifying, needing the greatest human skill and industry to restore. The map of the world was again greatly altered. Germany was divided up into zones of occupation for the armies of the victors, and although the three western zones have regained unity and independence as the Federal Republic of Germany, the eastern zone (the German Democratic Republic) remains a Russian puppet. Germany's principal allies, Italy and Japan, were less severely treated. The Italians, who surrendered in 1943, and who themselves subsequently disposed of Mussolini and other leading Fascists, were allowed to form an independent democratic republic, and the Japanese, whose emperor was not deposed, regained their independence after a period of American occupation and tutelage in 1951, as a result of the Korean War.

SURVIVAL OF MONARCHY

The Second World War, like the First, was fatal to many European monarchies. Kingship was abolished in Rumania, Yugoslavia, Bulgaria, and Italy. Apart from Britain there are only six countries where it survives: Denmark, Norway, Sweden, Holland, and Belgium, where the defeat of Hitler was followed by the re-establishment of constitutional monarchy; and Greece, where a formidable task of rehabilitation had to be undertaken after ten troubled years (1941–51) of invasion by both Italians and Germans, followed by civil war. In France, which, for over four years (1940–4) was literally a German province, liberation was followed in 1947 by the establishment of the Fourth French Republic, which was conducted in much the same way as the Third. After many ministerial crises the Fifth French Republic was proclaimed in January 1959 with the wartime hero Charles de Gaulle as President. In Spain, which was technically neutral during the war, Franco's dictatorship remained unshaken despite separatist tendencies in Catalonia and the Basque province, and a strike among the miners of Asturias in 1962.

Great Britain emerged from the war with enormous prestige, but with reduced wealth, and her position as a world power diminished. Her empire shrank; her resources were so impaired that some forms of food rationing were still necessary eight years after the conclusion of hostilities. Most war restrictions were by then removed, but because of the unsettled state of the world military conscription was not at once abolished. The monarchy is as strong as ever, as was strikingly demonstrated by the nation-wide rejoicings at the coronation of the young Queen, Elizabeth II, in June 1953. But high taxation has depleted the numbers of the landed gentry, and considerably lessened the power and influence, if not the prestige, of the aristocracy. There is greater equality of wealth; and insurance against old age, sickness, accident, and unemployment has become a government obligation in what has come to be known as the 'Welfare State'.

The two most powerful world powers after the Second World War were the United States of America and Russia. Co-operation in war and the generally friendly contacts of the supreme leaders at Teheran and Yalta gave hopes of friendship and understanding when the fighting came to an end, and of the establishment of a world government, which would eventually lead to the outlawing of war. The conclusion of hostilities was quickly followed, after many preliminary discussions, one of which had taken place in Moscow two years previously, by the formation of a new international body, the United Nations Organization (U.N.O.), pledged 'to maintain international peace and security—to develop friendly relations among nations based on respect for the principle of equal rights and self-determination of peoples', and 'to promote and encourage freedom for all without distinction as to race, sex, language, or religion'. The United States was one of the original founder members of U.N.O., which began with fifty members; the charter of inauguration was signed in San Francisco; and its permanent headquarters were subsequently established in Manhattan, New York. There was no recurrence of the policy of isolationism which kept the Americans out of the League of Nations. The Organization has a General Assembly where all member nations are represented, and a Security Council of fifteen members of whom five—the United States, Great Britain, Russia, France, and Nationalist China—are permanent members, and since the Security Council is predominant, and any one of the permanent members can veto any of its decisions, it is obvious that if they cannot work in harmony permanent peace can never be achieved. Unfortunately, Russia has been even less co-operative than in wartime, and she has negatived much of the work of the Council by frequent use of the veto. This has undoubtedly been partly due to suspicions of her former allies, who have not, for example, shared atomic secrets with her. But the fundamental cause is that Russia

AGGRESSIVE COMMUNISM

represents a philosophy and a way of life which is alien to American and British ideas. Russia is a Communist state, and after the war there were indications of a return to the rigidity of early Bolshevist doctrine, and of a desire to convert the world to communism. Poland, east Germany, Hungary, Rumania, Bulgaria, Yugoslavia, and Albania became satellites of Russia, though Yugoslavia under Marshal Tito broke away in 1948 to become an independent Communist republic; the Czechoslovakian democracy was in 1947 replaced by a Russian-directed Communist dictatorship; the poverty and ignorance of Asiatic peoples were exploited to further Communist power; and conferences with the great democracies broke down after much useless talking and recrimination. The presence of large Soviet armies in Europe and the fear which they inspired led to the formation in 1949 of an organization of mutual defence against possible aggression known as the North Atlantic Treaty Organization (N.A.T.O.). Ten European countries, subsequently increased to thirteen with the admission of Greece, Turkey, and the German Federal Republic, and the United States and Canada formed the membership. A big test for the United Nations came in 1950 when the Communist state of North Korea invaded South Korea, which was under American protection. Despite the opposition of the Communist members the Assembly decided to repel the aggressors and sixteen nations sent troops, the bulk of these being American. The North Koreans would have been completely defeated if China had not come to their aid. As it was, the battle-line became stabilized near the frontier of the two countries and a truce was eventually signed in the summer of 1953. The signing of this truce, together with the removal of restrictions in many Communist countries and a moderation in the tone of Russian propaganda, led to occasional relaxations of tension after the death of Stalin in the spring of 1953.

The principle of nationality which was stimulated by the

First World War was still farther advanced through the Second World War, particularly in Africa and in Asia, where there was the greatest room for its development. To some extent this was due to Communist propaganda, which used national aspirations to foster discontent as a step towards world revolution. But there were deeper causes too, especially the spread of education among native populations, and the natural desire which it brought to destroy race barriers and to establish social and political equality. Some colonial powers have shown a tendency to oppose this, or to give reluctant consent to changes which had become inevitable. Thus France resisted Tunisian and Algerian demands until 1962, and while in 1950 she recognized her former colonies of Tonkin, Annam, and Cochin China as the independent state of Viet Nam within the French Union, it was largely because of the rise within the same regions of a rival Communist authority, Viet Minh (North Viet Nam). It was force of circumstances too which obliged Holland in 1949 to recognize the independent republic of Indonesia, consisting of former Dutch possessions in the East Indies, including the rich islands of Java and Sumatra, the Moluccas, and part of Borneo. Generally speaking, Great Britain's attitude has been more generous. The British Empire has become a British Commonwealth of Nations, with self-government a logical and attainable goal for all its members. Some like India, Pakistan, Ghana (Gold Coast), Nigeria, and Cyprus are completely independent; others like Canada, Australia, New Zealand, and Ceylon are independent but acknowledge the British monarch as their sovereign; they are free at any time to repudiate this obligation and remain within or without the British Commonwealth. By the end of 1966 all Britain's former African colonies were independent states within the Commonwealth, except Rhodesia (the former Southern Rhodesia) and South Africa. South Africa, with its policy of permanent rule of the Negro majority by the white minority, had been refused permission to remain a member of the Commonwealth when it became a republic in 1961; the white minority in Rhodesia illegally seized independence in 1965 in order to perpetuate their rule over the Negro majority. British troops have been withdrawn from Egypt, although together with France and Israel they tried to re-occupy the Suez Canal zone when the Egyptians seized control of the canal in 1956. All three withdrew when requested by the U.N. with both the United States and Russia denouncing this action by force. Great Britain gave early recognition to the republic of Israel, which in 1949 was established in Palestine, formerly a mandated British colony; and when in 1951 the government of Iran (Persia) nationalized the oil industry, the British Government made no attempt to use force to recover valuable British refineries.

But probably India affords the most striking example of the change which has come over British imperial policy. During the First World War demands for self-government received encouragement when the Lloyd George government promised increasing use of Indians in every branch of the administration, and 'the development of self governing institutions with a view to the progressive realization of responsible government in India as an integral part of the British Empire'.[1] In fulfilment of this the India Act of 1919 put into force a system which divided powers between the British government and various elected Indian councils and assemblies. This did not satisfy Indian nationalists, of whom the most notable was the ascetic Mahatma Gandhi, who disapproved strongly of industrial civilizations imported from the West and their effect on his country. Strikes, self-imposed fastings, and other devices to undermine British authority followed, and further concessions increased Indian responsibility but failed to satisfy the nationalists, who made it clear that

[1] The Montagu Pronouncement, 1917.

they would be content with nothing short of complete independence. The problem was further complicated for the British government by a serious religious cleavage among the Indians themselves. The Muslims wanted a country of their own free from Hindu influence, whereas the Indian Congress, dominated by Hindus, demanded an undivided India. During the Second World War the British government, anxious to retain Indian loyalty, particularly because of a possible Japanese invasion, made proposals of complete self-government, either within or without the British Commonwealth. After the war these promises were faithfully observed; in 1947 the British Empire of India came to an end, and its place was taken by two self-governing Dominions, India and the Muslim state of Pakistan. In 1950 India, whose Prime Minister was Pandit Nehru, one of Gandhi's staunchest admirers, chose to become an independent republic; Pakistan also became a republic in 1956. Both states are democracies, with popularly elected assemblies and ministers responsible to them. They have difficulties to overcome greater than those which usually confront democratic governments, arising out of widespread illiteracy; a great deal of chronic poverty; under-development of agricultural and industrial resources; over-population; religious differences often amounting to fanaticism; the position of minorities—Muslims in India and Hindus in Pakistan; frontier problems and territorial adjustments; the persistence of caste, particularly in Southern India; and communism, which has made deep inroads into both India and Pakistan. It will be difficult to communicate the sanity and judgement of the leaders of the Indian democracies, which has often been demonstrated in the United Nations Organization, to vast and clamorous populations until education becomes general and effective.

Far different has been the history of China, the other great power of the Far East. The end of the First World War was

1. A Meeting of the Security Council of the United Nations Organization

2. Some of the devastation caused in Hiroshima by the explosion of one atomic bomb on 6 August 1945

PEACE OR WAR?

here followed by a period of intensive Japanese penetration, and the Chinese delegates at Versailles refused to sign the treaty because it gave them no redress against the invaders of their country. China subsequently became the prey of civil war between rival war lords; banditry and piracy became profitable occupations; in 1931 the great province of Manchuria became a Japanese dependency; and communism secured a firm hold. In these troublous times two leaders emerged as champions of nationalism: Sun Yat-sen, who was proclaimed President of the Chinese Republic in 1921, and Chiang Kai-shek, who succeeded him in 1925. Four years later the government established itself in a new capital at Nanking. A seven years war with Japan ended in 1945, and disputes immediately arose between the Communists and the central government. Chiang certainly had a hard task because of war strains, the illiteracy of the people, and the size of the country, which made it very difficult to exercise authority in places remote from the capital. But there was no excuse for the widespread corruption at which he connived, the misuse of generous American aid, and the neglect of American advice. The result was the complete conquest of China by the Communists in 1949. Their leader Mao Tse-tung, became President of a newly constituted 'People's Republic of China' with its capital at Peking; his government was recognized by Great Britain in 1950; but the United States of America still recognizes Chiang's government, which has established itself in the island of Formosa, and still represents China at meetings of the United Nations Organization. This is due mainly to the fact that the Peking government has not been content to keep communism within its own borders. Its intervention in Korea saved the Communists from defeat, and it has been responsible for Viet Minh victories in Indo-China; it invaded Tibet and in 1959 deposed the Dalai Lama; in 1962 it forcibly disputed the northern boundary of India.

THE UNITED NATIONS ORGANIZATION 557

The two decades which have followed the end of the Second World War and the founding of the United Nations in 1945 have been years of unrest and apprehension. As the world has been divided into two major groups, one dominated by the United States of America and the other by communist Russia (maintaining a not completely happy alliance with communist China) the United Nations has been more successful in its humanitarian than its political capacity. The powers and prestige of the General Assembly have increased but the veto which can be imposed in the Security Council can still be an absolute bar to the will of the majority. The number of members has more than doubled, but China, the largest state in the world, is still excluded, mainly because of the opposition of the United States, which continues to regard the government of Formosa as the legitimate Chinese government. In the Assembly the principle of one vote for each country whatever its size has tended to decrease the influence of the great powers, and to increase that of the Afro-Asian group one of whose representatives, the Burmese U Thant, was elected as Secretary-General in 1962. Nevertheless, the United Nations is not a democratic institution and is not comprised only of democratic countries. It includes dictatorships like Spain and some of the South American republics, the Union of South Africa where there is discrimination against coloured people, and Saudi Arabia where there are still slaves.

Removed from the stress of politics, the humanitarian work of the United Nations, conducted through subsidiary organizations, has achieved notable successes. U.N.E.S.C.O. (United Nations Educational, Scientific and Cultural Organization) has brought education and technical knowledge to undeveloped countries; the World Health Organization has reduced the ravages of malaria and other diseases; F.A.O. (Food and Agricultural Organization of the United Nations) has disseminated the most modern agricultural methods, which have achieved such results as the saving of the grape crops of Afghanistan, and a greatly increased yield from the cotton fields of Egypt.

The political activities of the United Nations have been less spectacular, but, depending on the importance of the problems and powers involved, useful work has been done in at least two cases by the intervention of United Nations troops. In 1956 Egypt took over control of the Suez Canal, which had previously been administered by an international company, and British, French, and Israeli forces invaded the country. Their action was condemned by the United Nations (with the United States and Russia prominent among the critics), the invading forces were withdrawn, and United Nations troops were sent to the affected areas to restore peace and order. But when in the same year permission was sought to enter Hungary to investigate the manner in which a revolution had been suppressed by Russian troops, it was peremptorily refused. The United Nations was able to intervene more effectively in the Congo civil war of 1960, and its troops, drawn from many nations, were here engaged in active fighting. Despite the bloodshed the presence of international forces had the effect of limiting the local conflicts before the interests of major powers could seriously collide. On the groupings and alliances of individual countries for their own interests, the United Nations has had little effect, but its meetings provide an international forum where grievances can be ventilated and where a majority opinion can be made known even if little action may be taken. The dissemination of such opinion, especially with regard to colonialism and racial problems, has had a great but not always a fair and beneficial effect.

The break-up of the colonial empires and the emergence of new nations have been accepted as inevitable by the European colonizing powers, with the exception of Portugal, which put up all the resistance it could to the seizure by

THE END OF COLONIALISM 559

India of Goa in 1961, and which still clings tenaciously to its African colonies of Angola and Mozambique. The French fought a war lasting seven and a half years to retain Algeria, but gave up the struggle in 1962; and in the same year the Dutch, who thirteen years before had very reluctantly acknowledged the independence of Indonesia, agreed to West New Guinea being put under United Nations trusteeship until the inhabitants could decide their own future. Great Britain has been the most realistic of all. Education has been widely spread, university and technical training extended, and local inhabitants prepared for the work of government, so that the transitions were smooth and orderly except in the case of India and Pakistan in 1947; there disputed borders and religious fanaticism resulted in the deaths of 300,000 people and the flight of a total of 14 million from one state to the other in a couple of months (the greatest exodus in human history). But in Africa the new governments were not always able to maintain the law and order and unity they had inherited: Nigeria in particular suffered the murder of two successive prime ministers in 1966 and the threat of breaking up into its main tribal divisions. The Belgians transferred the Congo Free State in 1960 to a people unprepared and with hardly any experience of handling even the simplest instruments of government. Chaos soon followed, and the rich province of Katanga tried to break away. United Nations troops were sent in to restore order, a task which took five years.

It must be recognized that the future of the British Commonwealth as a political and economic force in the international scene is somewhat uncertain at the present time. The issue of communism still divides the world into two principal power blocs, led by the U.S.A. and the U.S.S.R. respectively, but neither bloc is solid in its allegiance and interests. On the Communist side Russia has her differences, more or less serious from time to time, with her European satellites on the one hand and China on the other. On the Western side, both economic and political needs have resulted in closer co-operation between the nations of Western Europe, which recovered rapidly from the devastation of war with aid under the Marshall Plan from the U.S.A. (1948–51). The customs union between France, Western Germany, Italy, the Netherlands, Belgium, and Luxemburg as a 'European Common Market' has already greatly stimulated the commercial prosperity of these countries, and is likely to lead to closer political ties in future. This has placed Britain in a quandary. Her geographical proximity to Europe and the advantages of being able to sell her goods widely in the Common Market incline her to join; her independent traditions, peculiar relationship with the U.S.A., and reluctance to harm the interests of Commonwealth farmers, hold her back. Whatever the outcome, it is difficult to be confident that the Commonwealth will still hold together as an effective force. If it does manage to do so, in spite of the conflicting interests of its members, it will be an inspiration to the world and a most valuable stabilizing factor in the cause of peace.

In the U.S.S.R. the death of Stalin in 1953 was followed by a period of some confusion and uncertainty until in 1956 Nikita Khrushchev, the Secretary-General of the Communist Party, openly denounced Stalin as a criminal and a murderer, and shortly afterwards became Chairman of the Council of Ministers with virtually supreme power. His great energy found frequent outlets in travel and in long speeches extolling the virtues of communism, the glories of Russia, and the evils of capitalism. But by 1964 his boastfulness, unpredictability, and increasing taste for arbitrary personal power had united his colleagues against him. Catching him unawares, they replaced him by Leonid Brezhnev as First Secretary of the Party and Alexei Kosygin as Chairman of the Council of Ministers, and forced him into impotent retirement. In the meantime in the U.S.A. the presidency

THE U.S.A. AND THE U.S.S.R. 561

of General Eisenhower (1953–61) had seen the end of the Korean War and the admission of Alaska and Hawaii into the Union, bringing the total number of states to fifty. The bright promise of his successor's presidency (John Fitzgerald Kennedy, the youngest and the first Roman Catholic president) was suddenly cut off by his assassination in 1963.

Both the United States and the U.S.S.R. have shown a disposition to interfere in the affairs of other nations, particularly if they consider such interference necessary for their security. Russia resents American military bases in Europe; to balance this, Cuba, north of the Caribbean Sea and not far from the United States, has received much help from Russia, and was put under an economic embargo by President Kennedy's administration. In 1961 there was an unsuccessful attempt at invasion by a mixed force of exiled Cubans and American volunteers. In the late autumn of 1962 the Russians established missile bases on the island. The Americans demanded their withdrawal, imposed a blockade, and were on the point of invading Cuba, when the Russians agreed to dismantle the bases and withdraw their missiles. The most protracted clash has been over the city of Berlin, which is geographically in East Germany but has a West German section kept in being by American, British, and French forces. In 1948 Stalin tried to starve out the West Germans, but was defeated by an airlift organized on a very large scale. In 1961 the East Germans built a wall to prevent their people from crossing over to the more prosperous Western sector of the city.

Between the two most powerful rivals common interests have led to the formation of a third bloc in the U.N.—a loose association known as the Afro-Asian group. India and many of the newly emerging states of Africa, the Near East, and South-East Asia had to a varying degree the same problems of inexperience, poverty, over-population, or under-development. Although they might accept economic aid from the prosperous rivals ready to court their support, these countries felt that their true interests lay in non-involvement with either the Eastern or the Western group. But this did not mean that they were immune from war, as could be shown by Indian border disputes and by Chinese intervention in Laos and elsewhere. In South-East Asia China showed no intention of letting Russia mould her policy, particularly when she almost openly backed North Vietnam against American resistance to Vietcong (communist) infiltration in South Vietnam (1961–). An even more dangerous prospect opened in 1964 with China's explosion of her first nuclear device. Furthermore China was outside the restraining influences of the U.N., had the largest population in the world, and unlike Russia claimed that she would gain rather than lose from the outbreak of full-scale warfare.

The twentieth century will always be notable as a great age of scientific and technical achievement. There has been an enormous increase of air travel, and the invention of the jet engine has made it possible for aeroplanes to fly faster than the speed of sound. New machines like the helicopter and the amphibious hovercraft have added to the wonders of transport. The productivity of the earth has been made greater by vast irrigation enterprises like the Kariba Dam harnessing the waters of the Zambesi in central Africa, the building of the Aswan High Dam in Upper Egypt, and the conservation of the waters of the Ganges and the Indus in India. French engineers have made the barren Sahara into a land of plenty by the extraction of oil and natural gas.

At the end of the fifteenth century European civilization burst the bounds of its own continent and for three centuries set the pattern and the pace for the development of the whole world. In the second half of the twentieth century mankind burst the bounds of his own planet and began travelling in inter-planetary space. The Russians led the way in 1957, and launched the first man into space in 1961; the Americans matched this achievement the next year. Since then these two nations, leading the world in strength, wealth, and technology, have raced neck and neck towards the goal of landing men on the moon and bringing them safely back to earth.

But in spite of these startling technical achievements man is threatened today by an increase in his own numbers beyond what his own planet can support. On the eve of the Industrial Revolution in 1750 the population of the world numbered between 650 and 850 million people, and was increasing at the rate of 0·3 to 0·4 per cent. per year. By 1959 it had reached about 2,907 million, and had been increasing for some time at the rate of 1·7 per cent. per year. If this rate of increase is maintained until the end of the present century, world population will then reach approximately 6,000 million inhabitants. Improved medical knowledge and practice and better hygiene have eradicated many diseases which formerly limited the rate of increase, particularly by killing over half the children born before they reached the age at which they could in their turn have children themselves. The resulting almost unrestricted growth of population in the industrially under-developed countries of the world is already having two consequences: it is estimated that at least 2,000 million of the world's inhabitants are either insufficiently or unsuitably fed; and the struggle to provide, however inadequately, for the ever-increasing swarm of people is holding back the industrial development of the under-developed countries. There is a grave danger of the permanent division of the world into rich and poor nations, and of the gap between the standards of living of the rich and the poor becoming even wider than it is today. Voluntary limitation of births has always accompanied industrialization and the improved living standards which result from industrialization; the problem facing the world today is how to enable the peoples of the poor lands to limit the number of their children in order that they may industrialize and enjoy the resulting improved standard of life.

The civilization of the twentieth century is, in many respects, the fitting culmination of the endeavours and aspirations of the past. In some ways, such as in art and in literature, the world of today cannot claim superiority over the world of centuries ago. The literary achievements of the Greeks and the artistic works of the great painters of the Renascence have never been surpassed. Biologically man has not advanced for 30,000 years. The Cro-Magnons were physically superior to the human beings of today; their brains were heavier, and their average height was 6 feet 3 inches. But the scientific wonders of modern times—wireless, television, the telephone, the gramophone, the cinematograph, the motor-car, aviation, the release of nuclear energy, space travel—have no counterparts in the past; in these respects our civilization is immeasurably superior to any which has preceded it. Socially too there have been great advances, exemplified by widespread movements against slavery, the sense of duty towards backward races, the extension among progressive peoples of the franchise and of education, the provision of pensions for the aged, state insurance against accident, sickness, and unemployment, acts improving the conditions of factories, regulating hours of labour, and ensuring greater safety for those engaged in dangerous occupations. Governments show increasing concern for public health, and the death-rate has been substantially reduced. Life under normal conditions is much more secure than it was a hundred or even fifty years ago. Medical science is advancing rapidly; many diseases have practically disappeared, and many others are far less prevalent; and the work of great doctors like Pasteur, Lord Lister the initiator of antiseptic surgery,

MODERN CIVILISATION

Morton and Simpson who introduced anaesthetics, and Sir Alexander Fleming the discoverer of penicillin, has done an incalculable amount towards the relief of physical pain. The zeal for knowledge and the spirit of exploration are as keen as ever. The discovery of the North and South Poles, the conquest of the air, and the successful ascent of Mount Everest, the world's highest mountain, in May 1953 by the New Zealander Hillary and the Sherpa Tensing, are as glorious examples of courage and endurance as the exploits of Columbus or Francis Drake.

But there is still much about modern civilization that is ugly and disquieting, such as pauperism, unemployment, slums, and worst of all, war, the most enduring relic of barbarism. The hopes which enabled mankind to endure the two most devastating wars of all time are still far from fulfilment. Europe has lost its supremacy in the world; Asia is a seething cauldron; there are many dark shadows over Africa; and the menace of militant communism has caused the world to be divided into two hostile camps, the one dominated by the United States and the other by Russia in the West and China in the East. The genius of scientists has been used to devise more and more terrible weapons of destruction such as the atom bomb, two of which wiped out the Japanese cities of Hiroshima and Nagasaki in 1945; the hydrogen bomb which has since been discovered is far more destructive, and another World War may mean the end of civilized society. The United Nations Organization, like its predecessor the League of Nations, has done much excellent social work, but it has still to solve the problem of the over-mighty nation which menaces world peace. Selfishness and fear still dominate men's minds; Reason's greatest conquest is yet to come. John Stuart Mill once predicted that all the great sources of human suffering would ultimately be overcome. This would mean not only an advance in medical science, where it may not unreasonably be expected, but also in political and social science. It would mean the abolition of war, the disappearance of crime, the end of slums, the breaking of racial barriers, the extinction of class hatred, the control of the growth of population, and a degree of individual wisdom and unselfishness which may appear beyond the realms of possibility, but which must be the aim of all progressive civilizations. Real progress is almost invariably the result of attempts to attain the apparently unattainable.

SOME IMPORTANT DATES IN MEDIEVAL AND MODERN HISTORY

A.D.

527–65 The reign of the Emperor Justinian.
570–632 The Life of Mohammed.
732 Charles Martel defeated the Mohammedans at Tours.
771–814 The reign of Charles the Great.
800 Charles the Great crowned Emperor at Rome—the beginning of the Holy Roman Empire.
1066 The Norman Conquest of England.
1095 The First Crusade.
1198–1216 Innocent III, Pope.
1215 Magna Carta signed by the English King John.
1226 Death of Francis of Assisi.
1227 Death of Jenghiz Khan.
1271–95 The travels of Marco Polo.
1309 The Papacy shifted from Rome to Avignon.
1348 The Black Death.
1378–1417 The Great Schism in the Papacy, ended by the acknowledgement by all Roman Catholics of one Pope, whose headquarters were to be at Rome.
1384 The Death of John Wycliffe.
1415 John Huss burned at Constance.
1453 Constantinople captured by the Ottoman Turks.
1492 Columbus's first voyage to America.
1498 Vasco da Gama discovered a sea route to India.
1519 Leonardo da Vinci died. Magellan's expedition started to sail round the world. Cortez entered the city of Mexico.
1521 Luther at the Diet of Worms.
1525 The Mogul Empire founded in India.
1539 The Jesuit Order founded.
1546 Death of Martin Luther.
1547 Ivan the Terrible took the title of Czar of Russia.
1556–1605 The reign of Akbar the Great in India.
1564–1616 The Life of William Shakespeare.
1609 Dutch independence secured.
1618–48 The Thirty Years' War.
1620 The Pilgrim Fathers left England in the *Mayflower*.
1642–60 The Great Rebellion in England.

IMPORTANT DATES

1643 Louis XIV of France began his long reign of 72 years.
1644 The beginning of the Manchu Dynasty in China.
1688 The 'Glorious Revolution' in England.
1689–1725 Peter the Great Czar of Russia.
1707 End of the Mogul Empire in India.
1740 Frederick the Great became King of Prussia.
1756–63 The Seven Years War. England and France fought for supremacy in North America and India.
1775–83 The American War of Independence.
1776 (4 July) The American Declaration of Independence.
1789–94 The Great French Revolution.
1795 Napoleon embarked upon his career of conquest.
1815 The Battle of Waterloo and the final overthrow of Napoleon.
1830 The First Passenger Railway (Liverpool to Manchester).
1832 The First Reform Bill passed by the English Parliament.
1840 China began to attract the serious attention of Europeans.
1848 The great year of revolutions in Europe.
1853 Japan opened to foreign nations.
1859 The beginning of the struggle for Italian Independence.
1871 William I of Prussia became German Emperor. The Third French Republic established.
1912 China became a republic.
1914–18 The First World War.
1917 Establishment of the Soviet Republic of Russia.
1920 The first meeting of the League of Nations.
1922 The Fascist March on Rome.
1923 Proclamation of the Turkish Republic.
1934 Hitler became head of the German State.
1935–6 Italian Conquest of Abyssinia.
1936 Civil War in Spain.
1939–45 The Second World War.
1945 Formation of the United Nations Organization (U.N.O.).
1947 The Fourth French Republic established. India and Pakistan became self-governing Dominions.
1948 Burma became a republic, and Ceylon a Dominion.
1949 Establishment of the People's Republic of China. Israel and Indonesia became independent states.
1950 Vietnam became an independent state.
1950–3 The Korean War.
1953 Death of Stalin.
1954 First hydrogen bombs in the U.S.A. and the U.S.S.R.
1955 Risings in French North African possessions.

IMPORTANT DATES 569

1956 Israel, Britain, and France attacked Egypt—the 'Suez Incident'. Hungarian rebellion against Russia.
1957 The U.S.S.R. launched the first space vehicle.
1958 The European Economic Community (Common Market founded. The Fifth French Republic established.
1960–5 Civil war in the Congo.
1961 The U.S.S.R. launched the first manned space vehicle. South Africa left the British Commonwealth. Beginning of American resistance to Vietcong in South Vietnam.
1962 The first American manned space vehicle. France recognized the independence of Algeria.
1963 Assassination of President Kennedy in the U.S.A.
1964 Dismissal of Khrushchev in the U.S.S.R. China's first nuclear explosion.
1965 Rhodesia's Unilateral Declaration of Independence.
1966–7 Serious disorders in China.
1967 Arab-Israeli War. Civil war in Nigeria.

TIME CHARTS

B.C.	MEDITERRANEAN COUNTRIES West	EGYPT	BABYLONIA & PERSIA	INDIA	CHINA
3400		First Dynasty			
3200					
3000					
2800		PYRAMID AGE	Sumerian Empire overthrown by Sargon		
2600					
2400		FEUDAL AGE			
2200			Hammurabi conquers Babylon		
2000	Copper in general use				
1800					
1600	Zenith of Cretan Civilisation	End of Hyksos domination IMPERIAL AGE	Palestine settled by the Jews		SHANG
1400				Rig Veda	DYNASTY
1200					
1000	Cnossos destroyed		Zoroaster founds his religion		CHU DYNASTY

TIME CHARTS

B.C.	MEDITERRANEAN COUNTRIES West	EGYPT	BABYLONIA & PERSIA	INDIA	CHINA
1000	Cnossos destroyed	Shishak plunders Solomon's temple	Saul king of Israel, David, Solomon. Separation of Israel and Judah	STRUGGLES OF ARYANS AND DRAVIDIANS	Y
900	Building of Carthage		TWO INDEPENDENT EMPIRES – ASSYRIAN & BABYLONIAN		T S
800	Rome Founded — First Olympiad		Tiglath Pileser III conquered Babylon. ASSYRIAN Sennacherib		A N
700	PERIOD OF THE KINGS — Homeric Songs written	Egypt conquered by Assyrians under Assurbanipal	Esarhaddon. EMPIRE Fall of Nineveh		Y
600	OF ROME — Age of Greek Tyrants		CHALDEAN Nebuchadnezzar EMPIRE Cyrus the Great conquers Babylon		D — Confucius
500	Battle of Marathon, Thermopylae, Salamis. Age of Pericles — Peloponnesian War	Jerusalem destroyed. Egypt conquered by Persians under Cambyses	Darius Xerxes PERSIAN EMPIRE Retreat of the Ten Thousand	Buddha	H O
400	Ascendancy of Sparta — Battle of Chaeronea. PERIOD OF CONQUESTS OF ALEXANDER the GREAT				
300	CONQUEST Laws codified – Twelve tables OF ITALY BY THE ROMANS	PTOLEMIES	SELEUCIDS	Chandragupta	
200	First Punic War — Second Punic War			King Asoka	Shi-Kwang-Ti Great Wall

TIME CHARTS

B.C.	EUROPE Western	EUROPE Eastern	ASIA MINOR	CHINA
-200			Battle of Magnesia	
	Destruction of Carthage	Destruction of Corinth by the Romans		
100	The Gracchi			HAN
	All Italians become Roman citizens		Mithridates	
	Death of Marius			
	Death of Sulla			
	Julius Caesar is murdered			
A.D.	Augustus			
	Tiberius		Jesus of Nazareth	DYNASTY
	Nero		St Paul	
100	Vespasian	ROMAN	Jerusalem destroyed by Titus	
	Titus			
	Domitian			
	Trajan			
	Hadrian			
	Antoninus Pius			
	Marcus Aurelius			
200	Septimius Severus	EMPIRE		
	Caracalla			
	Decius		SPREAD AND	UNREST
	Aurelian		TRIUMPH OF	
300	Diocletian	Constantinople built	CHRISTIANITY	AND
	Constantine			
	Theodosius			
400	Rome sacked by Visigoths	INVASIONS OF ATTILA AND THE HUNS		DISUNION
	Fall of Rome			
500				

ROMAN EMPIRE 27 B.C.–476 A.D.

TIME CHARTS

A.D.	England	EUROPE Western	EUROPE Southern	EUROPE Eastern		ASIA
500	SETTLEMENT OF ANGLES, SAXONS AND JUTES IN ENGLAND St. Augustine's landing	Clovis SETTLEMENTS OF FRANKS IN	} St. Benedict	} JUSTINIAN		Turks invade China
600	PROGRESS —Cædmon & TRIUMPH OF CHRISTIANITY	FRANCE AND WESTERN EUROPE	} Gregory the Great PERIOD OF LOMBARD RULE		} MOHAMMED ERA OF MOHAMMEDAN
700	} Bede MERCIAN SUPREMACY Offa	—Battle of Tours	IN NORTH ITALY End of Lombard rule in north Italy Crowning of Charles as Emperor		B Y Z A N T I N E E M P I R E	} CONQUESTS
800	WEST SAXON SUPREMACY } Egbert	CHARLES THE GREAT Louis the Pious crowned Emperor at Rheims Charles the Bald [First King of France] Treaty of Mersen	GROWTH OF FEUDALISM Arabs in Italy			} Haroun-al-Raschid Caliph of Bagdad DECAY OF MOHAMMEDAN
900	NORSE INVASION } Alfred the Great Edward the Elder Athelstan } Edgar	Rolf the Ganger Founds Dukedom of Normandy Otto the Great } Hugh Capet	Hungarians in Italy Saxon Emperors			POWER
1000	Ethelred the Unready					

TIME CHARTS

A.D.	Northern	England	France	E U R O P E Spain	Empire & Papacy	Eastern [Byzantine] Empire	ASIA
1000		Canute King of England, Norway and Denmark — Edward the Confessor — Battle of Senlac	CAPETIAN KINGS				Seljuk Turks conquer Syria & Palestine
1100		NORMAN PERIOD — Henry i — Richard i		THE FIRST CRUSADE	Emperor Henry iv — Gregory vii Pope		
1200		PLANTAGENET PERIOD — Magna Carta — De Montfort's Parliament — Roger Bacon — Edward i	Albigensian Crusade	THE SECOND CRUSADE — St. Dominic — THE THIRD CRUSADE	Frederick Barbarossa — Lombard League — Frederick ii — Innocent iii Pope	LATIN EMPERORS	Saladin — Jinghiz Khan, Kublais Pekin — MONGOL CONQUESTS — Kubla Khan — Travels of the Polos
1300		John Wycliffe — Peasant's revolt	Morgarten — HOUSE OF VALOIS–1589 — NATIONAL CONSOLIDATION & RISE OF ABSOLUTE MONARCHY — 100 YEARS WAR	THE BLACK DEATH	Dante — Boniface viii Pope — Rienzi — Hanseatic League — FLORENCE — VISCONTI·IN·MILAN — Francis of Assisi — Rivalry of Venice and Genoa	BYZANTINE EMPERORS	
1400	Ivan the Great of Russia	LANCASTRIAN PERIOD — Caxton — YORKIST PERIOD — TUDORS	Louis xi	Union of Castile and Aragon — Fall of Granada — Columbus — Vasco da Gama	Hussite Wars — Printing — MEDICI·IN — Wars between Venice & Milan — Leonardo da — Michel Angelo	Fall of Constantinople	Timurlane — OTTOMAN CONQUESTS — MING DYNASTY — YUAN DYNASTY
1500							

TIME CHARTS

A.D.	Northern	England	France	EUROPE Spain	Germany
1500		Henry vii {TUDOR PERIOD: Henry viii, Edward vi, Mary, Elizabeth} {REFORMATION}	Louis xii / Francis j / Wars of Religion	Death of Ferdinand of Spain / Magellan / Emperor Charles v / Jesuits founded / Philip ii, King of Spain	Luther starts the Reformation {REFORMATION & COUNTER REFORMATION}
	Netherlands revolt from Spain	Spanish Armada / Shakespeare			
1600	Gustavus Adolphus, King of Sweden	{STUART PERIOD: James j, Charles j, Cromwell/Great Rebellion/Milton, Charles ii, James ii, William iii}	Henry iv / Richelieu / The Fronde / Louis xiv	Expulsion of Moors from Spain / Portugal independent of Spain	Thirty Years War / The great Elector of Prussia
	Wars between England and Holland / French invasion of Holland / Peter the Great of Russia {Charles xii of Sweden}	Newton			First King of Prussia
1700	{HOUSE OF ROMANOV IN RUSSIA}	Anne / George j / George ij / {George iij}	Molière / Louis xv / Racine / Voltaire / Louis xvi / French Revolution	War of Spanish Suc—	War of Austrian Succession / Seven Years War {Frederick the Great}
	Catherine ij of Russia	{HANOVERIAN PERIOD} {INDUSTRIAL REVOLUTION}			
1800		George iv / William iv / Victoria	THE CAREER OF NAPOLEON / Waterloo / Napoleon iij / Franco-German War / THIRD		Year of / GERMAN EMPIRE {Francis Joseph of Austria}
		{DEMOCRATIC LEGISLATION}			
1900	Russian Revolution	Edward vii	REPUBLIC ←	← FIRST WORLD	
	Stalin	George v			
		George vj / Elizabeth jj	← SECOND WORLD — Hitler		
		United Nations Organization, predominance new independent nations in Asia			

TIME CHARTS

Italy	Eastern Europe	ASIA	AFRICA	AMERICA	AUSTRALIA
Foreign invasions { Sack of Rome { End of the Council of Trent — Battle of Lepanto	Sulieman the Magnificent	Akbar the Great English East India Co. founded	Hawkins gets slaves from Guinea coast	Columbus' last voyage { Spanish conquest of Mexico { Pizarro conquers Peru { Jacques Cartier claims Canada for France { Drake and others fight Spaniards on Spanish Main { Raleigh's expedition to Virginia	
— Galileo dies Venice, the Empire, Poland & Russia fight the Turks	EMPIRE	Dutch take the Moluccas { French East India Company	Dutch take possession of the Cape of Good Hope	Virginia colonised { Pilgrim Fathers { New Amsterdam becomes New York	
— cession BUONAPARTE Revolutions { Italy a Nation	OTTOMAN EMPIRE Period of Polish Partitions { Greece Independent DISMEMBERMENT OF TURKISH EMPIRE	MOGUL IN INDIA Death of the Great Mogul Period of unrest and confusion in India Battle of Plassey INDIA RULED BY THE ENGLISH EAST INDIA COMPANY Indian Mutiny Rise of Japan BRITISH EMPIRE OF INDIA China a Republic	Napoleon in Egypt Conquest of Algiers by France ENGLISH COLONISATION OF SOUTH AFRICA Africa partitioned among great European powers	Wolfe takes Quebec { American Declaration of Independence { Brazil and Mexico independent { American Civil War	{ Captain Cook in Australia { English colony of New South Wales founded { English colony of Tasmania { Western Tasmania { New Zealand annexed by England
WAR 1914 – 1918					→
{ Mussolini { WAR	1939 – 1945				→
of U.S.A. and Russia, Europe divided by "Iron Curtain" nationalist feeling in Africa					

p P

INDEX

AACHEN (Aix - la - Chapelle), 288, 297
Abbasids, 280, 282
Abdul Hamid, 520
Abelard, 384
Abraham (Patriarch), 48, 244, 275
Abu Bakr, 274, 278
Abu Simbel (temple), 44, 159
Acre, 84, 320, 322, 453
Actium, 182, 255
Adrianople, 518, 522
Aegospotami, 137, 140
Aeschylus, 118, 131, 394
Afghanistan, 68, 155, 376, 558
Agricultural Revolution, 472
Akbar the Great, 376-7
Akhnaton, 34-43, 64, 254
Alabama (cruiser), 527
Alaric (the Goth), 213-19, 227, 255
Albania, 483, 520, 522, 551
Albigenses, 326, 328
Alcibiades, 135-7, 138
Alexander VI (Pope), 306, 356, 402
Alexander the Great, 15, 46, 71, 77, 108, 116, 140, 144-52, 154, 238, 255, 421, 464
Alexandria, 142, 150-2, 199, 240, 345
Alfred the Great, 360
Algiers, 382, 496, 552
Alhambra, 280
Alphabet, 18, 54, 63, 79, 85, 90, 104-5, 161, 234
Alsace, 496, 534, 535
Altamira, 6, 9
Alva (Duke of), 411
Amarna (Tel el), 34, 39, 42
Amenhotep III, 32, 34, 44
Amen-Ra, 34, 36, 39, 42, 148, 152
Amerigo Vespucci, 400
Amiens, 316, 349
Ammonites, 241, 253
Amorites, 50, 254
Amos (Prophet), 108, 242
Amphitheatre, 186, 199
Anaxagoras, 132, 151
Angles, 219, 360
Anglo-Saxon Chronicle, 302
Ankara, 523, 541
Antioch, 150, 246, 250, 318
Antiochus the Great, 171
Antiochus Epiphanes, 238, 244
Antony (Mark), 180, 182, 184, 255
Aphrodite (Venus), 52, 85, 106, 140
Apocrypha, 240

Apollo, 67, 100, 105, 116, 124, 141, 268
Aqueducts, 199, 206
Aquinas (Thomas), 332
Arabia (and Arabs), 46, 68, 85, 141, 199, 252, 273-4, 316, 345, 370, 400, 522
Arabian Nights Entertainments, 280, 285
Arameans, 54-55, 63, 234
Arbitration, 134
Archimedes, 142, 150
Architecture, 32, 64, 97, 104-5, 116, 128, 151, 198, 206, 232, 261, 265, 270, 276, 280, 284, 348-50, 353-4, 356, 390
Argentine Republic, 466
Ariovistus, 231
Aristagoras, 66
Aristophanes, 137
Aristarchus, 142
Aristotle, 140, 144, 147, 148, 158, 249, 384, 387, 425, 464
Armada (Spanish), 369
Armenia, 68, 192, 382
Aryan, 46, 59, 79, 82, 83, 98, 144, 160, 166, 233, 377
Asia Minor, 39, 60, 64, 68, 69, 89, 98, 104, 112, 124, 134, 141, 166, 170, 182, 199, 210, 213, 250, 254, 267, 370, 371, 380, 523
Asoka, 155, 255
Assembly (American), 432; (Frankish), 292; (French National), 438; (Ancient Greek), 99, 100, 115, 126, 127, 135-6; (United Nations), 550, 551; (of the Roman Plebs), 164; (Teutonic), 227
Assurbanipal, 56
Assyria, 44, 54-58, 60, 64, 85, 90, 97, 110, 233, 234, 236, 242-3, 254, 278, 376
Astronomy, 54, 58, 59, 132, 151, 261, 285, 392
Athena (Goddess), 104, 106, 128, 130, 132, 188
Athens, 66, 67, 69, 71, 90, 92, 100, 102, 104, 112, 114-19, 122-44, 147, 164, 171, 172, 175, 184, 206, 250, 254, 394, 464
Atomic bomb, 548, 558
Aton (God), 34, 36, 38, 39
Atreus (Treasure House of), 96
Attila the Hun, 219-20, 255, 264

Augsburg, 310, 312 345, 350
Augustus (Emperor). *See* Caesar (Augustus)
Augustine, Saint (of Hippo), 203, 288
Augustine, Saint (Missionary), 267, 272
Austerlitz, 454, 458
Australia, 447, 502, 509, 543, 552
Austria, 358, 368, 412, 418, 424-8, 437, 445, 452, 453, 454, 456, 460, 461, 465, 466, 467, 475, 479, 482, 483, 484, 486, 488, 489, 492, 494, 515, 517, 520, 522, 533-4, 535, 540, 547
Austrian Succession (War of), 426
Avesta, 64
Avignon, 336, 354, 365, 559
Aztecs, 402
BAAL, 84, 241
Baalbec, 199
Babel (Tower of), 48
Babylon, 44, 47, 48, 50, 54, 56, 58, 60, 147, 236, 254, 278
Babylonia, 12, 14, 42, 46-59, 63, 64, 69, 90, 92, 94, 199, 234, 236
Bacon (Sir Francis), 410
Bacon (Roger), 332, 384, 386
Bagdad, 280, 282, 284, 285, 286, 370, 371, 382, 505
Balkans, 166, 468, 516-22
Barca (Family), 168, 169
Basilica, 265, 266, 350, 354
Bastille, 438, 447
Bath (England), 199
Baths, 92, 194, 198, 199, 206, 212
Bavaria, 288, 294, 368
Beast (Roman wild beast shows), 184-6
Becket (Thomas à), 325
Bede (The Venerable), 272
Belgium, 184, 263, 297, 345, 350, 416, 424, 461, 463, 467, 474, 475, 483-4, 500, 534, 546, 547, 549
Benares, 153
Benedict (Saint), 267-72
Benes, 546
Berlin, 424, 517, 518, 561
Bernard of Clairvaux, 323
Beza (Theodore), 408
Bible, 55, 58, 94, 104, 203, 231, 234, 238, 240-6, 294
Bismarck, 480, 486, 490-5, 496, 498

INDEX

Black Death (plague), 364
Boccaccio, 353, 386, 387
Boers, 497
Bohemia, 290, 315, 336, 424, 479, 484
Bolivar, 466
Bolshevism. *See* Communism
Boniface (Archbishop of Mainz), 272
Boniface VIII (Pope), 335–6, 365
Borodino, 458
Botha (Louis), 497
Botticelli, 354
Brahmans, 77, 82, 154–5
Bramante, 356
Brazil, 467, 482
Britain. *See* England
British Commonwealth and Empire, 468, 482–3, 497–8, 502, 505, 543, 552–4, 559–60
Brunellesco, 353
Buddha and Buddhism, 80, 82, 152–9, 254, 267, 268, 374, 375
Bulgaria, 66, 378, 516, 520, 522, 549, 551
Burgundy (and Burgundians), 214, 219, 220, 297, 365, 366
Burke (Edmund), 447, 509
Byzantine Empire, 261–2, 291, 380
Byzantium, 212
CAESAR (Augustus or Octavius), 180, 182, 189–90, 195, 200, 222, 255, 291
Caesar (Julius), 155, 166, 178–81, 200, 226, 231, 255, 421
Cairo, 280, 284
Caligula, 190, 194, 208, 248
Caliph (origin of title), 276
Calvin (John), 407–8
Calvinism, 408, 410, 411, 416
Cambyses, 60, 63
Cameroons, 498
Canada, 426, 430, 432, 435, 482, 497, 509, 532, 543, 552
Cannae, 168
Canning (George), 460
Canossa, 310
Canute, 360
Cape Colony, 468, 497, 500
Capitalism, 112, 472, 474, 475, 476, 478, 479–80, 500, 502, 505, 530
Capitularies (Frankish) 292, 300
Capua, 169
Caracalla, 212
Carnac, 6, 89
Carthage, 59, 88, 134, 136, 147, 166, 168–71, 175, 183, 219, 220, 254, 255
Cassiodorus, 260
Caste, 77, 79, 82, 97, 154, 377

Catherine II of Russia, 424, 428
Catholicism (Roman), 203, 240, 259, 264–72, 306–38, 372–4, 377, 383, 384, 388, 392, 404–12, 414, 416, 430, 438, 486, 495
Cato (Marcus), 170, 195
Caves and Cave-dwellers, 2, 3, 5, 6, 8
Cavour, 486, 488, 489, 490
Caxton, 388
Cellini (Benvenuto), 390
Cesare Borgia, 306, 356
Ceylon, 509, 552
Chaeronea, 140, 146, 255
Chaldea, 44, 54, 58, 59, 60, 236, 253
Chandragupta, 154
Charlemagne (Charles the Great), 155, 259, 262, 287–96, 298, 300, 301, 306, 313, 418, 559
Charles Albert of Sardinia, 484, 486
Charles the Bold of Burgundy, 366
Charles I (of England), 413, 417
Charles II (of England), 413, 414, 430
Charles V (Emperor), 218, 369, 406, 416
Charles Martel, 278, 287, 559
Chartists, 476, 484–6
Chaucer (Geoffrey), 334, 362, 387, 475
Chiang Kai Shek, 556
Chile, 466
China, 14, 72–78, 147, 154, 155, 158, 213, 254, 255, 286, 344, 370, 371, 372, 374, 410, 502, 503, 504, 550, 551, 554–6, 558, 560, 562, 565
Christianity, 40, 130, 152, 189, 190, 192, 203, 208–12, 218, 222, 230–1, 240, 241, 246–52, 255, 263, 264–72, 273, 290, 298, 372, 374, 377, 410, 449, 502
Churchill, 548
Cicero, 180, 183, 184, 186, 202–3, 386
Cimon, 126
Cities and Citizenship (Ancient), 86, 100, 110, 124, 160, 162, 165–6, 175, 176, 183, 198, 212, 232, 236
Civil War (American), 233, 524–8; (English), 411, 417, 559; (Fronde), 417; (Roman), 176, 180
Cleisthenes, 115, 126
Cleon, 135, 137
Cleopatra, 180, 182
Clermont, 316
Clovis, 261, 262, 263

Cnossos, 90, 92, 254, 517
Codes of Law (Draco), 114; (Hammurabi), 50; (Jewish), 238; (Justinian), 200, 261–2; (Napoleon), 462, 463–4; (Solon), 114–15; (Theodosian), 222; (Twelve Tables), 162
Colombia, 466
Colonies, 86, 88, 108, 110, 429–34, 496–510, 528, 530, 533, 552
Colosseum, 186, 192, 198
Columbus (Christopher), 372, 374, 396–400, 565
Communism, 437, 442, 481, 515–16, 536–8, 540, 551, 552, 554, 556, 558
Confucius, 76, 156, 158–9, 254
Congo State, 500, 509, 559
Congress (U.S.A.), 433, 434, 435, 526
Constance (Council of), 338
Constantine (Emperor), 211, 212, 231, 255, 265, 266
Constantinople, 212, 220, 222, 227, 258, 260, 261, 266, 267, 320, 345, 353, 371, 378, 380, 382, 387, 505, 519, 517, 518, 522, 523, 541, 559
Consul (Roman), 612, 180
Consulate (French), 453, 454, 475
Copernicus, 142, 392
Cordova, 252, 278, 280, 284
Corinth, 96, 134–7, 141, 172, 206, 250, 255
Corsica, 159, 168, 213, 450
Cortez, 402, 559
Cotton, 58, 85, 469, 470
Counter Reformation, 408–12
Crete, 14, 44, 85, 90–96, 97, 159, 234, 254, 517
Crimea, 212, 488, 517
Croesus (King of Lydia), 60
Cro-Magnon, 5, 6, 8, 14, 564
Cromwell (Oliver), 413
Crusades, 259, 315–25, 340, 344, 352, 382, 559
Cuba, 398, 404, 531, 561
Cunaxa, 71
Cuneiform Writing, 47, 55, 63, 90, 104, 233, 234
Cynoscephalae, 171
Cyprus, 44, 86, 110, 208, 388, 520, 552
Cyrus the Great, 58, 60, 236, 254
Czechoslovakia, 535, 546–7, 551
DAEDALUS, 92
Dalai Lama, 156, 556
Damascus, 54, 55, 280
Danes, 286, 297–8, 360
Dante, 353, 386
Danton, 444

INDEX

Dardanelles, 68, 89, 378, 517
Darius I (the Great), 63–68
David, King of Israel, 86, 234, 241
Davis (Jefferson), 526
Davis (John), 402
Dead (Book of the), 28, 37
Declaration of Independence (American), 433, 434, 560
Delos, 67, 100, 124, 134
Delphi, 71, 100, 115, 116, 138
Democracy, 115, 127, 136, 138–9
Demosthenes, 140, 144
Denmark, 89, 297, 346, 360, 392, 546, 547, 549
Diaz (Bartholomew), 394
Dictator (Roman), 164, 168, 176, 180
Diderot, 421, 422
Diet (German), 368, 467; (Polish), 428
Diocletian (Emperor), 211, 212, 222
Directory (French), 452, 453
Disraeli, 253, 517, 518
Divine Right of Kings, 287, 413, 418
Dolmens, 9
Dominic (Saint) and Dominicans, 268, 330, 332, 334, 403, 408
Dominions, 509, 543, 552
Domitian (Emperor), 194, 210, 211
Draco, 114, 254
Drake (Sir Francis), 403, 558
Drama (comedy and tragedy), 131, 137, 144, 205
Dravidians, 377
Druids, 12
Duma (Russian), 515
Dürer (Albrecht), 393
EDGAR (King of England), 360
Edward I (King of England), 322, 335
Edward III (King of England), 364
Egbert, King of the West Saxons, 360
Egypt, 12, 14, 15–46, 48, 54, 55, 56, 58, 60, 63, 64, 68, 72, 77, 85, 86, 88, 89, 90, 92, 94, 97, 110, 126, 147, 148, 150–2, 156, 159, 180, 182, 188, 196, 199, 208, 232, 233, 234, 241, 242, 253, 254, 267, 273, 278, 280, 285, 370, 376, 377, 382, 453, 497–8, 500, 510, 553, 558, 560
Eisenhower, President, 561
Elba, 461, 462
Electors (Imperial), 315
Electricity, 470
Elgin Marbles, 128

Elizabeth I (Queen of England), 364, 403
Elizabeth II, 549
Encyclopédie (French), 421, 422, 437
England (and the English), 12, 189, 192, 199, 205, 253, 263, 266, 267, 272, 287, 288, 298, 300, 301, 302, 304, 308, 309, 312, 318, 320, 322, 325, 335, 336, 345, 346, 348, 350, 359, 360–4, 365, 366, 367, 392, 393–4, 396, 402, 403, 404, 407, 412–16, 417, 418, 421, 423, 426, 429, 430, 433, 434, 435, 437, 440, 442, 445, 446, 447, 453, 454, 458, 460, 461, 466, 469–78, 481, 482, 483, 484–6, 497–8, 500, 502, 505, 509, 510, 517, 518, 520, 522, 527, 532, 541, 542–3, 547, 549, 550, 552–4, 556, 559–60
Entente Cordiale, 510
Epaminondas, 140
Ephesus, 66, 227, 246, 250
Epictetus, 142
Epicurus, 141–2
Erasmus, 393, 404, 406
Eratosthenes, 151
Etruria (and Etruscans), 112, 159–60, 165, 188
Euclid, 142, 150, 151
Euphrates, 29, 46, 47, 110, 146, 147, 150, 190, 278
Euripides, 131, 249, 387, 394
European Economic Community (Common Market), 560
Everest, 557
Ezra, 236, 238, 245
FABIUS (Quintus Fabius Maximus), 165, 168–9
Factories, 88, 112, 195, 196, 469, 470, 472, 474, 475–9
Faraday, 470
Fascism, 538–9
Fashoda, 498
Fatehpur-Sikri, 377
Ferdinand of Aragon, 367, 396, 397, 398
Feudalism, 26, 30, 72, 73, 259, 298–306, 307, 323, 383, 437, 449, 450, 502
Filippo Lippi, 353
Finland, 467, 483, 516
First World War, 428, 480, 496, 505, 510, 515, 516, 522–3, 533–5
Flaminius, 206
Flanders, 320, 345, 365, 366, 392
Florence, 352, 353–4, 356, 358, 387, 396, 400
Flying machines, 92, 386, 392

Formosa, 556
France (and the French), 2, 3, 9, 14, 108, 178, 199, 205, 206, 252, 253, 263, 278, 297, 298, 308, 314, 316, 318, 320, 322, 328, 345, 348, 350, 358, 359, 362, 364, 365–6, 368, 393, 396, 402, 404, 410, 411, 412, 414, 416–22, 423, 426, 427, 430, 435–68, 470, 472, 474, 475, 479–80, 482, 483, 487, 488, 489, 492, 494, 495, 496–7, 498, 500, 501, 502, 509, 510, 515, 517, 522, 524, 526, 541, 542, 543–4, 547, 549, 550, 552, 553
Francis of Assisi, 156, 267, 268, 330–4, 404, 559
Franco, 541, 549
Franco-German War, 480, 494–5, 496
Franks, 220, 226, 232, 259, 260, 262–3, 278, 289–97
Frederick I (Barbarossa), 312–14, 318
Frederick II (Emperor), 314–15, 322
Frederick II (the Great) of Prussia, 422–3, 424, 425, 426, 428, 560
Frobisher (Martin), 402
Fronde, 417, 418
GALILEO, 392
Gama (Vasco da), 396, 400, 502, 559
Gandhi, 553, 554
Garibaldi, 354, 489
Gates (Egyptian Book of), 37
Gauls, 166, 176, 178, 183, 199, 216, 219, 220, 226, 227, 255, 260, 263, 291, 295
Geneva, 407–8, 527, 544
Genoa, 160, 324, 345, 352, 372, 394, 396
Genseric (the Vandal), 219, 220, 226
Geographical discoveries, 15th and 16th centuries, 259, 353, 394–404
George III (of England), 429, 435
Germany (and the Germans), 1, 3, 10, 183, 190, 200, 213, 219, 220, 226–33, 262, 263, 264, 272, 288, 290, 291, 294, 298, 307, 308, 310, 312, 313, 314, 315, 320, 322, 345, 346, 348, 350, 358, 359, 360, 368, 369, 371, 392, 393, 404, 406, 407, 411, 422, 423, 424, 425, 442, 445, 456, 460, 463, 467, 474, 475, 479, 480, 486,

581

INDEX

490–5, 496, 498, 502, 505, 509, 510, 515, 522, 534, 539–40, 541, 547–8, 551
German East Africa, 498, 500
German SW. Africa, 498, 505
Ghent, 345, 350
Ghiberti (Lorenzo), 390–2
Gibraltar, 86, 88, 89
Gilds (guilds), 82, 340–4
Gipsies, 377–8
Girondins, 442
Gladiators, 177, 184, 186, 192, 198, 205, 214
Gladstone, W. E., 517, 518
Godfrey of Bouillon (King of Jerusalem), 318
Gold Coast (Ghana), 497, 552
Good Hope (Cape of), 394, 400, 502
Gothic Architecture, 350, 390
Goths, 212–13, 226, 227, 230–1, 232, 255, 260, 261, 262
Gracchi (Tiberius and Caius), 174–5, 255
Granada, 280, 290, 367, 397
Grant, (General), 527
Great Charter (Magna Carta), 418, 559
Great Elector of Prussia, 422, 423
Greece (and the Greeks), 30, 46, 52, 59, 60, 64, 66–72, 76, 85, 86, 90, 92, 94, 97–144, 146, 150, 152, 154, 158, 159–62, 165, 166, 171–2, 183, 184, 188, 189, 195, 198, 200, 202, 203, 205, 206, 216, 232, 238, 244, 245, 249, 252, 253, 254, 255, 264, 273, 284, 290, 295, 320, 345, 371, 380, 390, 393, 425, 468, 483, 520, 522, 535, 549, 551, 564
Greek language, 382–3, 387
Gregory the Great, 267
Gregory of Tours, 261, 263
Gregory VII (Pope), 266, 309–12
Grimaldi, 5, 6
Guinea Coast, 394, 396
Gunpowder, 374
Gustavus Adolphus (King of Sweden), 411
Gutenburg of Mainz (inventor of printing), 350, 388
HABSBURGS, 368, 424, 456, 484, 488
Hadrian, 192, 208
Hague (The Hague), 484
Hamilton (Alexander), 434
Hammurabi, 50, 53, 254
Hannibal, 165, 166, 168–70, 255
Hanno (Carthaginian), 88
Hanseatic League, 346, 348

Harappa, 78
Harun al Rashid, 282
Hatshepsut (Egyptian Queen), 30
Hawkins (Sir John), 403
Hebrews, 28, 29, 38, 39, 55, 233–6, 241
Hedjaz, 522
Henry I (King of England), 294, 312, 362
Henry II (King of England), 294, 301, 302
Henry IV (Emperor), 310–12
Henry IV (King of France), 420
Henry V (King of England), 364
Henry VIII (King of England), 407
Henry the Navigator, 394
Hera (Juno), 106, 188
Herculaneum, 192
Heresy, 222, 328
Herod Antipas, 240
Herod the Great, 240
Herodotus, 68, 69, 70, 88, 108, 120, 131, 137, 138, 144, 261, 387
Hesiod, 106, 108, 114
Hijira (Mohammedan), 274
Hipparchus, 115, 116
Hippias, 115
Hippocrates, 142
Hiram, King of Tyre, 86
Hitler, 539–40, 547
Hittites, 39, 54, 55, 90, 241
Hohenzollerns, 422, 424
Holbein, 393
Holland (and the Dutch), 263, 288, 367, 393, 402, 404, 410, 413, 414, 416, 418, 420, 423, 456, 463, 467, 483–4, 500, 502, 524, 546, 547, 549, 552
Holy of Holies (Jewish), 208
Holy Roman Empire, 290, 291, 424, 454
Holy Sepulchre, 315, 318
Homer, 98, 102, 105, 106, 171, 195, 254
Honduras, 400
Honorius (Emperor), 212, 213, 214, 216, 219, 224
Horace, 195, 203, 204, 384
Horus, 34, 154, 250
Hosea (Prophet), 243
Huguenots, 410, 420, 423
Hundred Years War, 362, 364, 366
Hungary, 220, 297, 307, 318, 382, 424, 425, 479, 484, 486, 551, 558
Huns, 73–74, 213, 219–20, 255, 264, 370
Hunters (ancient), 2, 6, 14, 73, 76, 82, 231
Huss (John), 336, 338, 559
Hyksos kings of Egypt, 29
ICE Ages, 1, 2

Iceland, 298, 396
Ictinus (architect of the Parthenon), 128
Imhotep (Egyptian architect), 20, 25
Imperialism (Modern), 496–510
India, 14, 58, 63, 77, 78–83, 147, 152–7, 184, 199, 255, 278, 344, 345, 376–7, 383, 394, 396, 400, 402, 403, 410, 426, 453, 502, 509, 517, 547, 552, 553–4, 559, 561–2
Indians (North American), 14, 16, 398
Indonesia, 552, 559
Industrial Revolution, 469–82, 504, 523
Innocent III (Pope), 322, 325, 328, 330, 559
Innocent IV (Pope), 314
Inquisition ('Holy Inquisition'), 328–30, 334, 377
Ionian Greeks, 64, 98, 104, 105, 110, 112, 138
Ireland, 295, 360, 484, 486, 543
Irrigation, 15, 26, 286
Isabella of Castile, Queen of Spain, 367, 396–7, 398
Isaiah (Prophet), 242–3
Isis (Goddess), 34, 79, 154, 208, 209, 250, 251, 252
Islam, 151, 273–87, 290, 297, 306, 314, 315–16, 318, 320, 323, 325, 344, 367, 370, 374, 377, 378, 380, 382, 498, 542, 554
Isocrates, 140, 158
Israel, 553, 558
Israelites, 43, 233–6, 242, 243, 244, 252
Italy, 86, 92, 94, 110, 136, 141, 147, 159–225, 227, 252, 253, 255, 260, 261, 262, 263, 284, 291, 297, 300, 307, 308, 310, 312, 314, 315, 322, 324, 336, 339, 344, 348, 352–9, 368, 382, 384, 385, 386, 387, 389–92, 396, 410, 425, 437, 445, 450, 452, 453, 454, 463, 467, 479, 483, 484, 486–90, 492, 494, 495, 497, 501, 509, 520, 535, 536, 538–9, 541, 548, 549
Ivan the Great (of Russia), 375
Ivan the Terrible, 375, 559
JACOBINS, 444, 452
Jains, 80
Jamaica, 413
James I (King of England), 413, 417
James II (King of England), 414, 446
Janissaries, 378, 380

INDEX

Japan, 147, 155, 372, 502, 504, 505, 509, 514, 515, 536, 547–8, 554–6, 558
Jefferson (Thomas), 433, 436
Jehovah (Jahveh), 241, 242, 244, 328
Jenghiz Khan, 370–1, 375, 376, 377, 378, 557
Jerome (Saint), 203, 219
Jerusalem, 192, 234, 236, 240, 241, 243, 245–6, 254, 278, 315–23
Jesuits, 377, 404, 408, 409, 506, 559
Jesus Christ, 55, 72, 158, 159, 190, 240, 241, 245–8, 250, 251, 263, 275, 328
Jews, 55, 56, 58, 141, 150, 152, 158, 208, 211, 233–53, 254, 273, 314, 362, 397, 412, 514, 540
John (King of England), 325, 362, 365, 418, 559
Jonson (Ben), 394
Joseph Buonaparte (King of Spain), 456, 460, 466
Joseph II (of Austria), 425, 426
Joshua, 233
Judah (Judea), 44, 233, 236, 238, 240, 243
Judaism, 238, 249
Jugurtha, 175–6
Julius II (Pope), 354
Juno (Hera) (Goddess), 188
Jupiter (Zeus) (God), 188, 189, 408; (Planet), 59
Justinian (Emperor), 200, 252, 261–2, 559
Jutes, 219, 360
Juvenal (Roman satirist), 196
KADESH, 43
Karnak, 29, 30, 32, 34, 43
Kemal (Mustafa Kemal Pasha), 523, 541
Kennedy, President, 561
Kenya, 552–3
Kepler (astronomer), 392
Khrushchev, N., 560
'Kingdom of God' (Jewish Doctrine), 244–6
Kingship (Egyptian), 26; (Early Greek), 98–99, 102; (Hindu), 154; (Roman), 160
Knox (John), 408
Köln (Cologne), 315, 339, 345, 346, 368, 384
Koran, 275–6, 377
Korea, 74, 504, 505, 551, 556
Kubla Khan, 371, 372, 374
LAKE villages, 10
Land-owning, 99, 100, 115, 172–5, 224, 298–306, 417, 436–7, 512, 518
Lao-tse, 156, 158
Las Casas, 404

Latin language, 262, 263, 264, 326, 362, 384, 386, 388, 393
Latins (and Latium), 160, 165
Laurium (silver-mines), 134
League (Delian), 124, 126, 134, 135; (Hanseatic), 346, 348; (Spartan), 137; (of Nations), 204, 505, 509, 532, 533, 536, 540
Lebanon, 84
Lee (Robert E.), 526, 527
Leipzig (battle), 461
Lenin, 515, 536, 538
Leo the Great, Bishop of Rome, 220, 264, 266
Leo X (Pope), 356
Leonardo da Vinci, 354, 356, 358, 392, 559
Leonidas, King of Sparta, 69–71, 119, 120
Leopold, King of the Belgians, 184, 500
Lepidus (Triumvir), 180, 182
Liberia, 88, 501
Libraries (Assurbanipal), 56; (Alexandria), 151; (Mohammedan), 284; (Vatican), 356
Licinian law, 164, 174
Lincoln (Abraham), 526–8
Lister (surgeon), 565
Livingstone (David), 500, 505
Livy (Roman historian), 202, 386
Lloyd George, 553
Lollards, 338
Lombardy (and Lombards), 213, 262, 290, 294, 313, 488, 489
London, 92, 339, 474, 475
Louis IX (Saint Louis), King of France, 322, 365
Louis XI (King of France), 366
Louis XIV (King of France), 411, 414, 417–20, 422, 423, 447, 560
Louis XV (King of France), 420, 421
Louis XVI (King of France), 435, 440, 442, 446, 461
Louis XVIII (King of France), 461
Louis Philippe (King of France), 466, 484, 496
Loyola (founder of the Jesuit Order), 408
Lucretius (Roman writer), 200, 203, 204–5
Lucullus (Roman general), 177, 178
Luther (Martin), 369, 404–7, 559
Luxor (Temple of), 32, 44
Lydia, 60, 112, 120, 172
Lysander, 137

MACCABEES, 238, 244
Macedonia, 97, 140, 144–52, 154, 171, 172, 183, 206, 227, 250, 255, 273, 378, 520, 522
Machiavelli, 356, 358, 426
Madagascar, 497
Maecenas, 195
Magellan (Ferdinand), 396, 400–2, 559
Magna Carta. *See* Great Charter
Magnesia (battle), 172
Magyars, 220, 425, 483, 484, 486
Mahabharata, 80
Mahdi, 498
Mainz (Mayence), 272, 287, 288, 315, 339, 350, 351, 388, 442
Malay States, 502, 505
Malta, 86, 468
Manchuria, 504, 536, 556
Mandarins (Chinese), 77
Mandate, 505
Mao-tse-tung, 556
Marathon, 67, 68, 102, 116, 118, 126, 131, 255
Marcel (Étienne), 366
Marcellus (Roman general), 206
Marcus Aurelius (Emperor), 142, 189, 192–4, 210, 211, 255, 502
Maria Theresa (of Austria), 424, 425, 426, 428
Marie Antoinette (Queen of France), 440, 442, 446, 472
Marius (Caius), 176
Marlowe (English poet), 205, 394
Marriage, 79, 99, 162, 243, 252, 260, 265, 268, 300, 304, 308, 362, 380
Marseilles (Massilia), 184, 322, 474
Marshall Plan, 560
Martyrs (Christian), 190, 210, 211, 231, 250
Marx (Karl), 437, 479, 480, 481, 536
Mary (Queen of England), 414
Masaryk, 546
Masinissa, 169
Mauritius, 468
Maximilian (Emperor of Mexico), 492, 494, 526
Mazarin (Cardinal), 417
Mazzini, 354, 486
Mecca, 273, 274, 276, 280, 522
Medes, 44, 58, 59–72; (and Persians), 148
Medici (Cosmo), 353, 354
Medici (Lorenzo), 353, 354, 356
Medici (Piero), 354
Medicine, 28, 74, 140, 142,

151, 155, 198, 246, 285, 332, 508, 557
Medina, 273, 274, 280, 522
Mediterranean Sea, 2, 5, 24, 28, 44, 48, 54, 60, 84, 85, 86, 89, 108, 150, 171, 174, 178, 324, 346, 394, 461, 517
Memphis (ancient capital of Egypt), 22, 26, 86
Mersen (Treaty of), 297
Mesopotamia, 46–72, 192, 233, 278, 282, 374, 375, 376, 522, 540
Messiah (Doctrine of), 28, 243–6
Metals (age of), 10, 20, 89, 96
Metellus (Roman general), 176
Metternich, 465–6, 484, 496, 510
Mexico, 372, 402, 403, 466, 492, 494, 524, 527, 546, 559
Michelangelo, 354, 356, 390, 392
Midianites, 253
Milan, 211, 212, 224, 264, 313, 352, 354, 358, 369, 424, 425, 452, 484
Miletus, 66, 116, 131, 134
Militarism, 56, 58, 180, 232, 302, 448, 454, 464, 465, 490, 509
Military service, 172, 224, 300, 378, 462, 492
Millennium, 248
Miltiades, 67, 126
Milton, 205, 394
Minos, 90
Minotaur, 90, 92
'Missi Dominici' (Frankish), 294, 295
Missionaries, 155, 156, 231, 249–52, 267, 404, 410, 505–8
Mithras, 64, 188, 208
Mithridates, 176, 177
Moabites, 241
Mohammed (Prophet), 273–6, 278, 280, 282, 559
Mohammed II (Sultan), 380, 382
Mohenjo-daro, 78
Molière, 205, 420
Monasteries (and Monasticism), 156, 264, 267–72
Money-lending, 183, 252, 325, 346
Mongols, 370–8
Monotheism, 34, 158, 241–3, 273, 275
Monroe Doctrine, 466, 492, 527
Montcalm, 430
Montenegro, 483, 516, 518, 520, 522
Moors, 182, 287, 325, 367, 396–7, 402

More (Sir Thomas), 393
Morgarten (battle), 368
Morocco, 497, 501, 510
Moscow, 375, 423, 458, 460
Moses, 233, 241, 243, 275
Mummius (Roman), 172
Museum (Alexandria), 151; (British), 16, 18, 56, 128; (Cairo), 33
Music, 24, 76, 88, 116, 131, 171, 194, 261, 298, 510
Mussolini, 538–9, 548
Mycale, 71
Mycenae, 94, 96, 98
NANTES (Edict of), 411
Naples, 110, 160, 268, 314, 369, 384, 440, 454, 456, 465, 489
Napoleon I (the Great), 29, 66, 146, 148, 169, 290, 424, 447, 448, 449, 450–68, 469, 474, 480, 487, 488, 510, 532, 560
Napoleon III (Louis Napoleon), 480, 487–9, 492, 494, 495
Natal, 497
Naukratis, 110
Navigation Acts, 429
Nazis, 535, 539–40
Neanderthal, 2, 3, 5
Nebuchadnezzar, 44, 58, 60, 236, 254
Nefertiti (wife of Akhnaton), 39, 42
Nehemiah, 236, 238
Nehru, 554
Nelson (Admiral), 458
Neolithic Age, 9–14
Nero (Emperor), 190, 194, 203, 210, 250
Netherlands. (*See also* Holland and Belgium), 367, 369, 411, 416, 418, 424, 425, 442, 445, 452, 467
Newspapers, 414, 462–3, 508
Newton (Sir Isaac), 392, 421
New York, 470, 523, 539, 550
New Zealand, 502, 505, 509, 543, 552
Nibelungenlied, 298
Nicaea, 224, 227
Nicaragua, 400
Nicholas I (Czar of Russia), 478, 483, 511, 512
Nicholas II (Czar of Russia), 512
Nicholas II (Pope), 309, 514
Nicholas V (Pope), 354, 356, 388
Nicias, 135, 136
Nile, 14, 15, 16, 17, 18, 20, 24, 26 (Nileometer), 29, 30, 34, 46, 60, 63, 86, 89, 147, 174, 199, 453, 498, 500
Nîmes, 199, 206
Nimwegen, 288
Nineveh, 44, 54, 56, 58, 60
Nippur, 47, 48

Nirvana, 154
Nomads, 14, 48, 98, 234, 236, 370, 375
North Atlantic Treaty Organization, 551
North Pole, 557
North-West Passage, 402
Normandy (and Normans), 298, 300, 350, 360, 362, 365
Norway, 89, 226, 297, 360, 467, 546, 547, 549
Nubia, 32, 44, 69
Numantia, 172
Numidians, 169, 170, 175
Nuremburg, 345, 350, 368
Nyasaland, 497, 552
ODOACER, 220, 260, 290
Odysseus (Ulysses), 105
Oligarchy, 136, 352
Olympia, 130, 132, 141, 184
Olympic games, 100
Olympus (Mount), 105
Omar (Caliph), 278, 280, 315
Omayyads, 280
Orange River Colony, 497
Oratory (ancient), 131–2, 140, 203
Osiris, 34, 37, 38, 44, 152, 156, 188, 252
Ostracism, 115, 126, 127
Oswiu, 266
Otto the Great, 306, 313
Ottoman Turks, 378–83
Ovid (Roman poet), 203, 204
Owen (Robert), 478, 482
PAINTING, 6, 7, 8, 9, 12, 22, 90, 92, 96, 105, 130, 141, 354, 356–8, 388, 390, 392–3
Pakistan, 509, 552, 554, 559
Palaeolithic (Old Stone) Age, 3–9, 10, 14
Palestine, 30, 39, 42, 55, 58, 68, 108, 190, 233–46, 248, 254, 273, 315–23, 345, 370, 397, 505, 522, 553
Pan (God), 118
Panama Canal, 530
Pan-American Congress, 546
Pan-Athenaic Festival, 128
Paper, 73, 285–6
Papyrus, 18, 21, 54, 234
Paris (city), 30, 92, 263, 284, 366, 384, 411, 440, 444, 450, 460, 461, 462, 474, 479–80, 494, 496, 535, 544
Parliament (English), 362, 412, 413, 414, 416, 417, 432, 433, 435
Parsees, 64
Parthenon (Athens), 104, 128–30
Partitions of Poland, 428
Pasteur, 565
Patricians (Roman), 162
Patriotism, 100, 127–8, 222, 238, 460

INDEX

Paul (Saint), 134, **246**, 248, 249–52, 266
Pausanias, King of Sparta, 120
Peace Doctrines, 40, 76, 94, 128, 155, 244, 245–6, 302, 404, 421, 509
Peasants' War (German), 406
Pearl Harbour, 547
Peloponnesian War (1st), 126; (2nd), 135–7, 138, 255
Peninsular War, 460
Pericles, 100, 124, 126–35, 162, 164, 175, 255, 353, 387
Persepolis, 63, **147**
Persia (and Persians), 44, 46, 48, 58, 59–72, 85, 102, 116, 118–22, 124, 126, 128, 131, 134, 136, 138, 140, 144, 146–8, 188, 236, 254, 255, 273, 278, 282, 284, 328, 345, 370, 371, 374, 375, 483, 553
Peru, 402, 403, 466
Pestilence, 56, 135, 183, 192, 211, 214, 231
Peter (Saint), 251, 266, 308
Peter the Great of Russia, 375, 423–4, 510, 560
Peter the Hermit, 316, 318, 322
Petrarch, 353, 386
Pharisees, 244
Pharos of Alexandria, 151
Pharsalus, 180, 255
Pheidias, 128–30, 132, 141
Pheidippides. *See* Philippides
Philip I (of Macedon), 140, 144, 146, 158, 255, 387
Philip II (of Macedon), 171, 206
Philip II (of Spain), 369, 410, 416
Philip II (of France) (Augustus), 318, 320, 365
Philip IV (of France), 335, 336, 365–6
Philippi, 246, 250
Philippides, 116, 118
Philippines, 402, 532–3
Philistia (and Philistines), 44, 86, 94, 234
Philosophy, 114, 116, 132, 137–44, 158, 203, 249, 250, 314
Phoenicians, 24, 63, 64, 84–89, 104, 105, 110, 147, 234
Pilate (Pontius), 240
Pilgrims, 315, 316, 335
Piraeus, 124, 137
Piracy, 174, 178, 346, 403
Pisa, 324, 352
Pisistratus, 115
Pius II (Pope) (Aeneas Silvius), 350, 354

Pius IX (Pope), 486, 495
Pizarro (conqueror of Peru), 402
Planets (discovery), 54, 59
Plataea, 67, 71, 120
Plato, 138, 144, 158, 238, 249, 387
Plautus (Roman dramatist), 205
Plebeians (Roman), 162, 164
Pliny (the Elder), 195, 203
Pliny (the Younger), 194, 196, 210
Poitiers (battle), 366
Poland, 252, 272, 371, 423, 424, 428, 458, 483, 492, 496, 511, 516, 535, 547, 551
Polo (Marco), 324, 372–4, 396, 398, 502
Polo (Nicolo and Maffeo), 372, 502
Pompeii, 192, 221
Pompey, 177–8, 180, 238, 255
Pont du Gard, 206
Pontifex Maximus Roman, 189
Pope (origin of title), 266
Port Arthur, 502, 504
Portrait Sculpture (Ancient), 24, 42, 206, 208
Portugal, 263, 345, 367, 369, 394, 396, 398, 400, 402, 430, 467, 482, 500, 559
Potsdam, 423
Pottery, 5, 8, 9, 22, 73, 78, 82, 90, 104, 105, 112, 286
Praetor (Roman), 162, 190
Praxiteles, 140, 141
Prester John, 372
Printing, 374, 388
Prophets (Hebrew), 28, 240, 241–4
Protectorate (Colonial), 505, 510
Provincial government (Roman), 183–4, 190, 194
Prussia, 226, 272, 383, 412, 422–3, 424, 425, 426, 428, 437, 440, 445, 455, 456, 460, 461, 467, 472, 475, 484, 486, 490–5, 496, 560
Psalms (Hebrew), 234, 240, 244
Ptolemies (Rulers of Egypt), 30, 150, 151, 155, 180
Public Safety (Committee of), 444
Puerto Rico, 530, 532
Punic Wars (First), 168, 255; (Second), 168–70, 255; (Third), 170–1, 255
Punjab, 78
Pyramid (of Zoser), 20; (Great), 20, 22
Pyramid Age, 22–26, 254
QUAKERS, 421, 430
Quebec, 430

Quintilian, 203
RA (Egyptian Sun God), 16, 34, 36. *See also* Amen-Ra
Rabbis (Jewish), 238
Rabelais, 393
Racine (French dramatist), 420
Railways, 470, 498, 500, 505, 528, 560
Ramadan, 276
Ramayana, 80
Rameses II, 43, 159
Raphael (artist), 356, 392
Ravenna, 214, 216, 218, 260, 262
Reformation (Protestant), 259, 314, 338, 374, 384, 404–12, 416, 449
Reform Bill (English Parliamentary), 414, 560
Religion (Wars of), 410, 411
Rembrandt (artist), 393
Renascence, 246, 259, 306, 325, 358, 384–94, 404, 557
Republic (English Commonwealth), 413; (First French), 442, 444; (Second French), 480; (Third French), 480, 543–4; (Roman), 159–89; (Russian), 515–16; (Turkish), 523; (U.S.A.), 433–5; (Venetian), 352–3
Resurrection (Doctrine of), 250, 251–2
Revolution (American), 429–35; (French of 1789), 146, 287, 417, 418, 422, 429, 435–50, 452, 467, 469, 515, 560; (French of 1830), 484; (of 1848), 484–6; (Polish), 511; (Russian Bolshevik), 437, 442, 481, 515–16
Rheims, 296, 339, 350
Rhodes, 86, 141
Rhodesia, 5, 497, 500, 552–3
Richard I of England, 318, 320
Richelieu, 417
Rienzi, 315
Rights of Man, 438
Rights (English Bill of), 414
Rigveda, 79–80, 82, 83, 254
Road-making, 63, 68, 147, 172, 192, 200, 462
Robespierre, 444, 452
Rome (and Romans), 46, 52, 54, 59, 110, 134, 150, 159–225, 226, 227, 230, 231, 232, 238, 240, 244, 245, 246, 250, 253, 254, 255, 259, 260, 262, 264, 265, 266, 268, 273, 290, 294, 295, 297, 306, 309, 312, 313, 315, 330, 339, 352, 354, 356, 365, 382, 384, 386, 390, 398, 406, 486, 489, 490, 495, 502, 539

INDEX

Roosevelt, 530, 546, 548
Roses (Wars of), 364, 366
Rosetta Stone, 453
Roumania, 66, 516, 518, 520, 522, 535, 549, 551
Rousseau, 422, 437
Rubens (artist), 393
Rubicon, 180
Russia, 66, 169, 252, 286, 346, 371, 374, 375, 376, 383, 412, 422, 423–4, 428, 437, 440, 442, 445, 454, 458–60, 461, 467, 475, 478, 481, 482, 483, 484, 486, 492, 502, 504, 505, 509, 510–16, 517, 518, 519, 520, 522, 532, 533, 534, 536–8, 541, 547, 550–1, 553, 557–8, 559–62, 565
SACK of Rome (Charles V), 218; (Goths), 218–19; (Vandals), 220
Sadducees, 238, 244, 245
Sagas (Norse), 297–8
Saguntum, 168
St. Bartholomew (Massacre), 411
St. Helena (Island), 461, 463, 464, 465, 488
St. Peter's Church (Rome), 290, 336, 356, 406
St. Petersburg (Petrograd, Leningrad), 423, 515
St. Simon (author), 420
St. Sophia (Church), 261, 382
Saladin, 318, 323, 370
Salamis, 71, 115, 119, 131
Salisbury (Cathedral), 350; (Oath of), 300
Samarcand, 286, 371, 376
Samaria, 56, 236, 242
Samnites, 160, 165, 166
Samson, 234
Sanskrit, 79
Sappho, 116, 144
Saracens, 318, 320, 323
Sarajevo, 522, 533–4
Sardinia, 159, 168, 174, 208, 213, 369, 440, 486, 487, 488, 489, 490
Sargon I, 48, 54, 254
Satrap, 63
Saturnalia, 188, 189
Saul (Hebrew king), 234
Saxons, 219, 226, 290, 298, 310, 360
Saxony, 288, 290, 315, 368, 404, 406
Schools, 52, 144, 200, 288, 344, 377, 387–8, 393, 410
Science, 28, 58, 140, 142, 205, 246, 285, 392, 469–75, 557
Scipio (Aemilianus, conqueror of Carthage), 172
Scipio (Lucius, brother of Publius), 171

Scipio (Publius, conqueror of Hannibal), 169–70, 172
Scotland, 360, 362, 478
Scribes (Jewish), 238, 245
Sculpture, 12, 24, 48, 50, 55, 76, 96, 105, 116, 128, 130, 140–1, 150, 172, 206, 358, 388–92
Scylax (navigator), 63
Scythians, 66, 127, 169, 199
Second World War, 547–8
Sedan, 494
Seleucids, 150, 154, 155
Semites, 29, 46, 48–59, 79, 84–89, 233–53, 370
Sempach (battle), 368
Senate (Roman), 162, 164, 168, 170, 176, 178, 180, 182, 190; (United States of America), 526, 533
Seneca, 142, 203, 205, 248 (quoted), 249
Sennacherib, King of Assyria, 54, 56, 110, 243
September Massacres (French Revolution), 442
Septuagint, 150
Serbia, 378, 483, 516, 518, 520, 522, 533
Serfdom, 228, 304, 306, 383, 406, 436, 437, 460, 502, 511–12
Sertorius, 177
Seti I (Pharaoh), 43
Seven Years War, 426, 429, 430, 432, 560
Severus (Emperor), 212
Sévigné (Madame de), 420
Sforza (Francesco and Ludovico), 358
Shakespeare, 205, 252, 364, 394, 557
Sherman (General), 527
Shi-Hwang-ti, 73, 74, 76, 213, 255
Ships (and Sea Power), 14, 24, 63, 64, 78, 85, 89, 104, 108, 112, 119, 126, 136–7, 146, 150, 160, 168, 169, 174, 182, 199, 219, 220, 297–8, 323, 346, 386, 394–404, 458, 470, 471, 474, 498, 502, 503, 504, 517, 519, 527
Shishak, 44
Siberia, 376, 505, 511, 514
Sicily, 86, 88, 94, 110, 136, 168, 171, 174, 183, 262, 297, 314, 325, 369, 489
Sidon, 84, 86, 87, 104
Siege (Carthage), 170–1; (Florence), 357; (Jerusalem), 208; (Medieval), 363; (Rome), 216, 218; (Tuileries), 441
Sigurd the Volsung, 298
Silbury Hill, 12
Silesia, 371, 422, 424, 426, 472

Simony, 308, 309
Sindh, 78
Slavery, 20, 48, 86, 100, 112, 114, 115, 127, 132, 134, 171, 172, 174, 176, 177, 182, 195–6, 211, 228, 231, 250, 320, 322, 403, 421, 433, 450, 524–6, 557
Slave Trade, 403, 433, 468
Slavs, 290, 292, 297, 425, 483, 486, 516
Social conditions, 22, 24, 28, 48, 52, 77, 78, 80, 82, 92, 98, 99, 100, 106, 108, 115, 126–8, 172–5, 182–6, 195–7, 228, 242, 245, 248, 304–5, 332, 406–7, 435–8, 475–82, 541–2, 549, 554, 557–8
Socialism, 437, 478–82, 492, 515, 536, 538, 544
Social War (Roman), 176
Socrates, 131, 137–9, 151, 158
Solomon, 86, 236, 241
Solon, 114–15, 254
Somaliland, 505
Sophists, 131–2
Sophocles, 131, 394
South Africa, 497, 505, 543, 552
South Sea Islands, 505, 530
Spain, 6, 9, 85, 86, 88, 108, 147, 168, 169, 172, 175, 176, 183, 192, 199, 216, 226, 227, 252, 260, 263, 267, 278, 279, 280, 284, 287, 290, 325, 330, 333, 345, 348, 367, 369, 393, 396, 397, 398, 400, 402, 403, 408, 410, 412, 416, 418, 430, 437, 440, 458, 460, 461, 465, 466, 482, 497, 506, 532, 540–1, 549
Spanish Main, 403
Spanish Succession War, 418
Sparta, 60, 66, 69–71, 98, 100, 102, 115, 116, 118, 120, 122, 124, 125, 126, 134, 135–40, 171, 255
Spartacus, 177
Sphinx, 24, 30
Spices, 85, 344, 345, 394
Stalin, 538, 548, 551, 560–1
Stanley (explorer), 500
States - General (French), 366, 417, 438; (Dutch), 416
Steamboat, 470–1
Steam-engine, 151, 469–70, 474
Stephen, King of England, 300, 301, 302
Stephenson (George), 470
Stilicho, 213–14, 216, 224
Stoics (and Stoicism), 142, 192, 196, 248, 249
Stonehenge, 9, 13, 89
Stuart Dynasty (England), 287, 413–14

INDEX

Sudan, 18, 24, 69, 498
Suez, 28, 64; (Canal), 553
Suleiman the Magnificent, 382
Sulla, 176, 177, 188
Sumerians, 46–48, 72, 78, 254, 370
Sun-worship, 12, 34–36, 44, 82, 84
Susa (capital of Ancient Persia), 63, 66, 71, 121, 147
Sweden (and Swedes), 89, 226, 297, 346, 360, 411, 423, 456, 461, 467, 483, 546, 549
Switzerland, 10, 159, 366, 367–8, 407–8, 474
Syracuse, 110, 136, 141, 142, 158, 206, 299
Syria, 29, 30, 39, 42, 43, 44, 54, 55, 68, 69, 87, 150, 171, 182, 192, 199, 234, 238, 240, 273, 276, 280, 282, 322, 345, 370, 371, 374, 375, 453, 522

TACITUS, 200, 202, 203, 226, 228, 230 (quotation), 248, 290
Tamerlane, 376
Tarquinius Superbus, 160
Tartars, 74, 375
Tasmania, 3
Taxation, 15, 16, 52, 224, 278, 292, 335, 377, 413, 416, 418, 432, 433, 434, 435, 438, 464, 480, 518
Telegraph (electric), 470
Temple (Jewish), 208, 236, 241
Terence, 205
Terror (French Reign of), 442–4, 446, 480
Testament (New), 238, 240, 245–6, 266; (Old), 150, 152, 240–5, 328
Tetzel (seller of Indulgences), 406, 407
Thales of Miletus, 116
Thamagudi (Timgad), 199
Theatre (ancient), 131, 150, 174, 184, 199
Thebes (Egypt), 26, 29, 30, 34, 39, 40
Thebes (Greece), 67, 70, 102, 135, 140, 146
Themistocles, 118, 119, 124, 126
Theocritus, 150
Theodoric, the Great, 227, 260
Theodosius the Great, 212, 213, 222, 224, 255, 264
Thermopylae, 69, 71, 119, 120, 255
Theseus, 92
Thessaly, 69, 96, 97, 105, 180
Thirty Years Truce, 135
Thirty Years War, 411, 559

Thothmes III, 29, 30, 32, 43, 94
Thrace, 142, 213, 227, 266, 380
Thucydides, 122, 131, 138
Tiberius (Emperor), 190, 208
Tibet, 155, 156, 157, 556
Tiglath Pileser III, 55, 56, 254
Tigris (river), 46, 54, 60, 110, 147, 280, 370
Tiryns, 94
Tito, 551
Titus (Emperor), 186, 192, 208, 240
Toleration (religious), 151–2, 208, 222, 328–30, 377, 410–12, 413, 414, 420, 421, 423, 430, 438, 450, 464
Tools (ancient), 2, 3, 5, 6, 8, 9, 10, 20
Towns (medieval), 313, 332, 338–59
Town Halls, 340, 348, 350
Trade Unions, 197, 476, 478. *See also* Gilds
Trade and Commerce, 24, 50, 78, 85–86, 88, 90, 94, 96, 97, 102, 104, 112, 197, 198–9, 286, 306, 323–4, 340–6, 353, 429–30, 506–8, 530
Trafalgar (battle), 458
Trajan (Emperor), 192, 199, 208, 210, 223, 229, 255, 291
Transvaal, 497
Trasimene (battle), 168
Trent (Council of), 410
Tribune of the Plebs, 162, 164
Tribute, 54, 56, 63, 220, 278
Trinil (Java), 1
Tripoli, 278, 318, 520
Triumphal Procession (Roman), 177, 189
Triumvirate (First Roman), 178; (Second Roman), 182
Troy (and Trojans), 89, 94, 96, 98, 102, 105, 195, 253
Tudors (English Dynasty), 364, 412, 413
Tuileries, 440, 442
Tunis, 496, 552
Turkestan, 147, 285, 371, 374, 375, 376, 378
Turks, 46, 130, 222, 278, 282, 286, 287, 315–16, 318, 320, 353, 369, 370, 376, 378–83, 387, 394, 454, 468, 482, 483, 497, 505, 509, 516–23, 534, 541–2, 551
Tutankhamen, 32, 39, 42, 44
Twelve Tables (Roman Law), 162
Tycho Brahe, 392
Tyranny, 114, 115, 116, 117, 254, 353–4, 425–6

Tyre, 84, 86, 104, 146, 241
UGANDA, 497, 505
Ulphilas (Bishop of the Visigoths), 231
Unifying influences, 100, 102, 222, 259
Union of Soviet Socialist Republic, *see* Russia
United Nations Organization, 550, 551, 553, 554, 556, 558, 559, 561, 565
United States of America, 287, 433–5, 466, 475, 481–2, 492, 504, 505, 514, 523–32, 534, 536, 541, 542, 544–6, 547–8, 550, 551, 553, 556, 558, 559–61, 565
Universities, 252, 261, 280, 284, 285, 384, 411
Ur, 48, 78
Urban II (Pope), 316, 325
VALMY, 440
Vandals, 212, 214, 219, 220, 226, 232, 255, 261, 262
Van Dyck (artist), 393
Van Eycks (artists), 392
Varennes, 440
Vasari (artist), 357
Vases (ancient), 32, 86, 112, 141
Vatican, 356, 495
Velasquez (artist), 393
Venetia, 488, 489, 490, 492, 494
Venice, 130, 313, 320, 324, 345, 346, 348, 352–3, 358, 372, 374, 394, 396, 452, 484
Venizelos (Greek statesman), 520
Verdun (Treaty of), 296
Verocchio (artist), 354
Verres, 183–4
Versailles, 420, 423, 424, 440, 494, 540
Vespasian, 192, 240
Vesuvius, 177, 192
Victor Emanuel II (King of Italy), 486, 489, 490, 495
Victoria, 478
Vienna, 384, 424, 454, 484
Vienna (Congress of), 467–8, 496, 510, 516
Viet Nam, 552
Virgil, 195, 200, 203, 204, 384, 386
Virginia, 430, 433, 523
Visconti family, 354
Vittorino da Feltre, 387–8
Volsunga Saga, 298
Voltaire, 420–1, 422, 423, 437
Votes (Franchise), 115, 127, 166, 174, 228, 342, 367, 414, 432, 438, 445, 476, 481, 515, 528, 560
Voyages, 24, 28, 30, 84–89, 108, 110, 147, 197–8, 394–404, 500

INDEX

Vulgate, 203
WAGNER (musician), 298
Waldenses, 326, 328
Wales, 360, 362, 364
Wall (Great Wall of China), 73–74, 192, 213; (Hadrian's Wall), 189, 192
Washington (city), 523, 527, 530; (Conference), 544
Washington (George), 433, 434
Waterloo (battle), 461, 465, 467, 475, 560
Watt (James), 469–70
Weaving, 5, 9, 22, 73, 82, 112, 474
Wellington (Duke of), 460
West Indies, 398–400, 413, 468
Westminster, Statute of, 543
Widow-burning, 79, 377

Wilfrid (of Ripon), 272
William I (King of England), 302, 304, 309
William III (King of England), 414
William I (German Emperor), 490, 494, 560
William II (German Emperor), 481
William the Silent, Prince of Orange, 416
Wilson (President of U.S.A.), 530, 532, 535–6, 544
Wireless Telegraphy, 532
Wolfe (General), 427, 430
Women's rights, 132, 155, 231, 250
Wool, 86, 470, 474
Writing, 12, 14, 16, 18, 42, 47, 54–55, 63, 73, 90, 94, 99, 104, 110, 160, 234

Wycliffe (John), 336, 338, 362, 559
XENOPHON, 71, 131, 138
Xerxes I, 68–71, 102, 118, 119, 120, 255, 378
YOUNG Turk Movement, 520
Yugoslavia, 535, 549, 551
ZAMA, 169, 170
Zanzibar, 400, 407
Zeno (first of the Stoics), 141–2
Zeus (Jupiter) (God), 106, 116, 130, 132, 152, 188
Zeuxis (Greek painter), 141
Zimbabwe (ruins), 500
Zion (Mount), 208
Zipangu, 398
Zoroaster, 64, 82, 119, 208, 254, 326, 328
Zwingli (Swiss reformer), 40